ANCIENT
CHRISTIAN WORSHIP

ANCIENT
CHRISTIAN WORSHIP

EARLY CHURCH PRACTICES IN SOCIAL, HISTORICAL,
AND THEOLOGICAL PERSPECTIVE

Andrew B. McGowan

Baker Academic
a division of Baker Publishing Group
Grand Rapids, Michigan

Published by Baker Academic
a division of Baker Publishing Group
P.O. Box 6287, Grand Rapids, MI 49516-6287
www.bakeracademic.com

Printed in the United States of America

Library of Congress Cataloging-in-Publication Data

McGowan, Andrew Brian, 1961–
    Ancient Christian worship : early church practices in social, historical, and theological perspective / Andrew B. McGowan.
        pages cm
    Includes bibliographical references and index.
    ISBN 978-0-8010-3152-6 (cloth)
    1. Worship—History—Early church, ca. 30–600. I. Title.
BV6.M39 2014
264.009′015—dc23   2014009065

Unless indicated otherwise, Scripture quotations are from the New Revised Standard Version of the Bible, copyright © 1989, by the Division of Christian Education of the National Council of the Churches of Christ in the United States of America. Used by permission. All rights reserved.

Scripture quotations labeled KJV are from the King James Version of the Bible.

Unless indicated otherwise, translations of other ancient texts are those of the author.

14   15   16   17   18   19   20   7   6   5   4   3   2   1

In keeping with biblical principles of creation stewardship, Baker Publishing Group advocates the responsible use of our natural resources. As a member of the Green Press Initiative, our company uses recycled paper when possible. The text paper of this book is composed in part of post-consumer waste.

For Brian and Cate

CONTENTS

ACKNOWLEDGMENTS

This book contains original scholarship, but it also synthesizes the work of many other scholars who have done so much over recent decades to advance knowledge of ancient liturgy, meals, ritual, and other aspects of early Christianity. I am honored to have had many of them among my teachers, colleagues, and friends. While I hope dependence on others' research is properly acknowledged, the intended audience of this volume has necessitated that many notes point to resources in English that will elucidate complex questions, and not necessarily to the whole of a wider body of scholarship.

I particularly thank those who offered various forms of direct advice and assistance, especially Harold Attridge, Paul Bradshaw, Felicity Harley-McGowan, and Alistair Stewart, who each read one or more chapters. James Ernest, a colleague in early Christianity as well as a patient and conscientious editor, also offered important questions and improvements in reading the drafts. I have had important and helpful conversations with Joan Branham, Patout Burns, Jeremy Hultin, Robin Jensen, Clemens Leonhard, Jodi Magness, Hindy Najman, and Gerard Rouwhorst. My colleagues in the Society of Biblical Literature Meals in the Greco-Roman World Group have been stimulating and supportive colleagues over some years; I mention among them, representatively rather than comprehensively, Dennis Smith, Hal Taussig, Angela Standhartinger, and Matthias Kinghardt. My own limits, rather than theirs, are reflected in the results.

Most of this book was written while on a sabbatical from Trinity College, Melbourne, spent at Yale Divinity School. Those who allowed me to leave the one and be welcomed at the other, particularly my Trinity colleagues Campbell Bairstow and Bill Cowan, and again Harold Attridge, who was dean of Yale Divinity School at the time, all have my gratitude.

I offer this to those in whose company I first experienced the distinctive life of the Christian community, my parents.

Abbreviations

General

ABRL	Anchor Bible Reference Library
AT	author's translation
BCE/CE	Before the Common Era/Common Era
BCP	Book of Common Prayer
ca.	circa (about, approximately)
CCSL	Corpus Christianorum: Series latina. Turnhout: 1953–.
cf.	confer (compare)
chap./chaps.	chapter/chapters
ICC	International Critical Commentary
KJV	King James Version
LXX	Septuagint
NHC	Nag Hammadi Codices
NRSV	New Revised Standard Version
NT	New Testament
OT	Old Testament
PG	Patrologia graeca. Edited by J.-P. Migne. 162 vols. Paris, 1857–86.
PO	Patrologia orientalis
v./vv.	verse/verses
WUNT	Wissenschaftliche Untersuchungen zum Neuen Testament

Old Testament

Gen.	Genesis	Lev.	Leviticus
Exod.	Exodus	Num.	Numbers

Deut.	Deuteronomy	Eccles.	Ecclesiastes
Josh.	Joshua	Isa.	Isaiah
1–2 Sam.	1–2 Samuel	Jer.	Jeremiah
Ps./Pss.	Psalm/Psalms	Dan.	Daniel

New Testament

Matt.	Matthew	1 Thess.	1 Thessalonians
Rom.	Romans	1–2 Tim.	1–2 Timothy
1–2 Cor.	1–2 Corinthians	Heb.	Hebrews
Gal.	Galatians	1–2 Pet.	1–2 Peter
Eph.	Ephesians	Rev.	Revelation
Col.	Colossians		

Old Testament Apocrypha and Pseudepigrapha

| 4 Macc. | 4 Maccabees | *Odes Sol.* | *Odes of Solomon* |
| *Let. Aris.* | *Letter of Aristeas* | Wis. | Wisdom of Solomon |

Dead Sea Scrolls

1QH^a	*Thanksgiving Hymns*
1QS/1QSa	*Rule of the Community/Rule of the Congregation*
4QD^b	*Damascus Document*[b]

1QH[a] *Thanksgiving Hymns*
1QS/1QSa *Rule of the Community/Rule of the Congregation*
4QD[b] *Damascus Document*[b]

Josephus

| *Ant.* | *Jewish Antiquities* | *War* | *Jewish War* |

Philo

| *Contempl. Life* | *On the Contemplative Life* |
| *Spec. Laws* | *On the Special Laws* |

Mishnah and Talmud

| *b.* | Babylonian Talmud | *t.* | Tosefta |
| *m.* | Mishnah | | |

Ber.	*Berakot*	*Roš Haš.*	*Roš Haššanah*
Meg.	*Megillah*	*Taʿan.*	*Taʿanit*
Pesaḥ.	*Pesaḥim*		

Apostolic Fathers

Barn.	*Letter of Barnabas*
1–2 Clem.	*1–2 Clement*
Did.	*Didache*
Herm. Mand.	*Shepherd of Hermas, Mandate(s)*
Herm. Sim.	*Shepherd of Hermas, Similitude(s)*
Herm. Vis.	*Shepherd of Hermas, Vision(s)*
Ign. *Eph.*	Ignatius, *To the Ephesians*
Ign. *Magn.*	Ignatius, *To the Magnesians*
Ign. *Phld.*	Ignatius, *To the Philadelphians*
Ign. *Pol.*	Ignatius, *To Polycarp*
Ign. *Rom.*	Ignatius, *To the Romans*
Ign. *Smyrn.*	Ignatius, *To the Smyrnaeans*
Mart. Pol.	*Martyrdom of Polycarp*

Patristic and Other Early Christian Sources

Ambrose

Myst.	*On the Mysteries*

Ap. Const.	*Apostolic Constitutions*
Ap. Trad.	*Apostolic Tradition* (attributed to Hippolytus)

Augustine

Conf.	*Confessions*
Exp. Pss.	*Expositions on the Psalms*

Clement of Alexandria

Paed.	*Paedagogus (Christ the Teacher)*
Strom.	*Stromateis*

Ep. Apost.	*Epistula Apostolorum*

Eusebius

Comm. Ps.	*Commentary on the Psalms*
Eccl. Hist.	*Ecclesiastical History*

Gr.[1]	*[First Greek] Life of Pachomius*

John Chrysostom

Hom. on Col.	*Homilies on the Letter to the Colossians*

Justin Martyr
    1 Apol.   *1 Apology*
    Dial.   *Dialogue with Trypho*

Mart. Perp. *Martyrdom of Perpetua and Felicitas*

Methodius
    Symp.   *Symposium*

Socrates of Constantinople
    Eccl. Hist. *Ecclesiastical History*

Tertullian
    Apol.   *Apology*

New Testament Apocrypha

Acts Thom. Acts of Thomas   *Gos. Pet.*   *Gospel of Peter*
Frag. Oxy. Fragment Oxyrhynchus

Papyri and Inscriptions

CIJ   *Corpus inscriptionum*   P.Ryl.   Greek Papyri in the John
      judaicarum   Rylands Library,
P.Oxy. Oxyrhynchus Papyri   Manchester

1

INTRODUCTION

The Origins of Christian Worship

Christian worship—the set of communal practices of prayer and ritual characteristic of the followers of Jesus—is as fundamental to the church as its doctrine. Yet worship has also been contentious just as long as it has existed. The earliest surviving discussion of a Christian assembly is not a clear description of common order but an exasperated judgment of liturgical failure: "When you come together, it is not the Lord's supper that you eat" (1 Cor. 11:20 AT).

Early Christian literature about worship tends to emulate Paul's ambition, if not his exasperation: much of what has come down to us was written to encourage, critique, and change what Christians were doing, not to describe it. There is nothing quite like a Book of Common Prayer (BCP), Directory of Worship, or a hymnal from the ancient church. A historical picture of ancient Christian worship is thus constructed not only from records of praise, ritual, and prayer but also from witnesses to debate, development, and instruction.

This makes the tasks of the historian and reader more complex, but more interesting too. The history of early Christian worship may not be a serene tour through idealized house churches full of believers "of one heart and soul" (Acts 4:32), as even a very early account nostalgically put it, but a diverse and challenging journey through the history of Christianity itself. For what these Christians confessed and contested when they wrote about "going to church" is not just about what might now be called "worship," but involved their deepest beliefs and aspirations, and their embodied practice as well as their inner faith. Then as now, worship practices could be problematic and divisive, as well as engaging and inspiring.

The Challenge of "Worship"

Tracing "Worship"

If worship has always been contentious, the modern reader brings a particular unwitting difficulty to ancient Christian practice. Not only is ancient worship different from our own (whichever "our" that might mean), the language we use has shifted, even in quite recent times, sometimes without a corresponding awareness of that change.

This challenge is illustrated by tracing how the English word "worship" has changed drastically in meaning. Today "worship" can often mean communal prayer and ritual, as it will be used for the most part in this book; but for some, "worship" is more like a personal belief or orientation, which is inward in essence, if necessarily expressed in outward and communal forms.[1] In some parts of contemporary Christianity, however, "worship" means a particular genre of music, often used in gatherings (as in the first definition) but intended to express and affirm personal devotion (as in the second). If the last of these definitions is most strikingly specific or even idiosyncratic, all of these uses are actually quite modern; not very long ago, "worship" meant something rather different.

The form for Holy Matrimony in the first English BCP in 1549 included these words at the time of the giving of a ring by groom to bride: "With this ring I thee wed; this gold and silver I thee give; with my body I thee worship; and withal my worldly goods I thee endow." Although these spousal duties were religiously grounded, "worship" here does not imply some overly romantic devotion, nor does it play fast and loose with what pertained properly only to God. The sixteenth-century groom was referring not to "worship" of his wife as some inward disposition that he would manifest from that point on but to what he was actually doing by giving his bride tokens of his property,

---

1. Note, for instance, the way "worship" is used in Larry W. Hurtado, *At the Origins of Christian Worship: The Context and Character of Earliest Christian Devotion* (Grand Rapids: Eerdmans, 2000); this study pays little attention to communal practice but emphasizes how Jesus was viewed and understood.

including a ring. This sharing of wealth was itself "worship"—a ritual, but also a literal form of reverent service, the founding example of a set of acts and dispositions inherent in marriage rather than merely a sign pointing to them.

A little later, "worship" is deemed appropriate by the translators of the King James Version of the Bible (KJV) to render a particular set of Hebrew and Greek words about obedience, service, and bodily performances related to them; God or gods are the sole referent. The actions described as "worship" are not those noted as modern definitions (rituals, beliefs, or songs); "worship" in the KJV is not a synonym for "praise" or for "faith." As in the BCP marriage service, it refers to a whole set of dispositions, a relationship rather than just a ritual; but it also refers to physical performances that both reflect and enact such relationships, and most often to literal practices of bowing or prostration (see the series of "worship" actions in Gen. 24; cf. Matt. 4:9; 8:2; 28:9; etc.). "Worship" includes participation in sacrificial rituals such as those of taber- nacle or temple (Gen. 22:5; 1 Sam. 1:3), within a broader notion of obedience or service, but does not equate to them or derive its meaning from them.

The bodily acts at the center of "worship" in these early modern cases, primarily of prostration and gift, are not merely signs pointing to something else called "worship" but really are "worship"; they may be said to "effect what they signify," to borrow from well-known language about sacraments. These performances thus exemplify theorist Catherine Bell's suggestion that "the molding of the body . . . primarily acts to restructure bodies in the very doing of acts themselves. Hence, required kneeling does not merely communicate subordination to the kneeler. For all intents and purposes, kneeling produces a subordinate kneeler in and through the act itself."[2]

In these cases, and also in the ancient ones underlying the KJV, "worship" refers not only to specific ritual performances but also to a wider reality they create and represent. That wider reality, or "worship," is obedience or service, not gatherings, nor beliefs, nor song, nor ritual, except within that wider whole. Prayer and communal ritual nevertheless served, along with personal and physical acts of bodily "worship," to create and express that obedience and service. For the ancients, therefore, such language was not specifically about liturgy any more than it was about music, and it had as much to do with what we would call politics and ethics as with what we call worship.

Although a millennium separates these two early modern texts from even the most recent ones discussed in the body of this book, their thought world

2. Catherine M. Bell, *Ritual Theory, Ritual Practice* (New York: Oxford University Press, 1992), 100.

seems closer to that of the ancient church (and to the usages reflected in the Bible) than to our own. Not just semantically but at a deeper conceptual level, activities for which words related to "worship" were used in the premodern world denote not a specific realm of activity like "liturgy" but the orientation of all forms of human activity, including the liturgical or ritual, toward a particular allegiance.

Modern participants and practitioners of the somewhat different actions now variously labeled "worship" could all properly insist that their activities are still, or at least should be, intimately related to such reverence and service to God. Yet there is an unmistakable difference between these various metonymies and the older senses of "worship." The old is about embodied life and ethics, the new about inner life and aesthetics. No one in the ancient church could have asked about "styles" of worship.

"Worship" in Translation

"Worship" has nevertheless in the modern world become a distinct kind, or kinds, of practice, forms of human activity whose relationship to faith and discipleship is constructed along quite different lines from those that prevailed in ancient Israel, early modern England, or—most important for our purposes—the ancient church that appeared and grew in the Mediterranean world in the first few centuries of the common era.

Language, like ritual, exists in history and necessarily changes, and so these differences are matters for reflection rather than refusal. What can be problematic, however, is the failure to acknowledge the change, and thus (for example) to imagine that references to "worship" in ancient settings are about the same things we may call "worship" now. Such slippage is common, and indeed hard to avoid, given that the Bible itself is still usually rendered into English using the same equivalences made familiar when the KJV was translated. When patriarchs, kings, and apostles are now depicted "worshiping" God, something is arguably lost in translation.

Where modern translations attempt to depart from those early modern patterns of rendering the biblical text, however, they can confuse things further. So, for instance, a ritual prescribed in Leviticus for the grain offering (*minḥah*) is rendered thus in the KJV: "And when any will offer a meat offering unto the LORD, his offering shall be of fine flour; and he shall pour oil upon it, and put frankincense thereon: And he shall bring it to Aaron's sons the priests" (Lev. 2:1–2a). The modern reader is likely to be confused by the KJV reference to "meat" in the older sense of "food," and the New Revised

Standard Version (NRSV) fixes that; however, the new translation transports the ancient Israelite sacrificer to the world of twentieth-century Protestantism by gratuitously inserting its own idea of "worship": "When anyone presents a grain offering to the LORD, the offering shall be of choice flour; *the worshiper* shall pour oil on it, and put frankincense on it, and bring it to Aaron's sons the priests" (Lev. 2:1–2a, emphasis added). Leviticus, the book of the Bible most concerned with acts of communal ritual, does not actually use any word translatable as "worship" here or otherwise, with one problematic exception: in reference to making idols and prostrating or bowing to them (Lev. 26:1). The modern translators introduced this idea to gloss the type of activity they saw going on in the text.

Where ancient talk of "worship" was about the whole of service or devotion, modern "worship," even though diverse, refers to more distinctive and discrete things. While then as now there was communal eating and drinking, music, symbol, prayer, Scripture, teaching, and those other things that now constitute "worship" as variously understood, we must admit something difficult at the outset: in the ancient world, what we now call "worship" did not quite exist.

Augustine of Hippo (354–430), whose works are a valuable source for the liturgical practice of his own North African church and others in the late fourth century, indicated that this puzzle about the language of "worship" was real in his time also, and suggested that the semantics of Latin were no more adequate to the task than we find modern English:

> To make offerings and sacrifice, and to consecrate our possessions and our-selves . . . is the worship [*cultus*] that is due to the divinity . . . and since no Latin term sufficiently exact to express this in a single word occurs to me, I shall avail myself, where needed, of Greek. *Latreia*, whenever it occurs in Scripture, is rendered by the word "service" [*servitus*]. But that service that is due to humans, referring to which the apostle writes that servants must be subject to their own masters, tends to be referred to by another word in Greek, whereas the service that is paid to God alone by worship [*cultus*], is always, or almost always, called *latreia* in the usage of those who wrote down the divine oracles for us. So if we only used the word "worship," it would not seem to be due exclusively to God; for we also speak of "worship" of humans, whom we celebrate with honors, whether in memory or in the present. (*City of God* 10.1.2)

It may by now seem faintly encouraging to find the problem of translating "worship" arising in ancient as well as in modern contexts. Augustine's reflection suggests two things: first, that, as already seen, language itself changes and may not be completely adequate to convey the same ideas or describe the same practices across cultures or over time; and second, that there may nonetheless be a recognizable (if not readily defined) commonality of action and purpose across these same barriers, through which women and men are seeking to enact divine service.

"Worship" in the New Testament

It should not now come as a surprise that words usually translated as "worship" in English versions of the New Testament (NT) are not primarily concerned with the conduct of Christian assemblies or communal rituals. Like their equivalents in the Hebrew Bible, these terms are concerned either with reverence and obedience or with bodily performances that enacted them; of the references to "worship" in most English translations, a great many in Greek are actually related to *proskynēsis*, prostration. So when, for instance, the apostles are depicted "worshiping" the risen Christ, they are not singing, reciting prayer, or (only) experiencing a feeling or attitude; they are flat on their faces (Matt. 28:17). Of course this is ritual—but not ritual intended to convey something else. "Worship" is about the body and about service.

"Worship" language in the NT can also indicate dispositions of piety and reverence on the part of a person or community (Rom. 12:1). This includes specific utterances, actions, or events, including ritual (John 4:20; 12:20; Acts 8:27; 24:11), as well as acts of charity and justice (James 1:27). "Worship" in the NT texts is not, however, tied strongly or distinctively to prayer or to Christian gatherings or communal activities. Of course practices traced to the command of Jesus (1 Cor. 11:24b, 25b; Matt. 28:19) or to apostolic authority might be regarded as "worship" in the senses outlined above, as a part of obedience and service. Still, the fact that this possibility is not directly taken up in NT documents is striking. There are various reasons for this silence, including the issues already raised, and also the continued existence of other gatherings and practices (especially the rituals of the temple, initially) that were more customarily regarded as communal forms of "worship" or service to God. Whatever its basis, however, this acknowledgment takes us to something of a fork in the road.

On the one hand, there is the biblical language or concept of "worship," which suggests the reverent orientation of the whole person and of communities toward God—and sometimes just being flat on your face to make that real. This "worship" does include both speech acts and physical performance and may take place in the domestic and personal realm, as well as in the communal and public; but communal rituals of the Christian community are not actually presented as "worship" in the NT. "Worship" language in the NT texts suggests a great deal about ethos or a Christian way of life, but relatively little about the specifics of distinctive liturgical practice or performance.

On the other hand, there is a collection of distinctive practices attested and urged in Scripture, specific actions characteristic of the Christian community, which assume and embody proper reverence and service toward God, even if not always or anywhere labeled "worship." Christians eat (1 Cor. 10:16–17; 11:17–34; Jude 12), baptize (Acts 2:41; Rom. 6:4; 1 Cor. 1:13–17; 15:29; etc.), fast (Matt. 6:16–18; Acts 13:2–3; 14:23), pray (Acts 1:14; 6:4; 14:23; Col. 4:2), teach or proclaim (1 Cor. 12; Col. 3:16), and more; these actions all have ritual elements such as prescribed forms of words, bodily performances, and use of particular objects and substances. Their uneasy relationship with the language or concept of "worship" does not make them any less essential to the emerging Christian movement. This list could be expanded to include less clearly communal or ritual actions, such as practical acts of concern for the poor (Gal. 2:10; 1 Cor. 16:1–2; James 1:27); if for present purposes we focus on the foundations of liturgical practice, or "worship" in the narrower modern sense rather than the ancient one, this is not to say that such a limitation best expresses the understandings of the earliest Christian communities about their distinctive actions.

Baptism and Eucharist have a particular place among these practices, and their continuation by the Christians was connected with the example and teaching of Jesus directly through NT texts. Each of these has its own rationale(s)— that is, sets of meanings that flesh out the ways it is constitutive of Christian identity for individuals and communities. So, for example, Paul suggests that baptism effects the incorporation of its members into the body (1 Cor. 12:13), which is itself made by sharing in the one broken bread (1 Cor. 10:17).

Creating Worship

In this book, "worship" henceforth means these practices that constitute Christian communal and ritual life, as reflected in the NT itself and thereafter, not merely or specifically what the NT itself calls "worship." As the story of how this sort of "worship" develops, however, we may continue to bear in mind the other sense or senses in which the word was used. Since the Christians of the first four centuries did not have a concept of "worship" as a distinct form of human activity that linked these practices over against other forms of ritual or obedience, to narrate early Christian life entirely as though it did would be misleading. We will also use the term "liturgy," which, while it has a clearer modern set of references in the communal rituals of some Christian groups, has also changed in significance, originally referring to forms of public service or philanthropy, but in the early Christian period came gradually to be applied to the "service" that was Christian communal prayer and practice.

If the more specific idea of worship or liturgy as communal ritual and prayer is recent in some respects, we can see it beginning to form at least conceptually in early Christianity itself. In his *First Apology*, written in the mid-second century, the Christian teacher Justin Martyr (ca. 100–ca. 165) addresses a defense and description of Christian practice to the Roman emperor, linking some of these characteristic performances and gatherings such as Eucharist and communal prayer and comparing them favorably to Roman sacrifices:

> We praise [God], to the best of our ability, through prayer and thanksgiving for all we have been given to eat, as we have been taught is the only honor worthy of him; not to consume by fire what he has created for our sustenance, but to use it for ourselves and those in need. And in thanksgiving for our existence, and for all the means of strength, for the various kinds of created things, and for the changes of the seasons, we offer him prayers for our persistence in immortality through faith in him in verbal processions and hymns. (*1 Apol.* 13.1–2)

Justin's references to "thanksgiving" (*eucharistia*) in relation to food alludes to the Eucharist, as he makes clearer later in the same important work, which we will encounter at various points in what follows. He thus places the distinctive sacramental actions of the Christians within a bigger picture, with the ritual and the worldview as two sides of the same coin; "thanksgiving" among a small group of Christ-believers is both the whole of their life and a meal of bread and wine.

Sources and Method: Diversity and Development

Texts and Objects

"Worship" in the sense employed here is about bodies and spaces and objects, as well as about words. Words, however, are most of what survives to give direct indications of early Christian practice, at least until the third century; and we cannot always be entirely clear how typical or representative these words are. Nevertheless, a rich set of surviving texts will be the first resort for much of this book.

Material evidence and the results of archaeology do contribute fundamentally to imagining the world in which Christianity emerged. The earliest Christian objects may actually be texts, or rather manuscripts, such as the many papyri found a century or so ago at Oxyrhynchus in Egypt; many of these had some sort of ritual or communal use, as sacred texts for reading.[3] If until the third century it is difficult to point to other material evidence that relates to actual Christian ritual, some of the activities of the early communities can be illuminated by evidence for common practices in the wider world of the ancient Mediterranean, such as for communal dining.

When objects and spaces with specifically Christian origins do become available for examination, they are often funerary in character; catacomb paintings and sarcophagi provide a disproportionate amount of the earliest Christian art. The images and symbols they bear emphasize the hope of resurrection and how the afterlife was imagined, rather than how worship was conducted. If we should avoid romantic fantasies about persecuted Christians huddling in the catacombs for regular worship, we can nevertheless glean some wider elements of ritual practice from such places and objects, in addition to the more immediate sense these give of actual funerary observances.[4]

From the third century on we are also able to begin considering actual spaces and their use by groups of Christians. The oldest surviving "church"—a misnomer by most counts, but at least a space dedicated to the activities of Christian communal rituals—from Dura-Europos in Syria provides a new sort of opportunity to consider baptismal ritual. From the fourth century, architectural and other evidence starts to become considerably more common, but few other accoutrements of worship—vessels, books, and such—from the period within the scope of this study have survived.

The New Testament Texts

The most valuable texts for examining the origins of Christian worship are those collected in the NT. For our purposes their value is twofold. First, they are, as a group, the oldest set of texts illustrating any aspect of early Christian gatherings; there are only a few others that can claim to be as ancient as even the latest of these. Second, they are themselves artifacts or elements of Christian worship; their collection and preservation, and even composition,

3. See now the discussion in AnneMarie Luijendijk, "Sacred Scriptures as Trash: Biblical Papyri from Oxyrhynchus," *Vigiliae Christianae* 64 (2010): 217–54.

4. Robin Margaret Jensen, *Understanding Early Christian Art* (New York: Routledge, 2000), esp. 8–31.

owe much to the liturgical practices of the ancient communities among whom these works came to be read as Scripture.[5]

This does not mean, however, that NT documents can be read as simple windows onto the earliest Christian practice. Much depends on genre. The Gospels themselves may be more valuable than some assume as evidence for communal practice after the emergence of the Christian movement, since their composition and use reflects not only the practice and teaching of Jesus but also the concerns of his followers subsequently. On the other hand, it is tempting for some to imagine that prescriptive texts in the NT—such as many of the letters are in part—give a straightforward indication of what was actually done. The fact that Paul advocates or criticizes a certain custom in a letter may or may not actually mean that his readers instantly complied with his wishes; it probably does mean that they were not doing what he wanted to begin with.

Modern efforts to create or reform liturgical practices in terms such as "NT worship" reveal a different sort of problem. There are principles that can be discerned about issues such as order, participation, edification, and mutual regard (1 Cor. 12–14), yet the contexts in which these virtues were sought cannot always be established straightforwardly. Baptism and Eucharist are grounded in specific injunctions of Jesus (1 Cor. 11:24–25; Matt. 28:19), and otherwise assumed or discussed, but the forms they took are hardly specified. So these documents manifestly do not present a systematic description or prescription for Christian gatherings; they do assume various practices as available for assessment and critique. Reading the NT as a liturgical source thus requires some imaginative construction of these assumed practices; such construction must of course be accountable to the evidence for what actually took place, and appropriate critical attention must be given to how imagination tends to favor present experience and preferences.

Jewish Evidence

In 1949 a leading scholar of Christian liturgy, Gregory Dix, famously stated that "our understanding of our forms of worship underwent a radical transformation when it finally occurred to someone that Jesus was a Jew."[6] Most of a century later, there have been many important developments in the study of early Christian worship that reflect this obvious but long-underemphasized

---

5. See further chap. 3 on reading and preaching, below.
6. The quip is recounted by one of the hearers, Thomas J. Talley, in "From Berakah to Eucharistia: A Reopening Question," *Worship* 50 (1976): 115.

reality. Yet our sense of what it meant to be a first-century Jew has also changed significantly.

In the same year that Dix spoke about Jesus and Judaism, archaeologists were undertaking the initial excavation of Cave 1 at Qumran, the source of the Dead Sea Scrolls.[7] The library discovered at Qumran revealed a diversity and richness of Jewish thought that was contemporary with Jesus and whose character was often quite distinctive over and against better-known texts, such as the rabbinical monuments of Mishnah, Tosefta, and Talmuds, on the one hand, and the Hellenized reflections of urbane Jews like Philo and Josephus, on the other.

Consideration of the Jewish matrix within which Christianity emerged remains fundamentally important to consideration of early Christian ritual practice, but this is not a simple matter. Many published works simplify or objectify Jewish practice, however sympathetically, as a neat backdrop against which the actors of early Christian liturgy can be imagined performing their rituals. Ancient Judaism was in fact a diverse and dynamic set of traditions; all of the sets of texts just mentioned are potentially important as evidence for Jewish belief and practice, but none provides a simple or uncontested picture of such.

The Dead Sea Scrolls themselves were initially hailed by some as shedding direct light on the milieu of Jesus, or at least on John the Baptizer. Among the texts found at Qumran, those particularly concerned with the life of the sectarian community that produced them expand our sense of how diverse Jewish thought and practice may have been, but invite only indirect comparison with John or Jesus. They do, however, corroborate and enrich evidence from some of the other texts regarding forms of Jewish prayer and a widespread interest or concern about the temple and its rituals.[8]

Rabbinic literature may be the most often misused of Jewish sources. Voluminous in scope, and systematic in some respects but celebrating indeterminacy in others, these tractates include traditions as old as Jesus or older, but also reflect the continuing realities of the periods up to their compilation: around 200 CE for the Mishnah and Tosefta, but much later for the Talmuds.[9] This does not make them less important texts, but they are documents of an ongoing tradition that continued to interact with Christianity after the time

---

7. James C. VanderKam, *The Dead Sea Scrolls Today*, 2nd ed. (Grand Rapids: Eerdmans, 2010), 9.

8. Ibid., 61–96.

9. See the discussions in Jacob Neusner, *The Classics of Judaism: A Textbook and Reader* (Louisville: Westminster John Knox, 1995).

of Jesus, and are not merely depictions of a homogenous Judaism from which
Christianity departed. As we will note below, rabbinic evidence for practices
such as the Passover seder, baptism of proselytes, and patterns of scriptural
reading, which around Dix's time were sometimes treated simply as direct
influences on Christianity, must now be viewed more as parallel or, better,
interwoven strands of later ritual development.

Church Orders

There is Christian literary evidence not in the NT canon, some of it perhaps
as old as some scriptural writings, that provides more specific information
about liturgical practices and concerns. Preeminent, at least in liturgical focus,
among these documents is a "church order" genre, which offers a sense not
only of what was regarded by its real authors as the appropriate or ideal forms
of worship practice but also of what kind of implied authority was deemed
appropriate to establish it.

The oldest of these church orders is generally known as the *Didache* ("Teaching"), which has been transmitted along with suggestions (in varying titles)
that its "teaching" came either from the twelve apostles or from the Lord
himself, through them, to the nations.[10] The *Didache* (ca. 100?) includes a
catechetical summary, instructions for baptism and Eucharist, and rules for
leadership practice. Its successors predictably add more detail and substance,
including principles and texts for other forms of gathering, for daily prayer,
and for what we might see as ethical and organizational matters and not
just the narrowly liturgical—another reminder that their categories and ours
may not coincide. Church orders written or compiled across the third to fifth
centuries—prominent among them the works known as the *Apostolic Tradition*, *Didascalia Apostolorum*, *Apostolic Constitutions*, and *Testamentum
Domini*—not only attempt to prescribe proper worship practices but also
continue to place their ambition for good liturgy in the hands of older and
higher authorities, to whom the works or their contents are earnestly if im-
plausibly attributed. Over time, general attributions to apostolic authority
in these works give way to supposed direct quotes from the apostles, and in
some cases to teachings ascribed to Jesus himself.

The names of these works, confusing as they are to the newcomer, are all
intended to be rather transparent; the church orders do not present themselves

---

10. Kurt Niederwimmer, *The Didache: A Commentary*, ed. Harold W. Attridge, trans.
Linda M. Maloney, Hermeneia (Minneapolis: Fortress, 1998), 57.

as distinct compositions but as records of apostolic or even divine sanction for what they describe. The authors and communities whose interests they represent were generally not conscious inventors of liturgical practice, but, in their own minds at least, inheritors and defenders of acts and words whose antiquity and authority were far greater than their own. A modern reader may reach different conclusions about both of those claims, but ought not blithely to ignore their significance. This also means that these documents fit awkwardly into typical modern ideas of original authors or autographs; they are rather "living literature," among which every version and every manuscript has its significance.[11]

The most interesting and problematic of all these may be the work often referred to as the *Apostolic Tradition* and associated with Hippolytus, a presbyter and would-be bishop in Rome early in the third century. This is a text that can only be reconstructed with moderate certainty from fragments and borrowings, but which was (or versions of which were) certainly used by a number of other later works dating from about 400 onward. Scholars in the early twentieth century established a likely form and content of this "Egyptian Church Order," as it was initially and more modestly referred to; they also grew more confident it could be attached to a place and a name, to the extent that it became routinely referred to as the work of one Hippolytus of Rome and called the *Apostolic Tradition*. That confidence—not so much about a basic form of the document but about its specific origin—now seems excessive, and the supposed assurance of an early Roman provenance needs to be considered critically.[12] Still, this *Apostolic Tradition* (as we will continue to refer to it, for convenience, at least) was certainly an early and very influential work of the church order genre, and is a precious witness to some (probably) fourth-century compiler's highest liturgical and pastoral ideals, as well as to those of earlier writers or communities—some even as early as the elusive Hippolytus—who provided its sources.

Other Works

Few other literary works from the early church are as directly focused on worship as these, but few have no relevance at all. Writings of apologists

11. Paul F. Bradshaw, *The Search for the Origins of Christian Worship: Sources and Methods for the Study of Early Liturgy* (London: SPCK, 2002), 5.

12. A circumspect position is taken in the most comprehensive recent commentary; see Paul F. Bradshaw, Maxwell E. Johnson, and L. Edward Phillips, *The Apostolic Tradition: A Commentary*, ed. Harold W. Attridge, Hermeneia (Minneapolis: Fortress, 2002); a plausible revision of the case for Roman origin is made in Hippolytus, *On the Apostolic Tradition*, ed. Alistair Stewart-Sykes (Crestwood, NY: St. Vladimir's Seminary Press, 2001).

like Justin, whom we have already encountered, include attempts to defend Christian practice from ignorance or slander. From the third century on there are extended exegetical works, such as those of Origen of Alexandria (ca. 185–ca. 254), that began life in homiletical contexts and thus provide us with direct evidence for what will come to be seen as the ministry of the Word and with incidental evidence for other practices. Letters from significant figures like Cyprian (d. 258) and Augustine sometimes address questions of worship practice directly.

These rich resources of patristic literature offer various possibilities for reading and reflection. Some readers today have and will seek to draw prescriptive theological pictures from them; some of these "fathers" whose more extensive writings have survived certainly offer sacramental theologies whose similarities and differences from later ones are important. While sacramental theology will appear in this book from time to time, our concern is descriptive more than prescriptive. That is, these chapters attempt to reconstruct a sense of what was said and done in various ancient churches, not of what ought to have been done, even in the view of the most persuasive or authoritative ancient writers.

There are also surviving liturgical texts in the more immediate sense—that is, words used in worship. Apart from those contained in the church orders, some prayers and hymns have come down from well-known authors like Ephraem of Nisibis (ca. 306–73) and Ambrose of Milan (ca. 339–97), but others have come without attribution, speaking with a collective voice of the past rather than an individual one. These are all words composed by a relative few, but spoken or sung by many, women and men, young and old, speakers and hearers in Latin, Greek, Syriac, and Coptic, among other languages.

In addition to these relatively well-known and authoritative texts and authors, there were others that were looked at askance by them but that are not necessarily less interesting to us. Early Christianity was characterized by processes of community formation, involving both ritual and theory, from the earliest times; a strand that we know as "catholic" or "orthodox" emerged in and through a variety of controversies and contests across the period that is the subject of this book, but was not always and everywhere the most or only obvious way to be Christian. And what characterized that orthodoxy, as it emerged in the period of the creeds and councils, cannot be assumed to have been part of the thought or the practice of every earlier group.

Losers rarely write history, so the evidence for early Christian diversity in worship is as difficult to establish as for other things. There are important reports and critiques of certain practices passed on by the victorious—by Irenaeus of Lyons (ca. 130–ca. 200), Tertullian (ca. 160–ca. 225), and Cyprian for the second and third centuries, and by Augustine and John Chrysostom (347–407) for the fourth. Some of the other voices have survived more directly, however. These include works of a quasi-scriptural nature, such as apocryphal gospels and acts, which reflect a variety of positions often not in keeping with the eventually normative tradition, and some of which contain indications of how their authors and early readers thought, sometimes surprisingly, about matters such as baptism and Eucharist. The movement sometimes referred to as gnosticism has left some direct literary remains, such as those documents that survived in the cache of Coptic texts from Nag Hammadi in Upper Egypt.[13]

We will consider the practices of these groups as they arise, and their importance is not merely a matter of curiosity. As the Christian movement grew and developed, its ritual, like its theology, was in formation. The particular forms of gatherings and the actions and utterances that came to characterize them were not always the organic development of what was already obvious to the earliest Christians, but involved dialogic processes—controversies, often—both internal and external. Jewish and Greek and other communities and traditions provided points of contrast, imitation, and competition. Internal differences—about the extent of Scripture, the elements of the Eucharist, and the forms of baptism—all gave shape to the practices that were to emerge in more or less familiar forms; and these emergent practices were to some extent choices, reflecting decisions about what to do and what not to do.

There are also texts conveyed as inscriptions, whose witness has a different and very significant character. Specifically Christian inscriptions, like other material evidence, take some time to appear and are few in number until the fourth century; and like other material evidence, they are somewhat skewed toward the funereal. However, these texts, whose audiences were somewhat different from those of literary works, add some remarkable thickness and diversity to the picture—for example, witnessing to the existence of at least some women who were clergy at periods when this has often been regarded as impossible,[14] or indicating that the difficulty of holding some traditional

13. On this see the different positions held by David Brakke, *The Gnostics: Myth, Ritual, and Diversity in Early Christianity* (Cambridge, MA: Harvard University Press, 2010), whose discussion includes some important treatments of ritual and sacramental issues, and Michael Allen Williams, *Rethinking "Gnosticism": An Argument for Dismantling a Dubious Category* (Princeton: Princeton University Press, 1999).

14. Ute E. Eisen, *Women Officeholders in Early Christianity: Epigraphical and Literary Studies* (Collegeville, MN: Liturgical Press, 2000).

beliefs along with the new ones of the gospel was not always so self-evident to those mourning the departed.[15]

Scope

This study begins with the earliest evidence for Christian belief and practice, and ends not long after 400. The reasons for this chronological scope are those that have often led to a working definition of the "early church" that spans those centuries; just as this period sees the emergence of relative clarity around the canon of Scripture and creedal definitions of doctrine, it also sees the formation of liturgical patterns that would remain fundamental to Christian practice thereafter.

Nevertheless, the picture constructed here has not been formed purely with the intention of explaining those practices that persisted and that underlie present ones. There are paths pursued in this book that go nowhere in terms of subsequent liturgical history, but that were walked on with faith and hope by the ancients: dancing, foot washing, and kissing are some examples whose inclusion is important to construct an ancient picture and not merely to illuminate a modern one.

It may be clearer how these early centuries are fundamental to present Christian identity in the cases of creeds and canon—which continue to have widely acknowledged authority across modern Christian traditions—than that of liturgy. While in Roman Catholic, Eastern Orthodox, and some mainline Protestant traditions the connections between the rituals of Eucharist and baptism as traced here will be easy to see, the forms of worship in many other Christian groups today are not consciously based on these models. This raises some interesting questions regarding how each of these forms of Christian practice (including intellectual practice) really are or should be determined; some Protestants would be surprised to know that many of the Reformers understood their liturgical task as being to restore ancient models rather than to construct worship anew purely from NT texts—a problematic notion in any case.

However, even the varied forms of baptism and Eucharist, or Lord's Supper, across the enormous diversity of contemporary Christianity allow some perception of older shapes and texts; every Christian liturgical practice is, after all, "reformed" in some sense, not really invented from whole cloth or

15. For instance, the epitaph of Licinia, which invokes Jesus as "fish of the living" on a stele, also refers to the Roman *Dii Manes*; see Jensen, *Understanding Early Christian Art*, 51.

outside of history. Ancient approaches to words spoken and sung are at least of comparative interest for modern preachers and performers; and the practice of daily prayer, which will be considered here in some detail, arguably underlies the typical Protestant service of the Word, even if its practitioners are often unaware of the precedent.

The story of Christian worship across this time involves both continuity and change. This book does not seek to present the change either as minimal (as though the shape of Christian worship was always and immediately obvious, and merely gathered some inconsequential detail as it went along) or as so radical as to amount to discontinuity (as though the Constantinian revolution imposed ritual practice on a group previously characterized only by spontaneity and freedom of action).[16] The history of Christian worship, like the history of Christianity itself, is probably ill served by either of these grand narratives. Christian worship does, however, have a real story, which like any other worth telling has foundational elements that are developed, others that appear as genuine novelties, and some that appear and then fade or die. Within this narrative, the efforts of Christians to seek, serve, and praise the Maker of all things as revealed in Jesus Christ is the sustained theme.

---

16. On the Constantinian revolution see Paul F. Bradshaw, "Ten Principles for Interpreting Early Christian Liturgical Evidence," in *The Making of Jewish and Christian Worship*, ed. Paul F. Bradshaw and Lawrence A. Hoffman, Two Liturgical Traditions 1 (Notre Dame, IN: University of Notre Dame Press, 1991), 3–21.

2

⁓

MEAL

Banquet and Eucharist

Then they told what had happened on the road, and how he
had been made known to them in the breaking of the bread.
(Luke 24:35)

T he oldest account of ancient churchgoing describes the first Christian
community in Jerusalem as devoted to "the apostles' teaching and fellowship, to the breaking of the bread and the prayers" (Acts 2:42). We
lack the details of these elements, but one thing in particular is surprising,
relative to more recent patterns of worship: Christians met for meals. A distinctive meal tradition—here called the "breaking of the bread"—was not a
social event additional to worship, or a programmatic attempt to create fellowship among the Christians, but the regular form of Christian gathering.

These assemblies, where bread was broken, cup blessed, and various forms
of discourse shared among the community and offered to God, were of course
the forerunners of what Christians have known as the Eucharist, Lord's Supper,
Holy Communion, or Mass. We begin consideration of these meals not because
of the prominence the descendants have for some Christians now, however,
but because of their place then. They were not merely one sacramental part

of a community or worship life but the central act around or within which others—reading and preaching, prayer and prophecy—were arranged.

Ancient Eating

The Banquet[1]

Although modern Christians are accustomed to understanding their own versions of this meal largely through the story of Jesus' final meal, the term "Last Supper" itself implies a whole series of previous suppers. The first Christians remembered not just the last but many meals of Jesus as models for their own eating. Those meals also belonged to a wider cultural tradition of shared eating and drinking, within which the emerging eucharistic meal tradition took its place and claimed its significance.

The Christians were also not unique or peculiar in the ancient world in having common meals as a central event. In fact it would have been strange had they not shared food together in both a festive and a formal way, since most other definable social groups in the ancient Mediterranean world did the same. In 1 Corinthians, Paul compares and contrasts a "Lord's supper" with the "private suppers" his readers celebrated at other times. The Greek word usually translated "supper" is *deipnon*, which would be better rendered as "banquet." A *deipnon* (or in Latin, a *cena* or *convivium*) was an evening meal with certain expected formalities and a tradition of proper conduct; as an institution, the ancient Greco-Roman banquet includes and defies modern categories of secular and sacred, familial and public, celebratory and solemn.

Ancient banquets were relatively formal and purposeful events, held often but nonetheless distinguished from merely incidental eating. They could be large or small, ostentatious or austere, civic or familial. They were also an integral part of Greco-Roman (including Jewish) sacrifices, since the flesh of animal victims was often consumed straight after ritual slaughter in a festive atmosphere. Groups bound by kinship and by professional, social, religious, or ethnic ties celebrated such meals together to create and express their identity and their beliefs when need or opportunity for celebration arose.[2]

Apart from the Last Supper itself, the most famous banquets of Mediterranean antiquity may be the philosophical feasts of Plato, whose dialogues

---

1. See further Dennis E. Smith, *From Symposium to Eucharist: The Banquet in the Early Christian World* (Minneapolis: Fortress, 2003).

2. Modern scholars often use the Latin term *collegia* as a way of referring to these ancient clubs or guilds, wherever they were found and whatever language was spoken among them.

were often set during the after-dinner conversations of the great Socrates and his associates. These literary meals and those depicted in ancient visual arts are somewhat idealized, yet they reflect much of what was seen as typical or proper. Subsequently, those famous "symposia" (from the name for the drinking course or party, *symposion*, following the meal proper) have come to serve as models not only for many diners but also even more for scholars, conversationalists, and students.

There were expected features of ancient formal dining, although much variety in detail. We hear of participants gathering in a dining room, or *triclinium*, often reclining on couches arranged around the room as three sides of a rectangle like an angular U. In some places, and especially in later antiquity, diners might form their party around a C- or crescent-shaped table, or *stibadium*; the earliest surviving depictions of Christian meal scenes, such as those in the Roman catacombs, present such curved assemblies, as do the oldest images depicting Jesus' Last Supper.[3] Places for guests in these configurations reflected the relationship of diners to host, or their social status. Gender roles were often clearly expressed. The classical Greek banquet tended to be a male-centered affair, with women's participation defined somewhat carefully—women other than attendants and entertainers usually sat, rather than reclined, with the men, unless at women-only events. Roman customs, and later Greek ones, were somewhat more inclusive or egalitarian than those of the classical period.[4] Gospel accounts of Jesus' meals reflect interest in some of these issues of status and participation, not only as they occurred in his own ministry but also in the early Christian settings to which the stories were subsequently applied (see Luke 11:37–54; 14:1–21). Who should sit where? Where and how could women as well as men participate?

Preliminaries for the banquet could include washing of hands, offering of an opening prayer or hymn, and libations. The meal proper followed, with the variety and quality of foods depending on the means of the host or group and on the nature of the occasion. After eating, tables were removed and wine was brought and mixed with water, typically in a large bowl, or *kratēr*, and then shared by the diners in individual cups after further prayers or libations to the relevant deity. A number of such large bowls of mixed wine might be prepared over the evening—three was regarded as ideal. Entertainment and/or conversation was expected during this time, its form depending on the group.

---

3. Jensen, *Understanding Early Christian Art*, 53–55.
4. Katherine M. D. Dunbabin, *The Roman Banquet: Images of Conviviality* (New York: Cambridge University Press, 2003), 19–30.

Such diversions ranged from the subdued conversations of philosophers to more raucous events involving flute girls and courtesans.

The communal suppers of the earliest Christians followed this or similar patterns, with the after-dinner conversation centering on issues and forms of speech (including song) appropriate to their faith. An account of the Christian meal from North Africa as late as 200 CE would still have been recognizable to any ancient Greek or Roman reader as a banquet, if a rather restrained one:

> We do not recline until we have first tasted of prayer to God; as much is eaten as to satisfy the hungry; only as much is drunk as is proper to the chaste. They are satisfied as those who remember that they have to praise God even in the night; they talk as those who know that the Lord is listening. After water for washing the hands, and lights, each is invited to sing publicly to God as able from holy scripture or from their own ability; thus how each has drunk is put to the test. Similarly prayer closes the feast. (Tertullian, *Apol.* 39.17–18)

This was a very conventional way to meet and celebrate shared values and common commitments. Yet to do so not by pouring libations for the emperors but by remembering a crucified victim of their rule was a more remarkable and indeed countercultural thing.[5]

Ancient Food

The story of the Last Supper depicts Jesus sharing bread and wine with his disciples. A meal consisting largely of bread and wine (mixed with water, as it almost always was) would not have seemed remarkable to ancient eaters, although a banquet would have involved other foods too. The three Gospel accounts that include the "institution narrative" present that fateful meal as a celebration of Passover, which also would have included bread and wine, like other meals; none of the more specific and desirable foods that were later to characterize the seder of the Passover are mentioned, but some of them may be assumed.

Grains were staple food across the Greco-Roman world, and economics as well as convenience determined that many people at many times—not just Jews at Passover—ate unleavened bread. Leavened bread took longer to make and was more desirable and expensive; those with even less time or fuel might just boil their grain or flour to consume it, or eat parched grain. At banquets on

---

5. Hal Taussig, *In the Beginning Was the Meal: Social Experimentation and Early Christian Identity* (Minneapolis: Fortress, 2009), 115–43.

whatever scale, however, bread was at the center of the meal. Smaller amounts of highly seasoned foods such as fish (often in preserved form), salt, vegetables, legumes, oil, cheese, and sometimes meat accompanied the bread to make a meal. The more festive the occasion and the more resourceful the host, the greater the variety, quantity, and quality of these accompanying elements.

Meat was expensive, and access to it was relative to wealth and power. It was also thoroughly associated with sacrifice, and much of the meat came via temples; devotees offering a sacrificial animal would eat part of it in the ritual and take some away, but often sold a surplus through the priests, too. In cities other than Jerusalem, Jews and Christians felt they had to avoid regular meat markets, knowing the meat could have been "offered to idols" on its way to sale. Paul's attempt to deal with this unknown threat via a sort of dietary "don't ask, don't tell" strategy (1 Cor. 10:25) would not have convinced every scrupulous Christian or Jewish eater.

Wine was also drunk, and not only on special occasions; it completed a standard Greek meal triad of bread (*artos*), side dish or relish (*opson*), and wine (*oinos*).[6] In an agrarian society where many struggled to achieve the necessary food intake to stay alive, the food value of wine was significant. Even quite poor people, such as slaves and widows, could expect some form of wine in their diet, although the quality of the vintages may well have been unimpressive. Wine was a focus at banquets for reasons beyond aesthetics or nutrition, since libations (offerings poured onto the ground) or, in Jewish circles, blessings over wine were regularly offered to initiate and sanctify the whole proceedings. Thus wine, like meat, had religious significance. Scholars have referred to these elements together, meat and wine, as a "cuisine of sacrifice" in the Greco-Roman world.[7]

Early Christians did not live by bread and wine alone; other foods (*opsa*) sometimes played an important part in their "eucharistic" eating as well, as we will see. Yet the normative pattern of bread and wine central to the Christian communal meal reflects the staple food and drink of the ancient Mediterranean, not just a specific ritual or tradition associated with Jesus. Their character as the most ordinary foodstuffs, universally accessible and necessary, underlay their importance in a meal ritual that was associated with spiritual benefits of the most extraordinary kind.

---

6. Andrew Dalby, *Siren Feasts: A History of Food and Gastronomy in Greece* (London: Routledge, 1997), 22–24.

7. Marcel Detienne and Jean Pierre Vernant, *The Cuisine of Sacrifice among the Greeks* (Chicago: University of Chicago Press, 1989).

Jewish Meals

Jesus' own eating, including his Last Supper, involved sensibilities and rituals specific to Jewish tradition. Jewish dining, including of course observance
of the Mosaic dietary laws, should, however, be understood as one part of an
ancient Mediterranean banqueting tradition rather than as a totally separate
reality.

The relationship between the Last Supper and the Passover banquet, or
seder, has already been mentioned. Although it is not entirely clear exactly
how the death of Jesus and/or a last meal with his followers related historically to the celebration of Passover (cf. John 18:28; 19:41), most scholars
are inclined to see the meal as a formal Passover banquet, as the Synoptic
Gospels present it. Christians certainly went on celebrating a form of Passover in their new feast of Easter, and used paschal imagery to interpret the
death and resurrection of Jesus. This made the seder at least an important
point of reference.

The Mishnah, the collection of oral law compiled around 200 CE, depicts
the seder of that time as a complex meal where significant foods were eaten
in a specific order, with accompanying discourse. That much would have been
expected in any ancient banquet. The influence of the broader Greco-Roman
banqueting tradition on this rabbinic seder has often been noted; for instance,
Jewish diners are required by the Mishnah to recline (*m. Pesaḥ.* 10.1), just as
their pagan neighbors would have done. Yet instead of a meal followed by
a *symposion* in the expected Greek manner, the seder involves various cups
of wine taken and blessed along the way between courses, with eating and
explanations. The contrast with the Greek model is real but not necessarily
radical. The repetition of a pattern (wine, food, and conversation) means that
later, the seder becomes almost a series of "mini-banquets," courses whose
complexity reflects the significance of the feast.

Luke's account of the Last Supper does have, uniquely, a cup (22:17) shared
by Jesus *before* the familiar bread-cup sequence of the Greco-Roman banquet.
This has led some scholars to see the NT narrative as excerpted from that
more complex seder ritual.[8] Yet the seder as depicted in the Mishnah may not
have been fully developed, let alone universally observed, at the time of Jesus;
the later rabbinic form may even owe something to the Christian eucharistic
tradition and reflect responses to it.[9] If the Last Supper was a Passover banquet

8. Joachim Jeremias, *The Eucharistic Words of Jesus* (London: SCM, 1966).
9. I. J. Yuval, "Easter and Passover as Early Jewish-Christian Dialogue," in *Passover
and Easter: Origin and History to Modern Times*, ed. Paul F. Bradshaw and Lawrence A.

as seems likely, it is nevertheless misleading to see the Eucharist as a sort of Christianized seder in that later and more developed sense.[10]

The opening of a meal with blessing of a cup (as in Luke) is, however, a characteristic Jewish tradition attested much earlier and more broadly. Meals described in the Dead Sea Scrolls, which are as old as the Gospels or older, as well as in the later Mishnah, involve blessings for an opening cup with a characteristic prayer of *berakah* ("blessing") form: "Blessed are you Lord God, King of the universe," followed by a specific petition (see *m. Ber.* 6.1). Although blessing the cup at the outset parallels how libations opened a banquet where Greek gods were honored, in these Jewish instances the cup blessing seems also to have preempted a *symposion* after the meal. This pattern may have become a conscious point of contrast to dubious behavior associated with that later part of the Greco-Roman banquet and to other practices identified with gentiles.

There are other examples of particular Jewish groups close to Jesus' time celebrating meals as a means of expressing and creating bonds of social obligation and divine obedience. The Qumran community envisaged present and future ideal banquets (1QS; 1QSa), and the later Mishnah considers proper blessings and other conduct for the common meals of *haburot*, or associations. These are useful comparisons for early Christian eucharistic eating but do not provide answers to the questions of how or why the followers of Jesus ate while reflecting on his presence and promise.

All these Jewish meals are useful for comparison with the evidence for Christian communal eating; none of them provides a simple model adopted or adapted for Christian use, however. The Eucharist emerges in the same world as these forms, aware of some of the earlier ones, but developing alongside rather than merely out of them.

Meals in the New Testament

Many Suppers

The story of Jesus' "Last Supper" has been received and recited by innumerable Christians as the basis for their own sacred meals. The power and poignancy of the scene, and Jesus' words identifying a meal of bread and

Hoffman, Two Liturgical Traditions 5 (Notre Dame, IN: University of Notre Dame Press, 1999), 98–124.

10. See Joel Marcus, "Passover and Last Supper Revisited," *New Testament Studies* 59 (2013): 303–24.

wine as a participation in his body and blood, have created an authoritative and enduring example. If, then, it would be hard to exaggerate the Last Supper's importance, its importance has nevertheless been misconstrued. The earliest Christian communities were certainly eating together before any of the documents that now convey the story were written, and although it must have circulated orally before that, some almost certainly gathered to eat even without knowledge of this parting advice from Jesus.

The Last Supper was obviously not the first supper, either. The Gospels themselves present that final meal of Jesus as the climax of his practice as a frequent, significant, and controversial eater. Jesus dines with tax collectors and sinners (Mark 2:15–17; Matt. 11:19; Luke 7:34), receives hospitality from unlikely characters (Luke 14:1–24; 19:1–10), uses banquets as the venue for teaching (Luke 11:37–54; 14:7–14), and acts as a miraculous and generous host under unlikely circumstances (Mark 6:34–44, etc.). These many not-last suppers were an important part of Jesus' ministry and contributed both to his popularity and to his conflicts; one scholar has said pointedly, "Jesus was killed because of the way he ate."[11] In reality, Jesus' eating may not have been quite so exceptional or controversial as that—but it reflected the content of his message and the ethos of the group that followed him.

If the "Last" Supper was not the first significant meal to which Jesus' later followers could look for an example, according to the Gospels it was not strictly the last, either. Stories of the resurrection depict an eating Jesus sharing food with disciples as a sign of his renewed life (John 21:12–13), and even as the means of revealing his presence and identity (Luke 24:30–31). These narratives reflect the early Christians' sense of their community meals as the continuation of a whole series of Jesus' suppers or banquets, not just a response to or memorialization of one.

In conveying their pictures of the historical ministry of Jesus, the Gospels also reflect the concerns of the Christians a generation or two later (60–100 CE) who wrote and received them, and are therefore sources in our quest for the meals of those communities. A good example is the regular pattern of meal blessing that occurs across the Gospel tradition and is particularly prominent in Luke-Acts. From the miraculous feeding stories (Luke 9:16), to the Last Supper (22:19), to the resurrection meal at Emmaus (24:30), a familiar sequence of taking bread, blessing or giving thanks, breaking it, and distributing it for eating is present.

11. Robert J. Karris, *Luke: Artist and Theologian; Luke's Passion Account as Literature*, Theological Inquiries (New York: Paulist Press, 1985), 70.

One remarkable example of this pattern takes place in Acts on board a ship at sea, with Paul, the host, exhorting his frightened shipmates:

> Therefore I urge you to take some food, for it will help you survive [lit.: "this is for your salvation"]; for none of you will lose a hair from your heads." After he had said this, he *took* bread; and *giving thanks* to God in the presence of all, he *broke* it and *began to eat*. Then all of them were encouraged and took food for themselves. (Acts 27:34–36, emphasis added)

This fourfold shape may reflect very early ritual practice (including that of Jesus and his followers) that may have in turn influenced subsequent eucharistic prayer and action.[12] The pattern of thanksgiving or blessing further reminds us that the Last Supper stories, which also all include it, belong in a wider meal tradition rather than being completely unique.

The Last Supper was therefore not the sole basis for celebrating Christian meals, even if it often came to be seen as the most important reason for them. The meal gatherings of the earliest church had many memories and stories attached, and the first Christians may have understood their meals in terms considerably more varied than the familiar remembrance of Jesus' death. The risen Jesus of the road to Emmaus was present to these meal participants along with the Last Supper's doomed host, and the words of the prophetic feeder of the Galilean crowds were recalled at table as well as those of the crucified Savior.

Over time, however, the Last Supper would demand particular attention. Viewed in relation to other Gospel meal traditions, and to the prominence of shared meals as a means of expressing and forming community in ancient Mediterranean societies, the Last Supper narratives can be better understood not as a curious quirk of ritual practice instituted by Jesus in isolation but as an original expression and interpretation of familiar and widespread meal customs.

The Last Supper and the Eucharist

The complex and difficult symbolism of eating Jesus' body and drinking his blood has been fundamental to most eucharistic eating and drinking ever since, although perhaps less so in the first decades of the Christian movement

---

12. Gregory Dix, *The Shape of the Liturgy*, new ed. (London: Continuum, 2005); Dix's proposal has been justly criticized by Paul F. Bradshaw, "Did the Early Eucharist Ever Have a Sevenfold Shape?," *Heythrop Journal* 43 (2002): 73–76, but the fourfold notion can be sustained in the modest terms suggested here.

than often assumed. Its exact significance is of course controversial; here we are concerned with how the first Christians understood those words from Jesus rather than with some supposed original form or meaning, or with later disputes.

That "institution narrative" for the Christian meal is found in three of the Gospels, but the oldest written version is that from the apostle Paul, in 1 Corinthians 11. Only two of those four versions actually have Jesus commanding the continuation of the meal in his memory (Luke 22:19; 1 Cor. 11:24–25), and there are subtle if important differences across all four.

A comparison between what may be the two earliest versions, found in 1 Corinthians and the Gospel of Mark, illustrates the most important differences as well as core similarities:

. . . the Lord Jesus on the night on which he was handed over	And as they were eating,
took bread, and having given thanks, he broke it and said,	he took bread, and blessed, and broke it, and gave it to them, and said,
"This is my body which is for you. Do this in memory of me."	"Take; this is my body."
Similarly also the cup after supper, saying,	And he took a cup, and having given thanks he gave it to them, and they all drank of it. And he said to them,
"This cup is the new covenant in my blood. Do this, as often as you drink, in memory of me." (1 Cor. 11:23b–25 AT)	"This is my blood of the covenant, which is poured out for many.
	Truly, I say to you, I shall not drink again of the fruit of the vine until that day when I drink it new in the kingdom of God." (Mark 14:22–25 AT)

Paul's account and Luke's seem closely related, as Mark's and Matthew's are likewise; these two broad traditions we will call PL (Paul/Luke) and MM (Mark/Matthew). The similarities and differences are immediately apparent in the words used to describe Jesus' actions presiding and praying over bread and cup: on the one hand PL has Jesus *giving thanks* before breaking and giving the bread to his companions, where MM has Jesus *blessing* bread before breaking and giving it to them; on the other hand, MM has Jesus explicitly *giving thanks* over the cup, where PL merely implies ("similarly," etc.) thanksgiving again.

From a certain distance, "blessing" and "thanksgiving" may not seem very different; they are both ways of acknowledging God's grace for the meal. Up closer, the differences are also important. Blessing, or *berakah*, was a well-developed genre of Jewish prayer, typically addressed to God ("Blessed are you, Lord our God . . ."); one whole tractate of the Mishnah is dedicated to the appropriate blessings to offer at various times, including at meals. The *Birkat ha-mazon*, an extended prayer based on blessing but giving way to thanksgiving and supplication, became standard at Jewish meals not long after this time. While there were also forms of Jewish thanksgiving, or *hodayah*, prayers, these were less closely connected with meals; yet ongoing evidence for Christian prayer at meals emphasizes thanksgiving over blessing—as reflected in the prevalence of the term *eucharistia* ("Eucharist," but first and literally "thanksgiving"). So the differences between these two versions of the Last Supper story may reflect a point where this shifting terminology has not yet become so distinct; memories of Jesus' "blessing" are merged with the Christians' own experience of "thanksgiving."[13]

The identification of the bread—or rather, of the actions including its eating—as Jesus' body is common to all versions, although only PL adds words of interpretation and/or command; for MM it is merely that "this is my body." "This" (*touto*) is neuter in Greek, while "bread" (*artos*) is masculine; the implication is that "this" is not (or not only) the bread itself but the whole action undertaken or the community established thus.[14] It is the narrative context rather than the mere reference to "body" that makes a connection with Jesus' death.

The command to "do this in remembrance of me" is only in PL. MM is more expansive about the word over the cup, which is (identically, to begin with) "my blood of the covenant, which is poured out for many <for the forgiveness of sins>"—the longer version is Matthew's. Perhaps the most intriguing difference of all is that for PL the cup is not "my blood" at all, as in MM and most liturgical versions of the recitation, but rather "the new covenant in my blood." Thus while MM presents a neat if confronting parallelism of "body" and "blood" between bread and cup, PL identifies the cup not as Jesus' blood but as a covenant made in blood—as covenants were indeed generally made, with animal sacrifice (cf. Gen. 8:20–22). The cup need not be understood as alluding to the blood of the sacrifice, which after all was not drunk, but to the

---

13. See Talley, "From Berakah to Eucharistia."

14. Matthias Klinghardt, "Gemeindeleib und Mahlritual: *Sōma* in den paulinischen Mahltexten," *Zeitschrift für Neues Testament* 27 (2011): 51–56.

celebratory drinking that would accompany the sacrificial feast (cf. Ps. 116:13). In this context, the word over the cup still refers to Jesus' approaching death, but emphasizes its covenantal character and the meal itself as the festive banquet of that covenant.

The formulaic character of these stories has long been recognized as reflecting a communal use of some kind, usually imagined as a kind of prayer over the meal, as it would become in later liturgical texts. However, the earliest explicit evidence for eucharistic prayer—rather later than these NT texts, as we will see—does not include the institution narrative at all. That absence suggests some other use, such as a recitation intended to explain or interpret the meal;[15] Paul's own earliest presentation of the story has precisely such a use, and to this we turn.

Commensality at Corinth

Although many NT stories and traditions reflect the beliefs and practices of the early Christians about their shared meals, the first explicit discussion of them is in Paul's First Letter to the Corinthians. The oldest surviving work to include the story of Jesus' own last meal, this letter also reflects issues of communal dining among the Christians at Corinth, two decades after Jesus' ministry.

The Corinthians' regular meeting was a eucharistic meal, providing the first clear indication that eating characterized the earliest Christian gatherings. In chapter 11, where Paul is certainly discussing the meal and its proper conduct, he refers to the event simply as "com[ing] together" three times (1 Cor. 11:17, 18, 20) before adding the qualification "to eat" at verse 33. Of course they did not just eat and drink; Paul uses the same language in chapter 14, where other activities are described:

> When you come together, each one has a hymn, a lesson, a revelation, a tongue, or an interpretation. Let all things be done for building up. If anyone speaks in a tongue, let there be only two or at most three, and each in turn; and let one interpret. But if there is no one to interpret, let them be silent in church and speak to themselves and to God. Let two or three prophets speak, and let the others weigh what is said. If a revelation is made to someone else sitting nearby, let the first person be silent. For you can all prophesy one by one, so that all may learn and all be encouraged. (1 Cor. 14:26b–31)

15. Andrew B. McGowan, "'Is There a Liturgical Text in This Gospel?': The Institution Narratives and Their Early Interpretive Communities," *Journal of Biblical Literature* 118 (1999): 73–87.

These forms of inspired speech may seem to have little to do with meals or sacraments, but a meal as event was about more than food; eating and drinking at the banquets of associations and coreligionists was also accompanied, or followed, by discourse among the participants.[16]

When the table of the Lord was shared at Corinth, other questions and problems from the wider world of dining were brought along. Those who could afford to bring food were clearly eating a substantial meal (1 Cor. 11:21). Paul uses the story of the Last Supper (vv. 23–25) not to give instructions for proper ritual or prayer, or to suggest consumption of mere crumbs and sips, but to shame a divided community at Corinth with the example of Jesus' humility and self-offering (vv. 27–30).

We do not know what resulted in this case but should not assume that Paul's intention was to separate out a token form of eating or have such replace the communal meal. The bread and wine to be shared in his ideal banquet are still staple foods, shared fairly—not odd, merely "sacramental," additions to the meal. His advice was for moderation and above all for mutual consideration at table. Discerning the body—not only the body of Christ identified with the bread, but the body thus constituted by those who shared the bread—was the condition for celebrating a meal worthy to be thought of as "the Lord's" (1 Cor. 11:27–29; cf. v. 20).

Sacrifice at Corinth

Food and drink themselves were important religious issues for the Corinthians and their neighbors. Dilemmas about eating meat were particularly prominent. Had the Christians refused all sacrificed meat, they would have lost not just dietary and aesthetic benefits but also much of their participation in wider social circles. Paul proposes that they avoid banquets directly linked to sacrifices (1 Cor. 10:21) but otherwise treat meat itself indifferently (10:25). The logic of his directive links the Christian banquet with both gentile and Jewish sacrificial meals:

> The cup of blessing that we bless, is it not a sharing in the blood of Christ? The bread that we break, is it not a sharing in the body of Christ? Because there is one bread, we who are many are one body, for we all partake of the one bread. Consider the people of Israel; are not those who eat the sacrifices partners in the altar? What do I imply then? That food sacrificed to idols is anything, or that an idol is anything? No, I imply that what pagans sacrifice, they sacrifice

16. Smith, *From Symposium to Eucharist*, esp. 173–218.

to demons and not to God. I do not want you to be partners with demons. You cannot drink the cup of the Lord and the cup of demons. You cannot partake of the table of the Lord and the table of demons. (1 Cor. 10:16–21)

This is the earliest known theology of what it actually means to participate in the Christian meal. Paul interprets it as receiving or sharing the body and blood of Christ (unsurprisingly, given the narrative that he will remind them of at 11:23–26). Unlike many later theologies, Paul's notion of the body eaten is focused communally rather than individually, finding the Savior's presence in the corporate consumption rather than in the elements taken in isolation.

Participants in any offering, Jewish, Greek, or Christian, are partners in the "altar," "cup," or "table," Paul argues. Each of these accoutrements functions to describe the whole meal, the experience of sharing it with others, and shared commitment to the deity. Paul thus for the first time offers a "sacrificial" understanding of the Eucharist, not merely in the sense of any relationship constructed between the meal and Jesus' own death or Passover but also in relation to ancient understandings of how sharing sacred food created a community of faith. This does not, however, imply that the meal had an expiatory or propitiatory character; sacrifices had purposes other than the forgiveness of sins.

The centrality of sacrifice for ancient Mediterranean societies is hard to exaggerate. Offerings of animals and other foods, as well as pouring libations and burning incense, were forms of gift or communication that expressed how closely believers—in one God or many gods—felt their own good depended on spiritual forces beyond their sight.[17] The practice of sacrifices was woven through daily life and marked the celebrations as well as the crises of communities of all kinds. The issues raised at Corinth were therefore not a local quirk but went to the heart of social and religious identity.

Sacrifice was important to all the early Christian writers, readers, and hearers, Jew or gentile. Israelite sacrifice, as reflected in the then-continuing functions of the Jerusalem temple, was a sort of parallel cultic universe to the more diffuse polytheistic practices of other Mediterranean peoples. Jewish sacrifice, like Greek and Roman, could serve to address problems of purity and propriety, but was often related to more general purposes or needs, including thanksgiving (see Lev. 1–7). Later Christian discourse about sacrifice regarding Jesus' death, or the Eucharist itself, has tended to focus on the role

17. Robert Parker, *On Greek Religion* (Ithaca, NY: Cornell University Press, 2011), 124–70.

of sacrifices as dealing with sin or impurity, but this was only one element of a complex system.

Although there were destructive offerings in both traditions, where the need to deal with sin or impurity seems to be linked closely with the complete annihilation of the victim (and hence its radical transfer to the deity), Paul here hints at shared offerings of thanks or celebration such as the Israelite *zebaḥ šelamim* or "peace offering" (cf. Lev. 3), where the meat of the victim was mostly returned to the worshiper for a feast. Paul's intention is not to suggest this meal is literally a Christian "peace offering," but he invokes a sort of early anthropological view of sacrifice generally, comparing the Christian meal with both Jewish and Greek cultus. The Christians' participation in the blood and body of Christ is for Paul concrete, communal, and cultic. Paul's presentation of the Corinthian common meal relies not on belief that it was a sacrifice per se but on the nexus between sacrifice and meal common in Jewish and Greek religion.

Paul also says this eating and drinking is to "proclaim the Lord's death until he comes" (1 Cor. 11:26), alluding again to the place of the Last Supper within a broader Passion Narrative. A reader of Luke or Acts might just as readily have seen the meal as a participation in Jesus' risen life (Luke 24:35) as in his death, but these were not exclusive alternatives. Paul's emphasis on Jesus' death should be understood in relation to the creation of a new covenant (1 Cor. 11:25), which binds him and those who have faith in him, celebrated in the Christian meal.

The First Eucharists

Naming the Feast

The oldest form of prayer and ritual for the Christian banquet comes from the *Didache*. This collection of teachings, perhaps from Syria, contains ethical material as well as instructions for baptism, church organization, and the meal it calls *Eucharistia* (chaps. 9–10, 14).

We have already seen that actions of *eucharistia* or "thanksgiving" (and "blessing") are prominent in the Gospel and Acts traditions, not only at the Last Supper but at other meals of Jesus. *Eucharistia* seems originally to have referred to the prayer offered over bread and/or cup, but was quickly extended to mean the food and drink for which thanks were given, as well as the event itself. This was to become, and remain, by far the most widespread term for the Christians' distinctive meal and/or the specific actions and elements of it, borrowed into Latin as well as continued in Greek.

The Acts of the Apostles suggests that a tradition of common meals known as "the breaking of the bread" was remembered as a central practice of the earliest Jerusalem community—and presumably was known in the author's own community, in Asia Minor or Syria decades later (2:42; cf. Luke 24:35). In that case, a phrase that refers to one specific ritual action gives its name to the event as a whole. While Christians continued literally to break bread, and to emphasize that act within their meal, this term did not continue as a prominent name for the event.

Another very early and widespread name for Christian meals is *agapē*, meaning "love" or "love-feast" (Jude 12; cf. 2 Pet. 2:13). *Agapē* was used in some communities or traditions of the first three centuries as a way of referring to the community banquet itself, but not to the prayers or to the food and drink (Ign. *Rom.* 7.1); but the extension of *eucharistia* to have a more comprehensive scope means the two end up as partially equivalent terms. *Agapē* and Eucharist were not two separate events or occasions; depending on the place and time, one or the other or both might refer to the same Christian meal.[18]

Despite Paul invoking the ideal of a "Lord's supper" when writing to the Corinthians (11:20), this was not a name for the early Christian meal in a sense comparable to *Eucharistia* or *agapē*. Paul contrasts the self-preoccupied eating of some Corinthian Christians ("your own supper," 1 Cor. 11:21) with their pretensions to be eating with the Lord; if they had regard for one another, they would indeed have been eating with Jesus (cf. "the Lord's supper," 1 Cor. 11:20), and not just alone. His related phrases "the table of the Lord" and "the cup of the Lord" function similarly, as theological reflections on the meal rather than as recurrent labels for the event. Christian writers of the next three centuries know the phrase only from Paul's text and terminology, and give no sign it was ever applied to the community meal or a part thereof. "Lord's supper" does not appear again as a way of talking about the Eucharist itself until the fourth century, when vestiges of an actual "supper" have fallen away, and the term can be used with a certain holy irony; even then, it is not a name so much as an epithet for the liturgical Eucharist. The tendency of modern scholars to imagine that Paul reflects some wider usage—for which there is no evidence at all—reminds us how influential our own liturgical experience can be in imagining that of the past.

18. Andrew B. McGowan, "Naming the Feast: The Agape and the Diversity of Early Christian Meals," in *Studia Patristica* 30 (Leuven: Peeters, 1997), 314–18.

Ordering the Meal

The meal of the Corinthian Christians was a banquet on Greco-Roman lines, a solid meal, or *deipnon*, followed by a drinking party, or *symposion*, featuring various forms of discourse and diversion. This is also the shape of meal implied in the Last Supper stories, particularly what we have called the PL tradition, where the cup is specifically taken "after the *deipnon*." The first Eucharists were such meals, where the other actions of singing, prayer, and inspired speech or sacred story often filled the expected place after eating. The history of the discourses, spoken and sung, associated with the meal is explored elsewhere in this book.[19]

Yet ancient Mediterranean dining traditions were not completely uniform in shape; the form of the meal, like the diet itself, could be an arena of debate and of differentiation among groups. Romans and Jews, to take two obvious subgroups within this ancient Mediterranean cultural tradition, both had means of distinguishing their own dining practices or their conversations about them. Cicero speaks of the Roman idea of the banquet as *convivium*, common life (*Ad familiares* 9.24.3); the Roman banquet was at least sometimes more gender inclusive than the Greek, and socially could be more egalitarian.[20]

The Roman version sometimes retained the morphology of the Greek model—meal followed by drinking party—but in other instances saw drinking through, as much as or more than after, the meal.[21] Jewish eating, while influenced by the same traditions, may have included other patterns of order. The meals of the Qumran community, depicted in ideal terms in the Dead Sea Scrolls, involve blessings of food and drink together at the beginning of a meal:

> They shall eat together, pray together, and deliberate together. Wherever ten men belonging to the council of the community are gathered, a priest must not be lacking. The men shall sit before the priest by rank, and in that manner their opinions will be sought on any matter. When the table has been prepared for eating or the new wine for drinking, the priest shall stretch out his hand

19. See chaps. 3 ("Word") and 6 ("Prayer").

20. Peter Garnsey, *Food and Society in Classical Antiquity* (Cambridge: Cambridge University Press, 1999), 136.

21. See further Matthias Klinghardt, "A Typology of the Communal Meal," in *Meals in the Early Christian World: Social Formation, Experimentation, and Conflict at the Table*, ed. Dennis E. Smith and Hal Taussig (New York: Palgrave Macmillan, 2012), 9–22.

first, blessing the first portion of the bread or of the new wine. (1QS VI, 2–6; cf. 1QSa II, 17b–22)

The Eucharist of the *Didache* has a shape that seems to contrast with that of the Greco-Roman meal—or that of the Last Supper, for that matter—but that may be comparable to that Qumran meal: "And regarding the *Eucharistia*, give thanks ["eucharistize"] thus: First regarding the cup, 'We give thanks to you. . . .' And concerning the broken bread: 'We give thanks to you. . . .'" (*Did.* 9). Despite the priority of the cup, the blessing of drink and meal elements at the beginning of the meal may actually serve to de-emphasize the place of wine, so elevated in the classical *symposion*. This order is found or implied in a few other Christian settings, and it fits with a community still observant of Jewish custom and law but seeking now to express these in relation to faith in Jesus.[22]

Another case where the cup has an unexpected prominence is recorded by Irenaeus, writing in late second-century Gaul. He reports on the activity of a leader named Marcus who was associated with the school of Valentinus and hence of a broadly "gnostic" tendency:

He makes as though to give thanks over mixed cups, and extending greatly the prayer of invocation, he makes them appear purple and red; with the result that it seems that Charis [Grace], who is from what is above all, drops her own blood into that cup through his invocation, and so those who are present should yearn to taste of that cup, so that the Charis lauded by this conjurer may also pour down on them. (*Against Heresies* 1.7.2)

This sort of liturgical sleight of hand was being reported to denigrate Marcus' activity and does not give a broader sense of his school's eucharistic meal. It does suggest a certain sense of theater and an emphasis on grace not so alien to later theologies.

When a Roman community of Syrian origin celebrates its communal meal in the mid-second century, we find them listening to Scripture and praying before the meal (see Justin, *1 Apol.* 67), apparently with the bread-cup order. Yet even after this, around 200 CE, the Christians of the great Roman city of Carthage were gathering for a *convivium* with the expected shape of meal followed by song, prayer, and other discourse (see Tertullian, *Apol.* 39).

22. Andrew B. McGowan, "'First Regarding the Cup . . .': Papias and the Diversity of Early Eucharistic Practice," *Journal of Theological Studies* 46 (1995): 551–55; McGowan, "The In-ordinate Cup: Issues of Order in Early Eucharistic Drinking," in *Studia Patristica* 35 (Leuven: Peeters, 2001), 283–91.

The Earliest Eucharistic Prayers[23]

The prayers of the *Eucharistia* in the *Didache* are the oldest that survive:

> And regarding the *Eucharistia*, give thanks ["eucharistize"] thus: First regard-
> ing the cup, "We give thanks to you, our Father, for the holy vine of David your
> child, which you have made known to us through Jesus your child; to you be
> glory forever." And concerning the broken bread: "We give thanks to you, our
> Father, for the life and knowledge you have made known to us through Jesus
> your child. To you be glory forever. As this broken bread was scattered upon the
> mountains, but was brought together and became one, so may your church be
> gathered together from the ends of the earth into your kingdom, for the glory
> and the power are yours through Jesus Christ forever." (*Did.* 9.1–4)

After the meal another set prayer is provided:

> But after you are satisfied, give thanks thus: "We give thanks to you, O holy
> Father, for your holy name, which you caused to dwell in our hearts, and for
> the knowledge and faith and immortality that you made known to us through
> Jesus your child. To you be glory forever. You, Lord Almighty, made all things
> for your name's sake, and gave food and drink to humans for their enjoyment,
> that they might give thanks to you, but you have blessed us with spiritual food
> and drink and eternal light through your child. Above all, we give thanks to you
> because you are mighty. To you be glory forever. Remember, Lord, your church,
> to deliver it from all evil and to make it perfect in your love, and gather it together
> in holiness from the four winds to your kingdom that you have prepared for it;
> for yours is the power and the glory forever. Let grace come and let this world
> pass away. Hosanna to the God of David. If anyone is holy, let them come. If
> anyone not be, let him repent: *Maran atha*, Amen." But let the prophets give
> thanks ["eucharistize"] as they will. (*Did.* 10)

This is not quite what we would expect if Christians had created their meal
ritual to imitate the Last Supper. The *Didache* does not mention the death of
Jesus, or his body and blood; Paul's interpretation of the Christian meal as
a proclamation and remembrance of Jesus' death does not feature. Yet other
passages in the work suggest that the *Didache* is closely connected with the
Synoptic Gospels or their sources. The compilers of the document and users
of these prayers probably knew and accepted the tradition of the Last Supper,
but their concern was with how to celebrate the meal rather than why. The

---

23. See further Enrico Mazza, *The Origins of the Eucharistic Prayer* (Collegeville, MN:
Liturgical Press, 1995).

prayers do suit the broader model suggested by various Gospel meal narratives, of giving thanks within a communal setting. Their brevity suggests that the meal itself—which, after all, had to be eaten and drunk—was more prominent than talking about it.

The prayers themselves are also rather like (other) Jewish ones. The formula "We thank you Father . . ." is almost a Christian "eucharistic" version of the blessing, or *berakah*, offered at many Jewish meals. The theology of the prayers draws from a variety of Gospel (and other) traditions: Jesus is remembered as "child" of God, as a descendant of David, and as the giver of life and knowledge. Over the cup, they give thanks for the "holy vine of David," a royal lineage into which Jesus has brought the participants themselves and reminiscent of the Johannine imagery of vine and branches.[24] For these Christians, the meal celebrated how Jesus had brought them into community to be children of God as Jesus was himself. Drinking and eating was realization and reiteration of their belief that they were God's own people, scattered now but ultimately members of a holy, united, and redeemed community.

In mid-second-century Rome, Justin Martyr implies that those who presided at the meal extemporized when they prayed. First he indicates that the president went on "at considerable length" (*1 Apol. 65*), but then in his second description says: "Bread and wine and water are brought, and the president likewise offers prayers and thanksgivings, according to his ability, and the people assent, saying 'Amen'" (*1 Apol. 67*).

Another early prayer is partly preserved in the late second-century apocryphal *Acts of John*:

> We glorify your name that turns us from error and pitiless deceit;
> We glorify you who have shown before our eyes what we have seen;
> We testify to your goodness, variously appearing;
> We praise your virtuous name, O Lord, which has judged those that are judged by you;
> We thank you, Lord Jesus Christ, that we believe in your mercy that is unchanging;
> We thank you who had need of our nature that is being saved;
> We thank you that you have given us this immovable conviction that you alone are God now and forever;
> We your servants, that are assembled and gathered for good reason, give thanks to you, O holy one. (*Acts of John* 85)

24. Johannes Betz, "The Eucharist in the Didache," in *The Didache in Modern Research*, ed. Jonathan A. Draper (Leiden: Brill, 1996), 244–75.

Here thanksgiving is addressed to the heavenly Christ for salvation he brought to believers. The Christians whose prayer is reported here saw themselves as rescued from a problematic social and religious context, characterized by error and decay. The opportunity to bless bread (no cup is mentioned—on this see further below) allows these affirmations about themselves and God. As with the *Didache*, there is little specific concern to interpret the sacred food itself; but this does not mean that they had no sense of its importance or power.

The absence of words regarding Jesus' body and blood is typical at this point. Although the evidence is very limited, no prayer involving recitation of the Last Supper story has survived from the first three centuries.[25] The prayers we do have indicate that set forms had already emerged, at least within some communities; the *Didache* offers the timeless advice that liturgical improvisation is for prophets, not for everyone (*Did.* 10). In that setting there were itinerant prophets as well as local leaders called bishops (*episkopoi*) and deacons, and it is implied that the locals were normally leading the community ritually and otherwise, except when prophets came to town. Liturgical leadership was therefore defined but not inflexible.

The first appearance of the Last Supper story within prayers over bread and cup comes from the compilation of prayers and instructions known as the *Apostolic Tradition*—a much more complex successor to the *Didache*.[26] This work may date from the later third or even early fourth century, but it contains sources older than its final form. In a eucharistic prayer that the *Apostolic Tradition* presents in association with a bishop's ordination, the events of Jesus' ultimate supper are presented not as the sole focus for consecration of bread and cup but as the highlight of an extended thanksgiving with greater historical and narrative emphasis than those earlier examples.

> We give thanks to you God,
> through your beloved child Jesus Christ,
> whom you have sent to us in the last times . . .
> who is your inseparable Word,
> through whom you have made all things
> who, being incarnate . . .
> who complying with your will . . .

25. See McGowan, "Liturgical Text?"

26. For a recent discussion of how and why this took place, see Maxwell E. Johnson, "Martyrs and the Mass: The Interpolation of the Narrative of Institution into the Anaphora," *Worship* 87 (2013): 2–22.

who, when he was handed over . . .
taking the bread, and giving thanks to you, said . . . (*Ap. Trad.* 4.4–9)

This prayer also has, for the first time in surviving evidence, many features familiar to more recent Christians: an opening dialogue between presider and others, a more extended prayer over both bread and cup, and a concluding "Amen." By this time the *Eucharistia* had become a more distinct event, separate from community banquets; the extended thanksgiving and the attenuated food and drink both contrast with the meal of the *Didache* or of Paul's Corinthian correspondents.

Across all these examples, the character of the prayer over the meal was still expressed in the word that had already become a technical term in the *Didache*; it was *eucharistia*, thanksgiving to God, for the meal itself and for the gifts of God known in and through Jesus. Some communities emphasized abstract or eternal aspects such as "life" and "knowledge"; others were more historically focused on the events of Jesus' ministry, death, and resurrection. But the character of the meal as "eucharistic" was established early and was a common factor across considerable diversity of meal practice and theology.

Roles

The earliest evidence suggests that leadership roles involving the ritual and in particular the prayers of the banquet belonged to those who had authority and responsibility in the community generally. Parallel evidence for Greco-Roman (including Jewish) meal practice suggests that order and leadership of some kind would have been expected at banquets, and depictions of Jesus or apostles leading prayer at meals give strong indications that Christians shared the expectation that this role at least was undertaken by a community leader (1 Cor. 11:23–25; Mark 6:1; Luke 24:30; Acts 27:34–36); but there is no reason to assume that this function was always limited to the exercise of a sort of proto-ordained ministry.

Leaders at meals might have been those holding offices such as elder (presbyter) or overseer (bishop) attested in the NT and other very early documents, but the earliest extant piece of evidence for liturgical leadership is the *Didache*, which refers to bishops and deacons (chap. 15), and indicates that an itinerant prophet might pray the *Eucharistia* spontaneously (10.7). Householders who welcomed the church to dine at their homes might also have been expected to preside at meals. This suggests as many as three groups of potential leaders at the meal: appointed officials of the community, those possessing "charismatic" authority, and those whose status and privilege was reflected in their roles as hosts and patrons. It is worth noting that women as well as men could have undertaken all these roles, at least in the first century or so, and probably later.[27]

Ignatius of Antioch, whose letters may be from closer to the middle of the second century than its beginning,[28] insists that the presence of the bishop is a necessity for the Eucharist to be celebrated (Ign. *Smyrn.* 8.1) but speaks of prayer in the eucharistic assembly as powerful because it was "of the bishop and the whole church" (Ign. *Eph.* 5.2), suggesting leadership in corporate liturgical prayer rather than an exclusive hieratic performance. Justin's account (1 *Apol.* 65) involves a "president" who not only composed a variable prayer of thanksgiving but also gave instruction, and hence was probably a specific officer such as a bishop—the terminology used by Justin is deliberately "secular," because the work was ostensibly for a non-Christian audience.

Alongside these signs of emerging clarity regarding offices with ritual, pedagogical, and organizational responsibility, there are signs that some preferred more flexible modes of authority; Ignatius' need to defend the bishop's office through his letters indicates as much. In Africa a little later, Tertullian complains of heretics whose hierarchy and associated liturgical functions are vague, even ephemeral—without suggesting they have none at all (*On the Prescription of Heretics* 41; cf. Irenaeus, *Against Heresies* 1.13.2).

Bread, Wine, and More

A meal of bread and wine was unremarkable; no particular historical origins or associations are required to explain the use of these staples by Christian communities. An early Roman critic and inquisitor of the Christians, Pliny the Younger, investigated Christian meal gatherings after hearing rumors of child sacrifice and cannibalism, but reported that the food was "everyday and prosaic" (*Letters* 10.96). Although contemporary Westerners may struggle to imagine bread and wine alone as a complete meal, these are precisely the elements ancient eaters would have expected for everyday fare. What was unusual was their use—or at least the use of bread, but not other foods—as central to such formal meals.

Early eucharistic meals were mostly simple, often even ascetic, despite their emphasis on thanksgiving to God, but need not have been merely token in

27. See further Eisen, *Women Officeholders*; Kevin Madigan and Carolyn Osiek, eds., *Ordained Women in the Early Church: A Documentary History* (Baltimore: Johns Hopkins University Press, 2005).

28. Timothy D. Barnes, "The Date of Ignatius," *Expository Times* 120, no. 3 (2008): 119–30.

quantity. The *Didache* introduces prayers after the meal with the words "after you have eaten your fill," and there is no reason not to take this literally. Paul's advice to the carousing Corinthians to eat in their own homes before coming to the Lord's table (1 Cor. 11:22) did not amount to advocacy of an insubstantial sacramental ritual instead of a potluck; rather, he was counseling those used to larger and better meals not to embarrass themselves and others by carrying this disparity into the conduct of a common meal.

Foods other than bread were sometimes used. Early Christian novels depict apostolic heroes eating eucharistic meals without wine (see below) but with vegetables and more; the *Acts of Judas Thomas*, for instance, mentions "bread, oil, vegetables, and salt" (*Acts of Thomas* 29) as blessed and as shared in an unmistakably "eucharistic" style. Other accounts include additional foods—milk or cheese, vegetables, oil, and perhaps even fish.[29] There is no hint that these other elements were thought of as the body and blood of Jesus, however. Like the communities reflected in texts like the *Didache* and the *Acts of John*, these worshipers were making sure that all their eating, and their eucharistic food in particular, reflected the purity and holiness to which they had been called, in contrast to those deemed hypocrites.[30]

In other cases, we should probably imagine that there actually were additional foods but that the bread and cup had acquired a symbolic significance that overshadowed the side dishes. Even around 300 perhaps, the *Apostolic Tradition* suggests that when a new bishop is chosen and ordained, oil, cheese, and olives be offered, and thanks be offered to God for them, along with the expected bread and wine (*Ap. Trad.* 6–7). When wine was drunk at the eucharistic banquet, as it commonly was, it would have been mixed with water, as was the ancient Mediterranean norm. There was a significant minority, however, who used water only or omitted the cup altogether.

These patterns of eucharistic eating should probably be understood as a sort of ascetic response to the common use of meat and wine. The problem of eating meat we have already noted; but it is clear that many of those who rejected all meat were also avoiding wine, and vice versa.

---

29. The importance of fish has sometimes been exaggerated based on the Gospel references and (much later) artistic evidence, but fish escaped the negative connotations of meat and may have been a desirable feature at some Christian meals; see Alistair Stewart-Sykes, "Bread and Fish, Water and Wine: The Marcionite Menu and the Maintenance of Purity," in *Marcion und seine Kirchengeschichtliche Wirkung/Marcion and His Impact on Church History*, ed. Gerhard May, Katharina Greschat, and Martin Meiser (Berlin: Walter de Gruyter, 2002), 207–20.

30. Andrew B. McGowan, *Ascetic Eucharists: Food and Drink in Early Christian Ritual Meals*, Oxford Early Christian Studies (Oxford: Clarendon, 1999), 89–142.

This pattern was not a Christian innovation. Some Jews seem also to have felt that after the destruction of the Jerusalem temple (70 CE), meat and wine—but not other foods offered, like grains or oil—ought no longer to be eaten.[31] Hints of this approach among Christians are already present in the NT texts; writing to the Romans, Paul expresses a certain sympathy for those who believe "it is good not to eat meat or drink wine" (14:21). First Timothy exhorts its recipient not to "drink only water" (5:23), referring to an established pattern of abstinence.

Such objections must have extended to the eucharistic meal, even though it is not singled out in those texts. Where the contents of a cup are mentioned in second-century Christian evidence, water (alone) is there as often as wine. Perhaps groups that avoided wine made a point of stating their preference; otherwise a "cup" probably implies wine, even though some wine avoiders were happy to exploit the ambiguity of the Last Supper stories (which only mention "the cup") to argue their case.

Modern disputes about wine or grape juice for Communion make for interesting comparison but are quite different. Although ancient Christian avoiders of wine were quick to point out the perils of drunkenness, moderate wine drinkers did the same. There was no ancient movement in favor of using unfermented grape juice; without refrigeration or pasteurization to keep "juice" in its pristine state, the difference would quickly have been a moot point; water was the only real alternative.

In its more common form, however, focused on bread and mixed wine, the Christian meal tradition was a compromise relative to the festive "cuisine of sacrifice" that prevailed for most other Greeks, Romans, and Jews, centered on consumption of meat and wine. Leaving meat to one side and using bread as a sort of symbolic flesh, on the one hand, but allowing and giving thanks for wine, on the other, the Christian meal was both like and unlike many other religious banquets.

Holy Food, Holy People

The most characteristic addition to the confronting simplicity of the eucharistic meal was not to load it with other literal food elements but to interpret it theologically. Although bread and wine contrasted with the copious food and drink of some sacrificial banquets, they could convey similar or even stronger meanings than the literal meat and wine of the "cuisine of sacrifice"—they could be holy food or even the body and blood of Jesus.

31. Ibid., 67–86.

Living close to others who also claimed to be the true people of God, and striving to find and preserve their distinct identity, the Christians of the *Didache* regarded the meal as the exclusive preserve of the faithful without theorizing the actual significance of its food and drink very far. There is a parallel between the exclusivity of their food and that of priests of the temple (cf. Lev. 21), since in the *Didache* Eucharist is also a "sacrifice" (*Did.* 14).[32] Although it is unclear just how the food of their Eucharist became holy, it was set apart from regular use or from being shared outside the circle of believers. Baptism, the sign of induction into the community, was also the requirement for participation in the meal.

Such exclusion is typical of early eucharistic meals; but insistence on initiation before joining the community and sharing its food reflected the rules and expectations of ancient dining societies and was not a Christian oddity. There may have been structured exceptions, as it were, where outsiders were invited; in 1 Corinthians 14, Paul speaks of outsiders being present for what seems to be the postprandial discourse of the Christian *symposion*, using the same description of the assembly "coming together" as in 1 Corinthians 11:

> If you say a blessing with the spirit, how can anyone in the position of an outsider say the "Amen" to your thanksgiving, since the outsider does not know what you are saying? . . . If, therefore, the whole church comes together and all speak in tongues, and outsiders or unbelievers enter, will they not say that you are out of your mind? But if all prophesy, an unbeliever or outsider who enters is reproved by all and called to account by all. After the secrets of the unbeliever's heart are disclosed, that person will bow down before God and worship him, declaring, "God is really among you." (1 Cor. 14:16, 23–25)

This passage would make no sense unless the presence of an unbeliever at the gathering were conceivable, but this does not mean it was typical; such an onlooker might have been a member of the host's household rather than representative of an open-door policy otherwise unsupported by the ancient evidence. Nor does the passage suggest the "outsider" ate and drank, for that matter.

32. Andrew B. McGowan, "Eucharist and Sacrifice: Cultic Tradition and Transformation in Early Christian Ritual Meals," in *Mahl und religiöse Identität im frühen Christentum*, ed. Matthias Klinghardt and Hal Taussig, Texte und Arbeiten zum neutestamentlichen Zeitalter 56 (Tübingen: Francke, 2012), 191–206; Jonathan A. Draper, "Pure Sacrifice in Didache 14 as Jewish Christian Exegesis," *Neotestamentica* 42 (2008): 223–52.

Paul's warning about sickness and death for the unworthy eater (1 Cor. 11:30) need not have meant he himself saw the food as objectively dangerous, but his early readers and others were soon to draw this conclusion. There is certainly no reason to imagine that participation was a matter of indifference. The Pauline Epistles generally suggest far more anxiety about some attitudes to Jewish-gentile commensality, suggesting this was the pressing question of inclusion and boundary maintenance (Gal. 2:11–14).[33] Reflection on gender roles (1 Cor. 11:3–16) and wealth or social status (1 Cor. 11:17–22; 1 Tim. 6; James 2) makes clear that women as well as men, and poor as well as rich, took part. Holiness was not determined by segregation.

Body and Blood

Whether or not the Last Supper traditions originally alluded to eating a victim's flesh, the striking development of language in John 6 where Jesus speaks of the necessity of eating his flesh and drinking his blood—connected in the narrative not with a Last Supper but with the miraculous feeding—illustrates a rapid and complex reception of the language of the "institution narratives." The Johannine discourse is widely understood as alluding to eucharistic eating, but it seems to be making a point about faith more than about ritual; this suggests not only that the notion of the eucharistic food as "flesh" and "blood" was possible at an early point but also that this imagery could be used to make points of a different kind.[34]

Not much later, the implications of Jesus' words over bread and cup were pursued more directly regarding the meal elements. Ignatius warned that some who "did not believe in the blood of Christ" abstained from the Eucharist "because they do not confess that the Eucharist is the flesh of our Savior Jesus Christ" (Ign. *Smyrn*. 6.1, 7). He urges the Philadelphian Christians to "have only one Eucharist. For there is one flesh of our Lord Jesus Christ, and one cup for the unity of his blood" (Ign. *Phld*. 4). Ignatius can also speak of the food and drink of the Eucharist as the "medicine of immortality and antidote to prevent us from dying" (Ign. *Eph*. 20.2).

Ignatius' view of the eucharistic food as inherently powerful was typical at least from the mid-second century and had both negative and positive implications for diners; the food was desirable but dangerous. Food and medicine, drugs and magic, were not radically different things to his readers; the body

---

33. See the fuller discussion in Smith, *From Symposium to Eucharist*.
34. Harold W. Attridge, *Essays on John and Hebrews*, WUNT 264 (Tübingen: Mohr Siebeck, 2010; repr., Grand Rapids: Baker Academic, 2012), 18–20.

and soul were both affected by diet.[35] Meat from sacrifices also had a sort of spiritual food value, but the Christian claim about Jesus' body and blood was unusual because of the extraordinary value of the victim relative to the ordinary character of the apparent food. Where animal sacrifice offered an expensive and delectable means of feasting with a god, the eucharistic meal offered an accessible way of participating even more directly in God's saving power.

Realistic views about the sacred character of eucharistic food led quite quickly to direct interest in the consecrated elements of bread and wine, even in isolation from the meal. Justin Martyr indicates that after the eucharistic meal was shared, "there is a distribution and participation for each from that for which thanks have been given, and it is sent to those who are absent by the deacons" (1 Apol. 67. 5). Less than fifty years later, North African Christians were routinely carrying the broken bread away to break their fast with it (see Tertullian, To His Wife 2.5.3) and receiving it on occasions other than at the community meal (Tertullian, On the Soldier's Crown 3.3). These practices recall how sacrificial foods were taken away from temples for later consumption (cf. 1 Cor. 10:25–30).

Third-century African bishop Cyprian took realism to new heights (or depths), regaling his congregation with cautionary tales about unworthy recipients being confronted with exploding food boxes and poisonous bread crumbs:

> And a certain woman, when she tried with unworthy hands to open her box, in which was the holy [body] of the Lord, was deterred by fire rising from it lest she dare to touch it. And because another who himself was defiled, dared to receive secretly with the rest a portion from the sacrifice celebrated by a priest; he was not able to eat or handle the holy [body] of the Lord, but found ashes in his hands when he opened them. (On the Lapsed 26)

There were, however, skeptics about the Eucharist, its sacred food, and the potential of material things to convey spiritual power. The second-century Gospel of Judas retrojects such a view into the time of Jesus, and in one of its stories the disciples stand in for a thick-witted eucharistic church, while the Savior himself represents the enlightened view of a writer disdainful of the sacred meal:

> He found them gathered together and seated in pious observance. When he [approached] his disciples, gathered together and seated and giving thanks over the bread, [he] laughed. The disciples said to [him], "Master, why are you laughing at

35. Peter Brown, The Body and Society: Men, Women, and Sexual Renunciation in Early Christianity (New York: Columbia University Press, 1988), 219–24.

the *Eucharistia*? We have done what is right." He answered and said to them, "I am not laughing at you. <You> are not doing this because of your own will but because it is through this that your god [will be] praised." (*Gospel of Judas* 33.23–34.11)[36]

Some may have rejected the identification of the eucharistic food with Jesus' body and blood, as Ignatius disapprovingly suggests, or were uninterested in the sacrificial language of the tradition that focused on the Last Supper, but such views were not much like those of later reformers. Ignatius' opponents and the community reflected in the *Gospel of Judas* probably not only denied Christ's presence in the Eucharist but also thought of him as a spiritual savior no more likely to have come in flesh and blood in the past than in bread and wine at present.

Most Christian writings from the second century on suggest that the power and character of the eucharistic food were upheld with startling realism. There is no hint that they were merely signs to assist with the remembrance of an idea or understanding of a doctrine, or that their reality depended on the attitude of the recipient. On the other hand, the means of Jesus' presence in the food or in the act of sharing was not defined by any ancient writer in metaphysical terms like those of medieval theology.

From Eucharist to *Agapē*

From Banquet to Sacrament

Justin Martyr's description of sharing the meal after a baptism is the fullest account of a Eucharist from the second century:

Having ended the prayers, we salute one another with a kiss. There is then brought to the president of the brethren bread and a cup of water [and of wine mixed with water]; and he, taking them, gives praise and glory to the Father of the universe, through the name of the Son and of the Holy Ghost, and offers thanks at considerable length for our being counted worthy to receive these things at his hands. And when he has concluded the prayers and thanksgivings, all the people present express their assent by saying "Amen." This word "Amen" corresponds in the Hebrew language to "so be it." And when the president has given thanks, and all the people have expressed their assent, those who are called by us deacons give to each of those present to partake of the bread and wine

36. Rodolphe Kasser, Marvin Meyer, and Gregor Wurst, eds., *The Gospel of Judas*, 2nd ed. (Washington, DC: National Geographic, 2008), 30–31, modified.

mixed with water over which the thanksgiving was pronounced, and to those who are absent they carry away a portion. (*1 Apol.* 65)

Justin's prayer seems to be much lengthier than was the case for the *Didache* community, and spontaneous rather than fixed. Since this was a baptism, it may not have been typical. A few chapters later Justin offers a description of regular Sunday observance:

And on the day called "of the sun," when all who live in cities or in the country gather in one place, an assembly occurs, and the memoirs of the apostles or the writings of the prophets are read, as long as there is time; then, when the reader has finished, the president presents a verbal admonition and challenge for the imitation of these good things. Then we all rise together and send prayers, and, as we before said, when the prayer is ended, bread is offered, and wine and water. (*1 Apol.* 67)

There is no mention of the Last Supper as part of prayer here, although elsewhere Justin shows awareness that the Eucharist is a "sacrifice" that purifies from sin through Jesus' death (*Dial.* 41).[37] This meal may have been conducted without the accoutrements of a banquet and seems to depart from the Greco-Roman model by having discourse before, rather than after, eating. Yet it still seems to be a full meal. Justin describes eating staple foods, the participants were reclining or at least sitting, and portions were taken to the absent. Although a spiritual benefit was involved, the material needs of housebound members encouraged these sacramental food parcels.[38] Although Justin's pattern of Word before Sacrament in a Syrian community meeting in Rome resembles later practice, it may not have been typical at this point; in Carthage, Tertullian, even some decades later, still views the Christian banquet in more classical terms, with a modest and chaste symposium following the meal, rather than none (*Apol.* 39). This is one of many cases of ongoing regional diversity.

By the third century at least, and perhaps much earlier too, Christians were meeting not only in the *triclinia* of private homes, which would have accommodated just one or two dozen diners at best, but in spaces that could accommodate larger numbers. Reclining to eat became harder or impossible at meetings of a whole Christian community, even in larger rooms. This practical pressure, and reverence now being offered to the sanctified elements themselves independently of participation in the banquet, allowed or demanded changes in the Christian meal.

37. McGowan, "Eucharist and Sacrifice," 200–202.
38. Paul F. Bradshaw, *Reconstructing Early Christian Worship* (London: SPCK, 2009), 20–21.

Evidence from Carthage allows a possible reconstruction of this shift, at least in one place. Between the time of Tertullian and his later compatriot Cyprian—in effect the half century between 200 and 250—the eucharistic food came to be received primarily at morning gatherings at Carthage, not at evening banquets where only a fraction of the community could assemble. Tertullian knows of both practices (*On the Soldier's Crown* 3.3; cf. *Apol.* 39), but for him the evening meal gathering is still the primary assembly. For the Carthaginian Christians around 200, the evening gathering was formally an *agapē*, or "love-feast," but also more loosely a *convivium dominicum* or *cena Dei* ("Lord's dinner party" or "God's banquet")—which is the closest any writer of this period comes to reusing Paul's famous language, but in reference to the whole evening event rather than to the more strictly sacramental aspect, which could be celebrated separately. This was still the characteristic meeting, probably still the (or at least "a") primary venue for the blessing and consumption of the food generally known as "Eucharist," and certainly the event that gave rise to rumors about cannibalism and incest.[39]

Yet in addition to this main gathering there were other assemblies, and at least some—perhaps those associated with special fast days, or "stations"—where the Eucharist (apparently the blessed bread) was distributed too, although evidence suggests that it was as often carried away to be eaten later as consumed on the spot. Desire to receive the blessed elements (and the sanctified bread in particular) to break one's fast may have encouraged their distribution at a morning assembly (cf. Tertullian, *To His Wife* 2.5.3), whether one of the established hours of prayer or perhaps a gathering of Christians at the house of the bishop, parallel to those at the houses of wealthy patrons greeted by their clients and dependents at the start of the day.[40]

By Cyprian's time half a century later, however, the significance of evening banquets for the whole church had declined, perhaps because it was just not possible for the now-larger Christian community at Carthage to gather as one (granted that both in his time and in Tertullian's there were tensions and rivalries that may have led to separate gatherings anyway). Instead, the morning distribution of the Eucharist was the primary meeting. At those more specifically sacramental events, the quantity of food offered was not sufficient to be considered a meal, but involved small amounts that could be reverently carried in a bag or box around the believer's neck. This also reminds us that

39. Andrew B. McGowan, "Eating People: Accusations of Cannibalism against Christians in the Second Century," *Journal of Early Christian Studies* 2 (1994): 413–42.
40. I owe this suggestion about the morning *salutatio* to Professor Clemens Leonhard.

despite the emergence of more public forms of Christian ritual, the personal and domestic context was of great importance, and devotional practices centered there have their own, somewhat neglected, history.[41] The changes of these centuries do not constitute so much a move from private to public as the addition of a more public dimension to communal practice.

Banquets did, however, continue; and in Cyprian's time it is likely that in some places there were still eucharistic celebrations attached. Yet it seems clear that such gatherings came to be seen more as the preserve of particular subgroups than as assemblies of the Christian community as such. By the fourth century, banquets—sometimes still with the name *agapē*—were events linked not so much to the wider Christian community as to more specific networks of patronage and family, complicated as these necessarily were by the emergence of clerical and monastic influences. Some might be memorial banquets still held within cemetery churches and martyr shrines, where in the fourth and following centuries permanent picnic tables were installed (in the semicircular *sigma* form that had become more popular than the *triclinium* of earlier centuries), where the patrons memorialized their loved ones and heroes with inscriptions calling down peace and concord on their *convivium*.[42] These funerary meals were sometimes named in reference to the refreshment that Roman families had traditionally offered their departed loved ones, *refrigerium*; but like *agapē*, this word has sometimes been used beyond the scope given it by the ancients, and there was no particular meal form or ritual necessarily connected with the term.

In more comfortable and domestic settings, a member of the church might still invite leaders and those with particular needs, such as widows, to dine at home in a reverent atmosphere separately from the communal and sacramental Eucharist; this is the context of curious meal instructions preserved in late versions of the *Apostolic Tradition*:

> When the evening has come, with the bishop present the deacon shall bring in a lamp, and standing in the midst of all the faithful present, [the bishop] shall give thanks. He shall first greet all by saying,
>   "The Lord be with you."

41. See Kimberly Bowes, *Private Worship, Public Values, and Religious Change in Late Antiquity* (New York: Cambridge University Press, 2008).

42. See Robin Margaret Jensen, "Dining with the Dead: From the Mensa to the Altar in Christian Late Antiquity," in *Commemorating the Dead: Texts and Artifacts in Context; Studies of Roman, Jewish, and Christian Burials*, ed. Laurie Brink and Deborah Green (Berlin: Walter de Gruyter, 2008), 107–43.

And all the people shall respond,
  "And with your spirit."
Then the bishop shall say,
  "Let us give thanks to the Lord."
And they shall respond,
  "It is right and just. Greatness and exaltation and glory are due to him."
But he shall not say,
  "Lift up your hearts,"
because that is said at the oblation. (25[29C].1–6)

There follows a sort of thanksgiving prayer, not over food itself but over the light of the evening lamp. Then:

After the meal when they have risen and prayed, the children shall sing psalms, along with the virgins. Afterwards, a deacon holding the mixed cup of the oblation shall say a psalm from among those in which is written *"Hallelujah."* Then, if a presbyter orders it, more from the same psalms. After this, when the bishop has offered the cup, he shall say a psalm appropriate to the cup, all of them including *"Hallelujah."* When the psalms are recited, all shall say, *"Hallelujah,"* which is, "We praise the one who is God. Glory and praise to him who created all the world by a word!" Thus the psalm is completed, he shall give thanks for the cup and give of fragments to all the faithful ones. When they eat, the faithful present shall take from the hand of the bishop a piece of bread before taking their own bread, because it is a blessing, not the Eucharist, like the body of the Lord. (25[29C].11–16)

This meal has some "eucharistic" resonances, and is both like and unlike that "oblation" also known to the compilers of the work—in other words, the morning Eucharist. In their concern to establish the difference between meal and sacrament (the "oblation") they unwittingly make the connection clearer. While in the *Apostolic Tradition* as we have it, this meal is a sort of community supper (the term *agapē* is not used, interestingly), the source from which this description came might simply have known it as the Eucharist.

Such an ongoing mixture of meals reflects a process of continuing differentiation between sacrament and banquet; not very long before the text took this form, the evening meeting had apparently still included thanksgiving over bread and wine as the body and blood of Christ. The sacral food and drink elements are now blessed and received elsewhere, but the meal still bears their imprint.

Whatever the exact process, the result is clear. By 200 in some places and certainly by 300, these new eucharistic celebrations had many of the characteristics they would for centuries to come. Whereas the evening banquet had involved a meal followed by or interspersed with various forms of speech, music, or conversation, the morning sacramental assemblies had something like the reverse shape foreshadowed in Justin's Syro-Roman community: readings from Scripture, teaching, and prayer all preceded the reception of the sacred food. So the Syrian *Didascalia Apostolorum*, reflecting fourth-century practice but perhaps earlier also, urges its readers to "assemble on the Lord's day to hear the word of life and be nourished with the divine food that lives forever" (2.59[13]).

Sacred Space

The first Christian meals apparently took place in houses—including freestanding homes of wealthier members, and apartment-like *insulae* (see Acts 20:7–12)—whose dining areas were both functionally necessary and symbolically appropriate to the event. The larger freestanding house, or *domus* in Roman terms, had some flexibility; should groups be larger than normally accommodated in the dining room, or *triclinium*, they could spill out. Such well-appointed houses often had central pools that could have been used for baptism, allowing the demonstrated connection between initiation and meal to be ritualized in full, although NT stories and the flexible instructions of the *Didache* (chap. 7) suggest that more public and less domestic venues could have also been used for baptism at an early point.

Christians' use of different spaces parallels the development of different liturgical forms; again the fact of change is clear, but the form it took less so. The domestic character of the earliest meeting places is clear but can be romanticized, since the emerging Christian movement was less a family or household (except in some metaphorical sense) and more like other associations or clubs, and like them would probably have aspired to move from a member's home to their own dedicated venue when necessary or possible.

Some considerable variety of spaces must have been involved, based on practicality more than any domestic symbolism. Justin Martyr's trial narrative suggests his community met above a bathhouse (*Acts of Justin* 3), and some of the traditional sites of Roman churches have been connected with baths, too; these could have provided a sort of semipublic space for certain kinds of meeting.[43] Tertullian still refers to the venue of the Carthaginian *agapē* as a *triclinium* (*Apol.* 39.15); but *triclinia* were of different sizes and existed in various buildings.

43. Allan Doig, *Liturgy and Architecture: From the Early Church to the Middle Ages*, Liturgy, Worship and Society (Burlington, VT: Ashgate, 2008), 6–7.

The spectacular discovery of a house turned church in the Syrian border town of Dura-Europos almost a century ago provides one example of architectural adaptation for Christian communal use.[44] The largest room in the Christian building at Dura must have been used for prayer gatherings and for the Eucharist—probably in the more "liturgical" form by this time—but may also have been the scene of community meals, however performed or understood. This space is unadorned, in contrast to the rich decoration of the room for baptism; its small platform at one end seems designed for a teacher's dais, not an "altar."

The Dura building was literally a house turned into a church, but it cannot be assumed to be typical. More particularly, its ingenious adaptation makes no implied statement about evolution of Christian identity from household to church; the nearby synagogue at Dura had also been converted from a house, and both communities were probably doing what was most expedient to acquire functional spaces. Nor, in passing, should we imagine that synagogue architecture itself was sufficiently well developed to have provided direct models for Christian use; although synagogues and churches would continue to influence each other architecturally and liturgically, this process belongs not to the origins of either form but to their later development.[45]

The refocusing of communal activity in such church buildings did not make them sole centers for ritual expression of faith. Houses were not rendered irrelevant by the need to use larger spaces but continued to be important places for Christian gathering, more closely related to patterns of relationship connected with kinship and patronage.[46] Cemeteries and other open spaces were also venues for important meetings and performances; the remembrance of the dead was a particularly important focus. Such other points of gathering may not amount to a "second church," as has recently been claimed,[47] but it is true that gatherings led by bishops were not the only ones of significance.

Sacrifice

The Eucharist was proudly depicted by its Christian participants as a peaceable act, morally and religiously superior to the violent rituals of their pagan

44. Ibid., 1–19.

45. See the discussion in Lee I. Levine, *Ancient Synagogue: The First Thousand Years*, 2nd ed. (New Haven: Yale University Press, 2005); and on the parallel developments of sacred space in church and synagogue, see Joan R. Branham, "Sacred Space under Erasure in Ancient Synagogues and Early Churches," *Art Bulletin* 74 (1992): 375–94.

46. See Bowes, *Private Worship*.

47. Ramsay MacMullen, *The Second Church: Popular Christianity A.D. 200–400* (Atlanta: Society of Biblical Literature, 2009).

neighbors; and yet it was increasingly for them also a sacrifice par excellence, a sharing in flesh and blood not merely animal but human, or even divine. Christians could reject sacrificial imagery and ideas in relation to gentile religion and idolatry but still see their meal as fulfillment of the offerings once made at the Jerusalem temple.

We have seen that these dilemmas or creative tensions had already been present for Paul and the Corinthian Christians. As time went on, this tension grew into an ironic equilibrium of symbols; so by the mid-third century, Cyprian could speak without hesitation of the Eucharist—by then a separate morning celebration, intended for the whole church—as a literal "sacrifice." Despite the obvious contrasts, the Eucharist and its ministers were for him direct successors of the cultus and priesthood of the Jerusalem temple, and also superior equivalents to the demonic gentile sacrifices still being offered in their own city (see *Letter* 63). This was an especially bold attitude at a time of serious persecution, given that willingness to offer Roman sacrifice was often the means by which Christians were tested; the Eucharist was now a clear competitor to the rites that members of Cyprian's community might suffer for rejecting.

For Cyprian the bishop was thus literally a priest (Latin *sacerdos*), a "sacrificer," as the normal presider of the Eucharist; but associated elders could be delegated this role, and with the growth of the church they would in fact become the normal "priests"; so the English word "priest," while derived from the earlier and noncultic Christian term for an elder—*presbyteros*—has acquired a meaning that includes cultic functionaries across religious traditions.

The *Apostolic Tradition* calls its Eucharist the "oblation," or offering (chap. 4), and such language is typical after 300 or so. Through the third and into the fourth century, it became more and more likely that Christians would use such cultic ideas and images to describe their gathering, its food, and other accoutrements. The association with priesthood and sacrifice was to become fundamental in much subsequent Christian tradition, deriving from this sense of the Eucharist as a cultic act, but extending beyond it into ways of thinking about order and power.

These strong identifications with sacrificial religion made Christian ritual a more effective point of resistance or competition to Roman cultus, but also ultimately a more suitable tool for an imperial religion to use. After the changes heralded by the conversion of the emperor Constantine in the early fourth century, when spaces and symbols associated with the many gods might be reused for the eucharistic worship of the Christian God, Christian liturgy could itself become the most sacred ritual of Roman society.

Kissing

Christians and Kissing[48]

Words were an important means of exploring belief, creating social bonds, and celebrating faith, but so were (other) bodily dispositions and actions. The centrality of eating and drinking makes this more than obvious; to sing as an act of worship was common in the ancient church and is still familiar to many; acts such as kissing may be more surprising. While its subsequent history in Christian worship is less consistent, the importance to ancient Christians of kissing as a distinctive communal and ritual performance is clear.

Four of Paul's Letters close with reference to exchanging a "holy kiss" (Rom. 16:16; 1 Cor. 16:20; 2 Cor. 13:12; 1 Thess. 5:26; cf. 1 Pet. 5:14). He feels no need to explain or justify the practice, implying it was established and readily understood by his readers. Few letters from other ancient communities or traditions have comparable formulae. Kissing was associated with familial and sexual relationships as now, and also with other social interactions such as greeting colleagues. Kissing was not scandalous; literary examples from wider Greco-Roman sources indicate that familial and spousal or other sexually grounded relationships could be expressed thus publicly as well as privately, within limits.[49] The fact of the Christians' kiss was not as remarkable as who was doing it. The practice may already have been established among the followers of Jesus (cf. Mark 14:44–45; Luke 7:45). Membership in the Christian community brought believers into a relationship like that of family members, although no one precedent or model explains the prominence of Christians' kissing. It was a reworking of an existing practice or convention, for the new purposes of a genuinely new social grouping.

Justin Martyr's account of baptism and Eucharist indicates that the kiss had a specific place and function in many Christian assemblies by the mid-second century: "After we have washed the one who has been convinced and

48. For more detailed discussion, see L. Edward Phillips, *The Ritual Kiss in Early Christian Worship*, Alcuin/GROW Liturgical Study 36 (Cambridge: Grove Books, 1996); and Michael Philip Penn, *Kissing Christians: Ritual and Community in the Late Ancient Church*, Divinations (Philadelphia: University of Pennsylvania Press, 2005).

49. Penn shows that widespread assumptions that the kiss was scandalous are misconceived; see *Kissing Christians*, 12–15, 103–13.

agreed, we bring him to those who are called 'brothers' assembled, in order
to make earnest prayers in common. . . . Having ended the prayers, we salute
one another with a kiss" (*1 Apol.* 65.1–2). Tertullian similarly speaks of the
kiss as the "seal" of prayer, when expressing concern that those who undertake
fasts are abstaining from it:

> Those fasting, having prayed with the brethren, withhold the kiss of peace, which
> is the seal of prayer. But what better time is there for bestowing peace with the
> brethren than when the prayer has ascended with the additional commendation
> of the action? . . . What prayer is complete when divorced from the holy kiss? . . .
> What sort of sacrifice is it from which one leaves without the peace? (*On Prayer* 18).

A few decades later, Origen at Caesarea also notes that a "custom has been
handed down to the churches for brothers to kiss each other after the prayers"
(*Commentary on Romans* 10.33). He also connects the kiss specifically with
the "mysteries," meaning the Eucharist (*Commentary on Song of Songs* 1.1),
and he calls it an image of Christ's encounter with the pure soul. The kiss
was thus a ritual within the ritual; its own logic led to its use after prayer, and
especially at the Eucharist.

Kissing the Martyrs

Christian kisses were rituals but were not limited to communal worship
acts; devotional kisses were offered to the persecuted in their prisons. The *Acts
of Paul and Thecla* depicts Thecla bribing her way into the prison to listen
to Paul and kiss his chains (chap. 19), while Tertullian envisages a Christian
woman "creeping into prison to kiss a martyr's chains," suggesting that she
might want "to meet with the brethren to exchange the kiss, to offer water
for the saints' feet, to share a little of her food from her cup, to yearn for or
remember them"—all among proper but difficult acts of Christian service
(*To His Wife* 2.4.3).

Kisses feature in the *Martyrdom of Perpetua and Felicitas* in poignant ways
that connect familial, ritual, and communal modes of kissing. Three times in
dreams or visions Perpetua explicitly receives a kiss "of peace" (10.13; 12.4);
the one waking occasion is when the martyrs in the arena exchange it just
before death, creating an act of worship before the onlookers as they prepare
to become sacrifices (21.7).

There were dangers attached to such kissing; the late second-century apolo-
gist Athenagoras warned that "the kiss, or rather the devotion [*proskynēma*],

should be given with the greatest care, since if the slightest defilement in thought is mixed in, it places us outside of eternal life" (*Plea for the Christians* 32.5). A little later, Cyprian implied that the fervent kisses offered to martyrs had sometimes led to rather more happening in the dark (*Letter* 13.5). Clement of Alexandria (ca. 150–ca. 215) had also warned of lustful distraction, but was just as concerned about the opposite danger, of not getting past lip-smacking appearances: "Love is not proved by a kiss, but by goodwill. Yet there are those that do nothing but make loud noises in the churches with the kiss, while not having love within. For this, the unrestrained use of a kiss, leads to foul suspicions and slanders, but it ought to be mystical—the apostle calls the kiss holy" (*Paed.* 3.11).

Kissing and Initiation

Justin had described the kiss in the context of baptism; a repeated sign of a special relationship among the Christians, it was appropriately part of the initiation ritual. The importance of a baptismal kiss is also reflected in the curious case of African bishops around 250 expressing qualms about kissing the feet of young infants (Cyprian, *Letter* 64.4.1); perhaps this was how the very young were included in the kiss.[50]

The same power of expressing and creating affinity meant that the kiss was also a sign of reconciliation; Cyprian's *Letters* indicates that in times of stress, the exchange of this *pax* (peace) was the sign both of maintained and of recreated fellowship (see *Letter* 64.1). The kiss was thus also shared with the reconciled penitent, the newly baptized, and among those continuing to celebrate the Eucharist.

The *Apostolic Tradition* provides no fewer than four examples that confirm how the kiss was a sort of micro-liturgy, with a logic that determined its placement within events. The kiss is given to a new bishop after his ordination (*Ap. Trad.* 4.1); it is exchanged after prayers concluding a catechetical assembly (18.3–4); the bishop kisses the newly baptized after their postbaptismal anointing (21.23–26); and those baptized also share it after prayers (21.26). Catechumens (those undergoing instruction before baptism), however, did not kiss, because their kiss, or what lay behind it—physically or spiritually—was not yet pure (18.3). This fits with a very concrete understanding in the *Apostolic Tradition* about the breath and body themselves as pure or impure; only after baptismal sealing (cf. 21.23) could new Christians share in an exchange of breath or spirit.

---

50. See the discussion in connection with baptism and foot washing, chap. 5.

Further, the *Apostolic Tradition* specifies that men and women were not to kiss (18.4). This rule does not appear in earlier sources; while it reflects the same concerns behind Athenagoras' and Cyprian's observations, it also reflects an emergent tendency to separate men and women in Christian assemblies that seems to reflect more than anxiety about illicit romance. Gender was one aspect of a social hierarchy that was being inscribed in liturgical action more clearly than before, the assembly itself a map of a human community whose order was finely grained according to gender, age, and clerical or ascetic status.

Kissing at the Eucharist: The Fourth Century and After

The significance of an act that marked the baptized as a distinct group was bound to change across the fourth century, when Christianity became first accepted and then normative. Since the most unusual feature of the kiss was the group among whom it was shared, the mere fact of kissing Christians became less and less remarkable or significant as Christians came to dominate the Roman population, and changes in practice that developed here impacted those outside the empire too.

In the fourth century and after, the eucharistic kiss became the most important form, but its place literally shifted in some cases. Its role as the concluding and confirming act of intercessory prayers, as in Justin's baptismal gathering centuries earlier, was to remain or recur as one common position. Late in the fourth century, John Chrysostom and Theodore of Mopsuestia understood this placement in terms of the exhortation at Matthew 5:23—to be at peace prior to making an offering—which would have been a harder interpretive move for Justin, whose eucharistic table was not an "altar."[51] In any event, this eucharistic focus meant that the kiss was increasingly understood as prelude to what followed it rather than as "seal" to the prayer that had preceded it.

However, the older logic of the kiss as a "seal" still led some to place it after the eucharistic prayer and/or the Lord's Prayer but before receiving the Eucharist. This position after the eucharistic prayer was characteristically Western and is known first from Augustine, who explains it to a group of the recently baptized: "So at the point the consecration is completed we say the Lord's Prayer, which you have received and handed back. After that is said 'Peace be with you' and Christians kiss with a holy kiss" (*Sermon* 227). Pope Innocent I advocated the same pattern (acknowledging the other, older one

---

51. For John, see the *Catechetical Instructions* of the Papadopoulos-Kerameus series, 3.33; Theodore, *Baptismal Homilies* 4.40.

too), still seeing the *pax* as a seal of prayer: "Of course the Peace ought to be given after the completing of all those secret things I ought not reveal, by which it may be shown that the people assent to all that is done in consecrating the mysteries . . . with the closing seal of the Peace" (*Letter* 1). As in the East, however, this Western tradition came to focus less on what preceded the kiss than on what followed it, here meaning the reception of Communion (see, for instance, Gregory the Great's *Dialogues* 3.36).

Modern revivals of a "greeting of peace" reflect the interest of scholars and liturgists in recovering ancient practice, but contemporary Western rites in the English-speaking world have generally not made an actual kiss the "peace." While the ancient kiss was essentially a ritual action interpreted through the idea of peace, the modern "peace" is an idea, expressed in certain ritual actions.[52] The loss of the distinctive group that exchanged the kiss may have lessened its real significance as a sign of a strong and surprising kinship. As in some other areas of ritual practice, what had once been a Christian distinctive tended to be transferred to clergy or monastics; so in both Byzantine East and medieval West, the kiss became a vestigial action shared among clergy.

The Eucharist from the Fourth Century On

The Church in the Basilica

Participants in the eucharistic celebrations of the fourth century experienced something very different from those two centuries earlier, not least in the spaces where their gatherings occurred. Evening meetings in homes, small halls, or adapted houses had given way to morning assemblies in purpose-built structures, particularly the basilica, a form of public building that now often became the preferred setting for some types of Christian liturgy. The basilica form had had varied manifestations before the Christians adopted it, and Christian usage was also varied; but the basic form of an oriented hall with aisles and an apse has remained typical of much church architecture since.[53]

The growth in Christian numbers in the cities of the Roman Empire found its eventual climax in the adoption of Christianity as a hoped-for source of religious unity across civic and imperial structures. The significance of the conversion of Constantine can be exaggerated, and we have noted that the

52. Phillips, *Ritual Kiss*, 36.
53. The classic treatment of Richard Krautheimer remains valuable; see *Early Christian and Byzantine Architecture*, 4th ed. (New Haven: Yale University Press, 1986).

tendencies most characteristic of fourth-century Christian eucharistic liturgy originate before then. The changes in scale and in social opportunity within the empire, however, cemented and extended changes in eucharistic practice that had begun long before Constantine's conversion. This applies to characteristic uses of spaces and of buildings, as well as to what went on inside them.

There were already many purpose-built Christian halls in the latter half of the third century.[54] If the opportunity to use the basilica required precisely the formal and practical support provided by Roman emperors during and after that time, it was nevertheless the logical development of a pragmatic quest for space rather than tactical adoption of a piece of value-laden imperial architecture or avoidance of a more "religious" one such as the temple. Although Greco-Roman temples would sometimes be Christianized, and churches were themselves spoken of in increasingly cultic terms, the temple as an architectural form did not become the favored model for Christian sacred space, but arguably more for logistical reasons—temples were not gathering places for large assemblies under cover.

Going to Church in the Fourth Century

The character of these eucharistic events had changed as much or more than their surroundings. Instead of relatively intimate groups gathering for recognizable banquets, crowds now gathered to take and eat, or take away, token amounts of bread and wine; logistical necessity and theological possibility had worked together to transform the meal into what today's Christians would more readily recognize as a sacrament and its celebration as a liturgy. Some of the basic elements of this liturgy are still recognizable as continuing in or retrieved by modern churches of sacramental bent, while others might surprise.

Members of the church, of various ages and backgrounds, would gather in the church building prior to the celebration; Sunday morning was now the norm, but in many places the Eucharist was celebrated every day, if by a smaller group. The participants may often have brought food and drink from which the eucharistic elements would be chosen, the remainder made available for needy members of the community (Augustine, *Conf.* 5.9.17; cf. *Exp. Pss.* 129.7).

Congregations generally did not use chairs; most of the liturgy was spent standing. In most instances we know of, tendencies to separate the community according to gender and other factors had grown:

54. L. Michael White, *Building God's House in the Roman World: Architectural Adaptation among Pagans, Jews, and Christians* (Baltimore: Johns Hopkins University Press, 1990), 127–39.

Let the younger men sit by themselves, if there is room; if not, let them stand up straight. But let those that are already advanced in age sit in order. Let fathers and mothers take their own children to them. Let the younger women also sit by themselves, if there is room; if not, let them stand behind the adult women. Let those women that are already married, and have children, stand by themselves; but let the virgins, and the widows, and the women elders, stand or sit in front of all. (*Ap. Const.* 2.57.12)

Details of the liturgy did vary from place to place, although broad similarities were now clear. In what follows, a Western example that can be constructed reasonably fully and with confidence—Augustine's Hippo—is presented as an exemplar.[55]

The Eucharist began with the entrance of the clergy and the greeting by the bishop (or presbyter), "The Lord be with you." Readings from Scripture followed, sometimes from the OT, almost always from the NT writings, and inevitably from the Gospels. These were read by designated ministers, whether "readers," deacons, or priests. The bishop or a presbyter, usually addressing the readings heard or the feast or fast being observed, then gave a sermon.

The numerous catechumens could attend until this point, when they were dismissed and the doors of the church closed. The bishop and/or priests had been seated in the apse but now approached the altar (as the table could now typically be regarded), which might be placed in the body of the church rather than at the east end, and the gathered community came and stood close by, around low barriers, or *cancelli*. Prayers were offered, led by a deacon for the community and its needs, reflecting a belief that the imminent eucharistic offering enhanced the intercession.

The eucharistic prayer followed, the bread and wine having been on the altar from the beginning. An opening dialogue led into an extended but set prayer, now including the institution narrative, but still focused on expressing thanks and praise to God. The presiding bishop or presbyter made ritual gestures such as the sign of the cross over the bread and wine. The community responded with an "Amen" at the end.

The bread was broken and the Lord's Prayer said together before the kiss was offered. Then the eucharistic food and drink were distributed by bishops, priests, and deacons to those who pressed forward to the rails to receive them;

---

55. For this section I am indebted to Robin Margaret Jensen and J. Patout Burns, "The Eucharistic Liturgy in Hippo's Basilica Major at the Time of Augustine," in *Augustine through the Ages: An Encyclopedia*, ed. Allan Fitzgerald and John C. Cavadini (Grand Rapids: Eerdmans, 1999), 335–38.

generally the members of the church present, other than penitents, did receive Communion, but there was local variety of custom (see Jerome, *Letter* 48), and those outside urban areas, including monastics, might attend and receive very infrequently. The liturgy finished with a blessing from the bishop.

Some aspects of eucharistic celebration that now seem rather venerable were not yet present, even around 400. The Nicene Creed and the hymn *Agnus Dei* ("Lamb of God") became regular features much later, even though they are ancient texts.[56] The *Apostolic Constitutions* indicates that the *Sanctus* was a part of some Eastern eucharistic prayers by this point (8.12.27), but arising from later interaction with Judaism rather than as an original piece of Jewish inheritance, and hence not yet present in every liturgy.[57] Special liturgical dress was not yet evident, although clergy may generally have been distinguishable by sober garb, as were monastics; the vestments of later centuries were remnants of the formal or court dress from this period. Music, or rather singing, was an adjunct to the ritual meal rather than a central activity.

The Eucharist was celebrated often—daily in many places, but also on occasions where it seemed appropriate for pastoral need. Augustine recalls in his *Confessions* that when his mother, Monica, died, the company "offered the sacrifice of our redemption for her" (*Conf.* 9.12.32; cf. *Letter* 98.9). Funeral rites, we may note in passing, seem at this point to have drawn on the fundamental elements of sacrament, prayer, and psalmody appropriate to the practical needs of conveying the body to its resting place, rather than to have become a specific sort of rite; this would happen somewhat later.[58]

Conclusion

The Eucharist is a field of Christian practice characterized (like early Christian doctrine) by diversity and not just a single idea represented in bread and wine. It presents rich and varied themes of memory, presence, celebration, and sacrifice—and there is no stronger theme than thanksgiving, *eucharistia* itself. To use any one idea—particularly the later prevalent emphasis on remembering

56. Lizette Larson-Miller, "The Liturgical Inheritance of the Late Empire in the Middle Ages," in *A Companion to the Eucharist in the Middle Ages*, ed. Ian Levy, Gary Macy, and Kristen Van Ausdall (Leiden: Brill, 2011), 15–16.

57. Bryan D. Spinks, *The Sanctus in the Eucharistic Prayer* (Cambridge: Cambridge University Press, 2002), 194–96.

58. Another fourth-century example is Gregory of Nyssa's account of Macrina's funeral rites (*Life of Macrina*); see further the historical discussions in Richard Rutherford and Tony Barr, *The Death of a Christian: The Order of Christian Funerals* (Collegeville, MN: Liturgical Press, 1980).

the death of Jesus—as sole basis for interpretation of early eucharistic practice (let alone as a means to identify what we should recognize or accept as actually belonging to this eucharistic meal tradition) is apparently tempting but ignores the real feast of meanings offered by this evidence.

The Christian meal began as a form of ancient Mediterranean banquet, a varied but recognizable tradition fundamental to social and cultural, as well as religious, life. Banquets did not have a single or simple meaning inherent in their celebration, but might be venues for contest as well as celebration, for struggle as well as solidarity, for experimentation as well as consolidation. The Eucharist appears as a tradition within this tradition, with meanings and values attached, yet not simply as one single or simple "word" spoken within that "language" of communal and convivial signification. Its messages and its purpose are in fact those of communal Christian existence: of incorporation, challenge, transformation, and hope, centered on the message and meaning of Jesus.

This meal tradition did, however, change in striking ways even across the first few centuries of Christian history. The detachment of the eucharistic food and drink from an actual banquet with its attendant times, venues, and accoutrements, to be received in token form in separate morning assemblies, was the most important change, and probably happened somewhat later than usually presumed, from the mid- or late second century into the mid-third century. Theologically there were also important shifts: we have noted that ideas close to that of "real presence" are early, but that these, and in particular notions of sacrificial offering, become clearer and stronger over time, independent of communal eating itself, and had impacts on how person and place, as well as food and drink, play their part in early Christian eating.

It would be as misleading to dismiss the continuity, however, as to ignore the changes. Given that medieval Christian liturgy in the West would lose focus even on people's literal participation in the sacred meal, and that reformed churches would consequently inherit an assumption that eucharistic reception was not the distinctive and regular act of Christian communal life, the continued celebration of the eucharistic meal as the center of Christian life across these centuries is at least as striking as the remarkable change from, as it were, banquet to sacrament.

The first Christian meals were—like other ancient banquets—already highly ritualized occasions, centered on a form of sacred eating, and accompanied by prayer and formal discourse. There is no "fall" across early Christian history from commensality to ritual, or from feast to sacrament, despite the attractions such narratives seem to have for some. Even in sources of the fourth and later centuries there are persistent echoes of meals and banqueting practices in the celebration of the liturgical Eucharist. In the fourth century as in the first, a diverse group of believers gathered around a table to share simple food, and the Christians prayed and gave thanks to God for the life and work of Jesus, remembering his own acts of eating as they performed their own, affirming his presence in and at their meal.

3

⌒

WORD

Reading and Preaching

In the beginning was the Word, and the Word was with God,
and the Word was God. (John 1:1)

Words are an unavoidable medium for transmission of ideas and culture, but for Christians words have been more than just vehicles. Like Judaism and Islam, Christianity esteems Scripture as a unique source of revelation. Like them, it attributes creation itself to God's speech. Unlike either of these Abrahamic relatives, however, Christianity has also suggested that the divine Word is intrinsic to God's being and that the verbal instrument of creation is also the subject of the incarnation.

Words concerning this divine Word have been intrinsic to Christian communal ritual and practice from the outset. And while words feature in virtually every aspect of ancient Christian worship, they are of course the immediate focus in two related elements: the reading of Scripture and the forms of discourse that we know as preaching.

Consideration of reading and preaching could amount to a survey of early Christian literature as a whole, since virtually all ancient Christian texts are either concerned with scriptural interpretation, reflect homiletic practice, or were themselves read in liturgical settings. This chapter does not seek, however, to construct a history of ancient hermeneutics or explore the content of the earliest Christian kerygma, the message taken to the ancient Mediterranean world with such energy and success in the first few centuries; our concern is with the actual practices of speech—of reading and inspired utterance, of teaching and proclamation—that characterized the communal and ritual life of the Christian communities in the first four centuries or so. As we have already seen, while words were spoken in many settings, they were from the earliest times an important element of Christian meal gatherings, shared and consumed as surely as solid food.

The Word in the Synagogue

The Synagogue and Its Purpose

The synagogue has often been regarded as the starting point for Christian reading and preaching. The Gospels refer to Jesus as an active participant in synagogue assemblies (Mark 1:21; 6:2 and parallels; Luke 4:16–21); the Acts of the Apostles presents Paul and his companions attending synagogues as well (e.g., 13:5, 14; 14:1; 17:1–3, 10, 17).

Scholars assume that one aspect or another of Christian worship practice was borrowed from or influenced by the synagogue; but it is not unusual to find overconfident assumptions about the relationship, and about what there was to borrow. Recent scholarship urges caution about these connections; in the words of one recent study: "It is no longer possible to say with the certainty that marked the discussions of a generation ago that we know where Jews of the first century CE met, or what they did in their assemblies, or the nature of synagogue leadership."[1] In other words, what we know about first-century synagogues may actually be less than what we know about first-century churches.

"Synagogue" (*synagogē*) literally means "gathering" or "assembly." In the first few centuries CE it did not always refer to a building at all but could mean simply a group accustomed to gather in one place, whether that was a permanent architectural structure (adapted, purpose-built, or multipurpose) or simply a recognized point of assembly (cf. Acts 13:13, 43).[2] Not every first- or second-century Jewish community in Judea or elsewhere even had a synagogue, in either the sense of assembly or of building.

1. John S. Kloppenborg Verbin, "Dating Theodotos (CIJ II 1404)," *Journal of Jewish Studies* 51 (2000): 243.
2. Ibid., 247–48.

Synagogues rarely feature in early rabbinic literature,[3] suggesting that the emerging strength of the rabbinic movement was focused elsewhere at earlier times. The liturgical evidence of the Mishnah and the Talmuds, which has been fulsomely but sometimes uncritically used by scholars of Christian origins, actually reflects important changes from much later, when the rabbis became more prominent in synagogues. After the destruction of the Jerusalem temple in 70 CE, these local institutions gradually came to function in ways that not merely complemented the temple but even replicated or at least imitated it;[4] but that was not yet the case in the time of Jesus or Paul.

The Greek word used for the oldest attested "synagogue" buildings is actually *proseuchē* (literally "prayer" or "prayer-house"), which of course implies that prayer did take place in some of them, especially in the diaspora where distance from the temple required innovation by some even before destruction demanded it of all.[5] But first-century synagogues were not primarily liturgical centers; the temple was still the real hub of Jewish worship.

The dedicatory inscription of one synagogue built only meters from the Temple Mount in Jerusalem indicates how such a building might have functioned, in this case alongside the temple not just conceptually but literally. Theodotus, a priest and *archisynagōgos* (synagogue leader), probably funded the construction close to the time of Jesus:[6] "[He] built the synagogue for the reading of the Law and for the teaching of the commandments, and the hostel, the rooms, and the water fittings, as accommodation for those in need from abroad" (*CIJ* II.1404).[7] Theodotus' synagogue was not only a place of worship in the modern sense but also a community center and a pilgrim hostel. In Jerusalem, the need for hospitality for pilgrims may have been acute, but other early synagogues had comparably diverse facilities.[8] For that matter, similar multifunctional arrays of spaces and equipment

---

3. Günter Stemberger, "The Derashah in Rabbinic Times," in *Preaching in Judaism and Christianity: Encounters and Developments from Biblical Times to Modernity*, ed. Alexander Deeg, Walter Homolka, and Heinz-Günther Schüttler, Studia Judaica: Forschungen zur Wissenschaft des Judentums 41 (New York: Walter de Gruyter, 2008), 10.

4. Levine, *Ancient Synagogue*, 530–36; Branham, "Sacred Space."

5. The two terms also reflect different regional use, and even different functions; see Levine, *Ancient Synagogue*, 124–59.

6. The date is discussed in Kloppenborg Verbin, "Dating Theodotos"; although a later date is also possible, this was a fairly typical set of synagogue functions.

7. Text in ibid., 244.

8. See Levine, *Ancient Synagogue*, 135–36. The well-known Ostia Synagogue seems to have included a kitchen and accommodation for guests also; see L. Michael White, "Synagogue and Society in Imperial Ostia: Archaeological and Epigraphic Evidence," *Harvard Theological Review* 90, no. 1 (1997): 23–58.

might also be found in ancient architectural complexes like temples of the Roman gods, which by extension reflect the activities of social groups like guilds or collegia.[9]

First and foremost, however, what Theodotus had built was a place "for the reading of the Law." This focus on reading and study encourages further consideration of how synagogues may have been places from where early Christian knowledge and practice around use of Scripture stemmed.

The Torah and the Synagogue

Among the elements of Jewish communal prayer and ritual that were influential in earliest Christianity, the reading and interpretation of Scripture may be the most significant, partly because those activities were the real center of the earliest synagogue life. The "reading of the Law" that Theodotus expected in his synagogue preceded and accompanied the emergence of Christian practices of reading and preaching.

At the center of synagogue reading practice was the Torah, the first five books of the Hebrew Bible. The Torah had been regarded as a sacred text, or even object, before synagogues existed; the second-century BCE *Letter of Aristeas*, a fictionalized version of the Torah's translation, depicts the Egyptian king bowing solemnly before this newly produced Septuagint (*Let. Aris.* 177). Public and ceremonial readings of the Torah took place in the temple; at the Day of Atonement liturgy, the high priest read from Leviticus, describing the ritual itself, and recited from Numbers (*m. Yoma* 7.1 and *m. Soṭah* 7.1). Josephus and the rabbis agree that the king or high priest also read publicly from the Torah on the Feast of *Sukkot* after a sabbatical year (*Ant.* 4.209–11; cf. *m. Soṭah* 7.2).[10]

The centrality of reading the Torah in synagogues from the earliest times is clear from Josephus and his near contemporary, the Alexandrian Jewish writer Philo, who both describe reading and study of the Pentateuch as a distinctive Jewish communal activity and as the center of Sabbath observance.[11]

9. Levine, *Ancient Synagogue*, 134–35.

10. Lawrence A. Hoffman, "The Early History of the Public Reading of the Torah," in *Jews, Christians, and Polytheists in the Ancient Synagogue: Cultural Interaction during the Greco-Roman Period*, ed. Steven Fine, Baltimore Studies in the History of Judaism (New York: Routledge, 1999), 48.

11. See the texts and discussion in ibid., 46–47; and, further, Pieter W. van der Horst, "Was the Synagogue a Place of Sabbath Worship before 70 CE?," in *Jews, Christians, and Polytheists in the Ancient Synagogue: Cultural Interaction during the Greco-Roman Period*, ed. Steven Fine, Baltimore Studies in the History of Judaism (New York: Routledge, 1999), 25–27.

The impression these give, however, is not of reading as part of "services" but of long sessions of study and conversation. Philo refers to such Sabbath synagogue participation in scholastic terms:

> What then did [Moses] do regarding these seventh days? He commanded them to assemble together in the same place, to sit with one another with order and reverence to listen to the laws, so that no one should be ignorant of anything in them; and, in fact, they do always assemble together and meet with each another, the majority mostly in silence, except when it is appropriate to offer assent to what is being read. And then one of the priests present, or one of the elders, reads the sacred laws to them and interprets each of them separately till evening. (*Hypothetica* 7.12–13)

The Dead Sea Scrolls also refer to reading in their community (not a synagogue in the usual sense, admittedly) and reflect a practical concern familiar to those who have struggled with microphones or voice production: "And anyone who [speaks weakly or with a faltering sound], [without] separating his words to make [his voice] heard [should not read in the book of the Torah], so that he will not lead to error in a capital matter . . . to his brothers, the priests, in service" (4QD^b 6 II, 1–4).[12] Reading these texts meant reading them aloud. The ancient world contained quite a few books but fewer readers, in the modern sense at least; books were expensive, levels of literacy were not high, and although silent reading was known, oral recitation was a far more typical practice than we might otherwise assume.[13] Study of Scripture was thus not a matter of individuals poring over personal manuscripts but a communal activity focused on single copies of texts, with oral reading at its center, and shared conversation rather than individual reflection its corollary.

The pattern of reading in synagogues was apparently "in course," a segment or portion read each week on the Sabbath. Although there were portions allocated to certain festivals, no "common lectionary" can be spoken of for the synagogue until later centuries.[14] Theories suggesting that even the form of Gospel narratives might reflect formalized and predictable synagogue lectionary patterns are thus fanciful.

12. Translation from Florentino García Martínez and W. G. E. Watson, *The Dead Sea Scrolls Translated: The Qumran Texts in English* (Leiden: Brill, 1996), 52.

13. Harry Y. Gamble, *Books and Readers in the Early Church: A History of Early Christian Texts* (New Haven: Yale University Press, 1995), 1–41.

14. Hoffman ("Early History," 49–54) provides evidence of conflicting patterns and of problems where readings set for high days were repeated in an arbitrary course reading through the year.

Some of the best first-century evidence for such Sabbath study sessions comes from a surprising, if familiar, source:

> When he came to Nazareth, where he had been brought up, he went to the synagogue on the Sabbath day, as was his custom. He stood up to read, and the scroll of the prophet Isaiah was given to him. He unrolled the scroll and found the place where it was written: "The Spirit of the Lord is upon me, because he has anointed me to bring good news to the poor. He has sent me to proclaim release to the captives and recovery of sight to the blind, to let the oppressed go free, to proclaim the year of the Lord's favor." And he rolled up the scroll, gave it back to the attendant, and sat down. The eyes of all in the synagogue were fixed on him. Then he began to say to them, "Today this scripture has been fulfilled in your hearing." All spoke well of him and were amazed at the gracious words that came from his mouth. (Luke 4:16–22)

Jesus' reading and interpretation in Nazareth bears comparison with an account of Paul in the synagogue at Antioch from Luke's sequel, Acts:

> And on the sabbath day they went into the synagogue and sat down. After the reading of the law and the prophets, the officials of the synagogue sent them a message, saying, "Brothers, if you have any word of exhortation for the people, give it." So Paul stood up and with a gesture began to speak: "You Israelites, and others who fear God, listen." (Acts 13:14b–16)

The author of Luke-Acts uses these synagogue vignettes as "texts" to interpret and present his heroes' actions, but the presentation of how text and interpretation worked in synagogues must have some basis in experience. In both cases a public reading was undertaken, apparently of both Law and Prophets. In both cases interpretation takes place but with a certain spontaneity and openness to participation; "preaching" here was not a formalized, univocal activity led by one uninterrupted orator but a conversation in which those regarded as learned and articulate, or those who held a particular status in the community, were preeminent. Jewish homiletics at this time need not be imagined as normally a sort of one-sided rhetorical performance.[15]

What else this "preaching" was like we cannot readily tell. Jewish literature that includes the rabbis' distinctive exegesis, or midrash, probably derives from

15. Annette von Stockhausen, "Christian Perceptions of Jewish Preaching in Early Christianity?," in *Preaching in Judaism and Christianity: Encounters and Developments from Biblical Times to Modernity*, ed. Alexander Deeg, Walter Homolka, and Heinz-Günther Schüttler, Studia Judaica: Forschungen zur Wissenschaft des Judentums 41 (New York: Walter de Gruyter, 2008), 49–70.

oral teaching offered in the rabbinic schools rather than in the synagogues.[16] The Targums, interpretive translations of the Hebrew text into Aramaic, may also contain traces of early homiletic traditions but do not shed much light on just how Christians began to read and understand the sacred text communally.[17]

So Jesus' and Paul's synagogal Scripture events, as well as Philo's description of study there, seem more like communal Bible study with some authoritative input than "liturgy." There may be a ceremonial quality to them—Jesus stands to read, for instance, and Paul to speak—but this should not be exaggerated. Later evidence for synagogue worship is unlikely to fill in the gaps reliably; but after the destruction of the temple in 70 CE, synagogues were much more likely to be seen as spaces with an inherent sanctity, while the Pentateuch itself, both as text and as artifact, became even more a source of sacrality via the physical presence of Torah scrolls in shrines.

Church and Synagogue

The first Christians would have been familiar with some of these synagogal reading practices, but that does not allow us to prejudge how those actually influenced early Christian assemblies. Churches were not "synagogues," and in any case there was neither a recognizable "synagogue service" nor a lectionary nor an established homiletic form to adapt straightforwardly to Christian use.[18] Christian gatherings initially arose alongside the activities of the temple and of synagogues, not as a sort of liturgical double-duty for believers in Jesus but as qualitatively different and complementary events.[19] Christian churches, like synagogues, may have been understood as types of association or guild, of which there were many kinds in the ancient Mediterranean world based on common interest, faith, or purpose; but this is a different and more subtle sort of affinity to suggest between church and synagogue than either organic derivation or self-conscious modeling.

16. Gary Porton, "Midrash and the Rabbinic Sermon," in *When Judaism and Christianity Began: Essays in Memory of Anthony J. Saldarini*, ed. Alan J. Avery-Peck, Daniel J. Harrington, and Jacob Neusner (Leiden: Brill, 2004), 2:461.

17. Levine, *Ancient Synagogue*, 159–62.

18. *Pace* Hughes Oliphant Old, *The Reading and Preaching of the Scriptures in the Worship of the Christian Church: The Biblical Period* (Grand Rapids: Eerdmans, 1998), e.g., 1:226–27; O. C. Edwards, *A History of Preaching* (Nashville: Abingdon, 2004), 8; and Ronald E. Osborn, *The Folly of God: The Rise of Christian Preaching*, A History of Christian Preaching 1 (St. Louis: Chalice, 1999), 283. All assume both that Christian worship was based on synagogue practice and that such practice can be clearly reconstructed.

19. Use of "synagogue" at James 2:2 (and Rev. 2:9; 3:9) does not imply anything about procedure or ritual, or even relationship to Jewish gatherings; "synagogue" continued to have its simpler meaning of an "assembly."

The unquestionable connections at the earliest point are two, and related: first, the sacred writings of Judaism were undeniably known and interpreted in early Christian communities, as of course in Jewish ones; and second, the earliest Christians were themselves Jews who had in many cases participated in synagogues and continued in them even as followers of Jesus. Just how these elements were relevant to early Christian practice must be examined, however, rather than assumed.

The First Christian "Preaching"

Preaching to the Converted

Words like "preaching" and "sermons" have, like "worship," shifted in ways both massive and subtle. Talk of ancient "preaching" can mean the evangelistic activity of the apostles (or of Jesus) but also the quite different discourse or teaching within Christian assemblies.[20] It can then be tempting to imagine the earliest evangelistic oratory and the liturgical "preaching" we find in later centuries in terms of the other and to make either or both in the image of modern homiletics.

The confusion arises in part because Christians have continued to "preach to the choir." In recent times, texts and speeches that formally argue the claims of the Christian gospel have actually served the needs of the already convinced. In the early church, too, discourse phrased as though for mission may actually have been intended for maintenance. While the "good news" or its "proclamation" was fundamental to the existence of the church, its public performance to the outsider is not likely to have been as influential or central to conversions as might appear; rather, as in more recent times, most "preaching" may have been to those already connected to the community, the real basis of whose conviction and initiation was more complex and relational than imaginative pictures of primitive street preaching or ancient altar calls can sustain.[21]

If previously the history of the sermon has often been a quest first for oral performance related (really or ostensibly) to mission, and second for the real or supposed roots of familiar forms of ecclesial oratory, the present discussion concerns neither as such; rather, we are concerned here with the ways speech

20. E.g., David Dunn-Wilson, *A Mirror for the Church: Preaching in the First Five Centuries* (Grand Rapids: Eerdmans, 2005), 62–65. Dunn-Wilson situates preaching in a primarily liturgical setting only from the fourth century.

21. See Rodney Stark, *The Rise of Christianity: A Sociologist Reconsiders History* (Princeton: Princeton University Press, 1996); and Keith Hopkins, "Christian Number and Its Implications," *Journal of Early Christian Studies* 6, no. 2 (1998): 185–226.

or discourse was actually used in Christian communal settings, whether or not this included the presentation of the gospel to others, and regardless of whether it involved formal elements of rhetoric.

Preaching and the New Testament

The central and typical Christian gathering was the communal eucharistic meal. In the first century the "Lord's banquet," as Paul once called it, was not merely an opportunity for the sacral or social benefits of the meal proper but also a venue for various kinds of discourse, including reading and whatever forms of speech might first have passed for "preaching."[22]

In one sense the types of oral performance that characterized the earliest Christian meetings are obvious. Much of what is contained in the NT writings was certainly spoken, if not prior to being written then subsequently; it is true "that the New Testament sprang from early Christian preaching, rather than the other way around."[23] Writings such as those that came to be included in the NT canon, and other ancient Christian documents too, contain indications of the forms and content of discourse that characterized early Christian assemblies.

This assurance about the basic value of the NT and other early Christian literature as sources of ancient liturgical and, particularly, homiletical practice quickly gives way to doubt about the specifics. Nearly every part of the NT has been claimed as "liturgical" at one time or another, so that even literary structures of many texts have been claimed to map ritual practices otherwise unknown; however, such "panliturgism" is generally unconvincing, and thankfully now less favored.[24] The fact remains that we cannot be sure exactly which texts emerged in those gatherings, what other discourses were spoken and heard, or how these various speech events worked as part of a meeting or ritual.

Given this mass of material floating in the earliest Christian writings, with little to distinguish the genuinely homiletic from the rest, scholars have tended to sort by content (e.g., separating apparent kerygma, or proclamation, from supposed *didachē*, or teaching)[25] and/or by apparent rhetorical form.[26] In either

22. Taussig, *In the Beginning*, 36–40.

23. Alexander Olivar, "Reflections on Problems Raised by Early Christian Preaching," in *Preacher and Audience: Studies in Early Christian and Byzantine Homiletics*, ed. Mary Cunningham and Pauline Allen, A New History of the Sermon 1 (Boston: Brill, 1998), 21–22.

24. Bradshaw, *Search for the Origins*, 47–51.

25. C. H. Dodd, *The Apostolic Preaching and Its Developments; Three Lectures, with an Appendix on Eschatology and History*, 2nd ed. (New York: Harper, 1954).

26. See the survey in Alistair Stewart-Sykes, *From Prophecy to Preaching: A Search for the Origins of the Christian Homily* (Leiden: Brill, 2001), 23–39.

case, the quest for an ancient homily or sermon has then often become a matter of conformity to an ideal type, a method that may shed light on particular texts but is less useful in discerning how ancient Christian communal discourse might actually have worked.

We are on firmer ground with the relatively few explicit references in the earliest Christian texts to those first eucharistic meal conversations; we at least need to start with them, and two in particular are worth considering. Paul's attempt to coax the fractious Corinthians into better liturgical manners provides the earliest surviving account of a "ministry of the Word" in a Christian assembly:

> When you come together, each one has a hymn, a lesson, a revelation, a tongue, or an interpretation. Let all things be done for building up. If anyone speaks in a tongue, let there be only two or at most three, and each in turn; and let one interpret. But if there is no one to interpret, let them be silent in church and speak to themselves and to God. Let two or three prophets speak, and let the others weigh what is said. If a revelation is made to someone else sitting nearby, let the first person be silent. For you can all prophesy one by one, so that all may learn and all be encouraged. (1 Cor. 14:26b–31)

The idea of a whole set of contributions to a community conversation is not surprising at a banquet. Although communities with whom Paul worked had acknowledged teachers or others with some role of leadership, this critical review of communal discourse gives no hint of just one person dominating. Some of these utterances might have been ancient one-liners, formulae including the obvious "Amen" and "Hallelujah," and perhaps more developed or specific Christian phrases more along the lines of affirmation or praise than revelation or edification, needing no particular education or inspiration.[27] This is not to say there was completely open and equal participation, however; elsewhere in the letter, offices of apostle, prophet, and teacher are identified, along with others, suggesting a varied but real hierarchy in matters of human or inspired knowledge (1 Cor. 12:28–29).

While the Corinthians may have been particularly focused on charismatic utterance, prophecy was clearly important in many Christian communities, even if its forms might merge into other types of speech.[28] Nonetheless, Paul's own ideal suggests a whole procession of prophets, not one sole

---

27. Edward Foley, *Foundations of Christian Music* (Piscataway, NJ: Gorgias Press, 2009), 55–56.
28. See David E. Aune, *Prophecy in Early Christianity and the Ancient Mediterranean World* (Grand Rapids: Eerdmans, 1983), esp. 247–338.

teacher (at least when Paul himself was absent) or oracle. This picture of a collective set of inspired discourses, with neither "sermon" nor reading of Scripture, is the earliest direct evidence for how speech functioned in one Christian assembly.[29]

A second potential example comes from the later account of Paul's ministry in Acts, where Paul may give something more like a sermon. It is the first day of the week—perhaps already a conscious observance of Sunday—and the gathering is a eucharistic meal, the "breaking of the bread" (20:7). "Paul discoursed with them; since he intended to leave the next day, he continued his speech [*logos*] until midnight." This fearfully long "discourse" is interrupted by the death and resuscitation of Eutychus (vv. 9–10), only after which does Paul actually break bread, and then continues the conversation.

Although often seen as fatal long-windedness, this is probably a dialogue rather than one long speech, and to that extent compatible with the Corinthian conversation, granted that Acts must be somewhat later in date.[30] The apostle's prominence in the conversation may still reflect the historical experience of the Pauline mission, where Paul and other itinerants engaged in didactic conversations with converts and believers privately, and apologetic or evangelistic conversations more publicly. This can be seen as a "diatribe," or scholastic philosophical discussion; certainly Paul's activity would have been comparable to that of other ancient teachers and philosophers, and moreover his letters often show features of this method.[31]

These two examples suggest that the quest for an early Christian "sermon" may lead neither to a specific literary form, nor to a core kerygma, but rather to a conversation. Or perhaps, given the meal setting, we could simply call this a symposium (in the modern sense as well as the ancient), including oral contributions of different length, content, and form, from various participants. Such opportunities for shared discourse may have been more characteristic of the earliest Christian assemblies than any particular pattern of oratory.

Yet such occasions of collective, dialogical inspiration at the communal meal were also the crucible within which various discourses were shared, the extended as well as the brief, the scholastic as well as the charismatic; and

29. Stewart-Sykes, *From Prophecy to Preaching*, 11–14.

30. It is also an extraordinary event rather than a typical one, and the account is retrospective, intended for the author's later community rather than merely to chronicle Paul's career.

31. Stanley K. Stowers, "The Diatribe," in *Greco-Roman Literature and the New Testament: Selected Forms and Genres*, ed. David E. Aune, Sources for Biblical Study 21 (Atlanta: Scholars Press, 1988), 71–83.

indications are that some of these survived, in more and less obvious forms.[32] These were the predecessors of what later Christians have called homilies or sermons.

The Earliest Christian Sermons

Granted that the earliest Christian meetings included opportunities for various spoken contributions and not just one authoritative discourse, these occasions may nonetheless have often included more substantial and formal addresses or readings. We should not be distracted by Paul's own rhetorical self-deprecation, considering the clear evidence for his own effectiveness as a communicator; his letters may give some indication of what was heard in the flesh, and not just what was read when absent. And Paul was not unique as an articulate and energetic speaker; we also have the example of Apollos, whose reputation for eloquence must have arisen from rhetorical performance in the assemblies of communities he visited (Acts 18:24).

Aside from our knowledge of such articulate and rhetorically trained individuals, the very fact of some important candidates for identification as early Christian sermons or homilies adds to the sense that while the Christian assembly may not always have required oratory of any particular form, it often had room for it.

A term that seems actually to have been used about early homilies is "word of exhortation," a phrase used in reference to Paul's speech at the synagogue in Pisidian Antioch (Acts 13:16b–41; see v. 15b) as well as in Hebrews (13:22), where it refers to the work as a whole.[33] In the case of Acts 13, a set of examples or data (vv. 16b–25, concerning Israel; and 26–37, concerning Jesus) gives way to a conclusion drawn from them (vv. 38–39), and in turn some (terse) application or exhortation (vv. 40–41). Similar tripartite patterns are discernible within Hebrews, confirming that this is a recognizable rhetorical strategy. Since the same terminology also occurs in 1 and 2 Maccabees, some continuity with Jewish rhetoric (but not necessarily with synagogues in particular) can be assumed, although it may be a way of talking about

32. The charismatic aspect is emphasized by Stewart-Sykes, *From Prophecy to Preaching*; the scholastic aspect of the communities by E. A. Judge, "The Early Christians as a Scholastic Community," *Journal of Religious History* 1, no. 1 (1960): 4–15; and Judge, "The Early Christians as a Scholastic Community: Part II," *Journal of Religious History* 1, no. 3 (1961): 125–37.

33. See Lawrence Wills, "The Form of the Sermon in Hellenistic Judaism and Early Christianity," *Harvard Theological Review* 77, nos. 3–4 (1984): 277–99; C. Clifton Black, "The Rhetorical Form of the Hellenistic Jewish and Early Christian Sermon: A Response to Lawrence Wills," *Harvard Theological Review* 81, no. 1 (January 1, 1988): 1–18.

exhortation in general rather than necessarily a label for a very specific literary or rhetorical form.[34]

Parts of Paul's Letters presumably resemble the apostle's own speech; but stronger homiletic contenders in the NT writings include the Letter to the Hebrews, which apart from sharing the "word of exhortation" feature has elements of Greco-Roman rhetoric of the "epideictic" type, appropriate to formal gatherings.[35] Hebrews as received has been turned into a letter of sorts (see 13:22–25), which suggests this made it more authoritative, especially given Paul's corpus of letters (in which it was generally included in antiquity). Hebrews may even have begun life as a "desk homily," whose liturgical use followed its composition and thus really belongs as much or more to our consideration of reading as of preaching.[36]

We cannot extrapolate from the mere existence of a text like Hebrews to a whole genre of homily or sermon typical of Christian practice, but it demonstrates that there were individuals capable of sustained and sophisticated oratory, and that, by implication, there were real opportunities for composition and communal performance.

2 Clement

The ancient text known as the *Second Letter of Clement*, probably from the early second century, has a claim to being the oldest actual sermon or address surviving from ancient Christianity.[37] *Second Clement* is an exhortation to a congregation to act in justice and charity that fit their divine calling. It includes a number of explicit indications of its own communal performance: "We ought not merely to appear to believe and to be attentive now, while we are being warned by the elders [or "presbyters"], but also when we have gone home let us bear in mind the commands of the Lord" (*2 Clem.* 17.3). The author possibly refers to reading Scripture in the assembly, saying, "So, brothers and sisters, after the God of truth I am reading to you an address for paying heed

---

34. Wills, "Form of the Sermon," 280n10; Harold W. Attridge, "Paraenesis in a Homily (λόγος παρακλήσεως): The Possible Location of, and Socialization in, the 'Epistle to the Hebrews,'" *Semeia* 50 (1990): 216–17 (reprinted in Attridge, *Essays on John and Hebrews*; see p. 300).

35. Harold W. Attridge, *The Epistle to the Hebrews: A Commentary on the Epistle to the Hebrews*, ed. Helmut Koester, Hermeneia (Philadelphia: Fortress, 1988), 13–21.

36. Mary Cunningham and Pauline Allen, introduction to *Preacher and Audience: Studies in Early Christian and Byzantine Homiletics*, ed. Mary Cunningham and Pauline Allen, A New History of the Sermon 1 (Boston: Brill, 1998), 1.

37. See Michael W. Holmes, ed., *The Apostolic Fathers: Greek Texts and English Translations*, 3rd ed. (Grand Rapids: Baker Academic, 2007), 132–35.

to the writings, so that you may save yourselves and the one who reads among you" (*2 Clem.* 19.1). The curious phrase "God of truth" may be the same as the "writings," which makes it more likely that scriptural "writings" are in mind particularly;[38] what was read by one member to the others then might have been a homily, even *2 Clement* itself. In any case, the preacher's intention is linked not only with the repetitive moral urgings of this work but also with a body of revealed truth—and *2 Clement* does cite fulsomely from the Psalms, Prophets, and Christian writings. Somewhat like the "word of exhortation" model discussed, *2 Clement* moves from a theological affirmation to an ethical section, or *paraenesis*, and then to a conclusion encouraging patience in the end times.[39]

Evidence of the earliest Christian homiletics thus suggests no single model, but the situational adaptation of Greco-Roman rhetorical and other conventions to a version of the common meal or symposium. Some Christians were certainly capable of producing sophisticated compositions for proclamation within that somewhat flexible space, and some of these may have survived in literary form. At the earliest point, however, the opportunities for discourse and reflection were somewhat open.

From these less prescriptive beginnings emerge more pronounced rhetorical patterns and practices, as we will see. Before doing so, however, we need to address more explicitly the closely related question of reading Scripture.

Ancient Christian Reading

The Beginnings of Christian Reading

A famous story of early Christian readers has led to claims that the ancients generally did not, indeed could not, read silently at all. Augustine of Hippo describes his surprise on finding his mentor, Ambrose, doing just that: "But while he read, his eyes were led over the pages, and his heart searched out the sense, but his voice and tongue were silent. Often when we had come (for no one was forbidden to go in, nor was it his custom that arrivals be announced), we saw him thus reading silently, and never otherwise" (*Conf.* 6.3.3). In fact what was remarkable about Ambrose's silent reading was probably its continuation even when in company; he was not distracted by the arrivals

---

38. Karl P. Donfried suggests the writing is *1 Clement*, to which this writing was attached; see *The Setting of Second Clement in Early Christianity*, Supplements to Novum Testamentum 38 (Leiden: Brill, 1974), 14–15. However, the plethora of Gospel quotations (perhaps from a harmony or oral tradition) is also possible; cf. pp. 56–82.

39. Ibid., 42–48.

and, Augustine says himself, Ambrose did not want to invoke the interpretive conversation that reading aloud would have invited. The point of the story was thus not about technical ability—silent reading was actually well enough known—but of a "reading culture," wherein texts were typically performed and shared communally.[40]

The act of public reading in Christian or Jewish assemblies of the ancient world is different in character from modern study of books, and even from later liturgical readings in Judaism and Christianity. Hearing was for most people the only way to encounter a text at all, so reading and hearing were generally shared and were often the basis of interpretation and conversation.

The context for much of the earliest Christian reading was again the eucharistic meal. Readings at meals would hardly have surprised ancient diners. Pliny the Younger records his uncle's appetite for reading:

> After dinner a book would be read, and he would take sketchy notes. I remember that one of his friends, when the reader pronounced a word wrongly, called him back and made him repeat it, and my uncle said to him, "Surely you understood?" When the other said he did, he remarked, "Why then did you call him back? We have lost more than ten lines through your interruption." (*Letters* 3.5.11–12)

The elder Pliny's "reader" was apparently a servant—although few could read, not all readers were wealthy or free. The two diners had different expectations about the reading: Pliny, an inveterate multitasker and polymath, was focused on absorbing information and valued the sheer quantity of words heard; the friend (who seems to have been doing the more expected thing) attended to the aesthetics of the performance, which was something to savor during or after the meal.[41] Such varied pleasures of the text—hunger for knowledge, on the one hand, and desire for what was agreeable to the ear, on the other—were possible in Christian assemblies as well as in Pliny's *triclinium*.

"Reading" was thus usually "hearing." The act of reading itself was typically a performance of a work, the physical text something like a musician's score that invited or demanded not only rendering into voice but an interpretation of sorts by the very act of speaking what had been written.[42]

40. On this, and the Augustine anecdote, see William A. Johnson, "Toward a Sociology of Reading in Classical Antiquity," *American Journal of Philology* 121 (2000): 593–627.

41. Ibid., 616–17.

42. See the discussion by Peter Kivy, *The Performance of Reading: An Essay in the Philosophy of Literature*, New Directions in Aesthetics 3 (Malden, MA: Blackwell, 2006). Kivy makes this point about reading in general, but it is especially apt to ancient Mediterranean cultures.

Reading could have taken place in the earliest Christian meetings, but did it? A lack of direct evidence for the reading of Scripture—meaning, of course, Jewish Scripture—at the earliest Christian gatherings would perhaps be even more startling than the sparse evidence for preaching in the familiar sense, but it is just as true of Paul's account of the Corinthian banquet already mentioned (1 Cor. 14:26–31). While various Christians spoke there, there is no sign either that they read or that Paul wanted them to. At Corinth, the absence of scriptural reading could be related to the prevalence of inspired speech; "a hymn, a lesson, a revelation, a tongue, or an interpretation" (v. 26) certainly constituted a "ministry of the Word," to use the later term. If the word of God was available immediately through the words of prophets, then scrolls were arguably unnecessary.

This does not mean there was no reading at all. These same letters and other NT texts do provide clear evidence for early Christian liturgical reading, not of Scripture as then understood but rather of the Christian texts themselves. The Pauline Epistles were themselves intended for communal reading and listening, which would presumably have taken place even without Paul urging just this (1 Thess. 5:27). The later Letter to the Colossians conjures up a circulating library or book club: "And when this letter has been read among you, have it read also in the church of the Laodiceans; and see that you read also the letter from Laodicea" (4:16). The Revelation to John offers a blessing that implies the communal reading of the document itself: "Blessed is the one who reads aloud the words of the prophecy, and blessed are those who hear and who keep what is written in it; for the time is near" (1:3).

It is tempting to see these practices in retrospect as a different sort of "scriptural" reading, analogous to the study of Torah in the synagogue. Yet the NT writings were not initially "Scripture." By the time 2 Peter was written, Paul's writings do seem to have gained a certain problematic authority (3:16). First Timothy, later than the undisputed Pauline Letters, is mistranslated in some modern English versions as though it commends reading of "Scripture," but it actually urges the recipient simply to attend "to reading, to exhorting, to teaching" (4:13 AT). The author is at least as likely to have had Paul's own writings in mind as what was to become the Old Testament.

The Revelation to John claims an authority of a different and higher sort. That work's claim to an immediate glimpse into heavenly things is neither the legacy of an apostolic hero lending weight to his writings nor the evocation of "Scripture" as an established authoritative text. Its genre of a recorded heavenly vision implies a specific kind of revelatory authority, making it comparable with the oral prophetic discourses at Corinth, deriving power from origin and content rather than through participation in some as yet nonexistent category of canonical literature.

So the earliest Christian communal reading material may not typically have been what Christians themselves regarded as Scripture. Of course there is no way to be sure. The attempt made above to recast the relationship between Christian assemblies and synagogues, however, suggests that the evidence should not be interpreted in terms of false assumptions about continuity relative to reading the Torah and the Prophets.

What is clearer is that writings by the Christians themselves were read, not initially as Scripture or on the basis of inherited tradition, but as documents of present or recent charisma. Yet this serves to sharpen the question of scriptural reading rather than to dismiss it. It is clear that the earliest Christians did know and interpret the Jewish Scriptures; but how did they become part of Christian worship?

The Beginnings of Scriptural Reading

Of course the Jewish Scriptures were widely revered by early Christian believers and were reasonably well known too. The mere fact of the Jewish identity of the earliest followers of Jesus probably allows that much to be assumed, but an acknowledged reverence for Scripture does not necessitate a particular form of communal reading.

Paul's Letters themselves not only assume some form of biblical literacy but also assert that "whatever was written in former days was written for our instruction, so that by steadfastness and by the encouragement of the scriptures we might have hope" (Rom. 15:4). His and other early Christian authors' free use of scriptural citations indicates further that these relatively elite teachers not only valued biblical works but also had access to them.

The form of this access is not clear. Paul's own citations are too variable to encourage the awkward picture of an itinerant apostle with a whole library in tow, which is what a "Bible" in the modern sense would have amounted to. Memorization, access to local copies of books, and the use of *florilegia*, or collections of quotations, are all more likely sources of scriptural knowledge, for him and for others.[43]

43. The reference to "books" (i.e., scrolls) and "parchments" at 2 Tim. 4:13 is compatible with any of these possibilities; see further Christopher D. Stanley, "'Pearls before Swine': Did Paul's Audiences Understand His Biblical Quotations?," *Novum Testamentum* 41, no. 2 (1999): 127–28.

The synagogue would also have been an important resource for such early Christian teachers still organically connected to Jewish life. For less itinerant Christians, such "reading" of Scripture may initially have happened through the synagogue rather than in church. The reading of Torah in synagogues was already an established and characteristic practice by this time (cf. Acts 15:21), and if we abandon the dubious premise that churches were "Christian syna-gogues," we realize that it was less likely that such reading would be repeated in the Christian gathering.

While the common picture of many gentile sympathizers, or "god-fearers," attached to synagogues may be dubious,[44] many Christians were active par-ticipants in these assemblies at least for some decades (see John 16:2, and cf. Paul's activity in synagogues, noted above).[45] While even synagogues may not have consistently owned all the books we now call the Old Testament, the limits that economics and literacy placed on ownership of personal reading material should not be confused with isolation from the texts. In this communal reading culture, if one member could own and read a scriptural (or other) book, then all had access to it, if in different senses or to different extents.

Later NT writings suggest that a scholastic emphasis may have grown in Christian meetings, with a developing emphasis on reading Jewish Scripture. Second Peter asserts a normative scriptural focus and shows less enthusiasm for the charismatic interpretation of the Pauline community at Corinth, argu-ing that "no prophecy of scripture is a matter of one's own interpretation, because no prophecy ever came by human will, but people moved by the Holy Spirit spoke from God" (1:20–21 NRSV, modified). Again, this assumes access to the reading and hearing of Jewish sacred texts.

Second Timothy certainly has Jewish Scriptures in mind—if not quite the canonical "Old Testament"[46]—when positing that "all scripture is inspired by God and is useful for teaching, for reproof, for correction, and for train-ing in righteousness, so that everyone who belongs to God may be proficient, equipped for every good work" (3:16–17), apparently referring back to what the author has also just called "sacred writings" (v. 15). The apparent redundancy of this statement, given that Paul's own teaching had already been thoroughly grounded in the same Scriptures, reflects not so much a new doctrine of in-spiration as a desire to establish a pattern of reading and interpreting these

44. See A. T. Kraabel, "The Disappearance of the 'God-Fearers,'" *Numen* 28 (1981): 113–26.

45. Stanley K. Stowers, "Social Status, Public Speaking and Private Teaching: The Circum-stances of Paul's Preaching Activity," *Novum Testamentum* 26 (1984): 64–65.

46. Luke Timothy Johnson, *The First and Second Letters to Timothy: A New Translation with Introduction and Commentary*, Anchor Bible 35A (New York: Doubleday, 2001), 422–25.

writings communally. A few generations into Christian history, and with the synagogue perhaps at some greater distance, the need directly to engage the Jewish sacred writings in the Christian gathering would have grown with time, rather than being always and everywhere evident. The claim here that Scripture is "inspired" links the authority of the texts in the assembly with the same charisma that was evident in many of the early communities.

So even between the earliest known Christian gatherings of the mid-first century and the evidence for those of the early second, there may well have been a shift, from charismatic discourses at a communal banquet that complemented rather than imitated synagogue activity, to a more textual and scholastic emphasis involving scriptural readings and interpretation somewhat more like that of the synagogue. The influence of the synagogue therefore may have increased, paradoxically, with the strained relationships characteristic of the later first and second centuries, as Christian assemblies sought to incorporate more practices of reading and interpreting Scripture.[47]

Thus the commonly held view that Christian liturgical reading of Scripture has its origins in the synagogue may be broadly right, but wrong in the ways usually envisaged; it was not an organic, immediate, or universal bequest to the fledgling Christian movement but a later borrowing necessitated by a real (if sometimes exaggerated) "parting of the ways" wherein relations changed sufficiently for the synagogue no longer to be an obvious locus for Scripture to be heard and interpreted for Christians.

This account, where Scripture reading is a clearer phenomenon in a second generation of Christian ritual than at the earliest point, may also help explain the resistance by some strands of second-century Christianity to the use and authority of what became the earliest Christian "Bible," namely the Jewish Scriptures of the Septuagint. Teachers like Marcion and some of the groups often referred to as "gnostic" may have been liturgical conservatives, resisting the addition of readings from the Jewish Bible at gatherings traditionally characterized by charismatic or scholastic contributions of a specifically Christian kind.

The oldest clear description of an assembly with scriptural readings, and a "sermon" offered by a local leader, is from as late as 160:

> And on the day called "of the sun," when all who live in cities or in the country gather in one place, an assembly occurs, and the memoirs of the apostles or the writings of the prophets are read, as long as there is time; then, when the

47. Thus Stewart-Sykes (*From Prophecy to Preaching*, 17) speaks of the "synagogalization" of the Christian communities.

reader has finished, the president presents a verbal admonition and challenge for the imitation of these good things. Then we all rise together and send prayers, and, as we before said, when the prayer is ended, bread is offered, and wine and water. (Justin Martyr, *1 Apol.* 67)

This community at Rome—a group of Syrian expatriates like the author Justin himself, not necessarily exemplifying what all other Roman Christians knew or did—clearly had a diverse library to draw upon. These "prophets" could have included the writings attributed to Moses (i.e., the Pentateuch) and so this may just be a poetic way of saying "Jewish Scriptures" in general. The "memoirs of the apostles" (Justin Martyr, *1 Apol.* 66, cf. *Dial.* 103.8) are more or less the later-canonical Gospels,[48] in which case this is the oldest reference to their liturgical reading (granted that traditions about Jesus must also have been transmitted communally from the outset). Justin also knew Paul's writings but does not mention them being read;[49] even though we know they were read communally elsewhere, some diversity of preference and of possession continued.

Since Justin was a Syrian, and associated with his own compatriots, his liturgy may not have been "typically" Roman at all.[50] The neatness of his two-fold "lectionary" of Jewish Scripture and Gospel makes for a closer parallel to synagogue practice than does earlier Christian evidence, and Syrian Christians may have been more and sooner influenced by synagogal practice than some others; regional and cultural differences may have persisted in choices of reading, and other matters, for some time.[51]

If ancient Jewish Scripture thus makes its appearance in the mid-second century, and presumably had been used somewhat earlier, contemporary Christian letters continued to be read communally also. These might be from current

48. Justin may already have used a Gospel harmony; see Helmut Koester, "The Text of the Synoptic Gospels in the Second Century," in *Gospel Traditions in the Second Century: Origins, Recensions, Text, and Transmission,* ed. William L. Petersen, Christianity and Judaism in Antiquity (Notre Dame, IN: University of Notre Dame Press, 1989), 19–37. Justin seems to quote John once (John 3:4–5) at *1 Apol.* 61.4–5, but he may not view John in the same light as the Synoptics or the sayings in them; see Graham N. Stanton, *Jesus and Gospel* (New York: Cambridge University Press, 2004), 101–2.

49. On Paul in Justin, see Rodney Werline, "The Transformation of Pauline Arguments in Justin Martyr's Dialogue with Trypho," *Harvard Theological Review* 92, no. 1 (1999): 79–93.

50. McGowan, *Ascetic Eucharists,* 153–54.

51. Gerard Rouwhorst, "The Reading of Scripture in Early Christian Liturgy," in *What Athens Has to Do with Jerusalem: Essays on Classical, Jewish, and Early Christian Art and Archaeology in Honor of Gideon Foerster,* ed. Leonard Victor Rutgers, Interdisciplinary Studies in Ancient Culture and Religion 1 (Leuven: Peeters, 2002).

leaders as well as apostolic heroes, contemporary situational advice being heard along with the words of old apostolic favorites; a little after Justin, Dionysius of Corinth indicated to Christians at Rome (ca. 170) that *1 Clement* was still being read at the communal meal in his community, along with contemporary correspondence from the Roman church: "We passed this holy Lord's day, in which we read your letter, from the constant reading of which we shall be able to draw admonition, even as from the reading of the former one you sent us written through Clement" (cited in Eusebius, *Eccl. Hist.* 2.23.11). The Christians were eager producers and copiers, known for this even among outsiders (see Lucian, *On the Death of Peregrinus* 11); and while in some other circles the role of copyist was professionalized and somewhat distant, Christian scribes seem to have been enthusiasts who engaged with their texts as interpreters as well.[52]

An increase in reading from Jewish as well as Christian texts did not mean that this "ministry of the Word" was now purely text centered, or that charismatic and prophetic contributions were absent. Toward 200, Tertullian's defense of the Christian meal includes a description of postprandial discourse still varied enough to invite comparison with the Corinthian meal known to Paul:

> We do not recline until we have first tasted of prayer to God; as much is eaten as to satisfy the hungry; only as much is drunk as is proper to the chaste. They are satisfied as those who remember that they have to praise God even in the night; they talk as those who know that the Lord is listening. After water for washing the hands, and lights, each is invited to sing publicly to God as able from holy scripture or from their own ability; thus how each has drunk is put to test. Similarly, prayer closes the feast. (*Apol.* 39.17–18)

Tertullian elsewhere alludes to an intriguing mixture of liturgical order and chaos at Carthage, when a "sister" prone to charismatic revelations offered her insights even during the *dominica sollemnia* ("Lord's [Day?]" observances), probably here a Sunday morning assembly with the distribution of the Eucharist, when "scripture is read, or psalms are sung or speeches are made or prayers are offered" (*On the Soul* 9.4). Paul's advice about seeking order amid Pentecostal chaos might have occurred to the later Carthaginian elders too; in any case, this may be an accidental but more finely grained successor to the type of event the earlier Corinthians had shared. A century and a half later, Scripture apparently was now also read, or at least could be, and perhaps there

52. Kim Haines-Eitzen, *Guardians of Letters: Literacy, Power, and the Transmitters of Early Christian Literature* (New York: Oxford University Press, 2000), 129–32.

is even a liturgical *ordo* implied here in the morning event, with Scripture, psalm, homily, prayer; but the varied character of the symposium was still evident, even more so at the continuing evening gatherings.

It is also worth noting that the modes of reading or the uses of vocal performance referred to here may cross modern boundaries between speech and song. Tertullian refers to singing of Scripture; this may mean not just a "song" with a scriptural text but a sung "reading"; singing brought volume and gravity to the text as performed, and toward the end of the period covered by this book it becomes clearer that liturgical performance of Scripture was often what we might call chant; this may have been the case in many earlier instances too.[53]

Remembering and Reading Jesus

The Gospels were not the first Christian literature read in assemblies, because they were not written until some decades after the events they depict, and after the letters of Paul. Yet the Christian meal was certainly the locus for the oral tradition of stories and sayings of Jesus.[54]

The precise form of that sharing in assemblies remains uncertain. It has sometimes been constructed so as to foreground supposed "preachers."[55] We have already seen that those who remembered, recited, composed, or prophesied in ancient communities were a diverse group, both relative to the wider world and in the Christian community itself, rather than occupants of some such particular role.[56]

Paul, author of our earliest literary sources, had certainly shared some elements of a narrative about Jesus as crucified and risen, but not only that; his recapitulation of the Last Supper narrative shows that the Corinthians had "received" other traditions about Jesus that Paul had "handed on" (1 Cor. 11:23). The fact that written Gospels appear not very long after this provides us with one clear case of a transition from shared discourse in the mode of the ancient banquet to the later-normative reading of an authoritative text in Christian worship.

---

53. Foley, *Foundations of Christian Music*, 65; see the discussion in chap. 4, on music and dance.

54. Edgar V. McKnight, "Form Criticism and New Testament Interpretation," in *Method and Meaning: Essays in New Testament Interpretation in Honor of Harold W. Attridge*, ed. Andrew B. McGowan and Kent Harold Richards (Atlanta: Society of Biblical Literature, 2011), 21–40.

55. Assumed "preaching" as the context for transmission of the Jesus sayings has been criticized at least since the work of Krister Stendahl, *The School of St. Matthew, and Its Use of the Old Testament* (Philadelphia: Fortress, 1968), 19.

56. Joanna Dewey, "From Oral Stories to Written Text," in *Women's Sacred Scriptures*, ed. Pui-Lan Kwok and Elisabeth Schüssler Fiorenza, Concilium (London: SCM, 1998), 20–28.

The first account of reading Gospel stories in a literary form comes in the account already mentioned from Justin Martyr, who not only cites Gospel traditions in terms derived from the synoptic tradition but also refers explicitly to readings from the "memoirs of the apostles." This terminology, along with the character of Justin's Gospel citations, indicate that he viewed the texts not so much as inspired artifacts (like "Scripture") but as reliable sources for authoritative sayings and divinely ordered events; Jesus and his actions, not the literary witnesses to them, were what mattered.[57]

Irenaeus' writings a little later reveal both a further development of the collection that Justin knew into a more authoritative shape (on which see further below), but also that there were groups that wanted to read (and write) other Gospels too. Citations, fragments, and occasionally whole copies of such have survived, a reminder that diversity of authoritative reading would be a continuing reality in many Christian gatherings.

Codex and Canon

The emergence of Christian reading culture is paralleled by the appearance of a new reading technology, the codex. As Christianity itself emerged and grew, readers in the ancient Mediterranean were already voting with their fingers, away from the traditional scroll to this new quasi-book, wherein sheets of papyrus or parchment were folded and cut as quires, then bound together between boards. But Christian use of the codex was particularly enthusiastic, especially for the Christian writings that would come to form the NT collection.[58]

The advantages of the codex over the scroll for public reading of a collection of texts were considerable, since it allowed "random" rather than merely sequential access to the contents;[59] when various passages were sought rather than a continuous reading pattern followed, the desired text could be found and read much more easily. Codices also lent themselves to combining what would have been numerous scrolls into single volumes. This in turn allowed the collection of related texts, like the four Gospels and the Pauline Letters, which would have been useful anthologies for communal reading and hearing but which also catalyzed these collections into particular forms; a copyist might

57. See the discussion in Stanton, *Jesus and Gospel*, 92–105.
58. See Larry W. Hurtado, "Manuscripts and the Sociology of Early Christian Reading," in *The Early Text of the New Testament*, ed. C. E. Hill and M. J. Kruger (Oxford: Oxford University Press, 2012), 49–62.
59. Gamble, *Books and Readers*, 63.

now work from a codex collection rather than merely a single scroll-book, and communities would experience the codex, and hence the collection, as an artifact in their gathering.[60] Further, the codex was portable; and while this was not necessarily crucial for local liturgical use, it was fundamental to the transmission of literature, and particularly of an authoritative pattern of reading.

Irenaeus of Lyons stakes the first explicit claim for a fourfold Gospel collection, commending not only the inspiration but also the exclusivity of the familiar four. In doing so, he argues curiously (to us) from natural symbols of four winds and four corners or directions of the world, as well as correlating the four apocalyptic beasts, with whom he identified the perspectives of the texts (Rev. 4:7–8; see *Against Heresies* 3.11.8), to the familiar Matthew, Mark, Luke, and John.[61] The rather unconvincing character of these arguments actually suggests that the collection preceded and spurred Irenaeus' reflection; the reading practice must have preceded the theology. Justin's use of a similar data set, without the explicit reflection on its form, suggests that a similar collection could already have been available to some even in the 150s.[62]

Although Irenaeus tends to correlate libraries with what was to be called the "rule of faith"—later, orthodoxy—there were communities who saw themselves as part of that mainstream but who by Irenaeus' standards read too much, or too little, in church. One such case concerns Sarapion, a bishop in Antioch around 200, who was apparently uninfluenced by Irenaeus' notion of a closed quadruple Gospel collection, but who wrote gravely to the church at Rhossos in Cilicia about their use of a *Gospel of Peter*. Sarapion judged the matter solely on content; while at first he had judged this gospel harmless enough, he changed his mind:

> For we, brothers and sisters, receive Peter and the other apostles even as Christ; but the forgeries in their names we from experience reject. . . . When I was with you I considered you all to be attached to the right faith; and so without going through the Gospel attached to Peter's name, I said, "If this is all that leads to your squabble, why then let it be read." But now having learned that their mind was lurking in some heresy from information given me, I will make a point of coming to you again. . . . I was able to borrow this same Gospel from others—that

60. J. K. Elliott, "Manuscripts, the Codex and the Canon," *Journal for the Study of the New Testament* 19, no. 63 (1997): 107–11.
61. Stanton, *Jesus and Gospel*, 63–68.
62. Ibid., 82–86.

is, from the successors of those who originated it, whom we call Docetists (for most of its ideas are from that school)—and was able to go through it, and to find that most of it was from the true teaching of the Savior, but some things were additions. (in Eusebius, *Eccl. Hist.* 6.12.3–7)

The "squabbles" indicate that Sarapion was dealing with communal use, not some esoteric study by an individual. Sarapion's story suggests that what would later be regarded as an "apocryphal" document was no necessary mark of conscious theological or organizational departure from a norm. The Rhossians may simply not have had other Gospels to read.

The trash heaps of the Egyptian city of Oxyrhynchus indicate no lack of choice for liturgical reading there in the third century. Among discarded fragments, the *Shepherd of Hermas* was as popular as any text later regarded as canonical, and the *Gospel of Thomas* and *Gospel of Mary* were read alongside at least seventeen of the twenty-seven works that later came to be regarded as the canonical NT.[63] In Oxyrhynchus the material evidence underscores what the story of the Rhossians also suggests: that reading (and writing) choices could be theologically driven, but that the prosaic question of which books were actually known or owned was likely to be as important in the formation of an early Christian communal reading practice as some external measure of orthodoxy.

Canons, Rules, and Reading

The term "canon" is itself a modern one, at least as generally used to refer to an authorized collection of books (to be distinguished, by the way, from a collection of authorized books). Ancient Christian uses of "canon"—in Greek, *kanōn*, a ruler or yardstick—actually refer not to sets of books but to the "rule of faith," a doctrinal measure of orthodoxy used and discussed by authors such as Irenaeus (a "rule of truth" in his case—*Against Heresies* 3.2.1; cf. 1.10.1) and Tertullian, the content of whose rule was comparable to what would become the Apostles' Creed (*On the Prescription of Heretics* 13). These early writers imply the exercise of such a rule in scriptural interpretation and selection but do not explicitly link the two.

Most of the books that were to become the NT emerged fairly readily as popular and authoritative across the first few centuries, rather than just being

---

63. Eldon Jay Epp, "The Oxyrhynchus New Testament Papyri: 'Not without Honor except in Their Hometown'?," *Journal of Biblical Literature* 123 (2004): 5–55; Luijendijk, "Sacred Scriptures as Trash."

imposed arbitrarily at some late point.[64] Processes such as the previously noted aggregation of particular sets of books, aided by the technology of the codex, meant that many of these writings came to be widely accepted fairly quickly. There were important exceptions, where clarity took some time; some communities continued to use or produce different "scriptural" books. And the boundaries of what could actually be read in church were highly porous and may never have just reflected a supposed "canon."

Perhaps the oldest surviving list of books regarded as possessing authority proper to being read in church is that discovered in the early eighteenth century by Italian scholar Ludovico Muratori. This eighth-century manuscript reproduces a fragmentary list that some scholars date even to the late second century, others to the fourth. Its similarity to the writings of Victorinus of Pettau (d. 303) now makes a late third-century date attractive.[65]

Although this Muratorian fragment defends a list of NT works akin to the set later regarded as canonical, it does not mention Hebrews, 1 or 2 Peter, or 3 John, and includes the *Apocalypse of Peter* as well as the more familiar Revelation to John, but says of the former that some "do not wish [it] to be read in church." The other contested book is the *Shepherd of Hermas*, which was to be read,[66] but not as though it belonged either among the prophets or the apostles. This raises a question about different forms of reading or contexts for reading, which the Muratorian fragment does not answer. Yet it is clear that the real issue for the author was not the formation of a book called the Bible but the right practice of liturgical reading.

In 367 Athanasius, bishop of Alexandria, wrote his regular annual letter to his churches specifying the dates of Easter and its attendant fasting and feasting periods, and addressing current pastoral concerns. In this case he laid out his sense of the limits of proper scriptural reading for instruction in the church, and in doing so provided the oldest list of the twenty-seven books generally regarded since as the NT. This was not, however, the definition of a "Bible" in the modern sense. There was no single book, nor would most Christians ever own even parts of it, let alone the whole. The question was which books would be used in the actual practices of Christian communal life, and how.

---

64. John Barton, *Holy Writings, Sacred Text: The Canon in Early Christianity* (Louisville: Westminster John Knox, 1997), 1–34.

65. Jonathan Armstrong, "Victorinus of Pettau as the Author of the Canon Muratori," *Vigiliae Christianae* 62, no. 1 (2008): 1–34.

66. The Latin of the fragment is famously bad; it is hard to tell whether the implication is that the *Shepherd* should be read, but only privately, or should not be read publicly in specific ways the prophets or apostles were.

Athanasius introduces in the *Festal Letter* a distinction between books "measured by [the] rule [of faith]," or "canonized," and others that are "not measured by rule, but merely read" (*Festal Letter* 20). "Read" here means, as previously, read aloud and, in particular, communally. In the former category are the books of the Hebrew Bible and the NT as we know them, while the latter contains most of the books of Jewish Scripture preserved only in Greek and often now referred to as deuterocanonical (or, less helpfully, as the OT "Apocrypha"), although Athanasius includes Esther in this group, along with the *Didache* and (again) the *Shepherd of Hermas*.

Athanasius rejects a third category of book called by him "apocryphal," or hidden (*Festal Letter* 21). These are books that his opponents—"Meletians," "Cataphrygians," and others—saw as requiring a measure of spiritual maturity to access. It seems unlikely that these were being read publicly in churches under Athanasius' pastoral rule anyway, but rather that they were a kind of higher curriculum for an academic or scholastic network of Christians that sat uneasily under episcopal authority.[67] Athanasius' claim regarding the "canonized" books was less the imposition of some new rule than associating his episcopal authority with what was established practice in churches.

All the books (other than his "apocrypha") were suitable for some liturgical use. Yet within that category of books read—a liturgical canon (in the later sense)—he establishes a sort of doctrinal canon, those "measured by rule." These books seem both to be authenticated by the rule of faith (which is the meaning of "canonized" here) but are also the sources of definitive doctrine, "springs of salvation" (*Festal Letter* 19).

The secondary or "read-only" category are, interestingly, not marginalized as far as public reading goes but are actually favored by Athanasius for reading "to those who recently join us and want to be catechized in the word of piety" (*Festal Letter* 20). This makes explicit that these books were favored in catechetical assemblies of some sort—perhaps precisely because they were not "springs of salvation," and hence their catechetical use did not compromise the distinction between prebaptismal education and the mystagogy that followed initiation.

While Athanasius has no time or respect for the "apocrypha," the implication of his decree is not book burning or even self-censorship; people would

67. David Brakke, "Canon Formation and Social Conflict in Fourth-Century Egypt: Athanasius of Alexandria's Thirty-Ninth Festal Letter," *Harvard Theological Review* 87, no. 4 (1994): 395–419; Brakke, "A New Fragment of Athanasius's Thirty-Ninth Festal Letter: Heresy, Apocrypha, and the Canon," *Harvard Theological Review* 103, no. 1 (2010): 47–66.

have continued to read these books more privately, no doubt, in their discussion circles, separate from the more public assemblies. Some other texts, such as martyr acts (perhaps including the books of the Maccabees), might have been read too, but Athanasius is silent about them. Athanasius' letter is thus not really an attempt to establish a "canon" of Scripture in the later sense, but rather, on the one hand, to make sure his readers understood what was appropriate for liturgical reading, and, on the other, to understand his own authority as judge of a good book.

Roles and Readers

Who read? The earliest texts are either silent or unclear; but since literacy was limited, reading could not be assigned or performed randomly or according to charisma, but required skills initially likely to accompany social status and/or professional training. Since slaves or freedpersons trained for the task could often be readers, the capacity to read and other indications of social status cannot always be used as simple evidence for one another. As time went on, Christian communities seem to have developed a more distinctive culture of roles and readers, not merely reflecting wider patterns of power and literacy, but where literacy became a sign of and means of leadership.

A passage from 1 Timothy urging attention to reading may imply that the addressee, a local leader, is involved in reading, exhortation, and teaching (4:13). The author of 2 Clement may also be presented as reading (19.1). Neither of these cases requires the reader to have a formal or ordained role, or directly associates reading with the other offices attested in these documents (bishops or overseers, 1 Tim. 3:1–2; and elders, 2 Clem. 17.3), but both do imply that reading was associated with leadership. Justin Martyr's 1 Apology, a few decades later than these, distinguishes the person who reads from the apostles or prophets and the presider who then expounds the reading, hinting at further differentiation of roles (chap. 67).

The idea of a "reader" as holder of a specific office appears only in the third century. Cyprian of Carthage refers to readers as at the bottom of a ladder of attainment for a now-professional clergy, comparable to the career path of Roman officials. These African lectores apparently read the Gospel at the Eucharist (Letter 38.2, 39.4) and were expected to progress to the rank of presbyter. Literacy was now a mark of, and qualification for, ordained Christian leadership. The extended and differentiated readings of the more developed eucharistic liturgy of the fourth century came to be embedded in this clergy hierarchy; while "readers" continued to have roles, the preeminence accorded to the Gospels led to the assertion in the *Apostolic Constitutions* that "a presbyter or deacon [should] read the Gospels" (2.57.7).

The developing emphasis on reading in Christian assembly involves more than absorption or repetition of the assumptions about roles and readers shared in the wider Greco-Roman milieu; it also involves the construction of a different culture (or cultures) of reading. While few Christians read or wrote, even the forms of surviving texts suggest the accommodation of manuscripts to a more diverse group of public readers than the classical specialists such as the elder Pliny's mealtime reader. Known codices with Christian writings show a distinctive emphasis on word divisions and other aids to the semi-trained reader, arguably now more a generalist than a specialist. This can certainly be seen as a sign of the social diversity of the early Christian communities,[68] but it also reflects the establishment of new structures in which literacy itself, and not merely the social status that might otherwise have led to it, became a source of authority. The reader was not first and foremost a specialist performer but a leader whose authority came to be associated with the texts proclaimed.

Assemblies for the Word

Praying Together

Given that the eucharistic meal was the main communal event and included forms of teaching and discourse from the beginning, and reading or interpretation of Scripture at least from a certain point, we need also to consider events or assemblies where Scripture, preaching, or other discourse was the primary or sole focus.

The evidence is inconclusive for the earliest times. Reference in Acts to the "apostles' teaching and fellowship, to the breaking of the bread and the prayers" (2:42) could conceivably point to different gatherings, where the "prayers" are the periodic prayers discussed elsewhere and the "breaking of the bread" is the eucharistic meal, leaving the reference(s) to teaching and fellowship as another form of communal event. A case for a gathering apart from the meal could also be made from the contrast between discussion of the banquet in 1 Corinthians 10 and 11, where failure to eat worthily is dangerous, and the undefined events in chapter 14 (cf. also chap. 12), where apparently there may be unbelievers present; for various reasons, however, these Corinthian instances are more likely to be the same type of event, viewed from different

68. See Hurtado, "Manuscripts and Sociology."

perspectives.[69] However, while we can assume that there were other meetings—for example, for organizational purposes—there is no clear sense of anything amounting to a primitive Christian "worship service," or of meetings of an entire local Christian community, separate from the eucharistic meal itself at the earliest times.

The earliest evidence for other assemblies seems to be linked not with discourse or Scripture but with Christian observance of specific times of prayer, which are discussed at greater length elsewhere in this book. Pliny the Younger reported to the emperor Trajan from his governor's post in Bithynia in 111 CE that the Christians there "were accustomed to meet on a fixed day before dawn and sing responsively a hymn to Christ as to a god, and to bind themselves by oath" (*Letters* 10.96). This is not a Eucharist, since he later indicates that in the evening they met for the meal; the earlier event sounds like a communal prayer meeting. The "fixed day" could be Sunday, but collective observance of Wednesdays and Fridays as fasts (later, "stations") is just as well attested, particularly for sharing the fixed hours of prayer.[70] The character of Pliny's account, crafted for his imperial patron and not for liturgical historians, allows no very firm conclusion.[71]

Sometime later in Africa, Tertullian's bitter arguments with less rigorous Christians indicate they managed to agree on the idea of communal gatherings for the set hours of prayer, at least on fast days. These included a morning assembly where the Eucharist was distributed (*On the Soldier's Crown* 3.5) but with no sign of extended reading or even conversation. Later in the day, when some of the Carthaginians explained their custom of praying at the ninth hour by the example of Peter and John attending the temple (Acts 3:1), they seem to have been looking for a model of gathering, not just of praying.[72]

Origen also extols the virtues of praying at the prescribed hours in the regular place of assembly, by now probably a place built or converted for Christian use, where he encourages his readers to think they will find not just human but angelic company (*On Prayer* 31.5–7). This is something like the theory of later monastic practice, with individuals offering what is essentially

---

69. See the discussion in chap. 2.

70. See chap. 7.

71. Note the comments regarding use of this text from J. Albert Harrill, "Servile Functionaries or Priestly Leaders? Roman Domestic Religion, Narrative Intertextuality, and Pliny's Reference to Slave Christian Ministrae (Ep. 10,96,8)," *Zeitschrift für die neutestamentliche Wissenschaft und die Kunde der älteren Kirche* 97, nos. 1–2 (2006): 111–30; see bibliography at 111n4.

72. Paul F. Bradshaw, *Daily Prayer in the Early Church: A Study of the Origin and Early Development of the Divine Office* (London: SPCK/Alcuin Club, 1981), 67.

their personal prayer, but together. So the first fairly clear pattern of assemblies other than the eucharistic celebration is of these shared times of prayer at the set hours; and even then these are not so much assemblies of a whole community but some individuals seizing opportunities to share their common desire and obligation to pray.

Catechesis

Origen and Tertullian are also witnesses—through the sheer bulk of their writing that explores Scripture, faith, and ethics—to a culture of teaching or catechesis that had its own communal expression. Both these writers, it is also worth noting, were (at least initially) laypeople; this was at this stage no impediment to certain forms of leadership, and to teaching in particular.

In both ancient and modern sources, "catechesis" can refer both to instruction in general as well as, more specifically, to teaching in preparation for baptism. In practice, the importance of instructing the already-baptized as well as the aspiring catechumens means these activities often overlapped. Teaching took place in gatherings for Eucharist and especially for prayer, but at times also had its own specific communal expressions.

In his defense of the Christians, Tertullian focuses on the evening *agapē* as the characteristic (and potentially suspicious) meeting, and knows also of morning prayer gatherings including distribution of the eucharistic food, but also hints at a different sort of event, apparently called on the basis of need or occasion rather than as a matter of course:

> We meet to call one another to remembrance of the Scripture, if some factor of the present times requires us either to be forewarned or to be reminded of anything. We staunchly feed our belief by holy voices, we raise our hope, we strengthen our confidence, we indeed consolidate discipline by driving home precepts. (*Apol.* 39.3)

He goes on to associate the exercise of pastoral discipline with this same sort of Scripture-focused meeting, but in itself it was more like a study session, whereas at the main meal assembly, Scripture may or may not have featured more prominently than other forms of discourse (including the occasional sister talking with angels). When he refers to a few reasons for which a Christian woman could be expected to leave the house, Tertullian includes both the daily prayers (which he calls "sacrifices") and some unspecified catechetical gathering: "some brother who is feeble is visited, or else sacrifice is offered, or else the word of God is dispensed" (*On the Apparel of Women* 2.11.2).

At least part of Origen's immense and sophisticated interpretive output implies a scholastic setting more specific than assemblies for daily prayer; much of his work is not education for a diverse audience but training for an elite one. Nonetheless, most of his *Homilies* may have been delivered in communal gatherings such as prayer assemblies on fast days; the later Christian historian Socrates says Origen often preached on Wednesdays and Fridays (*Eccl. Hist.* 5.22), which, if accurate, confirms that these stations or hours of prayer on fast days were becoming a focus for regular preaching and teaching.

At first, however, word-centered gatherings were probably structured around need (such as baptismal catechesis) or occasion (such as pastoral challenges) rather than being a regular part of a given day or week for most Christians.

Services of the Word

What may be one of the older parts of the *Apostolic Tradition* relates instruction to times for prayer:[73]

> The faithful, as soon as they wake up and have risen, before beginning work, shall pray to God, and then hurry to their work. And if there is any catechesis in the word, they shall give this priority and go there and hear the word of God for the comfort of their soul. They shall hurry to go to the assembly, where the Spirit flourishes. (*Ap. Trad.* 35)

Nothing is said explicitly about reading Scripture here, but catechesis usually involved the expounding of scriptural texts.

More details of another catechetical gathering in the *Apostolic Tradition*, this time more specifically related to baptismal preparation, give it a prayerful or even liturgical feel (and imply a scriptural focus):

> Let catechumens hear the word for three years. Yet if someone is earnest and perseveres well in the work, the time is not judged but the conduct. When the teacher finishes instruction, the catechumens are to pray by themselves, separate from the faithful. Let the women stand praying in a place in the assembly by themselves, whether faithful or catechumens. When they have finished praying, they do not give the kiss of peace, for their kiss is not yet holy. But let the

---

73. Chap. 35 is repeated in an expanded form at chap. 41, and its simplicity suggests it stems either from a source document or an early edition of the work; see Bradshaw, Johnson, and Phillips, *Apostolic Tradition*, 16.

faithful greet one another only, men with men, and women with women. Men are not to greet women with a kiss. Let all the women cover their heads with a pallium, and not only with a piece of linen, which is not a proper veil. When the teacher, after the prayer, lays hands upon the catechumens, let him pray and dismiss them. Whether a cleric is the teacher or a layperson, let him do so. (*Ap. Trad.* 17–19)

These morning assemblies were not only for catechumens; the other members were encouraged to take part—with some complexities arising around proper kissing and dressing as a result. A later version of the work shows an editor working hard to urge participation, but implying a somewhat elite listener and reader: "If there is a day when there is no instruction, let each one at home take a holy book and read enough of it to gain an advantage from it" (*Ap. Trad.* 41.4). At least some of the intended readers of this document were literate and reasonably wealthy; but the instructions are still ambitious. Later versions of the *Apostolic Tradition* define the text one should read more carefully as "the" holy book. And as the fourth century unfolds, we get a clearer sense that some Christians—not least some women of means—were collecting and exchanging scriptural and other religious works.[74]

If private ownership and therefore personal use of them grew, the Scriptures were still associated with the church itself and its gatherings, to the extent that during the Great Persecution under Diocletian (303), the destruction of scriptural texts found at churches was particularly pursued, and discovery of Scriptures in houses seems to have led to the presumption that Christians met there; those who handed them over to the persecutors—*traditores*—provide one origin of the modern word "traitors."[75]

So catechetical instruction at the daily hours of prayer seems to have been common by the third century. Not everyone celebrated this substantial spiritual fare; Origen complains about those who showed up only on feast days or who left before his catechetical sermons had finished (or even begun) (*Homily on Genesis* 10.3; *Homily on Exodus* 12.2). There were also seasonal fluctuations in the levels of participation, to the frustration of those who, like him, were more focused on eternal truths than temporal cycles.

74. Haines-Eitzen, *Guardians of Letters*, 77–104.
75. In the West, *traditio* was the definitive kind of apostasy and was central to the imminent Donatist schism; in Eastern sources more emphasis is placed on agreeing to pagan sacrifice, and the handing over of books was less significant; see G. E. M. De Ste. Croix, "Aspects of the 'Great' Persecution," *Harvard Theological Review* 47, no. 2 (1954): 75–113.

When Lent emerged somewhat later, it became a focus for catechesis, both because of the association with preparation for Easter baptism and also because of emphasis on fasting and self-examination. In fourth-century Antioch, a daily assembly in the afternoons of Lent included a sermon with moral exhortation, exemplified in John Chrysostom's *Homilies on the Statues* (on which see further below).[76]

So eventually there were various Christian gatherings, centered on Scripture, teaching, and prayer, as well as the Eucharist. Although it is reasonable to compare these events with later non-eucharistic "services," the differences are also important. These were generally weekday meetings with specific purposes and not the primary weekly expression of Christian identity. They belonged more to the pattern of daily time than of weekly, and were often related to communal observance of the daily hours of prayer. Catechesis—not solely or even primarily the education of candidates for baptism—was often conducted at these times for eminently practical reasons, as well as because of the importance that prayer and learning had for each other.

The importance of such events beyond the primary gathering of the community as a means of creating and expressing common beliefs and values may have increased over time. As the Eucharist itself changed from being a banquet for the community, its capacity for different sorts of discourse became more limited, or at least more focused. While scriptural readings came to be included at the Eucharist from an early point, the sacramental meal itself remained the primary focus. And as the Eucharist became more clearly "liturgical" and less a meal with opportunity for discourse, it was less well suited to being the primary locus of instruction or socialization; separate catechetical gatherings, and assemblies for the hours of prayer, thus became more important.

Across the third century a variety of assemblies or meetings became possible, or necessary. The most common and important term for these events in general was "synaxis" (gathering), which like *ekklēsia* was a common or secular word that took on specific significance. A "synaxis" in sources of the third and fourth centuries could mean either the Eucharist or another gathering for prayer and/or catechesis. The term can thus reasonably be translated as "service" in the modern sense, but the concept of synaxis was the product of various Christian assemblies for those other specific purposes, and not an idea prior to them.

---

76. Frans van de Paverd, *St. John Chrysostom, The Homilies on the Statues: An Introduction*, Orientalia Christiana Analecta 239 (Roma: Pont. Institutum Studiorum Orientalium, 1991), 161–201.

Patterns of Reading

Before Lectionaries

The early references to Christian communal reading suggest texts chosen according to occasion or opportunity, in keeping with more charismatic aspects of the communal discourse, rather than set patterns such as lectionaries. The common mistake of assuming that synagogue practice was the immediate source of Christian reading patterns has already been dealt with, but it may be worth reiterating that there was no lectionary cycle in the synagogue of Jesus' time.

Such freedom of reading—exercised increasingly by a clerical leadership, it must be added—was characteristic well into the fourth and even fifth centuries, granted the clearer emergence of canonical texts. Often this may have taken the form of an extended reading through a particular text or texts, not merely ephemeral or random choices (see further below regarding Origen). However, the appropriateness of certain authoritative texts to particular days or circum stances must always have been apparent. Fixed, or at least expected, patterns of reading emerged early through these points of celebrated significance.

One of the earliest known homilies, the *Peri Pascha* (*On the Passover*) of Melito of Sardis (on whom, see further below), opens with an explicit reference to a Scripture reading that would have formed part of the vigil of Pascha (not Easter Sunday, but a Christian observance of Passover): "The writing of the Hebrew exodus has been read, and the words of the mystery are made clear; how the sheep was slain, and how the people were saved" (*Peri Pascha* 1). This is perhaps the most obvious of all readings from Jewish Scripture to use at a particular Christian feast, and suggests a connection maintained (or remade) with the Haggadah that concerned the same story, although we are uncertain of the form and content of contemporary Jewish celebration of Passover. The exodus account may have been part of a longer set of readings, although clearer evidence for such extended readings at paschal vigils is much later.

So a measure of fixity probably developed around Easter in particular, then for martyrs' feasts (where the acts of the saints were read). These are likely to have been third-century developments, and they left the bulk of the year open to forms of course reading or more topical or thematic choices determined by local bishops and others.

Augustine's "Lectionary"

It is not until the fourth century that we have sufficient evidence to consider how such traditional associations of readings and feasts might have been expanded into a liturgical year—a concept that would not have been very meaningful much earlier. In fact, even in the expansive bodies of sermons from specific feasts and other times that have come down from such as Augustine and Chrysostom, there is still no sign of a "lectionary" proper but rather a richer set of norms, still focused around Easter, martyrs' feasts, and now also Christmas and Epiphany.

Augustine as bishop clearly had the discretion to choose most readings for his church at Hippo. He refers to his choice of readings for particular occasions (*Sermons* 362, 93). He sometimes preaches through a particular book in a sequence of homilies (like the *Tractates on the Gospel of John*), although not as a yearly or repeated pattern. He might also accept a lector's mistake as providential and preach accordingly (*Sermon* 352). More than once he had a Gospel repeated the next day to allow him to complete or reinforce a homiletic point (*Sermon* 68; *Exp. Pss.* 90; and *Sermon* 2).[77]

But at Christmas his community seems to have expected the Lukan infancy story to be read (*Sermons* 190, 193, 196), and the Matthean equivalent likewise at Epiphany (199, 202). At martyrs' feasts, the acts of the particular saints being celebrated could also be read liturgically, a reminder that "Scripture" was not so fixed a matter as we may assume.

During Lent, Augustine felt free to give a number of his *Tractates on the Gospel of John* (chaps. 7–12) in course, and similarly some of his *Expositions on the Psalms* (chaps. 128–33). There were readings that cropped up in relation to the rituals of baptismal catechesis, so that on the day the Lord's Prayer was to be recited by the candidates for baptism, the text of Jesus' advice to his disciples on prayer was read (*Sermons* 56–59). The Psalms were remarkably prominent in Augustine's preaching and in the liturgy; although some narrative and legal parts of the OT do occur in his readings, there was a psalm sung at every Eucharist, and this seems to have been widespread by the late fourth century if not earlier.

Unsurprisingly, the Triduum and Easter season did have established readings, but Augustine was not averse to some innovation, either. The church at Hippo had been used to hearing Matthew's Passion Narrative, but Augustine wanted to read different versions (or all?; see *Sermon* 232). At Easter each year, a walk through the various resurrection appearances from the four Gospels began, starting consistently with Matthew 28 at the vigil, but the order on the weekdays following was not fixed (*Sermons* 232, 235, 247).

77. Geoffrey G. Willis, *St. Augustine's Lectionary* (London: SPCK, 1962), 5–8; Willis overestimates the development of a set lectionary at this point.

While some of Augustine's series of readings and sermons were chosen at his own discretion, others had become associated with the major seasons. One year, the tradition of reading the various Easter Gospel stories made him adjourn his ongoing *Tractates on the Gospel of John,* since the Gospel readings would not work. Instead, he moved to expound the Letters of John that were read prior to the Gospel at the Eucharist (resulting in the parallel *Tractates* on those epistles). At Easter, a course reading through Acts (recently revived in some modern Western lectionaries) also began at Hippo, but neither the Acts readings nor the Johannine Epistles involved set passages for set days; rather, they simply progressed through the books at a pace that suited the need or mood of preacher and congregation.

The Lectionary and the Book

Although Augustine used neither a set order of readings for the year nor a book that contained them, both of these moved closer to reality in and after the fourth century.

When the pilgrim Egeria visited Jerusalem, she observed often that the readings at various assemblies were "appropriate" to the day or place, but she rarely says much more. Some assessment of her judgment is possible, though, because of the survival of Armenian and Georgian versions of the Jerusalem lectionary from the early fifth century. Although these probably include significant developments not witnessed by her, they confirm her general sense of readings chosen to complement an increasingly historicized liturgy in the mid-fourth century.[78] Like Augustine's implicit and inchoate "lectionary," these patterns do not yet reflect a grand narrative of the whole liturgical year focused in Scripture itself, but amount to a growing accumulation of focal points or celebrations, primarily for the celebration of the Eucharist, whose expansion begins to crowd the year, or at least parts of it, so as to leave less room for discretion and spontaneity.

The surviving lectionaries show liturgical reading at Jerusalem developing, focused on the major festivals related to the life of Jesus and to the saints and martyrs; in the fifth century, martyr acts were also still Scripture, at least on their heroes' feasts. Jewish Scriptures were read less than the NT, as we may now effectively call a clear set of Christian Scriptures; vigils, stational liturgies related to Holy Week, and feasts of ancient heroes provided the main

78. The Armenian Lectionary can be found in John Wilkinson, ed., *Egeria's Travels,* 3rd ed. (Warminster, UK: Aris & Phillips, 1999), 175–94.

appearances for OT readings. There are also signs of alignment with what we find in Augustine, even at some geographical distance; the consolidated Epiphany/Nativity feast still reflected in this Jerusalem calendar involves reading both Matthean and Lukan infancy stories; Good Friday involved reading all four Passion Narratives; Matthew 28 was the central Gospel narrative of the Easter vigil.

"Lectionary" can also refer to an actual book, constructed to provide a pattern of reading like these. Although many biblical manuscripts were for communal or liturgical use, books designed to provide more convenient (or more authoritative?) access to specific readings began to appear. The oldest of these that survives, from the fourth century, is fragmentary, and it is difficult to distinguish patterns or purposes from it or others of similar antiquity; we can simply tell from the close juxtaposition of texts from different books that some selection had been made for reading.[79]

Later patterns of liturgical reading began from that early period of elaboration and consolidation. Discretion and course readings gradually gave way to set patterns not merely in relation to feasts but to the wider liturgical year also.

Preacher and Text

Melito

Of the great preachers of the fourth century, notably John Chrysostom ("Goldenmouth") and Augustine of Hippo, a great deal has been written; but these represent the maturity of a Christian rhetorical tradition. There are, however, some earlier texts that give us a sense of how that tradition developed.

In 1936 the voice of a remarkable ancient preacher was heard again after many years of silence. A fourth-century papyrus containing a paschal sermon by one Melito was plausibly linked to a holy man of the same name who lived in the second century and is mentioned by Eusebius. This *Peri Pascha—On the Passover*—is powerful in its exposition of the resurrection, and confronting in its negativity regarding Judaism; the author's position can be better understood, if not excused, by contextualizing his preaching in a community where tensions between Jews and Christians were considerable.

79. The earliest lectionary texts do not conform to the later Byzantine pattern of readings; see Carroll D. Osburn, "The Greek Lectionaries of the New Testament," in *The Text of the New Testament in Contemporary Research: Essays on the Status Quaestionis*, ed. Bart D. Ehrman and Michael William Holmes (Grand Rapids: Eerdmans, 1995), 61–74.

For that matter, the character of Melito's prose and argument have a clear affinity with Jewish texts and authors:

> Therefore, note this, O beloved:
> New and old, eternal and temporal, corruptible and incorruptible,
> mortal and immortal is the mystery of the Passover thus:
> It is old insofar as it concerns the law, but new insofar as it concerns
>   the gospel; temporal insofar as it concerns the type, eternal because
>   of grace;
> corruptible because of the sacrifice of the sheep,
> incorruptible because of the life of the Lord;
> mortal because of his burial in the earth,
> immortal because of his resurrection from the dead. (chaps. 1–3)

Melito offers a series of antitheses—one of a number of lists or lists of pairs in the work—that serve to introduce his theme, in terms reminiscent of the poetic parallelism of the Psalms and Wisdom literature of Judaism. From these juxtapositions he proceeds to renarrate the exodus story (which had been read; see above) in dramatic terms:

> Listen to another and more frightful thing. In the tangible darkness, intan-
> gible death hid; and the ill-starred Egyptians touched the darkness, while
> death, keeping watch, touched the firstborn of the Egyptians as the angel had
> commanded. So if anyone touched the darkness, he was led off by death. If
> some firstborn, reaching out for a shadowy mass with his hand, and utterly
> terrified in his soul, called out in misery and in fear: "What has my right
> hand grasped? At what does my soul tremble? Who wraps my whole body
> with darkness? If you are my father, help me; if my mother, feel for me; if
> my brother, speak to me; if a friend, sit with me; if an enemy, go away from
> me, for I am a firstborn son!" And before the firstborn was silent, the long
> silence held him, saying: "You are my firstborn. I am your fate, the silence
> of death." (chaps. 23–25)

Melito's lively narrative style does not prevent an artful structure, as he proceeds from the story to draw conclusions via an explanation of his typological (and deeply supersessionist) approach to the text.[80] This dramatic narrative precedes and serves his point that the exodus, like the rest of Israel's history, points to the need for and the reality of Christ's triumph over death:

80. Alistair Stewart-Sykes, *On Pascha: With the Fragments of Melito and Other Material Related to the Quartodecimans* (Crestwood, NY: St. Vladimir's Seminary Press, 2001), 14–17.

This is the A and the Ω. This is the beginning and the end, an indescribable beginning and an incomprehensible end. This is the Christ. This is the king. This is Jesus. This is the general. This is the Lord. This is the one who rose from the dead. This is the one seated at the right hand of the Father. He bears the Father and is borne by the Father, to whom be the glory and the power to the ages. Amen. (chap. 105)

Melito sees history itself as an indistinct image that gives way to the reality of eternal truth. For him, as for second-century contemporaries like Justin, the text is a window to content, and to expound it is to reach in and interpret that reality.

Origen

Origen was one of the great thinkers of the early church, and of Christianity at any point. Although his reputation suffered after his death, the scope of his achievement, ranging from text criticism to interpretation to theology, is hard to exaggerate. This opus was achieved in circumstances that were both modest and harsh; he suffered during the persecution of Decius (250) and worked both as a private and an ecclesiastical teacher, with an ascetic outlook and ambition focused only on knowledge and his own salvation.[81]

Much of Origen's output may have been delivered orally, at gatherings for prayer or Eucharist and hence homiletic, although other works derive from more specifically scholastic settings. His homilies often amount to an oral running commentary, sometimes or perhaps generally composed on the spot, determined by the structure of the biblical text itself more than by any imposed rhetorical forms.

Although his own capacity makes these works somewhat unique, the influence of Hellenistic Judaism on Origen is important. Philo, whose works Origen knew, had described the exegetical and scholastic activity of the synagogue in terms of the activity of a priest or elder who "read the sacred laws to them, and interprets each of them separately till evening" (*Hypothetica* 7.13). Philo's own allegorical exegesis is also a powerful influence on Origen, whether or not this method was really widespread in synagogal interpretation.

Origen's homily on the story of the "belly-myther" of Endor is an interesting example of this preaching as exegesis, and we even know something

---

81. Anthony Grafton and Megan Hale Williams, *Christianity and the Transformation of the Book: Origen, Eusebius, and the Library of Caesarea* (Cambridge, MA: Harvard University Press, 2008), 22–85.

of its liturgical context. A long reading (1 Sam. [1 Kings in LXX] 25–28) was given at an assembly for one of the hours of prayer. There was, as we have seen, no lectionary system as such; Origen seems to have preached through the books of the OT in course at Caesarea (although this particular homily was preached in Jerusalem).[82] He begins by noting the literary structure of the text and the challenge of its scale, inviting the bishop to choose what to discuss: "Since there are four pericopes, each of which has not a few matters but which can also, for those able to examine them, take up hours not of just one assembly but of many, let the bishop indicate which he wishes of the four, in order that we may concern ourselves with it" (*Homily on 1 Samuel 28* 1.2). The "pericopes" correspond to four chapters in the later and familiar structure, but the lengthy reading suggests those divisions were not liturgical but based on sense. The bishop apparently chose the last.

Origen's treatment of the story is his own and was later controversial; but he illustrates uniquely well a shift in attitude to the text and implicitly therefore to preaching itself. Although he has a far stronger concern with the text as artifact than did Melito, Origen shares with him and most ancient Christian preachers a fundamentally typological approach to reading the OT. Samuel's descent is paired with Christ's ascent. But while he is traditionally seen as an exponent of allegorical or spiritualizing interpretations that downplay the literal meaning of the text, this piece illustrates how literal Origen could be.[83] Against attractive attempts to explain away the awkwardness of a spirit-medium apparently summoning the great Samuel, Origen insists on the text as it is: "See the kind of struggle going on in the word of God, which needs hearers also who are able to hear both great and holy words, and secrets concerning our departure, the first still unexplained, nor the second clear" (*Homily on 1 Samuel 28* 4.8). This "struggle" Origen sees as a feature of the inspired text that invites the capable reader and hearer into its embrace. Although not all biblical "history" is for everyone, this text has general relevance because of what it conveys or threatens about postmortem existence—our "departure" (*Homily on 1 Samuel 28* 2.1).

Origen's preaching is literal as well as allegorical, because rather than resolving the text into something else—events that might not have been what they

---

82. Adele Monaci Castagno, "Origen the Scholar and Pastor," in *Preacher and Audience: Studies in Early Christian and Byzantine Homiletics*, ed. Mary Cunningham and Pauline Allen, A New History of the Sermon 1 (Boston: Brill, 1998), indicates some of the other internal evidence for the liturgical setting and how Origen's teaching worked within it.

83. Patricia Cox, "Origen and the Witch of Endor: Toward an Iconoclastic Typology," *Anglican Theological Review* 66, no. 2 (1984): 137–47.

seemed—he insists that it is the text itself that demands to be read (or heard) and understood. While few preachers subsequently have employed comparable erudition, this notion of homiletics as a struggle with the text itself—of exegesis, in effect—has been enduring: "Hence there is nothing offensive in this passage, but everything is wondrously written and has been understood by those to whom God has revealed it" (*Homily on 1 Samuel 28* 10.1).

Preaching and the Psalms

Preaching and Place

With the growth and development of Christianity and its liturgy through the fourth century, the challenge of understanding and describing preaching changes significantly. One difference is the sheer quantity of undoubtedly homiletic material that has survived; a reasonable proportion of it has yet even to be translated.

Another difference is the existence of the first material evidence for Christian worship by which the texts can be contextualized in terms of space, objects, and, by implication, of bodies too. Apart from the remarkable Dura-Europos house church, a place perhaps as exceptional as its contemporary, Origen, we have little specific sense of the spaces created and occupied for Christian communal use prior to the opportunity created by the "Peace of the Church" and Constantine's patronage. After that point, churches appear, particularly on the basilica model, some of which still stand; these have been models for much subsequent church architecture also.

Two of the great preachers of the late fourth century, Augustine and Chrysostom, provide the opportunity to place homiletic text in a liturgical and wider context. Each has been the object of extensive study as preacher; here we merely note characteristic examples of their forays into what became the most popular book of the nascent Christian Bible, the Psalms. Chrysostom represents a high point in the application of ancient high rhetorical style to sermons; Augustine, although comparably trained, leans toward the more exegetical tradition of Origen.

John Chrysostom[84]

John, later known as *Chrysostomos*, or Goldenmouth, was active successively in Antioch and Constantinople, two of the great cities of the ancient

---

84. For further reading, see Wendy Mayer and Pauline Allen, *John Chrysostom*, Early Church Fathers (New York: Routledge, 2000), 26–33.

Mediterranean world. The churches of these cities were among the most prominent rhetorical platforms in the Roman Empire. His sermons are among the first examples of preaching as public theology, addressing questions of civic as well as spiritual significance; he is perhaps the most obvious ancient exemplar of the modern dictum to preach "with Bible in one hand and newspaper in the other." His sermons also reflect a level of rhetorical sophistication that presents a new height in the story of ancient preaching, even of ancient oratory.[85] Chrysostom's sermons reflect the matter-of-fact exegesis favored in Antioch, which contrasted with the allegorical approach common in Alexandria; these interpretive preferences would in time fuel two different ways of thinking about the person of Christ.

About eight hundred of John's sermons are extant, among them a set from the beginning of his career, in the midst of a massive social and political crisis that beset Antioch in 387. The *Homilies on the Statues* were delivered after riots responding to an unpopular tax levied by the emperor Theodosius, who had seen imperial monuments, including statues of the emperor and his family, toppled and subjected to acts reminiscent of modern scenes at the end of dictatorships. This ruler, however, remained very much in control of the wider world; and after order was reestablished, the city waited in fear for a brutal response.

Into this crisis and opportunity, during Lent, stepped the young presbyter. He used the sermons of the afternoon assemblies for prayer to encourage the fearful populace, urge them to repentance, and defend the claims of Christianity in what was still a diverse religious environment. The *Homily on the Statues* 17 was given partway through these events, after the emperor had stripped Antioch of its status as a "metropolis"; John uses this fact to reflect with the Antiochenes on the real significance of their civic identity.

In this instance he begins with the psalm that had been sung (Ps. 72) and verse 18, "Blessed be the God of Israel, who alone does wonders." First he argues that virtue, not status, is the real honor:

> Do you grieve that the honor of the city is taken away? Learn what the honor of a city is; and then you will see clearly, that if those who live there do not betray it, no one else will be able to take away the honor of a city! Not the fact that it is a metropolis; nor that it has large and beautiful buildings; nor that it has many columns, and broad porticoes and walks, nor that it is named in proclamations before other cities, but the virtue and piety of its inhabitants; this is a city's honor, and ornament, and defense. (*Homilies on the Statues* 17.10)

85. Ibid.

But John has another point to make that could not be made in any other city:

> Do you want to learn the honor of your city? Do you want to know its ancestry? I will describe these accurately, not just so that you know, but that you may also emulate them. What then is after all the honor of this city of ours? It happened first in Antioch, that the disciples were called Christians. This honor none of the cities of the world possesses, not even the city of Romulus! For this it can look the whole world in the eye; because of that love-charm for Christ, that boldness and that virtue. (*Homilies on the Statues* 17.10)

Chrysostom has not spent long on the text but pursues a basic insight from it—namely, that true honor, like "wonders," is God's alone.

Augustine

Augustine has many claims to ecclesial and theological fame. Known most often as the author of the remarkable *Confessions* and monumental *City of God*, his largest work—actually a collection—is his *Expositions on the Psalms*, which occupies nineteen hundred columns of the *Patrologia Latina* and multiple volumes in any modern translation.[86]

While Augustine's dogmatic works and controversies have earned him a reputation as "the inventor of original sin" and various other labels, his sermons reveal a thoughtful and pastoral bishop, as well as, of course, a considerable intellect. For him, the *Expositions* were part of a larger category of homilies; many of them were clearly taken down by secretaries from actual delivery as sermons.[87]

His basilica at Hippo and the surrounding complex of buildings have survived to the present day, if in ruins; it is possible to see the cathedra, or episcopal throne, in the apse. Some of the sermons come from daily eucharistic celebrations, others from the communal observance of daily prayer or catechetical assemblies that may have been held in a smaller chapel.

Augustine's treatment of Psalm 72 (for him, 71) is far more in the tradition of Origen than Chrysostom's, a rhetorically modest running commentary whose structure is determined by the psalm itself. Augustine does not seek to use this text for some specific point, but to claim this and every text for just one point; he sees the Psalms as addressed to Christ, about Christ, or spoken

---

86. The first complete translation into English is in six volumes: *Expositions of the Psalms*, ed. John E. Rotelle, trans. Maria Poulding, The Works of Saint Augustine: A Translation for the 21st Century (Brooklyn, NY: New City Press, 2000).

87. Perhaps not the one discussed here, though; his *Letter* 169 may refer to this on Ps. 72 (71) as a commentary dictated, not necessarily preached.

by him. He also reflects the tradition of typological interpretation; beginning with the title and traditional ascription to Solomon, he notes that its content does not fit Solomon, and hence claims that it really refers to Christ.

This single-mindedness of interpretative focus is not monotonous, however. Although avoiding rhetorical heights, he comments on rhetoric itself and engages with literary aspects of the Psalms with an acute eye, anticipating later commentators on poetic parallelism (and using it himself):

> Now it is customary in Scripture for the same thing to be repeated. So when it says, *your judgment* then it says differently *your justice*; and when it says *to the king*, then it says differently *to the king's son*. . . . Repetitions of this kind are frequently used to commend divine eloquence. The same idea is repeated, sometimes in the same words, sometimes in different words. Above all, these repetitions occur in the Psalms, and in that kind of discourse intended to move the state of the spirit. (*Exp. Pss.* 71.2)

At the end of his text-based exposition, Augustine comes to the verse with which Chrysostom had begun:

> Considering all that has been said, the hymn erupts, and the Lord, the God of Israel is blessed. For what was said to the barren woman is fulfilled: *the one who delivers you, the God of Israel, will be called the God of all the earth* (Isa. 54:5). He *alone works wonders*, because whoever performs them, he himself is working in them, *who alone works wonders*. (*Exp. Pss.* 71.20)

Conclusion

We have considered reading and preaching as two forms of practice, related insofar as they are both verbal discourse; but in fact we have seen they have a common origin in the ancient Christian banquet, and while both are characteristic activities of the Christians from the beginning, attention to words leads to distinct types of events only gradually.

At the earliest Christian gatherings, such as those of Paul's Corinthians, the difference between the divine word and its exposition was arguably unclear; prophecy and its interpretation were both given from above (1 Cor. 12; 14). There could also be reading, but the earliest texts read in such assemblies were probably Christian letters, not Jewish Scripture. The memory of Jesus' sayings and actions, and the proclamation of his death and resurrection, were initially matters of oral, rather than written or read, discourse.

The "scripturalization" of Christian worship, in the sense of Jewish Scripture—the Septuagint, in most cases—becoming an important or even central element of gatherings, seems to be a second- or third-generation phenomenon, accompanied by an increasingly textual, more than charismatic, approach to Jesus too. These changes were hardly uniform or neat; although an assembly of the mid-second century such as Justin's already involved a familiar-sounding use of literary prophets and of "memoirs of the apostles," still half a century later in Carthage prophets and even less-gifted members of the community contributed to the ministry of the Word from memory, or by inspiration, rather than from books.

Overall, however, there seems to have been an interdependent and complementary development of reading and preaching. The emergence of a more textualized and ultimately canonized approach to scriptural or revelatory discourse in the assemblies was accompanied by more authoritative, and indeed more clerical, exposition of those sacred texts. The interdependence of these two processes was liturgical, but more than that; for outside of communal events Scripture was generally not directly accessible to the individual, who was mostly neither reader nor interpreter but hearer, and so the development of an authoritative text implied the development of authoritative interpretation too.

Thus the emergence of a liturgical ministry of the Word is not merely a feature of worship; it is the key to understanding how the earliest Christians in general knew and received Scripture itself, and how they encountered the God who spoke in Scripture: not for the most part on the page perused privately, but in hearing amidst the communal assembly of the people called by that God.

4

~

Music

Song and Dance

Be filled with the Spirit, as you sing psalms and hymns and
spiritual songs among yourselves, singing and making melody
to the Lord in your hearts, giving thanks to God the Father
at all times and for everything in the name of our Lord Jesus
Christ. (Eph. 5:17b–20)

Worship," we have noted, is sometimes now a way of talking about
music. This would have baffled Christians of the first centuries;
music was often important for their communal gatherings, as were
buildings or food, but music was neither the most central or distinctive aspect
of their gatherings nor identified with "worship" as such, any more than other
ritual activities were. Yet sing they did.

Not a great deal is known of ancient Greco-Roman music generally, nor of
ancient Jewish or early Christian music in particular. The evidence we have is
largely of practices, roles, and attitudes toward music, and of the texts sung
to it rather than the music itself. Since music was a vehicle for the expression
of the thoughts and feelings of ancient Christians as prayer and praise, and,
as we will see, their focus was typically more verbal than musical, what has
survived is certainly among what was most important to them.

Yet there is an undeniable materiality of music that brings the body itself into view also, just as surely as communal eating does. Given that we have seen that ancient notions of "worship" began with the physicality of prostration or other forms of literal submission and service, singing—and even more so its close companion, dancing—raises the question of how the body itself, and not merely the soul or mind, was disposed toward God. Each of these—song and dance—evoked issues with which many early Christians struggled, perhaps because of the physicality of bodily performance or its availability for others to see and hear. Within these struggles, however, we can see important aspects of how early Christians experienced their embodied existence as a triumph over the limits of physical frailty and as anticipation of a renewed bodily life in a disposition of praise.

The Beginnings of Christian Hymnody

Music in the New Testament

The literature of the NT canon contains many passages that reflect the poetry and other verbal performances of the early Christian gatherings—as well as many more texts that have later been turned into musical compositions.[1] This double relationship between text and singing—and as we will see, singing is what we are concerned with rather than music in general—makes it difficult to be sure just which is which. Some NT hymnic texts, such as the Lukan canticles of Mary and Simeon (Luke 1:46–55, 68–79), are likely to have been literary compositions that later made their way off the page into communal use. Others, however, like the poetry embedded or adapted in John 1:1–16 and Philippians 2:6–11, are probably drawn from devotional hymnody known to the communities among whom the works arose and were adapted for use in the familiar books before traveling back into liturgical use.[2]

Actual singing was common Christian practice; musical instruments, however, were more "good to think with" than good to play for the early believers in Christ. Paul's exhortation to the Corinthians to offer intelligible and hence edifying praise involves both the literal song and the figurative instrument:

> [If] lifeless instruments that produce sound, such as the flute or the harp . . .
> do not give distinct notes, how will anyone know what is being played? And if

---

1. For a discussion of NT texts with poetic or hymnic character, see John Arthur Smith, *Music in Ancient Judaism and Early Christianity* (Farnham, UK: Ashgate, 2011), 183–87.
2. Bradshaw, *Search for the Origins*, 57–59.

the bugle gives an indistinct sound, who will get ready for battle? . . . There are doubtless many different kinds of sounds in the world, and nothing is without sound. If then I do not know the meaning of a sound, I will be a foreigner to the speaker and the speaker a foreigner to me. . . . Therefore, one who speaks in a tongue should pray for the power to interpret. For if I pray in a tongue, my spirit prays but my mind is unproductive. What should I do then? I will pray with the spirit, but I will pray with the mind also; I will sing praise with the spirit, but I will sing praise with the mind also. (1 Cor. 14:7–15)

The Revelation to John depicts heavenly instruments without hesitation; the living creatures and elders, each holding a kithara and a bowl of incense, fall down before the lamb (5:8); but since incense does not seem to have been used in Christian assemblies of the first century, we cannot assume too much about earthly harps, either. The seer's heavenly liturgy draws on the practice and accoutrements of temples known to his readers, not on the music or ritual of their domestic meal gatherings. This mixture of actual singing accompanied by metaphorical or heavenly instrumentation is fairly typical of Christian rhetoric and exhortation over the next few centuries.

Other NT texts reporting or urging song are few, but clear enough nevertheless: Paul and Silas sing in prison, indicating that there was a culture of song known to the author of Acts (Acts 16:25), but that work gives little further indication about its more regular communal use; however, the Letter of James urges the believers to join together in song, in a context that implies the communal eucharistic meal (5:13; cf. 2:3).

In parallel passages, the readers of Colossians (3:16) and Ephesians (5:19) are famously encouraged to sing "psalms, hymns, and spiritual songs." In contrasting musical sobriety with the dubious practices of the Greco-Roman banquet, Ephesians is implicitly pointing to proper conduct at the eucharistic meal again: "Do not get drunk with wine, for that is debauchery; but be filled with the Spirit, as you sing psalms and hymns and spiritual songs among yourselves, singing and making melody to the Lord in your hearts, giving thanks to God the Father at all times and for everything in the name of our Lord Jesus Christ" (Eph. 5:18–20). So this is liturgical and not merely ethical advice. It was perfectly applicable to personal and domestic life, though, as well as communal; and by the time of Pliny's account of Christian gatherings early in the second century, his reference to a morning song of praise (*Letters* 10.96) confirms that singing featured not only at the Christian banquet but also in gatherings for daily prayer.

The precise forms of that Christian singing, its performance in particular, remain mysterious; Paul's first-person-singular reference to singing "in the

Spirit" as an example in his extended musical discussion in 1 Corinthians 14 seems to imply individual rather than choral or communal singing, but we cannot be sure.

Psalms, Hymns, and Spiritual Songs

That familiar phrase "psalms, hymns, and spiritual songs" is less likely to refer to three specific kinds of song than to be three words or phrases combined to convey one complex idea. The songs of the earliest Christian assemblies could nevertheless have included scriptural texts, traditional hymns, and original compositions.

The very first Christian singing was also Jewish singing; like other aspects of communal worship, the very beginnings of Christian music must be understood within the matrix of Jewish practice. But what form, or forms, of practice? The Psalms come quickly to mind, but what we know about Jewish psalmody does not provide a neat model for continuation or adoption by Christians.

The word *psalmos* as used in Colossians and Ephesians need not refer exclusively to the Psalter; it literally means songs performed accompanied by a stringed instrument. However, it had already taken on a more technical meaning for Greek-speaking Jews (cf. Luke 20:42); the lack of other evidence for such performance in Christian contexts supports the possibility that here it was a way of referring to the biblical Psalms.

The earliest explicit reference to use of the biblical Psalter in Christian gatherings is from the second century, where "psalms of David" are included, with other songs, in a eucharistic meal shared "according to custom" as described in an apocryphal romance (*Acts of Paul* 9). This need not be a vestige of "original" practice, since Jewish and Christian communities continued to interact, influence, and compete with one another, not merely for years but for centuries.

The Psalms were used in the rituals of the temple as well as in later Christian worship, which has encouraged some to imagine a straightforward bridge between these two. There is, however, little sign that Christians saw their meetings as a literal kind of temple worship. For the first few decades, the temple and its sacrifices with their musical accompaniments continued and did not need replication; the influence of the temple on Christian liturgy was actually stronger after that great shrine was physically no more, but that influence was worked out over a long period rather than being an immediate or original feature of Christian gatherings. The temple could nonetheless have been a source of musical idiom for early gatherings of Christ-believers.

The synagogue is the other place where scholars have typically sought the connections between Jewish communal practice and the first Christian meetings. But the place of the Psalms in synagogue assemblies of the first century is by no means clear.[3] The rabbinic strand of Jewish culture and practice, represented in the Mishnah, does not refer to use of music. There are, however, inscriptions suggesting that an office of "psalm singer" did exist in some Jewish communities around the same time.[4] We have also noted that synagogue meetings were not the immediate or obvious source of how Christian gatherings were configured in other respects; there is no reason to think anything different applied to song. There may have been connections of genre and practice—apart from the use of instruments—between temple and some synagogues, and potentially, then, with Christian gatherings too.

Domestic devotion and ritual may be at least as important a source for understanding the first Christian gatherings and their Jewish connections, including psalm singing. The Psalms were part of domestic prayer and education in Judaism (see 4 Macc. 18:15). The set of psalms known as the Hallel Psalms (Pss. 113–118) was associated with the seder of the Passover, and might have had continuous use among Christians through their reinterpreted but continuing observance of that feast (cf. Mark 14:26).[5] In any event it seems likely that some forms of psalm singing already practiced in Judaism were known to Christians across the early centuries and that musical developments in both traditions may have been spurred by interaction, as well as by initial Christian borrowing. It is worth noting that, as practice in both early Christianity and the forms of Judaism located in synagogues emerges into clearer view, vocal music is in evidence far more than instrumental.[6]

Music in Second- and Third-Century Christianity

Dinner Music

Christians were encouraged to sing, and to sing the right hymns, as a part of their communal eating (see Eph. 5:19). Descriptions of eucharistic banquets where meal and sacrament were still one (or at least combined) confirm that there was often singing as well as spoken discourse.

3. See the discussions of Scripture reading and daily prayer in chaps. 3 and 6.
4. G. H. R. Horsley, "Epitaph for a Jewish Psalm-Singer," in *New Documents Illustrating Early Christianity* (North Ryde, NSW: Ancient History Documentary Research Centre, 1976), 1:115–17.
5. James W. McKinnon, "On the Question of Psalmody in the Ancient Synagogue," *Early Music History* 6 (1986): 159–91; Smith, *Music in Ancient Judaism and Early Christianity*, 117–34.
6. Foley, *Foundations of Christian Music*, 37–50.

The exact form of such singing is left largely to our imagination. Ignatius of Antioch speaks positively but vaguely about singing (Ign. *Eph*. 4.1–2). We have noted that the apocryphal *Acts of Paul* mentions the "customary" singing of a Davidic psalm after an ascetic meal. Tertullian's Carthaginian *agapē* around 200 involved slightly more varied fare, both in meal and music: "After water for washing the hands, and lights, each is invited to sing publicly to God as able from holy scripture or from their own ability; thus how each has drunk is put to the test" (*Apol*. 39.18). The balance of biblical, traditional, and composed song would have varied from place to place. Here Tertullian makes clear that Christian singing was not (merely) unison communal performance but a string of individual items. In another description, perhaps of the morning assembly that had emerged by this time, he notes that "Scripture is read or psalms are sung or speeches are made or prayers are offered" (*On the Soul* 9.4).

Between them, these events raise the possibility—which becomes much clearer over the following centuries—that singing was not just for what we might call songs or hymns, including psalms, but that the actual mode of performing scriptural texts was by what we might call chant. This may be another point of continuity and mutual influence with Judaism, where a rich tradition of chant and cantillation was also in formation across this period and beyond.[7]

The Hallel Psalms were used as a sort of adjunct to daily prayer by more conscientious Carthaginian Christians (Tertullian, *On Prayer* 27). Perhaps not much later, one of the sources of the *Apostolic Tradition* describes domestic eucharistic banquets where the same psalms featured again, or still:

> After the meal when they have risen and prayed, the children shall sing psalms, along with the virgins. Afterwards, a deacon holding the mixed cup of the oblation shall say a psalm from among those in which is written "*Hallelujah*." Then, if a presbyter orders it, more from the same psalms. After this, when the bishop has offered the cup, he shall say a psalm appropriate to the cup, all of them including "*Hallelujah*." When the psalms are recited, all shall say, "*Hallelujah*," which is, "We praise the one who is God. Glory and praise to him who created all the world by a word!" Thus when the psalm is completed, he shall give thanks for the cup and give of fragments to all the faithful ones. (*Ap. Trad*. 25[29C].11–15)

The biblical psalms were thus not simply a hymnal to be drawn on indifferently or occasionally; actual books are unlikely to have been the source of

7. See Smith, *Music in Ancient Judaism and Early Christianity*.

psalmody for many singers in any case. Certain texts, canonical or not, were more popular and more relevant than others.

The Singer and the Song

If singing is a universal human phenomenon, aptitude is less universal. This reality is often recognized by specialized roles and functions within groups. It takes some time for such differentiation of singers to appear in evidence for Christian worship, although we have noted cases of individuals sharing their performances communally; at first, to sing was in some sense a general prerogative.

The earliest Christian references to choirs are metaphorical, like the allusions to musical instruments. The idea of a choir as a harmonious blend of voices was often used by ancient Christian writers who had more than merely musical or liturgical points to make. Ignatius of Antioch uses musical metaphors freely, but in a passage where he compares bishop and congregation to lyre and strings he also refers to singing as an image of the community itself:

> Therefore in your agreement and harmonious love, Jesus Christ is sung. Become a choir, one by one, so that being harmonious in love, taking up the song of God in unison, you may sing to the Father with one voice through Jesus Christ, so that he may both hear you and perceive, because of what you do, that you are the members of his Son. (Ign. *Eph.* 4.1–2)

Clement of Alexandria takes up this choral motif. Although for him, as for Ignatius, communal singing is a metaphor for unity and obedience to God, his word picture again probably implies some real experience, whether or not in Christian gatherings:

> The unity of many out of polyphony and disorder, receiving divine harmony, becomes a single symphony, following one choir leader and teacher who is the Word, resting in the same truth, saying "Abba, Father"; God accepts this true sound from his own as firstfruits. (*Protrepticus* 9.88.3)

We know that the unity to which Ignatius and Clement urged their readers was often illusory; so too the existence of a musical ideal of communal singing in unison need not mean that it was realized in practice. These, however, are both referring, even theoretically, to a choral action of a whole group, not to a choir performing for a wider group; this was yet to emerge.

Tatian, an ascetic Syrian theorist of around the same time, refers dismissively to musical performances connected with Greek religion, not wanting "to stand agape at a number of singers" any more than to watch dramatic performances (*Oration against the Greeks* 22). There is no hint that Tatian yet knew of choral performance as something that had found its way into Christian practice; he would otherwise have been among the pioneers of the venerable custom of complaining about the music in church.

Such suspicion of contrivance or aestheticism was one factor that sustained communal singing ahead of more refined performance; but we have also seen that there was reflection on the unity that could be manifested in music. And individuals did sing songs, even though these are at first presented as sung discourses, both charismatic and scriptural, but not as musical performance per se.

But from the second century on there is also evidence for groups of singers. One of the earliest collections of hymns that circulated among Christians was the *Odes of Solomon*, probably of Syrian origin.[8] These sophisticated poetic texts imply by their very form a specialized performance of some kind, and one of the odes even refers clearly to a group that might have led them:[9]

> Those who sing will sing the
>   Grace of the Most High Lord
> And offer their psalms.
> And their heart will be like the day
> And their voices like the sublimity of the Lord. (7.22–23)[10]

A choral tradition was to develop further and famously in Syria; these hymns may be early evidence of both its fact and kind.

Not all emergent choral performance need have involved a group permanently set over against a congregation; they could have involved different subgroups in the community taking complementary roles in some more complex performance. Thus, for instance, in that evening meal of the *Apostolic Tradition*—what was once a community's eucharistic banquet, but from which the sacrament had been separated by the time the account was compiled into the work as we have it—specific musical roles are allocated: "After the meal when they have risen and prayed, the children shall sing psalms, along with

8. See Michael Lattke, *The Odes of Solomon: A Commentary*, ed. Harold W. Attridge, Hermeneia (Minneapolis: Fortress, 2009).

9. Smith, *Music in Ancient Judaism and Early Christianity*, 176.

10. Translation from Lattke, *Odes of Solomon*, 89.

the virgins. Afterwards, a deacon holding the mixed cup of the oblation shall say a psalm from among those in which is written '*Hallelujah*'" (25.11–12). The children and virgins—or perhaps "boys and girls"—seem to be singing (apparently canonical) psalms, not just to but on behalf of the congregation, prior to the deacon's recitation, which itself should probably also be understood as "sung."

It was only a short step from such division of labor to greater specialization. A collection of fourth-century rules attributed to the obscure Council of Laodicea stipulates that singers be properly appointed:[11] "No others shall sing in the church, except the regular ["canonical"] singers who go up into the lectern and sing from a book" (*Canon* 15). Those who chanted the Psalms in typical churches were now in effect "readers," not "singers," and the role of the people was to make a set response. Amid the emerging ascetic movement, psalms would be performed communally as chants, but still as a sort of Scripture.[12]

An Early Critic: Clement of Alexandria and Music

Clement of Alexandria offers plenty of advice to Christians about their morals and manners at both private and communal events, including on music.[13] His seamless, if complex, philosophy ties all these together in what is ultimately a theological vision rather than merely a ritual one. We cannot always be sure whether Clement is referring to liturgical rules or table manners—and indeed in his time these were not yet completely separate. Clement's strong emphasis on dining reflects the fact that meals were still central to Christian community life.

Clement writes more than any surviving ancient Christian writer about musical taste and the appropriateness of different musical idioms. Modern arguments often concern what music would be appropriate specifically to liturgical settings, over and against secular ones; Clement applied the same rules to both, not because of a "secularizing" approach to liturgy, but because of a "sacramental" approach to life. It is not so much that Clement sees the

---

11. This canon, of an initial group of similarly worded decrees, may indeed be from an original council of that name; see Hamilton Hess, *The Early Development of Canon Law and the Council of Serdica*, Oxford Early Christian Studies (New York: Oxford University Press, 2002), 48.

12. Peter Jeffrey, "Monastic Reading and the Emerging Roman Chant Repertory," in *Western Plainchant in the First Millennium: Studies in the Medieval Liturgy and Its Music*, ed. Sean Gallagher et al. (Burlington, VT: Ashgate, 2003), 45–49.

13. S. Blake Leyerle, "Clement of Alexandria on the Importance of Table Etiquette," *Journal of Early Christian Studies* 3 (1995): 123–41; Charles H. Cosgrove, "Clement of Alexandria and Early Christian Music," *Journal of Early Christian Studies* 14, no. 3 (2006): 255–82.

Eucharist itself as central to all life; rather, he views all of life—liturgy, labor, and leisure alike—as service to the true Word.

Clement's musings about music (*Paed.* 2.4; *Strom.* 6.11) reflect common philosophical notions about various Greek musical idioms and their supposed impact on the listener; different tones or modes (*harmoniai*) were thought to have inherent moral qualities and emotional impact. Like others, Clement favors the traditional Dorian mode (not to be confused with the scale used in later Christian chant that borrowed the same name) based on a diatonic scale; his criticisms of music based on chromatic scales may reflect conventional grumbles rather than any live issue of musical taste for Alexandrian churchgoers. Clement voices suspicion of music with too much "decoration" (*poikilia*), which might induce emotions ranging from sadness to ecstasy (*Strom.* 6.11.90); his own preference was for constant, thoughtful, and sober demeanor, in church or out.[14]

Could Clement have conceived of some instruments in church or elsewhere? The earlier Alexandrian philosopher Philo had made concessions to the string section within an otherwise negative attitude to the ancient orchestra. This distinction reflected the associations between certain forms of music and the sounds that accompanied pagan sacrifice. Lyres and similar instruments were associated with the domestic sphere, and less with sacrificial ritual, while percussion and wind instruments were played for the Greek and Egyptian gods.[15] In his own extended treatment of proper meal behavior, including music, Clement tells his reader that "even if you wish to sing and play with the kithara or lyre, it is not a matter of shame, since you will be imitating the righteous Hebrew king giving thanks to God." This could be read as a concession for use of "biblical" instruments. However, Clement, always an allegorizer, seems to have had something in mind other than (or in addition to) literal music; he continues, quoting that same Hebrew king's Psalter: "'Confess to the Lord on the kithara; play to him on the *psaltērion* of ten strings, sing to him a new song.' And does not the ten-stringed *psaltērion* indicate Jesus the Word?" (*Paed.* 2.4.43).

Clement probably did think that literal and not just spiritual stringed instruments could be played, at least at dinner parties. This should also have implied that they could be played—in the right way—at specifically sacramental events, given his seamless-garment approach to sacramental and substantial meals; but he never makes this quite clear.

14. Ibid., 270–76.
15. Johannes Quasten, *Music and Worship in Pagan and Christian Antiquity*, trans. Boniface Ramsey, OP, NPM Studies in Church Music and Liturgy (Washington, DC: National Association of Pastoral Musicians, 1983), 59–75.

He was somewhat clearer about singing. Clement discusses what and when to sing—again, more with dinner parties in view than the Eucharist as such—and waxes eloquent about both Davidic psalm singing (although *psalmos* may apply to songs beyond the canon for him) and ancient Greek scholia.[16] And intriguingly, at the end of one long work, *Christ the Instructor* (*Paedagogus*), he provides a hymn of his own, which calls on God for divine grace, parental care, and inspiration to sing:

> Bridle of untrained colts,
> Wing of steady birds,
> True rudder of ships,
> Shepherd of royal lambs,
> Gather your simple children
> To sing holy praise,
> To hymn without guile
> With innocent mouths,
> Christ the guide of children. (*Hymn to Christ the Savior*)

Singing a New Song

The oldest Christian hymn that has survived with its music was found among discarded waste from Oxyrhynchus in Egypt just over a century ago.[17] This fragmentary text (P.Oxy. XV 1786) is from the late third century and has retained enough of its notation—a very different system from that of today—to give a sense of both words and music. The text that survives is this:

> . . . together all the esteemed ones of God . . .
> . . . Let them be silent. Let the shining stars not . . .
> . . . let the [rushings of winds, and springs] of all surging rivers [cease.]
> While we sing
> Father and Son and Holy Spirit, let all the answering powers say
> "Amen, Amen."
> Might and praise
> [always and glory to God,] the only giver of all good things, Amen.
> Amen.

16. Cosgrove, "Clement of Alexandria," 258–66.

17. On what follows see Charles H. Cosgrove, *An Ancient Christian Hymn with Musical Notation: Papyrus Oxyrhynchus 1786: Text and Commentary*, Studien und Texte zu Antike und Christentum [Studies and Texts in Antiquity and Christianity] (Tübingen: Mohr Siebeck, 2011). My translation is based on the reconstructed text at p. 37.

Even in this fragmentary state, the text of the hymn has undeniable resonance. The "esteemed" ones are probably angels, so the hymn amounts to a participation by the singer in praise of God, led by angels and the whole of nature. The powerful reference to cosmic silence is reminiscent of the *Apostolic Tradition* and its reflection on prayer at night (*Ap. Trad.* 41.1–10; see further below).

The actual use of the hymn is unknown, but the musical notation encourages the thought that it was really sung. The third-century date could mean that it was intended for a now-distinct eucharistic assembly; the allusions to participation in angelic and cosmic worship are reminiscent of the angelic hymn, or *Sanctus*, whose adoption in eucharistic prayer is of similar date.[18]

Instrumental Anxiety

The fact that Christian music was predominantly a vehicle for uttering words of praise may help explain an evident lack of positive interest in instrumental music among most early Christian writers (Clement notwithstanding). There were, however, some actively negative associations too; various instruments were an important part of continuing gentile and former Jewish sacrificial rituals, the former demonic and the latter superseded, in the view of many Christians at least. Thus, despite plenty of biblical references to the use of instruments and abundant metaphorical notions of harmony, the most common attitudes among Christian writers toward actual instrumental music vary on a spectrum from indifference to suspicion.

Paul's use of an extended instrumental metaphor sets an example often followed among early writers. Ignatius of Antioch likened the Christian leaders themselves to strings of an ecclesiastic lyre, which was the bishop (Ign. *Eph.* 4.1; cf. Ign. *Phld.* 1:2), but gives no hint that there were real lyres in the hands of these congregants. The *Odes of Solomon* speaks of a divine kithara that will enable the devotee to praise God with "all the tones" (14.7)—spiritually, by implication, but not with literal strings.[19] We have already seen that Clement of Alexandria is a potential exception, if an uncertain one.

Explicit treatment of instrumental music by Christian writers comes fairly late, from the fourth century and after.[20] The tone of such discourse about actual music—when it is finally clear that real instruments are at issue—is

---

18. Ibid., 146–50; Spinks, *Sanctus in the Eucharistic Prayer*, 194–96.

19. Lattke, *Odes of Solomon*, 197.

20. The *Sibylline Oracles* may provide an earlier instance of instrumental critique, clearly related to pagan sacrifice (8.113–21), but the date and character of the work make it of uncertain use in this discussion.

universally negative. Instruments and the music they produce are rejected with vigor. Granted those associations with idolatry and immorality, to which these critics point, instruments are not treated merely as misused or tainted by association but as malign.

John Chrysostom, active first in Antioch and then Constantinople in the late fourth century, can suffice as an example. In a homily on Colossians, Chrysostom speaks in a way reminiscent of Clement's concern for meal decorum; he asks the listener to imagine two banquets, one with fine food and exalted company, and the other with Christ, the lame, and the blind. Like other accoutrements, the music of both parties is contrasted: "There [at the banquet of the wealthy] are flutes and *kitharai* and pipes, but here is no dissonant sound. But what is here? Hymns and psalms. There the demons are hymned, but here the Lord God of all" (*Hom. on Col.* 1.5). There is another striking feature of this fourth-century polemic, however; it is consistently directed at music outside the church, not framed as criticism of backsliders or heretics, or as a definitional issue for Christian liturgical practice. The obvious conclusion is that instrumental music was not actually known in the liturgy of Chrysostom and his contemporaries.[21]

Chrysostom also found himself having to sharpen the boundaries between Judaism and Christianity for his congregants in Antioch around 386–87. The synagogue in that city was particularly active, and its ceremonial, including at least some sort of music, was an attractant for many locals, not just the Jewish citizens. Chrysostom notes that some of the Christians apparently liked hearing the trumpeters—playing the shofar perhaps—who, he argues, should really have been made redundant along with the other practitioners and accoutrements of the temple.[22]

There is a mystery attached to this picture of a church that sings but does not play. Perhaps music had sometimes—but rarely at best—been accompanied by (stringed?) instruments when the meal itself was the sacrament or the site of it; but the stronger impression is that the musical idioms of the Christians were overwhelmingly vocal in nature from the outset.

There are various reasons this could have been the case; we have noted associations between instruments and sacrifice, and at least some clichés about

21. James W. McKinnon, "The Meaning of the Patristic Polemic against Musical Instruments," *Current Musicology* 1 (1965): 69–82.

22. Michael Peppard, "Musical Instruments and Jewish-Christian Relations in Late Antiquity," *Studia Liturgica* 33 (January 1, 2003): 25–32. Peppard suggests that Chrysostom's rhetorical references to tympani, lyres, and other instruments mean these were also used in the Antioch synagogue, but these seem less clear.

depravity at the banquet fostered by the wrong music. Yet the best explanation is—or includes—the likelihood that Christians had generally just been singing. This could reflect an inheritance from psalmodic traditions in Judaism, at least via a more domestic strand of performance that may also be represented in rabbinic literature. It may also reflect the implications of desire for communal (or at least varied) singing or participation, over against specialized performance. This robustly noninstrumental tradition, which was to remain characteristic of Christian churches into the Middle Ages (and beyond, in the East), is in any case clear as a feature of ancient Christian worship, even if its roots remain at least partly mysterious.[23]

Music and Singing in the Fourth Century

Fourth-Century Hymnody

Paul and Tertullian had both envisaged the vocalization of traditional or inspired texts outside of canonical writings, as well as of Scripture. The same impulses that led to increased definition of reading practices in churches after their time gave rise to a real, if less clear or universal, tendency to canonize singing too. This is partly because, as we have seen, singing was actually understood as a form of "reading" rather than as "music" in the modern sense; it was a means to the proclamation of a text, whether of praise, prayer, or edification.

The canons of Laodicea express concerns about songs as well as singers. Canon 49 (which may have been added to the original collection, but at an early date) prohibits the "reading of one's own [idiōtikoi] psalms in church" and allows only those of canonical books. This suggested not merely the Psalms but other scriptural texts (and only these) were to be used. Although they may have different origins, it is worth comparing this rule to Canon 15, which insists on authorized readers and the use of actual books—one obvious way to control liturgical content.

The Laodicean rules also indicate a push to keep psalmody within the bounds of a recognizable "ministry of the Word," to use later terminology, rather than become a sort of extended praise session; Canon 17 dictates that "psalms" not be performed in long sequences but be interspersed with Scripture readings.

23. See also Christopher Page, *The Christian West and Its Singers: The First Thousand Years* (New Haven: Yale University Press, 2010), 37–46.

Rules are, however, often better evidence for transgression than for compliance. We already know that there were other compositions being used in some Christian gatherings, as well as people not specifically authorized beyond their baptism who were offering their songs of praise (canonical or not). While the Laodicean canons do mark steps on a journey toward specialization of roles, attitudes toward the scope of hymnody itself seem to have varied over time and from place to place.

The singing of psalms in monastic and other forms of daily prayer in the fourth century has been noted elsewhere in this book. The Eucharist of this period was also a place for psalmody, which was increasingly incorporated into an ordered sequence of readings, granted local customs and variations. The *Apostolic Constitutions*, for instance, prescribes use of psalms after two readings from the OT, and before readings from the NT (2.57.6–7). As their popularity for exposition in surviving sermons of the fourth century shows clearly, these psalms were regarded not as a separate sort of activity such as a "hymn," but as part of the reading of Scripture; but their performance was distinctive and musical.

Athanasius of Alexandria wrote a sophisticated and influential treatise on the use of the Psalms in his *Letter to Marcellinus*, which was included in the famous Codex Alexandrinus, one of the most important early collections of Christian Scripture. The letter provides advice about use of the Psalms, including some theorizing about the significance of singing them:

> For some of the simple among us, although they believe the words to be inspired, think the Psalms are sung because of the melody and delight to the hearer. This is not the case. . . . Just as harmony creates a single sound from a group of flutes, so too, as different urgings appear in the soul (and all the movements of the body come from the stirrings of reasoning and yearning and desires in the soul), divine reason [*Logos*] does not wish humans to be at odds with themselves. . . . Thus as the plectrum acts in instrumental music, so a person in becoming a sort of stringed instrument completely given over to the Spirit may be compliant in all members and motives, and thus serve the will of God. (PG 27:39–40)

Using the familiar trope of imagined instrumentation, Athanasius makes his point about the real purpose of singing, for him at least; it is a sort of spiritual exercise, a workout for body and soul in close harmony. Of course, the need for this instruction reveals that there were others—perhaps not just the "simple"—for whom the music was beginning to be more important than the words.

There were new and different developments in Christian singing, though, that went beyond the Psalter. In his *Confessions* Augustine describes the introduction of new forms of hymnody in Milan as a custom drawn from the East (*Conf.* 9.7.15), implying that there had been more well-developed forms of communal singing there than in the Italy of his time. Yet in later writings he notes existing hymnic diversity even in his North African context, commending adoption of customs of other churches:

> For the singing of hymns and psalms . . . we have both the examples and the teachings of the Lord himself and of the apostles. In this practice, which is so useful for stirring the pious soul and inflaming the strength of divine love, there are different customs, and in Africa many members of the church are rather too sluggish about it; so the Donatists condemn us, because we sing the divine songs of the prophets in our churches solemnly, while they inflame their passions into revelry by singing psalms of human composition, which rouse them like the stirring notes of herald trumpets. When brothers are assembled in the church, when is it not time for sacred singing, except of course while reading or discourse is going on, whether a leader proclaims with a clear voice or common prayer is given voice by a deacon? (*Letter* 55.18.34 [*Ad Januarium*])

The difference in custom both between local versions of Christianity and from region to region did not end at this point, and hasn't since.

Hymnody and Daily Prayer

The Cappadocian theologians of the fourth century provide the first evidence for a famous hymn that is characteristic of the urban or "cathedral" style of prayer, and which has continued to be used in the evening assemblies of many Christians, particularly in the East. Known as *Phōs hilaron* ("Joyous Light"), this piece exemplifies how the pattern of the day itself became the basis for offering praise. It would have been used at the local equivalent of the *Lychnikon*, or Evening Prayer, like that described for Jerusalem by Egeria:

> Joyous Light of the holy glory of the immortal Father,
> Heavenly, holy, blessed Jesus Christ:
> Coming to the setting of the sun, seeing the evening light,
> We hymn Father, Son, and Holy Spirit, God.
> It is right for You at all times to be praised with blessed voices,
> Son of God, the Giver of life. Therefore, the cosmos glorifies You.[24]

24. Text and further discussion in Antonia Tripolitis, "Φῶς Ἱλαρόν: Ancient Hymn and Modern Enigma," *Vigiliae Christianae* 24, no. 3 (September 1, 1970): 189–96.

The hymn was already old when Basil of Caesarea quoted its venerable praise of "Father, Son, and Holy Spirit, God" to argue for the full divinity of the Holy Spirit in his own struggle to establish the doctrine of God as Trinity (see *On the Holy Spirit* 29.73).

Early Cappadocian sources also mention another hymn whose afterlife has been more famous in the West. *Gloria in excelsis* (usually known by that Latin title) was to become a prominent part of some later eucharistic liturgies, but in fourth-century Cappadocia it was part of morning prayers.[25] In the *Apostolic Constitutions*, the earliest surviving witness to the complete text, it appears thus:

> Glory be to God in the highest,
> and upon earth peace, goodwill among human beings.
> We praise you, we hymn you, we bless you, we glorify you,
> we adore you by your great High Priest;
> You, the true God, sole and unbegotten, the only inaccessible one,
> Because of your great glory, Lord, heavenly King, God the Father
>   Almighty;
> O Lord God, the Father of the Lord, the immaculate Lamb,
> who takes away the sin of the world, receive our prayer,
> You who are enthroned upon the cherubim.
> For you only are holy, you only are the Lord, God and Father of Jesus,
>   the Christ, God of all created nature, our King, by whom glory,
>   honor, and worship are to you. (7.47)

Hymnody in the Syrian Church[26]

The Syriac-speaking churches beyond the eastern end of the Mediterranean were particularly rich in hymnodic tradition and afford an important example of women's and lay participation in liturgical life, even as male and clerical leadership was otherwise becoming more definitive in many respects.

By the fourth century, East Syrian churches included separate men's and women's choirs, made up of participants in the distinctive form of committed asceticism found in that region. These "sons and daughters of the covenant" chanted hymns for edification of the congregation and praise of God, both at the Eucharist and in the local forms of daily prayer, such as vigils. Some of

---

25. Bradshaw, *Daily Prayer*, 102–3.
26. This section draws on the important work of Susan Ashbrook Harvey, *Song and Memory: Biblical Women in Syriac Tradition*, The Père Marquette Lecture in Theology 20 (Milwaukee: Marquette University Press, 2010).

these hymns told stories in narrative form, with the women's and men's choirs taking the parts of biblical characters. Within such songs there are cases where lament, a form of discourse where women's leadership was expected, is added to narratives even when not found (but plausibly interpolated) in the biblical text, incorporating into communal prayer an element of women's experience from the wider world.

Other Syrian hymns were explicitly doctrinal and pedagogical in character, and were allocated specifically to the women's choir, a tradition associated with the great teacher Ephraem of Nisibis. While writers in the Greek and Latin West were often ambivalent or even negative about women's liturgical participation even in such roles as these, the Syrian church tended to stipulate the use of the women's choir.

Women also play prominent roles in these hymns, including well-developed devotional references to Mary the mother of Jesus. In Ephraem's *Hymns on the Nativity*, Mary and other female figures of sacred history become the vehicles for the teacher's proclamation; the fact that many of Ephraem's opponents were groups that denied the materiality of the incarnation helps underscore the power of women's voices, both biblical and ecclesial, and implicitly reminded the hearer of how the flesh of Christ had come to be.

In many of these hymns, the experiences of these women across history and in the church became a vehicle for the message of salvation, and could arguably be "heard" differently as a result:

> She alone is your mother, but she is your sister with everyone else.
> She was your mother, she was your sister,
> > she was your bride too, along with all chaste souls
> You, who are your mother's beauty,
> Yourself adorned her with everything! (Ephraem, *Hymns on the Nativity* 11.2)[27]

Dancing

A Hymn and a Dance

The *Acts of John*, a novelistic account from the late second century expanding on the apostle's life, has John recall Jesus' Last Supper. This version centers not on words over bread and wine, or the washing of feet, but on a dance:

---

27. Translation from *Bride of Light: Hymns on Mary from the Syriac Churches*, Mōrān 'Ethō Series 6 (Kerala, India: St. Ephrem Ecumenical Research Institute, 1994), 18.

[Jesus] assembled us all and said "Before I am delivered to them, let us sing a hymn to the Father and so go to meet what lies ahead." So he told us to form a circle holding one another's hands, and himself stood in the middle and said "Answer 'Amen' to me." So he began to sing a hymn, and to say . . . (*Acts of John* 94)

This call and response opens with a trinitarian litany ("Glory to you, Father," etc.); then comes a series of paradoxical epithets or affirmations ("I will be saved and I will save"; "I will be born and I will bear"); as instructed, the others present respond with the "Amen." Nothing more is said about the form of the dance itself, but we infer that the circle moved with the responses, the participants keeping hands linked.

This story is intriguing, but we do not know quite how it relates to any actual liturgical practice—which is also true of the foot washing in the canonical Gospel of John.[28] The dance could represent a custom of the community in which the work was produced; in that case, it was apparently an accompaniment to a meditative hymn of praise, an adjunct to the song and vice versa. The *Acts of John* is often labeled as "gnostic," a term whose usefulness has increasingly been questioned in recent years;[29] however, the intended authorship would have had a streak of interest in esoteric and mystical matters, at least.

Although there are only a few parallels or pieces of supporting evidence, they share with the *Acts of John* that sense of an intellectually serious group engaged in a ritual that reflects or creates a coherence between the body and the inner self responding to the God encountered in Christ. "Dance" in the modern sense does not map perfectly onto the performances that might be grouped together in ancient Greek and Roman terms; music and poetry were typically accompanied by choral movement, and vice versa; Plato had suggested that the origins of dance lay in the addition of gestures to forms of utterance (*Laws* 816A). Although these actions could be performed by special groups, Plato had imagined the ideal community as dancing together (*Laws* 654A).

Such an ideal seems to have remained just that, as far as most dances and most dancers were concerned; in the late ancient world and among the Romans, dance was rarely seen in such rarefied terms.[30] Christians and Jews, or some of the philosophically minded among them, may have been among the exceptions. In a case of what may be both literary and literal imitation of that old ideal, Philo of Alexandria had reported in the first century on

28. See the discussion in chap. 5 below.
29. See Williams, *Rethinking "Gnosticism"*; but cf. Brakke, *The Gnostics*.
30. Penelope Murray, "Dance," in *The Oxford Encyclopedia of Ancient Greece and Rome*, ed. Michael Gagarin and Elaine Fantham (Oxford: Oxford University Press, 2009), 355–58.

the Therapeutae, an ascetic and philosophically minded Jewish community that sang "original hymns in honour of God in many meters and tunes, at one time all together, and at another in answering harmony, gesturing and dancing" (*Contempl. Life* 11.84).[31] The possibility that such dances really did occur among Christians is supported by an account from Clement—another philosophical Alexandrian—who adds his own explanation of some similar practice:

> So also we raise our heads and lift hands to heaven, and rouse [*airomen*] our feet at the closing sounding of the prayer, following the urging of the spirit toward the intellectual essence; and seeking to abstract the body from the earth toward the Word, raising the soul on high, winged with desire for better things, we direct it to advance to what is holy, wholeheartedly despising the fetters of the flesh. For we are well aware that the gnostic willingly passes over the whole world, as the Jews did over Egypt, demonstrating clearly that above everything he is to be as near as possible to God. (*Strom.* 7.7.40)

Clement's reference to "rousing" or stirring the feet to action suggests more than merely standing up, and the analogy with the passage of the Israelites out of Egypt also suggests motion. In any case, movement of the whole bodies of worshipers corresponding to the aspirations of the soul would have been understood as a sort of "dance," even were their feet still. The "gnostic" referred to here is not a member of some group outside the mainstream church as Clement understands it (although he does identify such people) but an elite Christian who, without condemning the other members of the community, pursues a more serious and ascetic discipleship.

A comparable dance appears in the *Symposium* of Methodius, a later third-century Christian writer who drew on classical models in conjuring a philosophical banquet where wise women exchanged profound thoughts. The *Symposium* reaches its climax as the conversationalists perform a sedate circle dance:

> When Arete had spoken, she told the others to rise and, standing under the *Agnos* tree, to sing a becoming hymn of thanksgiving to the Lord, and for Thecla to begin and lead. And when they had stood up, Thecla stood in the midst of the virgins at the right of Arete and she sang beautifully; the rest stood together in a circle like the shape of a chorus, and responded to her: "I keep myself pure for you, O Bridegroom, and holding a lighted torch I go to meet you." (*Symp.* 11.2)

31. Page, *Christian West*, 30–32, 43–44.

Methodius' dance—like his symposium—is imagined rather than historical, but, like the meal, it makes better sense if there were a referent in the lives of his readers for this ideal picture. The outdoor setting for dining and dance is part of the fantasy; Christian dances would have taken place indoors at this point, probably as part of the communal meal.

Before the changes of the fourth century, it is unlikely that Christians would have taken communal movement into outdoor or at least public settings, which were largely the preserve of religious ritual that reflected the belief of a wider community. This of course could and would change, when and where Christian belief itself became the norm. An early exception may have been cemeteries, where the hope of the resurrection was celebrated for the Christian departed, and the martyrs as exemplars were commemorated. When Roman emperors constrained the activities of the church during the persecutions of the mid-third century, cemeteries were sometimes included as no-go areas (see Eusebius, *Eccl. Hist.* 7.30). We have no evidence to suggest dancing was part of the cult of the martyrs before the fourth century or that it was specifically included in Christian ritual at graves; however, we will see that later evidence makes this connection, and it may have been an earlier one too.

Although dance may suggest a "popular" form of piety,[32] earliest Christian dance actually seems to be the domain of a fairly elite group, including at least some of those referred to (by themselves or others) as "gnostics." This may also be a localized tradition, more evident in places like Alexandria; for some time after this, there would be tensions there between Christianity based on scholastic culture and authority (where the dance would apparently have been at home) and a structure more like that which was emerging elsewhere, with a clerical hierarchy to the fore rather than the various merits of philosophers and teachers.

Other evidence for dance from the period before 300 is mostly hints or allusions; ancient and some modern critics have suggested that the New Prophecy movement, later labeled Montanism, adopted practices of traditional Phrygian religion, including dancing.[33] If this were so, it would probably have been a quite different form of performance, wherein the body was not so much disciplined to the will of the enlightened soul but given over to the ecstasy marking the presence of divine power; but the real practice of the New Prophets is hard to discern from polemical accounts.

32. MacMullen, *Second Church*, 29, 44.
33. Christine Trevett, *Montanism: Gender, Authority, and the New Prophecy* (Cambridge: Cambridge University Press, 2002), 8–10.

Dancing for the Saints

These hints about dancing in the first few centuries confirm the diversity of practice at the meal gathering. Dancing becomes a clearer, more public, and more controversial feature of Christian devotion in the fourth century, when commemorations of the saints took on forms related to local festivals and processions, and hence ushered in a new phase of cultural adjustment and identity formation.

In Antioch in 387, John Chrysostom referred approvingly to dancing on the feasts of martyrs: "You have reveled in the holy martyrs in these recent days; you have taken your fill of the spiritual feast. . . . You have danced a beautiful dance throughout the whole city, led by your noble general" (*Homilies on the Statues* 19.1). This may actually have been a procession—the metaphorical "general" at its head could have been the bishop Flavian or the relics of the martyrs themselves—but there is no reason to think they did not literally dance. Similarly, at Constantinople on the feast of the martyr Polyeuctes, obscure now but to whom Constantinople's largest basilica was dedicated, an unknown bishop of similar date called his community "to dance in our accustomed way."[34]

Victricius, bishop of Rouen in Gaul around the same time, also urged enthusiastic dance among acts of devotion to the martyrs, reminiscent of the ceremonial reception of an emperor, linking dance with song:[35] "You, too, holy and inviolate virgins, chant, chant, and in your choirs dance on the paths that lead to heaven. Those that rejoice in the everlasting springtime of paradise, in brilliant light, not darkened by any cloud—those, I say, you must wear out with your dancing, tire with your leaping!" (*Praising the Saints* 5). These examples all address a world of public Christian performance quite different from the sedate circles of Clement's true gnostics. In these imperial cities and *coloniae* the church was now providing civic rituals that could be compared without irony to the celebrations accompanying the arrival of victorious emperors. Dance was a medium employed within this new genre of the procession, wherein the Christians not only celebrated their martyrs in their own living bodies but also marked the space of the towns with monumental churches and with their stories of the victorious dead.

Although these dances had a civic character as well as an ecclesial one, they also had a personal and familial dimension, especially in relation to the care

34. Cited in Quasten, *Music and Worship*, 188n157.
35. Gillian Clark, "Victricius of Rouen: Praising the Saints," *Journal of Early Christian Studies* 7, no. 3 (1999): 365–99.

of the dead. These processional dances for the saints were performed not in the new Christian basilicas but in public venues—now effectively the possession of Christianized local communities—and in cemeteries where martyrs' relics were deposited.

Such Christian processions appeared in the lives of Mediterranean cities with varying speed. In Rome itself, source of the archetypal forms of *pompa*, or civic procession, for its own colonies, traditional patterns seem to have been very persistent, and it was not until the sixth century that Christian processions were sufficiently prominent to have left any evidence.[36]

The association of dancing and the dead lies in Greco-Roman custom and folk tradition; that fact, and associations with other aspects of revelry or carousing, added to the anxiety of other bishops (especially, it seems, in the West) who were less approving of the urge to dance, even or especially to celebrate faith and the saints.[37] Some tried to distinguish sober or spiritual dancing from the more uncontrolled and suggestive (see Ambrose, *On Penitence* 2.6.42); others thought it was all too much, wondering (or perhaps remembering) just where dancing might lead. The range of attitudes and approaches to celebratory dancing parallels attitudes that bishops took to the related question of meals with and for the dead, which also sometimes descended into immoderate revelry.

The connection noted between dancing and singing means that organized choirs may have danced in church at times too. Christians did continue to dance at festivals of saints, and in some places still do, but the history of such dances lies more in the realm of popular culture than in any distinct ecclesial and liturgical practice. Difficult as it is to access, the devotion expressed in these acts was nevertheless more closely related to faith than accounts of liturgical history have usually allowed.

Conclusion

Modern Christian worship is often likely to have the character of a spectacle, performed by specialists for onlookers, whose participation is predominantly aural and visual. Song is one aspect of practice where a communal dimension is frequently enacted.

36. Jacob A. Latham, "From Literal to Spiritual Soldiers of Christ: Disputed Episcopal Elections and the Advent of Christian Processions in Late Antique Rome," *Church History* 81 (2012): 298–327.

37. Ramsay MacMullen, *Christianity and Paganism in the Fourth to Eighth Centuries* (New Haven: Yale University Press, 1997), 103–6, 215–16nn1–10.

In ancient Christian worship, both participation and spectacle had their place, but the latter only gradually became a regular or central feature of liturgical gatherings. Granted that songs, as well as reading and charismatic utterance, could always be forms of action attended to by others, singing was a collective possibility, whether performed in chorus or by individuals; the ancient singers (and sometimes the dancers) are the Christians themselves. By the disposition of their bodies in the space occupied ephemerally for meal, catechesis, and prayer, the Christians perform an act of identity and community within which their particular acts of speech and eating take their place.

It will be apparent that early Christian approaches to these practices are distinctive in some important ways, even beyond the obvious and remarkable difference involved in the lack of instrumental music. The prominence of song involves a measure of cultural continuity with domestic Jewish piety, as well as aversion to the ways instruments were used in sacrificial cultus.

Despite Athanasius' vigorous opposition to an apparent (and perhaps widespread) aestheticizing approach to singing, his understanding about the harmony of the physical and spiritual self helps illustrate something about much of early Christian song and dance. While writers such as Athanasius or Clement evince distrust of any ecstatic or hedonistic engagement with music, and see song or dance as acceptable only for the body as disciplined by the soul rather than dominating it, they and those they scolded shared at least a basic understanding of these forms of worship; in these performances of faith by believers, the body itself is placed not merely at the disposal of the soul but in the service of God.

5

INITIATION

Baptism, Anointing, and Foot Washing

> Go therefore and make disciples of all nations, baptizing
> them in the name of the Father and of the Son and of the
> Holy Spirit. (Matt. 28:19)

aptism is linked to a command of Jesus yet is older than the ministry of
Jesus, let alone the church. To trace the origins of baptism is therefore not
to isolate or identify one act or command but to consider and interpret
rituals that began before Jesus and continued after him. These centered not
only on his remembered exhortation to baptize but also on his own baptism;
baptism would become a sign, variously, of his life, death, and resurrection,
and of the Christians' participation in them.

Baptism as an initiatory action was almost universal in earliest Christianity;
while there was diversity of specific practices and of theology, the fact of
baptism was generally assumed. The Greek words underlying the English
"baptism" (*baptisma*, sometimes *baptismos*) can mean "immersion" or "bathing," without religious overtones. Washing practices in early Christianity and
in ancient Judaism straddled the boundary between prosaic or functional
washing and rituals of cleansing and renewal. Christian baptism is a recasting

of ancient religious practice and of natural symbols involving water to serve new purposes and convey different meanings.[1]

The Origins of Christian Baptism

Baptism and Judaism

Water and washing feature in many stories and practices of the Judaism in which Jesus and John the Baptizer lived: the biblical story of creation began with God's spirit moving over the deep (Gen. 1); Moses led the Israelites through water out of Egypt (Exod. 14); Joshua led them through water into the promised land (Josh. 3). The Mosaic law also prescribed water rituals to establish purity and to accompany sacrifice (Exod. 30; Lev. 13–15). In Jesus' time, washing in everyday settings—for example, of hands before meals—was becoming a means by which the holiness associated with the temple and its workings was extended into daily life, especially by the emergent Pharisaic movement.[2]

Ritual baths, or *miqva'ot*, have been excavated at the entrance to the Jerusalem temple as it was rebuilt by Herod the Great. Devotees could readily wash in a *miqveh* as part of a journey to the temple, often undertaken from some considerable distance as pilgrimage. The placement of these pools at a liminal (cf. Latin *limen*, a threshold) point suggests that they enabled a symbolic transition for those coming to present offerings or to pray; the path to God's presence and promise, as often before, lay through the water.

The internal architecture of such a *miqveh* also indicates a sense of movement from impurity to worship. Some had internal dividers or walls that marked a path for the bather to follow, inviting movement into the water in one direction and out the other. Those coming to pray or offer sacrifice were not merely removing symbolic impurity by washing but were walking from everyday life into the different world of the temple.[3] The waters functioned, as in the exodus, both as a boundary between two states of being and as a path from one to the other.

---

1. Robin Jensen's *Baptismal Imagery in Early Christianity: Ritual, Visual, and Theological Dimensions* (Grand Rapids: Baker Academic, 2012) appeared after this manuscript was essentially complete, but should now be consulted on many of the issues discussed in this chapter.

2. Martin Pickup, "Matthew's and Mark's Pharisees," in *In Quest of the Historical Pharisees*, ed. Jacob Neusner and Bruce David Chilton (Waco: Baylor University Press, 2007), 82–84.

3. Joan R. Branham, "Penetrating the Sacred: Breaches and Barriers in the Jerusalem Temple," in *Thresholds of the Sacred: Architectural, Art Historical, Liturgical, and Theological Perspectives on Religious Screens, East and West* (Washington, DC: Dumbarton Oaks, 2006), 6–24.

Since the *miqveh* was used for persons and objects requiring purification, it is not surprising that converts to Judaism in late antiquity were also immersed ritually as part of their initiation—particularly because of presumed impurity from contact with corpses, according to later rabbinic texts (*m. Pesaḥ.* 8.8). However, the evidence for these immersions is later than the first evidence for Christian baptism.[4] The influence may even be partly the reverse—the rabbinic Jewish practice of immersing converts, or at least the emphasis placed on it relative to other aspects of conversion ritual (most obviously circumcision for males), may have been encouraged by the Christian example.

Jewish immersion of proselytes is not the immediate origin of Christian baptism, or even its immediate precursor. Yet both of these initiatory uses of washing, Christian and Jewish, build on practices in earlier Judaism, where ritual washing changed the status of individuals before God and made them ready for divine service.

Qumran and the Dead Sea Scrolls

Excavations at Khirbet Qumran in the Judean desert have revealed a settlement from close to the time of John and Jesus whose facilities included numerous *miqva'ot*. While they must have been in part for water storage, the number and prominence of these reservoirs, and the provision of steps within them, suggest they were also used for ritual washing.[5]

Washings are also prominent in the ancient sectarian library found near Qumran and known as the Dead Sea Scrolls. The authors of some of these documents—perhaps inhabitants of the settlement or their forebears—had separated themselves from mainstream Jewish society and from the workings of a temple they regarded as corrupt. Their lifestyle included regular ritual baths (see, e.g., 1QS III), which was also true of the Jewish groups known as "Essenes" (see Josephus, *War* 2.129), who may be the same as the authors of these scrolls and/or the inhabitants of the Qumran settlement.[6]

The prominence of such ablutions in a dissident wilderness community has inevitably led to comparisons with John the Baptizer. Like John, these Jews proclaimed and embodied a radical departure from the elite urban setting of

---

4. Shaye J. D. Cohen, "Is 'Proselyte Baptism' Mentioned in the Mishnah? The Interpretation of M. Pesahim 8.8," in *The Significance of Yavneh and Other Essays in Jewish Hellenism* (Tübingen: Mohr Siebeck, 2010), 316–28.

5. Jodi Magness, *The Archaeology of Qumran and the Dead Sea Scrolls* (Grand Rapids: Eerdmans, 2003), 134–57.

6. Thus, fully argued, VanderKam, *Dead Sea Scrolls Today*; see also Magness, *Archaeology of Qumran*, 39–44.

Jerusalem, condemned the iniquity of their contemporaries, and sought God in the wilderness. And they used water. Yet neither the Dead Sea Scrolls nor literary evidence for the Essenes suggests a unique baptism for initiation or even repentance or renewal. These desert baths were instead versions of the repeated ritual washing practices found elsewhere in Judaism.

The value of the scrolls and of the Qumran water tanks thus lies not in revealing the direct origins of John's or Jesus' practice but in adding to a sense of their ritual world, and in particular of the readiness with which water and washing could be employed in symbolic action by first-century Jews.

John

The Synoptic Gospels and Josephus all record John's title, "the Baptizer." When John began preaching the nearness of the reign of God and of the anointed one or Messiah, his practice of washing those who responded need not have been startling in itself. Yet John was certainly original in some ways; while opinion varies on the closeness of his practice to the ascetic texts and traditions discussed above, he was undoubtedly perceived as doing something unique, attractive, and dangerous.[7]

John's prominence in all the canonical Gospels, and also his respectful acknowledgment by the Jewish historian Josephus, indicates that he had widespread impact during his lifetime and ongoing influence after his early death. If many Judeans came to the Jordan to be baptized by John ("all" Jerusalem and Judea, according to Mark 1:5, while Luke 3:7 has the more circumspect "multitudes"; cf. Josephus, *Ant.* 18.118), the Gospels also record significant opposition to him (Mark 3:7–10; John 1:19–25). John's eventual execution affirms tragically that his baptism was viewed as important.

John was not "converting" anyone in the sense of changing their religious allegiance, or even necessarily making them his followers. His baptism was about God's demands and the nearness of judgment. Despite his own apparent asceticism, those baptized by John seem not to have separated themselves from everyday demands as the Qumran sectarians and/or Essenes had. The Gospels all present him teaching a righteousness capable of being sustained in daily life, within the existing structures of Judaism.

The character of John's "baptism of repentance for the forgiveness of sins" (Mark 1:4) is broadly supported by Josephus' report that John offered an inner

---

7. For a useful summary, see Catherine M. Murphy, *John the Baptist: Prophet of Purity for a New Age* (Collegeville, MN: Liturgical Press, 2003), 83–84.

cleansing (*Ant.* 18.117). Ethical renewal and forgiveness both were to remain firmly fixed to baptism in its subsequent history. At the outset, John's baptism was therefore a ritual of "conversion" only in the literal sense—of personal reorientation—and was not an entry into a different religious community or belief system.

As far as the ritual of baptism goes, John's unique bath in the desert is both like and unlike the repeated washings of the *miqveh*. It is like them in that the participant in John's washing passes from one status to the other; the bath is not merely a place for removal of material or spiritual taint but a place where the status of the participant is changed. However, John's baptism radicalizes this transformation; his proclamation of God's imminent judgment sharpened the perspective within which preparation for divine service must be undertaken. Where the *miqveh* was used as worshipers came and went from the temple or dealt with the impurities arising from day-to-day life, this one action at the Jordan, unique rather than repeated, was preparation for a new kind of divine presence. The citation of Isaiah 40:3 by all four Gospels suggests use of the passage by John himself: "The voice of one crying out in the wilderness: Prepare the way of the LORD, make his paths straight." This ancient prophetic call evoked the even-earlier Israelite history of the exodus and was a powerful message in a time of occupation and oppression. It also confirms that John's baptism was part of this "way" and preparation, a transition and not merely a transaction. The fact that John's baptism seems to have been administered by him, rather than performed by the one being washed, also recalls prophetic symbolic action like that of Jeremiah (13; 19; 32).[8]

The movement around John was part of the matrix within which Jesus' ministry was formed. The Gospel of John, otherwise the most circumspect about the connection between Jesus and the Baptizer, presents the apostle Andrew as initially a follower of that John. The prominence of John's teaching for the first Christians makes it reasonable to assume that Jesus' own followers, and later the emergent church, took over at least some of the meanings already inherent in the baptism of John. Of these, the most obvious are the reorientation of the self to justice and righteousness, the forgiveness of sins, and symbolic purification in the face of divine presence—all referred to in the Gospel accounts.

Yet the relevance of John's movement and its baptism should not be reduced to that of a stepping-off point for Christianity. John's followers continued to

8. Adela Yarbro Collins, "The Origin of Christian Baptism," in *Living Water, Sealing Spirit: Readings on Christian Initiation*, ed. Maxwell E. Johnson (Collegeville, MN: Liturgical Press, 1995), 35–57.

exist and to propagate his message, and this became a source of difficulty for
the followers of Jesus (see Acts 13:24–25; 19:3–4). Their continued baptismal
activity may also have been an ongoing influence on the thought and practice
of the earliest Christians alongside whom they lived.

The Baptism of Jesus

The most important link between the early church and the movement around
John the Baptizer is of course Jesus' own baptism. This is recounted in Mark
and Matthew as undertaken by John himself; the other two canonical Gospels
only imply it, de-emphasizing John's role other than as a witness to Jesus'
own experience.

A certain embarrassment about Jesus' initial deference to John is also reflected in the explanation provided in Matthew (3:14–15); the persistence
of John's movement years later may have pressed early Christians to clarify
or relativize the relationship. That Jesus was baptized by John, thus placing
himself publicly in the circle around the (other) popular teacher or prophet,
is not to be doubted. Not much else can be concluded about specific connections or influences between the two (granted the family relationship reported
by the Gospel of Luke), except the obvious continuity of belief or practice
and the overlap in participation already noted (John 1:35–42).

The accounts of Jesus' own baptism were very important for early Christian
belief and practice, and introduce the first clues to more specifically Christian
understandings of the rite. Across significant variations of detail, the Gospels avoid any implication that Jesus himself needed repentance or received
forgiveness, despite the emphasis of John's baptism; rather, the narratives
signal that in baptism he is revealed or acknowledged as Son of God. All four
accounts also present this revelation with the descent of the Holy Spirit in
the form of a dove.

Each of these elements—of divine adoption or proclamation and of the
giving of the Spirit—plays a significant role in subsequent Christian baptism,
along with forgiveness and repentance. Exceptional as Jesus' case was understood to be, sin and how to deal with it were not to be the only reasons for
Christian baptism.

All four Gospels also report John's own prediction that Jesus himself will
baptize others with the Spirit (Mark 1:8, etc.). This link with the Holy Spirit
is to remain a key theme in the early Christian appropriation and reshaping
of baptism, a clue not only to Jesus' unique identity as God's Son but also to
the meaning of following Jesus into the water.

Baptism in the New Testament and Earliest Christianity

Christian Baptism

The Gospel accounts of Jesus' ministry present baptism as a continued ritual sign and proclamation of the closeness of the reign of God and of the need and opportunity for change in the person and among the people. Baptism for the first followers of Jesus was still, in effect, the baptism of John.

The emergence of Christian believers as a more distinct group that proclaimed Jesus gave rise to crucial changes in the meaning and practice of baptism. The earliest Christian use of baptism was not, however, the creation of an initiation ritual for a religious group separate from Judaism, but was, like John's baptism, a sign of participation in God's renewal of Israel and the world. It was a means of repentance and forgiveness, of preparation for divine service, but now also of realizing belief in Jesus and of participating in the life of the Spirit—but initially still within the community of Israel.

Paul

The oldest evidence for distinctively Christian baptism comes from the writings of Paul of Tarsus, written from the 40s CE onward. Paul's and other NT references to baptism are largely incidental. While Christians have since given these texts unique theological authority, the baptismal practice to which he refers obviously preceded the letters and their reflections rather than stemmed from them.

By the time of Paul's writings, baptism had been linked with a gradual but radical change in the scope of the emerging Christian movement. The extension of the message about Jesus to non-Jews meant that baptism became more than a ritual of renewal within Judaism; it also became the means of entry into a movement that was beginning to transcend and transform Jewish identity for its members.

Paul's own practice and theology played a significant part in this change. He already knew of baptism as "into Christ" (Gal. 3:27; Rom. 6:3; cf. 1 Cor. 6:11; Acts 19:5); if such a christological focus preceded him, his development of it became crucial. Paul's bold advocacy of including non-Jewish women and (uncircumcised) men in the Christian community was fundamental to how baptism effectively became the sole initiatory ritual for the emerging movement. Applicable equally to men and women, baptism was perfectly suited to understanding Christian allegiance as a participation in Jesus that transcended divisions of all kinds:

Therefore the law was our disciplinarian until Christ came, so that we might
be justified by faith. But now that faith has come, we are no longer subject to a
disciplinarian, for in Christ Jesus you are all children of God through faith. As
many of you as were baptized into Christ have clothed yourselves with Christ.
There is no longer Jew or Greek, there is no longer slave or free, there is no
longer male and female; for all of you are one in Christ Jesus. And if you belong
to Christ, then you are Abraham's offspring, heirs according to the promise.
(Gal. 3:24–29)

Baptism "into Christ" still implied the ancient power of transition through
water from the shores of one state of being into another—the new being
participation in Christ and in his attributes. For Paul, Christians are defined
neither by elements of their own social status nor by the infancy of tutelage
of the Mosaic law, but are free adult heirs of God's promises in Christ.

Paul's most influential teaching about baptism, however, has been his emphasis on another element of this participation—Jesus' death and resurrection.
While the Synoptic Gospels linked Jesus' anticipated sufferings with baptism
(Mark 10:38–39; Luke 12:50), for Paul baptism itself is about dying and rising
with Christ (Rom. 6:3–4).

The significance of symbolic action depends not only on such expert theorizing but also in large part on the understandings brought by participants.
With a mission to the gentiles came a wider cultural context and new sets of
associations, including the wider religious and social significance of washing
in Greco-Roman culture. The understandings even of many people in Judea
would have owed something to other rituals for preparation and purification,
although the use of baptism for initiation seems to have been distinctive in the
Christian movement.[9] A pattern of initiation seen as death and rebirth may have
resonated for gentiles who had participated in Greco-Roman mystery cults,
whose rituals enacted dying and rising, but who did not perform baptisms.[10]

The idea of participating through baptism in Jesus' death and resurrection
was to remain or become central in much Christian understanding and practice;
but since baptism—even Christian baptism—was older and more widespread
than Paul's mission, baptism into Christ's death was far from being the only
idea through which the ritual was viewed in the ancient church.

9. Everett Ferguson, *Baptism in the Early Church: History, Theology, and Liturgy in the
First Five Centuries* (Grand Rapids: Eerdmans, 2008), 28–34.

10. The idea that such groups also "baptized" or that Paul's basic conception comes from
them has long been discredited; see Walter Burkert, *Ancient Mystery Cults* (Cambridge, MA:
Harvard University Press, 1987), 99–102.

New Birth

John's Gospel probably assumes knowledge of and participation in Eucharist and baptism in its fulsome use of images including bread (John 6) and water (John 4:1–42). It may also show some hesitation about the importance of rituals and seems particularly sensitive to the persistence of John the Baptizer's movement.

The Fourth Gospel, like Paul's Letters, presents baptism as transition to a new life, but as a second and different kind of birth related to the Spirit, rather than a death and resurrection in Christ:

> Jesus answered him, "Very truly, I tell you, no one can see the kingdom of God without being born from above [or "again"]." Nicodemus said to him, "How can anyone be born after having grown old? Can one enter a second time into the mother's womb and be born?" Jesus answered, "Very truly, I tell you, no one can enter the kingdom of God without being born of water and Spirit. What is born of the flesh is flesh, and what is born of the Spirit is spirit." (John 3:3–6)

Although baptism is not mentioned here in so many words, the reference to water and Spirit may well intend it; in any case, ancient Christians quickly read this exchange as about baptism and its centrality in becoming Christian. While Paul had presented baptism as a rite of adulthood and responsibility, here it is a kind of new infancy, given from above (and/or "again"—the Greek word means both), and reminiscent of the Synoptic Gospels' saying (Mark 10:15) where Jesus insists on the need to enter the reign of God as a child.

Baptism and the Holy Spirit

The Gospels present Jesus as both baptized and baptizing with the Spirit; in the stories of his own baptism, water and Spirit are both linked and distinguished. The "Great Commission" (Matt. 28:19) has the risen Christ command the eleven apostles to baptize disciples of all nations "in the name of the Father and of the Son and of the Holy Spirit." This is a significant change from John's baptism, incorporating the proclamation of Jesus himself as Savior and the work of the Holy Spirit. Matthew's and Luke's Gospels imply a connection between Jesus' and John's baptisms, but also a hierarchy (Matt. 3:11; Luke 3:16); John's Gospel insists on rebirth through both water and Spirit to enter the reign of God.

The Holy Spirit is a prominent actor in Acts, particularly in initiation and conversion. However, the Spirit seems to blow where it wills, sacramentally as otherwise; Christian baptism can precede the giving of the Holy Spirit (Acts 8:16), follow it (Acts 10:44–48), or coincide with it (Acts 19:1–7). Different doctrines of Christian initiation have been based on these passages, whether by traditional churches seeking the basis for laying on of hands and anointing (symbolic of the Holy Spirit) at confirmation, or by Pentecostal groups that have associated ecstatic experiences (again, linked with the Holy Spirit) with baptism and conversion.

In fact these stories do not present any consistent understanding about the precise relationship between baptism and the reception of the Holy Spirit, beyond the fact that they are indeed connected. Acts presents a unique history of the growth of the earliest communities, not models for initiation. What the stories do suggest more clearly (like the narratives of Matthew and Luke) is that the gift of the Holy Spirit was a distinguishing point between Christian initiation and the washings of John the Baptizer, which were by implication important but incomplete (cf. Acts 19:1–7).

The Earliest Christian Practice

What did Christians actually do when baptizing, and where and with whom were they baptized? The earliest stories of Christian baptism sometimes involve large groups of people (Acts 2:41), and so, like John's baptism, imply a public setting. The story of the Ethiopian eunuch and Philip sets baptism at whatever point their carriage "came to some water" (Acts 8:36), presumably intending a river or pond. Similarly, Paul and Silas met the merchant Lydia at a "place of prayer" that was "outside the gate by the river" (Acts 16:13), and she and her household seem to have been baptized even before going home (v. 15). Although these stories can be taken as exceptional, some of their elements must reflect expected practice.

Natural bodies of water, baths, or reservoirs accessible to the public (including *miqva'ot*, when possible) and pools in homes or other private settings were possibly all places for baptism at some point. All these could have allowed for sufficient water to immerse or totally wash the body, as the word "baptism" implies. This does not mean that the first Christians were watching for every part of the body to go under, and later controversies about immersion or sprinkling were obviously not yet in mind, but the symbol certainly starts from the assumption of complete bathing.

There is no very clear indication in NT writings of the actual ritual or words used in the first baptisms. The formula of the Matthean "Great Commission" might have been recited with a threefold pouring or immersion even at the outset, as certainly it was later; the *Didache* (see 7.1) is the first case where this is explicit. Some other early Christian baptisms may have invoked "the name of the Lord Jesus" (1 Cor. 6:11; cf. Acts 2:38) alone, although this phrase could also be a condensed statement of what Christian baptism meant, whether or not it reflects words with which it was performed.

Baptism seems often to have been performed by an authoritative figure or teacher, as was the case with John; that Paul laments the emphasis that Corinthian Christians placed on a baptismal lineage created by his own ministry (1 Cor. 1:13–17) confirms that it was typically administered by particular leaders, not randomly.

The question of just who was baptized is more controversial, and even less clear. Numerous references to the baptism of entire households (1 Cor. 1:16; Acts 11:14; 16:15, 34; 18:8) suggest that some of those baptized may not have been individuals who professed a deep faith, or who had undergone some dramatic personal conversion, but the dependents of a convert. It was not unusual in the ancient world for the loyalties of a householder patron—usually a free male (but cf. Lydia and others)—to impact spouse, children, other relatives, and slaves or servants. Some people may therefore have been baptized because of a communal decision made by the head of the household rather than because of a personal choice.

This may also mean that young children or infants were also baptized, as a sign of the new allegiance into which their whole social group had moved. Yet the baptism of children and infants remains an uncertainty for the first and much of the second century; there is simply no evidence on which to base a definitive judgment. Adults were for many years to remain the normal, if not necessarily sole, recipients of baptism.

A clearer but stranger practice, which also suggests that personal religious experience was not always crucial, was baptism on behalf of the dead. Paul refers to this almost incidentally when arguing for the reality of the bodily resurrection: "Otherwise, what will those people do who receive baptism on behalf of the dead? If the dead are not raised at all, why are people baptized on their behalf?" (1 Cor. 15:29). This seems to be a form of vicarious initiation: a living believer underwent baptism on behalf of a deceased person. The practice is otherwise mysterious, but it underlines the difference between ancient and modern views on the relationship between individual religious experience, community values, and ritual; if householders could make faith decisions for their slaves or children, the dead would certainly be more compliant still, but also perhaps in greater need. Baptism was not seen as a mere outward sign of a change that was really based in the mind or will, but as having objective power and as God's own action rather than that of either the participant or the minister.

The Didache

Although stories in Acts present baptism as an immediate and spontaneous response to God, even the first readers of that book were being reminded of a past apostolic age different in many ways from their own. As soon as we find evidence of actual practice in organized communities, preparation for baptism is revealed as a slower and more rigorous affair.

The *Didache*, or "Teaching of the Twelve Apostles," the earliest Christian document to give explicit instructions for baptism and Eucharist, begins with an extended ethical instruction (sometimes referred to as "The Two Ways") that probably served as a curriculum for those seeking baptism.[11] Reminiscent of the Wisdom literature of the Hebrew Bible, it presents a stark contrast between good and evil ways of life and their consequences. It does not include teaching about Jesus, although it draws on his own teaching in the form of Gospel-sayings tradition. We can assume more information was given to candidates in some way; yet the emphasis was initially on behavior, not doctrine. Conversion here was not primarily an intellectual choice or subjective experience but a practical willingness and capacity to live in a given community in humility and charity.

Preparation for baptism had its own ritual aspect. The *Didache* urges those about to be baptized, along with the baptizer (whose identity or role is otherwise unspecified, but is at least a designated person) and other believers who are able, to fast for one or two days (7.4). No specific reason is given for this, although the whole *Didache* community also fasted on Wednesdays and Fridays (8.1). Fasting marked the candidates as undergoing a change of status; such spiritual discipline might also have been understood to generate more effective prayer by the candidates, as later writers were to say more explicitly.

Although the immersion or saturation of the whole body in baptism remained normative, the *Didache* sets out a sort of flowchart to deal with situations where water was scarce or taking a convert to it was impractical: "Baptize in living [i.e., running] water. If you do not have living water, baptize in other water; if you cannot do so in cold, then in hot; if you have neither, put water on the head three times, in the name of the Father and of the Son and of the

---

11. Jonathan A. Draper, "Ritual Process and Ritual Symbol in Didache 7–10," *Vigiliae Christianae* 54, no. 2 (May 2000): 121.

Holy Spirit" (9.1–3). The trinitarian formula also found in Matthew's Gospel is to be recited, and a threefold dipping (or pouring) is the core symbol of baptism. Another document from the turn of the second century, the apocryphal *Letter of Barnabas*, sees movement through the water, rather than one or more immersions, as the central act: "We go down into the water full of sins and filth, and we come up bearing the fruit of fear in our hearts and having hope in Jesus in the Spirit" (11.11). This passage to purity recalls the logic of the *miqveh*—and the community of the *Didache* was still sufficiently Jewish in culture and belief to have seen it as that too.

Emergence from the water was not necessarily the end of the ritual. The *Didache* implies an immediate passage from baptism to participation in the sacred meal of the Eucharist, given its striking imagery applied to restricting participation in the sacred meal to the baptized: "Let no one eat or drink from your Eucharist except those baptized into the name of the Lord; for regarding this the Lord said 'Do not give what is holy to the dogs'" (9.5).

The *Didache* says almost nothing direct about the actual meaning of baptism, despite its emphasis on practical issues such as fasting and the need for baptism before admission to the Eucharist. The emphasis on these actions is eloquent in at least this respect: baptism actually created membership in this distinct community and offered participation in its benefits, and so required adherence to its ethical stances. As always, baptism had implicit meanings as well as explicit ones, and these implicit meanings suggest—as much as or more than do the sophisticated literary reflections offered by bishops and other teachers—what baptism meant to the typical participant.

Baptism in the Second and Third Centuries

Sin, Repentance, and Renewal

Justin Martyr, of Syrian background but living in Rome, gives an account of baptism that could have applied to many communities of that time. The baptism itself is straightforward, with apparent indifference to place, and trinitarian recitation or confession the only obvious ritual adjunct to the actual washing: "Then they are brought by us to a place where there is water, and are reborn in the same way we were ourselves reborn. For, in the name of God who is the Father and Lord of all that is, and of our Savior Jesus Christ, and of the Holy Spirit, they then undergo the washing with water" (*1 Apol.* 61.3). Yet the preparation and the consequences were extraordinary. Justin indicates as prerequisite not a particular faith experience, but assent to certain teachings along with commitment to the demands of Christian ethics. Like the Christians of the *Didache*, Justin's group had a pattern of ethical (and doctrinal) instruction and ascetic preparation: "As many as are persuaded and believe that the things we teach and say are true, and undertake that they are able to live accordingly, are taught to pray and to ask of God, with fasting, for the forgiveness of their previous sins, while we pray and fast with them" (*1 Apol.* 61.2–3).

The *Shepherd of Hermas*, written close to Justin's time and place, refers to would-be Christians "hearing the word and wishing to be baptized in the name of the Lord; but when they remember the chastity of the truth they change their mind and fall back into immorality, following their evil desires" (*Herm. Vis.* 3.7). Hermas was only referring to sexual restraint familiar in wider Christian tradition, but even the restriction of sex to marriage may have been confronting for those involved in forms of concubinage or to property owners accustomed to having sexual rights over slaves.

Others saw things even more dramatically and urged the renunciation of all sexual activity as necessary for authentic Christian faith, and hence for baptism. Marcion, Justin's and Hermas' contemporary renowned for his view that Jesus was the son of a hitherto unknown, higher God and not the OT Creator, demanded that candidates for baptism be virgins, widowed, celibate—or divorced (Tertullian, *Against Marcion* 1.29.1). Sex and baptism did not mix.

More generally, baptism was understood to begin a new phase of life, without (further) sin; this view, commonly expressed by authors of this period, may seem to indicate either a lack of realism or an unsophisticated doctrine of sin (or of baptism). Still, accommodations were cautiously made for those who transgressed in specific and significant ways later. The *Shepherd of Hermas*, for instance, suggests there might be a single opportunity for postbaptismal repentance (*Herm. Mand.* 4.3), apparently for major transgressions rather than just daily foibles.

Baptism was not merely a ritualized sign of a contract for moral righteousness agreed to before going into the water. For Justin it was a powerful and mysterious reality that provided an answer to deep-seated needs embedded in the human person from the outset:

And we have learned the following reason for this from the apostles. Since at our first birth we were born in ignorance and by necessity, from the wet seed of our parents' intercourse, and were brought up in bad habits and evil education; in order that we may not remain the children of necessity and ignorance, but may become the children of choice and understanding, and may undergo in the water the forgiveness of sins we previously committed, there is pronounced over him who chooses to be born again, and has repented of sins, the name of God the Father and Lord of all. . . . And this washing is called "illumination," because they who learn these things are illuminated in their understanding. (*1 Apol.* 61.9–10, 12)

Justin's earthy account contrasts unchosen natural generation with the choice and freedom of new birth; one wet, messy beginning requires another to fix its problematic consequences. His link between human reproduction and a somewhat negative assessment of life in the regular social order, including typical upbringing ("bad habits and evil education"), anticipates and helps interpret later ideas of "original sin"; this was not just a question of arbitrarily assigned culpability but diagnosis of a sort of genetic disorder.

While John the Baptizer's ancient emphasis on repentance and renewal is still recognizable here, there has certainly been a shift of focus from preparation for the imminent reign of God to escape from a world dominated by evil. Although Justin did not share Marcion's rejection of sex and marriage, his sense of reproduction as hopelessly compromised helps explain how sex could be seen as part of the problem to which baptism was the solution.

Yet baptism is not merely a sort of sacramental gene therapy; it was also referred to as "illumination" in Justin's community. This image of light, with its implication of growth in knowledge and understanding, suggests baptism not merely as removal of sin but as changing the believer's spiritual capacity or insight. Ignatius of Antioch also thought of baptism in terms of gain or gift—not merely the action once undergone to deal with sin but an abiding reality, a sort of spiritual armature (Ign. *Pol.* 6; cf. Eph. 6:10–18).

Who Baptizes?

Other communities and leaders of the time were more concerned about the relationship between baptism and church order. Ignatius of Antioch insists that it is not proper to baptize (or hold a eucharistic meal, or *agapē*) "without the bishop" (Ign. *Smyrn.* 8.2). This need not mean bishops always performed baptisms, but for Ignatius baptisms were properly to take place under episcopal authority. A tension was emerging between those who, like Ignatius and the compilers of the *Didache*, saw initiation as joining a close-knit community and others more focused on personal experience or enlightenment.

A fictional but important example appears in the ancient religious romance called the *Acts of Paul and Thecla*, written sometime during the second century. In this ascetically minded novel, a young woman named Thecla leaves home and family (and the prospect of marriage—again indicating the power of an un-compromising view of Christian discipleship) to follow Paul. Not only does she baptize herself, when on the brink of a martyr's death (*Acts of Paul and Thecla* 34), she survives and "enlightens" (presumably including baptizing) many others.

Tertullian was dismissive of this story a few decades after it was written, implicitly testifying to its influence and popularity, but explicitly excoriating the implication of women's leadership in baptismal ministry. The popularity of the work, and of Thecla herself, the first (if shadowy) Christian heroine after the canonical NT literature, persisted for centuries. It probably does reflect a historical reality of women as baptizers, and might also have provoked the idea where it had not already occurred; but this quasi-scriptural narrative presents exceptional stories (including the baptism of a lion!) rather than typical ones.

Women certainly exercised ministries that included participation in baptism and, particularly, anointing (on which more below);[12] other evidence suggests women may at least sometimes have held office as presbyters and bishops as well.[13] Clearer is that deacons, both male and female, came to play an impor-tant role in rituals that required practical assistance with both prosaic matters like clothing and profound things of the spirit.

Apparently a lay Christian himself, Tertullian argues not only that the right to baptize is technically held by all Christians (his view of Thecla notwithstand-ing) and could be exercised in an emergency but also that it was most properly exercised by the bishop, and otherwise at least by clergy (*On Baptism* 17). An "emergency" would probably have amounted to a deathbed conversion; although Christians might be persecuted, and there was a risk that unbap-tized catechumens would die violently, Tertullian envisioned martyrdom as a "baptism of blood" just as effective as a more peaceful and orderly plunge into water. This involuntary washing was also the only means to remedy apostasy; martyrdom was thus "a baptism that makes real a washing that has not been received, and gives back again one that has been lost" (*On Baptism* 16.2).

Preparation

Prolonged preparation with a strong ethical emphasis continued into the third century, often with an increasingly defined structure, the catechumenate. The Greek term "catechumen"—meaning "one receiving instruction"—was also borrowed by Latin-speaking Christians; so the young martyr Perpetua

---

12. Paul F. Bradshaw, "Women and Baptism in the *Didascalia Apostolorum*," *Journal of Early Christian Studies* 20 (2012): 641–45.
13. See Eisen, *Women Officeholders*.

and her companions, who had not yet been baptized when they were arrested in Carthage just after 200 for their Christian faith, were initially *catechumeni*.

It may not be surprising that astrologers, prostitutes, and gladiators could be refused admission to the catechumenate, but artists (who made pagan images) and public officials (who would be involved in enforcing measures against Christians) also fell at hurdles limiting acceptable professions; aspiring Christians working in these spheres would have to change their livelihood in order to seek baptism (Tertullian, *On Idolatry* and *On the Shows*; cf. *Ap. Trad.* 16).

Catechumens could be divided into two groups: those who had been enrolled with an eventual expectation of baptism or who were in the earlier phases of preparation, and others, often those who had been enrolled for some time, now moving more quickly or directly to baptism (Origen, *Against Celsus* 3.51). While catechumens could not participate fully in the eucharistic meals central to the life of the Christian communities, they attended other assemblies. There was also a ritual aspect to their own experience and instruction: Tertullian, who was also in Carthage when Perpetua, Felicitas, and their companions were martyred, admonishes catechumens "to pray, with frequent prayers, fastings, bendings of the knee, and all-night vigils, along with the confession of all their former sins" (*On Baptism* 20).

The catechumenate involved both negative and positive change, with accounting for former sins (not mere events or specific actions but whole ways of thinking and acting) and learning the specifics of Christian faith and life as two sides of the same coin. The somewhat later *Apostolic Tradition* says that (adult) catechumens remained so for three years (chap. 17), but this was a local or perhaps ideal practice rather than a universal pattern. Nevertheless, we should not imagine the catechumenate as a brief or merely formal requirement.

When baptism did beckon those preparing, further specific rituals often took place. In the *Apostolic Tradition* the bishop exorcizes the candidates at the end of their preparation (20.3) and again at the Sabbath prior to a Sunday baptism, laying on hands but also breathing and then "sealing" their ears and noses—acting on the identification in languages of the ancient Mediterranean of "breath" and "spirit" (21.23). This was a very concrete, ritualized removal of evil forces, followed by the substitution and consolidation of the good ones.

In Carthage, instruction and ritual as known to Tertullian and Perpetua continued to the very point of baptism. Immediately prior to washing, candidates made a threefold renunciation of "the devil, and his pomp, and his angels" (*On the Soldier's Crown* 3; cf. *On the Shows* 4), a prelude to a threefold profession of faith. The candidate was then immersed three times, in parallel with the threefold renunciation, and the trinitarian formula pronounced over them (cf. *Against Praxeas* 26).

Persons and Places

Some Christians could demonstrate a hearty lack of concern, at least in principle, for the niceties of venue or accoutrements for baptism:

> Consequently it makes no matter whether one is washed in the sea or in a puddle, a river or a fountain, a pond or a tub; and there is no difference between those John baptized in the Jordan and those Peter baptized in the Tiber—unless perhaps that eunuch whom Philip baptized in water chanced on during his travels obtained a greater, or a less, amount of salvation. (Tertullian, *On Baptism* 4)

Yet Tertullian is also the first witness to prayer offered over the water, in which angelic intervention was sought (cf. John 5:4); after this it seems to have been common for the water to be blessed. Despite his insistence that water was effective regardless of quality and quantity, by Tertullian's time baptisms in Carthage may already have been taking place in venues specifically set aside for the purpose.

One reason for the likely provision of dedicated places for baptism (even before any archaeological evidence for the same) is the common expectation that candidates strip. It was, after all, a bath. Evidence from this time reflects some anxiety about this, particularly regarding the roles of male clergy and the exposure of women's bodies; in some cases women may have worn a sort of linen undershirt to fulfill an expectation of shedding previous garments, naked before God but screened from male eyes.[14]

The *Apostolic Tradition*, which is late enough for us to be able to assume a dedicated place for baptism—a "baptistery" within some kind of church—reflects similar or greater concern for sanctity and modesty. Surviving versions of the text suggest baptism was always performed in a pool, but with water flowing into it (21.2). The preference for moving, natural water found in the *Didache* is recalled, but this has now become a way of referring to the source of the water, not the place for baptism. We can infer that the sanctified water of initiation now had to be contained in suitable ways.

Another reason that space and place became more important was the communal character of the rite, and especially its association with the Eucharist. Even the very early *Didache* had made an implied connection between

---

14. Bradshaw, "Women and Baptism," 641.

celebration of baptism and Eucharist, although it reflected a qualified preference for moving water and hence seems to have envisaged a ritual held outdoors
or away from obvious places for communal dining. In mid-second-century
Rome, Justin implied a baptismal site close to his community gathering, since
the "illuminated" ones moved promptly from the water to the meal. Tertullian also reflects an expectation that participation in the Eucharist was an
immediate consequence of baptism.

The *Apostolic Tradition* also has prayer offered over the water; the candidates are taken forward, in separate groups and without clothing: children,
men, and "finally, the women, after they have loosed their hair and removed
the jewelry of gold and silver they are wearing. No one shall take any foreign
object down into the water with them" (21.5). Inanimate objects might have
been thought to harbor demonic forces that would interfere with the power
of the water, or perhaps accoutrements that were incidentally "baptized"
would be seen to possess talismanic powers—or both. A river, spring, or pond
would not have been the right place for this community to baptize; but they
had probably left such behind long before.

The same work provides if not a clearer then at least a more elaborate picture of rituals immediately following the bath also, which should be included
with it to constitute "baptism"; anointing, laying on of hands, the exchange
of a kiss, and the Eucharist (21.19–40). The last two of these are discussed
elsewhere, but the first two require some more detailed consideration.

Sealing and Anointing

Baptism is often referred to in ancient texts as a "seal." This image refers
to the importance in antiquity of literal—typically wax—seals bearing the
owner's name or insignia, which functioned as signs of contracts and property
as well as for effective closure of vessels or of documents, establishing and
securing their contents.

Christian identity is already likened to a seal of the Holy Spirit in the NT
(Eph. 1:13; 4:30; cf. 2 Cor. 1:22). Circumcision, with which baptism was at times
compared and contrasted, was also termed a seal (cf. Rom. 4:13); as a literal
marking of the body, circumcision was also the sign of a covenant relationship, contract, or treaty. Baptism, while leaving no visible or outward mark,
was nevertheless a physical process, the ritual enactment of a contract through
which the participant entered into service of God as king, patron, and parent.

This language of seals encouraged the development of rituals more like
literal acts of signing or marking, including making the sign of the cross—but

these are not implied by the earliest literary and liturgical use of "sealing" language. Unless and until it is clearly otherwise, the "seal" is at first simply a way of talking about baptism itself.

Tertullian does report a widespread devotional practice of signing one's own forehead with the cross, performed by Marcionites as well as in his own Christian group (*Against Marcion* 3.22), hence an old and well-established act. This crossing the self (*signaculum*) was not specific to baptism but a persistent embodied prayer, performed (potentially) "at every forward step and movement, at every going in and out, when we put on our clothes and shoes, when we bathe, when we sit at table, when we light the lamps, on couch, on seat, in all the ordinary actions of daily life" (*On the Soldier's Crown* 3). It may nevertheless have echoed a baptismal practice that he does not record.

A few decades later, however, Cyprian uses the same word (*signaculum*) in a more clearly baptismal context: "They who are baptized in the church are brought to the prelates of the church, and by our prayers and by the imposition of hands obtain the Holy Spirit, and are perfected with the Lord's *signaculum*" (*Letter* 73.9). The cross may have been applied to the candidate's forehead then, and could already have been in Tertullian's time also.

Late in the second century the use of oil for anointing the candidate is first reported as part of baptism, and thereafter often becomes the focal point of "sealing." Imagery related to oil or anointing features often in the NT writings, most obviously in the designation of Jesus as Christ or Messiah, "anointed one." The connection between Jesus' messianic identity, baptism, and the Holy Spirit was important; two of the three were already linked by Paul writing that "it is God who establishes us with you in Christ and has anointed us, by putting his seal on us and giving us his Spirit in our hearts as a first installment" (2 Cor. 1:21–22; cf. 1 John 2:27–28). Given the association between baptism and "sealing," such texts could certainly be interpreted baptismally and subsequently applied to anointing in particular.

Yet while NT texts suggest literal anointing for healing (Mark 6:13; James 5:14), there is no indication that oil was used in baptism at the earliest times. Intriguingly, the first report of baptismal anointing relates to a group outside what would become mainstream or orthodox Christianity; Irenaeus of Lyons (ca. 180) reports on some Christians who anointed the newly baptized with balsam, and others who smeared oil and water on the heads of their candidates instead of going to the bath at all, calling this process "redemption" (*Against Heresies* 1.21.4).

Within a decade or two of these reports, there is evidence that oil was also being used around the Mediterranean as part of baptismal ritual by Christians closer to Irenaeus' own tradition, yet with various procedures and understandings attached. So Irenaeus was hardly revealing the beginnings of baptismal anointing, but happened to provide the first report.

Oil was used on the body in ordinary life in Mediterranean antiquity for therapeutic as well as cosmetic purposes, without necessary symbolic weight. In particular, anointing was regarded as an integral part of bathing;[15] the whole body might be anointed either before or after bathing, and the anointing of the head and/or face before a meal was a more specific act of festive and formal preparation.[16] It may well have been the case that oil was also used in very early baptismal ritual—incidentally, like towels or soap with a modern bath—without attracting comment or theological elaboration.

What comes into view around 200 is probably the conscious theologizing of older practices rather than a new set of constructed rituals intended to depict one or another dogma using oil as a teaching tool. Some esoterically minded groups—like those reported by Irenaeus—were prone to regarding all details of a text or ritual as having profound but hidden meanings. This made anointing, like everything else, a potential object of theological reflection; these became targets for criticism by writers like Irenaeus, not necessarily because their practice was distinctive but because their interpretation was. Nothing actually rules out the possibility that Irenaeus' own community anointed the baptized too; his plentiful theological reflections on Jesus' own baptism would have provided ample food for sacramental thought (e.g., *Against Heresies* 3.17).[17] But if they did so, the practice and the theory were different from those of Irenaeus' opponents.

Writing the first surviving treatise on baptism, Tertullian describes anointing as taking place after immersion and before laying on of hands by the bishop (*On Baptism* 6–8). Although this is only a few decades after Irenaeus, if across the Mediterranean, anointing is now presented as a venerable custom, derived from the anointing of priests and from the example of Jesus' own anointing with the Spirit. While these ancient theological rationales had probably not been attached to baptism very long before this, it is hard to imagine that oil of baptism itself was recent in Tertullian and Perpetua's Carthage.

In Syria around the same time, the apocryphal *Acts of Thomas* describes baptisms preceded by anointing, in which the use of oil seems to be at least as

15. Fikret K. Yegül, *Baths and Bathing in Classical Antiquity* (New York: Architectural History Foundation; Cambridge, MA: MIT Press, 1992).

16. Leonel L. Mitchell, *Baptismal Anointing*, Alcuin Club 48 (London: SPCK, 1966).

17. Kilian McDonnell, *The Baptism of Jesus in the Jordan: The Trinitarian and Cosmic Order of Salvation* (Collegeville, MN: Liturgical Press, 1996), 57–60, 116–23.

significant as the washing itself (*Acts Thom.* 26–27, 49, 120–21, 131–32; cf. *Gospel of Philip* 83). In one case in these acts it is not clear that washing takes place at all:

> And the apostle took the oil and poured it upon their heads and oiled and chrismed them, and began to say: "Come, holy name of Christ that is above every other name. . . . Come Holy Spirit and purify their innards and heart, and seal them in the name of the Father and the Son and the Holy Spirit." And when they were sealed there appeared to them a youth. (*Acts Thom.* 27)[18]

The "seal" Thomas administers may be baptism, and in other episodes from the same curious work that seems to be the case, but a waterless anointing for initiation could have been intended here.[19] In the *Didascalia Apostolorum*, perhaps reflecting later Syrian practice, anointing takes place yet seems to precede the bath, and oil is used both for the whole body and for the head, depending on circumstance (3.12[16]).[20] So even the relative closeness of the *Didascalia* and the *Acts of Thomas* does not guarantee a single or simple approach to how sacramental oil and water were mixed.

Meanwhile, the *Apostolic Tradition* gives a prayer for blessing oil (chap. 5), and also indicates that "oil of exorcism" and "oil of thanksgiving" were both blessed before use in baptism (chap. 21). Candidates are described as anointed with the former prior to being washed, and the latter immediately after; then after reclothing there comes still another anointing, on the head by the bishop along with laying on of hands, in the presence of the congregation.

The meanings attributed to these anointings in the *Apostolic Tradition* are complex; the first is with the "oil of exorcism" after renouncing Satan, his service, and his works, and relates to the removal of what was old and bad; the second, immediately after baptism, is with that oil "of thanksgiving";[21] the third is apparently with the same oil, but the bishop offers a prayer for grace at that point—later witnesses to the *Apostolic Tradition* have the bishop pray

---

18. This passage is from the Greek version, which probably reflects a version older than the extant Syriac. On this complex document see Harold W. Attridge, *The Acts of Thomas*, ed. Julian Victor Hills, Early Christian Apocrypha 3 (Salem, OR: Polebridge, 2010), 1–15.

19. See further Susan Myers, "Initiation by Anointing in Early Syriac-Speaking Christianity," *Studia Liturgica* 31 (2001): 150–70.

20. Bryan D. Spinks, *Early and Medieval Rituals and Theologies of Baptism: From the New Testament to the Council of Trent*, Liturgy, Worship and Society (Burlington, VT: Ashgate, 2006), 14–36. References to the text of the *Didascalia* are given with the numbering based on the comparable sections of *Apostolic Constitutions*, followed by the chapter number of the Syriac text in square brackets.

21. The Latin text resumes between these two anointings and refers to this second oil simply as "sanctified."

for the coming of the Holy Spirit, who in the Latin version is assumed to have already acted in the water.

This complexity could reflect the composite nature of the document, which may be a "desk exercise" in prescribing liturgical correctness rather than necessarily reflecting a widespread real set of practices; but it also shows how different traditions of anointing could later have been combined. When Christians or their liturgical documents traveled, a potential disconnect could appear between the known practice of one observer and what another church (or even the "apostles" in writing) advocated. Different understandings of when and why to anoint may sometimes have been resolved by choosing more than one right answer.

Anointing thus appears in the practice of Christian worship as a rich and complex reality from the outset. Some uses of oil seem closely related to and inspired by the idea of Jesus' own baptism and messianic identity, and by the ancient anointings of prophets, priests, and kings. The Syrian Christians who anointed the head as a seal—or more accurately as a "mark" or sign, since the ambiguity of "seal" did not apply in the Syriac language[22]—were emphasizing the messianic identity of the recipient. A connection with Jesus' walk into the river Jordan was obvious, but not strictly necessary; the earlier biblical examples were even more obvious, at least as ritual models. Other anointings, particularly of the whole body, may have had more contemporary and prosaic associations. The exorcistic emphasis (among others) in the *Apostolic Tradition* probably reminded those anointed of their own uses of oil as a medicinal and soothing substance, as well as for bathing and cleaning the skin.

Attempts to find a single origin for baptismal anointing, let alone an original form and meaning, are thus unnecessary and even misleading. As a widely known set of practices associated with bathing and the body, anointing (like baptism) is likely to be older than any of the specific theologies associated with it. It would have been more surprising if oil had *not* been used somehow in the process of ritual bathing.

Laying On of Hands

The foundational conversion stories in the Acts of the Apostles link water baptism with laying on of hands (e.g., 8:17). New Testament texts also link hand laying with prayer for healing and with commissioning for ministry (Acts 6:6; 9:17; cf. Heb. 6:2).

22. Gabriele Winkler, "The Original Meaning of the Prebaptismal Anointing and Its Implications," *Worship* 52 (1978): 26–27.

Like anointing, hand laying appears clearly in evidence for regular Christian baptismal ritual only from around 200, but it may have been used much earlier. It was, again, probably not so much a new phenomenon as an existing ritual practice that became more systematically applied, with more explicit and specific meanings; and unlike anointing, it is actually attested in Acts.

Tertullian offers very specific teaching about the connection between hand laying and the Holy Spirit: "In the water we are made clean by the action of the angel, and made ready for the Holy Spirit. . . . Next follows the imposition of the hand in benediction, inviting and welcoming the Holy Spirit" (*On Baptism* 6; 8). He therefore connects the giving of the Spirit at baptism directly with hand laying, not with washing or with the anointing. This view relates to some of the texts in Acts, and was to be highly influential in the Western church, especially when parts of the baptismal rite were later separated into the distinct event known as confirmation.

The *Didascalia* describes a similar rite being performed in the East, but with a different theological emphasis: "The Lord in baptism, by the imposition of hand of the bishop, bore witness to each one of you and uttered his holy voice, saying: you are my son: this day I have begotten you" (2.32[9]). So the imposition of hands makes real the participation of the baptized in Jesus' own baptism, and the key idea here is adoption, where the story of Jesus' baptism provides the background; but of course the Holy Spirit is prominent in that story too.

The *Didascalia* does link the Spirit more explicitly with the laying on of hands in the different case of ritualizing reconciliation for penitents:

> And as you baptize a pagan and then receive him, so also lay a hand upon this man while all pray for him, and then bring him in and let him communicate with the church. For the imposition of a hand shall take the place of baptism for him: for whether by the imposition of a hand or by baptism, they receive the communication of the Holy Spirit. (2.41[10])

The *Apostolic Tradition* still refers to the action of the Spirit as focused in the water, and the hand laying is basically an enacted prayer for grace:

> And let the bishop lay his hand upon them, invoking, saying: "Lord God, you who have made them worthy of the removal of sins through the bath of regeneration of the Holy Spirit, grant to them your grace, that they might serve you according to your will, for to you is the glory, Father and Son with the Holy Spirit, in the holy church, now and to the ages of the ages. Amen." (21.21)

Hand Laying and Ordination[23]

The acknowledgment or commissioning of men and women who held particular offices or orders was itself ritualized in the ancient church, even if not with the level of emphasis or accentuation familiar in some later cases. For much of early Christian history, baptism was by far the more significant sign of Christian identity; after the fourth century, when baptism was universal within the Roman Empire at least, both ascetic or monastic vocations and the status and role of the clergy developed more fully as specific identity markers. So while the laying on of hands was associated with commissioning various Christians for specific tasks from a very early point (Acts 6:6; 1 Tim. 4:14), this gesture would arguably have been understood in close relation to the more prevalent—and arguably more important—uses in baptismal ritual just discussed.

The first detailed account of ordination as a specific liturgical action comes from the *Apostolic Tradition*, which refers to the ordination of bishops, presbyters, and deacons (chaps. 2–8); of these, the first is clearly regarded as paradigmatic. It is to take place on "the Lord's day" along with the celebration of the Eucharist, not as a separate occasion. The candidate is to have been "chosen by all the people," as well as "named and accepted" by them, and then comes to an assembly on the "Lord's day" where not only local clergy and people but, in the extant versions at least, some number of other bishops are expected who also give assent (chap. 2); such involvement by visiting dignitaries, expressing connections across and within local churches, is otherwise attested from the mid-third century in, for example, Cyprian's letters (*Letter* 55.8). The reference here may have been added to an earlier version wherein just the local presbyters themselves, or perhaps the whole assembly of the church, were those who laid hands.[24]

Silent prayer accompanies this action at first, but then a single bishop lays hands again and prays aloud—the double hand laying is further evidence of an early editorial process, probably adding an individual bishop's spoken prayer to an original, silent prayer of the collected presbyters and/or people. The extended spoken prayer invokes the examples of Abraham, Israelite kings and priests, and the apostles. It gives strong emphasis to the priestly character of the role, invoking a "high priestly Spirit" (*Ap. Trad.* 3) and otherwise echoing themes also found in *1 Clement*; yet its identification of these roles with that of the bishop is more reminiscent of Cyprian and the mid- or late third century. The Eucharist that follows provides us with a eucharistic prayer

---

23. On later rites see Paul F. Bradshaw, *Ordination Rites of the Ancient Churches of East and West* (New York: Pueblo, 1990).

24. Bradshaw, Johnson, and Phillips, *Apostolic Tradition*, 26–27.

discussed elsewhere (*Ap. Trad.* 4), and the intriguing use of oil, cheese, and olives (*Ap. Trad.* 5–6), symbolic remnants of what might once have been the festive potluck as well as the sacramental meal.

The ordination of a presbyter (elder) in the *Apostolic Tradition* (chap. 7) shows similar signs of expansion or editing, but the versions of prayer have none of the sacerdotal character of the prayer for a bishop; the primary biblical model is that of the elders chosen by Moses (Num. 11:16–17). Presbyters join the bishop in laying hands on their peers. Instructions for deacons (chap. 8), somewhat convoluted as they are, reflect the view—still held in many contemporary settings—that only the bishop lays on hands, and that the diaconate is not "priestly" in a sense that the other two orders are. Given that the presbyteral section was not really priestly as such, this means the rubrics probably reflect a complex and late editorial process again, and reflect an interdependence of "priestly" character and presidency at the Eucharist, now increasingly seen as a literal sacrifice of some kind.[25]

The *Apostolic Tradition* in its various manifestations also presents what may be less familiar orders: confessors, widows, readers, virgins, subdeacons, and ministers of healing. Confessors—those who had been imprisoned because of their faith—are regarded as having been ordained (as presbyter or deacon) by that experience, without hand laying (chap. 9). Widows are also excluded from having hands laid on, but for different reasons; the text seeks to distinguish them from the ordained—which suggests that at least some saw them as precisely that. Yet there may also be a sense in which widows and virgins (as well as male ascetics) won their status through the quality of their life, and hence like confessors had less need of acquiring it at the hands of a bishop.

The *Didascalia Apostolorum* refers to women deacons but not to the ritual form of their appointment; the *Apostolic Constitutions* (whose compilers used both the *Apostolic Tradition* and *Didascalia*) includes the oldest known rite with hand laying for women deacons, invoking the Spirit who filled "Miriam and Deborah and Anna and Huldah" (8.20).[26] Both documents strongly associate the work of these women ministers with the rites of baptism.

Baptism and Eucharist: Milk and Honey

Eucharistic celebration had been closely related to baptism in some of the most ancient texts, such as the *Didache*; baptism was the means of entry into the defined community wherein the sacred meal was shared. It may also have been a part of the baptismal celebration itself. As more complex initiatory processes emerged,

25. Ibid., 64–65.
26. Madigan and Osiek, *Ordained Women*, 106–32.

participation in the Eucharist became a more clearly stated part of the ritual of baptism; but it also took on some specific characteristics for these occasions.

Tertullian's community, as well as local followers of his nemesis Marcion, fed the newly baptized a mixture of milk and honey (*On the Soldier's Crown* 3.3; *Against Marcion* 1.14.3). These were of course biblical symbols, but they had overtones of plenty and luxury for Greeks and Romans too. Perpetua, who was baptized into Tertullian's Christian community while a prisoner, would not have experienced every element of the baptismal ritual he describes elsewhere; her dungeon was small, dark, and foul, with little room for anything of pomp and ceremony (*Mart. Perp.* 1.2). Yet she probably alludes to this feeding practice in one of her visions:

> And I saw a great expanse of garden, and sitting in the middle a white-haired man dressed as a shepherd, large, and milking sheep. And standing around were many thousands in white robes. And he lifted his head, and looked at me, and said to me, "Welcome, child." And he called me, and he gave me from the cheese he was milking something like a mouthful, and I received it with joined hands and I ate, and all those standing around said "Amen." And at the sound of the voice I woke, still tasting something sweet, I do not know what. (*Mart. Perp.* 4.8–10)

Less clearly baptismal in origin but confirming the significance of milk are the *Odes of Solomon*, an early Christian collection of hymns with a mystical flavor, where milk can be a powerful and even startling image:

> Sprinkle on us your droplets,
> And open your abundant springs
> Which let flow milk and honey for us. (*Odes Sol.* 4.10)[27]

The image of a spring of milk and honey parallels the concrete postbaptismal feeding, but need not allude to baptism; the *Odes* seems less interested in ritual than in mystical union with God. This and plentiful similar imagery may, however, have encouraged use of the *Odes* in ritual contexts, and of milk and honey too.

While that particular ode was traveling the familiar terrain of milk and honey as symbols of agricultural plenty, another breaks striking new ground:

> A cup of milk was offered to me
> And I drank it in the sweetness of the Lord's kindness.

27. Translation based on that of Lattke, *Odes of Solomon*, 47.

The Son is the cup,
And he who milked was the Father,
And the one who milked him the Spirit of holiness . . .
[who] opened [the Father's] bosom
and mixed the milk of the two breasts of the Father. (*Odes Sol*. 19.1–2, 4)[28]

Here the imagery is partly that of the nursing child and God the androgynous parent. Again this need not be about baptism or literal sacramental milk, but it does illustrate the range of meanings that those who were washed and then fed might have experienced or formed.[29] Other ancient authors, such as Clement of Alexandria, confirm that this nutritive and maternal divine imagery could be used subtly and profoundly to reflect on eucharistic as well as baptismal practice (see *Paed*. 1.42–44).

The *Apostolic Tradition* provides some idea of how milk and honey were actually used for the eucharistic meal after baptism, and clarifies how they could be related to the expected bread and wine:

Let [the bishop] give thanks for the bread, for the representation . . . of the body of Christ; the cup of mixed wine for . . . the blood that has been shed for all who believe in him; and the milk and honey mixed together, in fulfillment of the promise made to the fathers, in which he said, "a land flowing with milk and honey" . . . and water also for an offering, as a sign of washing, so that the inner person, which is of the soul, may also receive the same as the body. (*Ap. Trad*. 21.27–29)

So there are actually three cups at this baptismal Eucharist: water, milk and honey, and the expected wine. The explicit meanings given are clear enough, but again may be secondary to the actual practice. The number of cups bears an implicit message of festivity; an ancient symposium worth attending would have had three mixed bowls of wine to share, as an indication of a proper party.[30] The distribution nonetheless has a sober feel:

Let the presbyters, and the deacons if there are not enough, hold the
cups and stand in good order and with reverence: first the one who
holds the water, second the one who holds the milk, and third the
one who holds the wine.
Let those who receive taste of each three times while the one who gives
says, "In God the Father Almighty."

28. Ibid., 268.
29. See further Teresa Berger, *Gender Differences and the Making of Liturgical History* (Farnham, UK: Ashgate, 2011), 72–88.
30. McGowan, *Ascetic Eucharists*, 108–9.

Let one who receives say, "Amen."
"And in the Lord Jesus Christ."
"And in the Holy Spirit, and in the holy church."
And let the one who receives say,
"Amen." Let it be done so for each. (*Ap. Trad.* 21.33–37)

While the other ritual elaborations of baptism—anointing and hand laying—involved an existing practice whose meaning was variously sought after and made more explicit, the feeding with milk and honey is more an "invented" ritual, where the innate significance of these dietary symbols encouraged their addition to the process. Yet the addition of food and drink other than bread and wine was not unheard of; and of course this milk-and-honey ritual was a eucharistic elaboration as much as a baptismal one.

Christianity without Baptism?

A noncanonical gospel (*Fragment Oxyrhynchus* 840) salvaged from ancient Oxyrhynchus in Egypt purports to depict an argument between Jesus and a certain Levi, identified—not very plausibly—as both a Pharisee and high priest.[31] Levi upbraids Jesus and his disciples for entering the temple precinct without washing. "The Savior" (the name "Jesus" does not appear in the text, but Jesus is certainly depicted) asks Levi about his own purity. He responds: "I am pure, for I have washed in the pool of David, and having gone down by one stair, I came up by the other; and I have put on white and pure clothes, and after that I came and looked upon these holy vessels" (*Frag. Oxy.* 2.5–6). "The Savior" responds scathingly to Levi's self-justification:

> Woe to you, blind ones who do not see! You have washed yourself in these running waters where dogs and pigs have wallowed night and day, and you have cleansed and wiped the outside skin that the prostitutes and flute girls anoint. . . . But I and my disciples, who you say have not bathed, we have bathed in waters of eternal life, which come down from the God of heaven. (*Frag. Oxy.* 2.7–9)

This text evokes Judea in Jesus' time (somewhat inaccurately), to address an issue of its own rather later period—perhaps the later second century. "Levi" probably represents mainstream Christianity, whose real or alleged concern with ritual is skewered as equivalent to Jewish practice; his "bath" then would be baptism rather than the *miqveh*. However, there is no evidence suggesting that white

31. See on this text and its interpretation François Bovon, "*Fragment Oxyrhynchus 840*, Fragment of a Lost Gospel, Witness of an Early Christian Controversy over Purity," *Journal of Biblical Literature* 119, no. 4 (2000): 705–28.

clothes were worn by the newly baptized at this point, or that the vessels of the Eucharist were comparable to the treasures of that or any other temple. These are not actual references to Christian ritual; the features of the temple itself, real or remembered, are here used as a means to criticize a church that would only later make such connections with temple worship more clearly and literally.

This "Savior" speaks for a group that saw the material character of Christian baptism and other ritual performances as missing the real and wholly spiritual point of salvation and enlightenment. Such implied opposition to baptism is spelled out in some of the documents found at Nag Hammadi (e.g., the *Paraphrase of Shem*, NHC VII,1) which expound the sort of world-renouncing, speculative theology often referred to as "gnostic."

Tertullian knew of a Christian teacher—a woman, which caused him additional problems—who argued that baptism was not necessary. Her influence was in fact the ostensible reason for his writing *On Baptism*:

> And in fact a certain viper from the Cainite group, who recently spent some time here, carried off a good number with her exceptionally poisonous doctrine, above all destroying baptism. Obviously this is according to her nature: for vipers and asps as a rule, and even serpents, seek out arid and waterless places. But we little fishes, following Jesus Christ our *ichthus*, begin our life in the water, and can only be safe remaining in water. (1.2–3)

This is the first report of the famous ΙΧΘΥΣ acrostic—Tertullian inserts the Greek word in his Latin text—presenting Jesus Christ as Son of God and Savior, but it seems already well known to his readers. Irenaeus also reports on a group of "gnostics" who saw Cain as a divine figure and who produced a *Gospel of Judas* (*Against Heresies* 1.31.1); if this is the same as the recently discovered work of that name, which rejects eucharistic celebration as a futile conjuring act with comestibles, it would not be surprising to find a similarly negative attitude toward water baptism.[32]

These "Cainites" may have thought baptism inconsequential as something merely physical, and viewed the material world itself as to be endured or escaped rather than as a good creation; yet other "gnostic" groups, rather than rejecting them, spoke more favorably of baptism(s), or of "sealing," and elaborated such rites in esoteric terms, perhaps suggesting repeated stages of ascent to mystical union.[33]

---

32. See *Gospel of Judas* (Kasser, Meyer, and Wurst, eds., 33–34), and the discussion in chap. 2 in this book; see also, on the "Cainites," Brakke, *The Gnostics*, 36–38.

33. On this see ibid., 74–83.

Baptism at Dura-Europos

The earliest material evidence for a permanent place of baptism—a baptistery or dedicated space with a purpose-built pool, or what would later be called a font—comes from the Christian building excavated at Dura-Europos in Syria.[34] This had been a fairly large house centered around a courtyard, was adapted for use as a church building in the 240s, and then was used until it was partially demolished (and in the process partially preserved) to form a defensive rampart against Persian attack in 256. The infill performed to buttress the city walls preserved part of the church, including all of its painted decoration, as well as a nearby and even more spectacularly decorated synagogue.

The small baptistery room, just a few meters across, had one end taken up by a bath dug partly into the ground and constructed similarly to the pools in the local bathhouse, a meter deep and wide, and a meter and a half long. The bath was covered by a handsomely decorated plastered canopy, of similar construction to the shrine for Torah scrolls in the neighboring synagogue. A niche on the wall may have been for storing baptismal oil.

The room was connected at floor level to two others, and opened onto the courtyard; but when it was first adapted and the pool built, the room had also been divided horizontally to create an upper chamber, accessible by an adjacent stair. It is thus possible to speculate about the performance of the ritual in the space of the house. The necessity of shedding clothes and the concern for modesty could have made the smaller upper room potentially useful as a waiting area for candidates of each sex while the other group stripped and were washed. As one group moved from the baptistery room into the larger adjacent room for postbaptismal anointing (which involved the whole body, and would probably have been performed by deacons of the same sex as the candidate), the group of the other sex could proceed down to the bath. All would finally move into the largest room of the house, where the Eucharist was celebrated.

The pool would have accommodated immersion only with some considerable effort, and the height of the canopy invites an image of the candidate standing, with water poured over the head and hence the whole body; but the structure was clearly intended to provide what a bath would—namely, complete wetting or washing. The baptistery room was decorated with a set of wall paintings evoking biblical images that these Christians associated with

34. Carl H. Kraeling, *The Christian Building*, vol. 2 of *The Excavations at Dura-Europos* VIII, ed. C. Bradford Welles (New Haven: Dura-Europos Publications, 1967), 141–55.

baptism, from the Good Shepherd over the bath itself to a mural depiction of women processing toward the font with the candidate. These have often been identified as the women approaching the tomb of Jesus at Easter, but the iconography may better be related to the wise and foolish virgins of the Gospel parable (Matt. 25:1–2).[35]

More Washings

The symbolic power of baptism depended on its uniqueness; yet the uniqueness of baptism and its power existed in a certain tension. If baptism was an effective means for dealing with sin, bestowing membership in the Christian community, and acquiring spiritual power and insight, might it not invite or require repetition in some circumstances?

The Letter to the Hebrews knows of "baptisms" (6:2; 9:10), but these were probably repeated ritual washings like those of the *miqveh*; its critical comments suggest these were not for initiation but purification, and the term used is *baptismos*, which has a more general use than the related *baptisma*.[36] The early Christian novels known as the Pseudo-Clementine *Homilies* use a source from around 200 that reflects the ritual and belief of Christian communities that retained a strong cultural connection with Judaism, including multiple washings or "baptisms" for purification, as well as for initiation. Followers of Elxai, an obscure Eastern Christian teacher whose influence had extended to Rome early in the third century, also advocated the repetition of baptism or perhaps other repeated washings comparable to those of Judaism (Hippolytus, *Refutation of All Heresies* 9.13–16).[37]

Repeated baptism (as opposed to repeated washings for purification) became an issue when external pressure created doubts about faith. Despite well-known earlier acts of violence against Christians by magistrates and mobs, it was not until the mid-third century that systematic persecution took place under Roman rule, spurred by the growth of the Christian movement and the tension between its exclusive practices and Roman expectations of civic responsibility and imperial religion. Stories of resistance and suffering are famous and

35. Michael Peppard, "New Testament Imagery in the Earliest Christian Baptistery," in *Dura-Europos: Crossroads of Antiquity*, ed. Lisa R. Brody and Gail L. Hoffman (Chestnut Hill, MA: McMullen Museum of Art, Boston College; distributed by the University of Chicago Press, 2011), 103–21.

36. Attridge, *Epistle to the Hebrews*, 164.

37. Oskar Skarsaune and Reidar Hvalvik, *Jewish Believers in Jesus* (Peabody, MA: Hendrickson, 2007); F. Stanley Jones, "The Pseudo-Clementines: A History of Research," *Second Century* 2 (1982): 1–33, 63–96.

inspiring, but there are less edifying stories as well. Some Christians bowed to the threat of violence and offered sacrifices before imperial statues. In the leadership, rival claims to ecclesial and sacramental legitimacy emerged when bishops themselves wavered or were thought to have done so.

Schism and apostasy both raised questions about the legitimacy of baptism. In the latter case, many Christians felt that those who had sacrificed to idols (or bought forged certificates stating they had) had lost the benefit of baptism, or worse. The different levels of severity with which the lapsed were treated then led to conflicts among the clergy themselves and to splits within the communities. This in turn raised the question of whether baptism into the wrong community was baptism at all.

The African bishop Cyprian and his Roman counterpart Stephen disagreed about the approach to be taken to those who sought to join or rejoin the Catholic Church. Stephen held that hand laying was adequate for these, and the sources of the *Didascalia*, among other works, suggest that many Christians underwent this ritual in cases of penitence. Cyprian, however, thought the efficacy of baptism depended on organic connection with one true church. He therefore insisted on (re)baptizing heretics, believing they had never really been baptized in the first place, however much water was used or whatever words intoned. Thus while neither Stephen nor Cyprian would have accepted the possibility of "rebaptism," they differed on what the earlier immersions had actually been.

Baptism in the Fourth Century

Constantine, Conversion, and Catechumens

The fourth century brought a new abundance of information about baptism. At least within the Roman Empire, it also involved a new context—the toleration and support brought by emperors from Constantine onward. Rituals continued to develop, and while regional diversity of baptismal practice continued, the patterns fall more clearly into a number of geographical strands or traditions, some of which have continued to the present day.

As Christianity became not only legal but favored, unsurprisingly it also grew. With adult conversion and baptism still normative, catechesis took place on an increasingly large scale. There are more examples from this period of Christians whose lives are known to us in enough detail to reveal choices they faced about whether and when to seek baptism. Such stories confirm the seriousness with which baptismal commitment was regarded, and that it was neither an immediate response even to the most genuine Christian conviction nor a slavishly followed ritual enacting the peer pressure of what was fast becoming a Christian society. Rather, baptism stood at the completion of a process wherein lifestyles, as well as beliefs, were examined and changed; yet it was not merely a symbolic confirmation of those changes but an objective encounter with divine grace, forgiveness, and renewal.

A famous example is Constantine himself, the first Christian emperor (see Eusebius, *Life of Constantine* 4.61–64). Whatever the motivation or sincerity of his much earlier personal conversion to belief in Christ, the delay of Constantine's baptism until his deathbed made eminent sense at the time. Ancient church orders specifying proper procedure for engaging adult converts are wary or negative about magistrates and soldiers seeking baptism at all, and the emperor's expected role in state-sanctioned violence sat particularly awkwardly with full initiation into a community professing peace and forgiveness.[38]

Augustine of Hippo is another famous convert whose baptism was delayed, under different circumstances, at a time when many Christian parents were now baptizing their children. He was born to a Christian mother and pagan father, and enrolled as a catechumen when a child. The ceremonies connected with his catechumenate included being signed with the cross and receiving blessed salt to eat (*Conf.* 1.11; cf. *On the Instruction of the Unlearned* 26.50). Yet Augustine did not proceed to baptism in his youth, apparently because of continuing concern—initially his mother's, and later also his own—about the dangers of postbaptismal sin.

Augustine instead became an adherent of another religious group, the Manichees, then drifted into a more urbane and less committed philosophical worldview before returning single-mindedly to the Christian faith of his conscientious mother. His famous conversion story (*Conf.* 8.12), in which he hears a child's voice calling him to "take and read" Romans 13:13–15, can readily be misunderstood; he had already been intellectually convinced of Christian faith by the sophisticated bishop Ambrose, but struggled with sexual renunciation, which seemed to him the corollary of his own commitment. The narrative is not one of propositional conviction or of personal encounter with Christ but of ascetic commitment. Augustine's contemporaries, however, would have said that he became a Christian neither while listening to Ambrose's sermons,

38. E. J. Yarnold, "The Baptism of Constantine," in *Studia Patristica* 26 (Leuven: Peeters, 1993), 95–101.

nor in that Milanese garden in August 386, but in the font of the Cathedral of Milan at Easter in 387.

Augustine, Infant Baptism, and Rebaptism[39]

Augustine's theological contributions to baptism were significant, and they had significant practical and pastoral consequences as well. Two of his most famous controversies stemmed in part from how to practice baptism and how to understand it.

Many infant baptisms were taking place by this time and had certainly been common in many communities for a century and more. Augustine himself provided impetus to that trend, or at least a clearer theological underpinning, through his development of the doctrine of original sin in polemical dialogue with the optimistic ascetic teacher Pelagius.

Augustine's response to this controversy gave more shape to a view hinted at by earlier Christian writers: that baptism was not only for forgiveness of sins committed but also addressed a fundamental flaw in the human condition, as real for infants as for emperors. Augustine used the well-established practice of baptizing infants as evidence for the truth of this view (see *On the Grace of Christ and Original Sin*). His thought that the sin dealt with in baptism is inherent, rather than just acquired through life's bad decisions, has its antecedents in earlier discussions like Justin's. Yet his more systematic and reflective approach has arguably made him the theorist of infant baptism, at least in Western Christianity.

This understanding of sin and baptism helped catalyze a shift toward the baptism of infants, but did not cause it. Since most people within the Roman Empire identified as Christians, baptism could become a rite of entry into that whole community, identified as coextensive with the church, rather than the distinctive sacrament of adult faith and discipleship in a mixed or hostile environment.[40]

Augustine also bequeathed to the Western church a more pastoral and accommodating framework for dealing with questions of baptism and disunity that had burdened the exchange between Cyprian and Stephen of Rome nearly two centuries earlier. Like his understanding of original sin, this framework was forged in controversy, this time with the local African movement Donatism. The Donatists, rigorists who looked to Cyprian for inspiration, felt that

---

39. For these issues, see further Ferguson, *Baptism in the Early Church*, 795–816.

40. David F. Wright, "Augustine and the Transformation of Baptism," in *The Origins of Christendom in the West*, ed. Alan Kreider (Edinburgh: T&T Clark, 2001), 287–310.

the wider Christian movement was compromised and its baptism accordingly invalid. Augustine, skirting arguments about whose ministers and sacraments were "purer," argued that the reality of baptism depended on God rather than the merits of ministers. Against Cyprian, he argued that the Donatists and other "schismatics" had valid baptism; but with Cyprian, Augustine regarded communion with the wider church as a prerequisite for its effective flourishing. His influence has meant that "rebaptism"—strictly an impossibility in any case, as we have already noted—was avoided in the Western church if water and the trinitarian name were used.

Catechesis and Mystagogy

The process of teaching and otherwise preparing candidates for baptism was never more important than during this century of transition. The somewhat earlier *Apostolic Tradition* tried to apply a filter of stability and seriousness in the face of an onrush of enthusiastic converts when it specified a three-year catechumenate, but the reality may have been quite variable.

We have already seen that some took much longer even than three years to wade into the water. It was relatively common, given these lengthy periods of reflection or dilemma, for those actually preparing for imminent baptism to be considered a special category among the catechumens; in the Latin of Augustine's Africa they were *competentes*, "fellow seekers"; in the Greek of Jerusalem they were *phōtizomenoi*, those "being enlightened," recalling Justin Martyr's language about baptism as illumination.

Not very long after taking office in 350 as bishop of Jerusalem, Cyril gave a set of addresses that are a uniquely valuable witness to that final and more critical educational process. A related set of postbaptismal, or "mystagogical," catecheses attributed to Cyril also reflects the fourth-century Jerusalem setting.[41] These can all be read along with the pilgrim diary of Egeria, probably from the later years of Cyril's tenure (380s), which provides valuable ritual cross-references to the rites associated with Easter baptism.[42]

What is most striking to the modern reader is the absence, in the prebaptismal catecheses, of information about baptism itself. Cyril's lectures are primarily about the creed that the *phōtizomenoi* were learning and would recite as part of the preparation. Only after they were baptized and had received

---

41. Ferguson, *Baptism in the Early Church*, 473–74.
42. See for further sources and their significance Juliette Day, *The Baptismal Liturgy of Jerusalem: Fourth- and Fifth-Century Evidence from Palestine, Syria and Egypt*, Liturgy, Worship and Society (Burlington, VT: Ashgate, 2007).

the Eucharist for the first time were they told exactly what had happened to them. This arcane approach to baptism itself was not universal; most teachers of the period offered some information prior to baptism and different "mystagogical" knowledge to the initiates. In nearby Syria, John Chrysostom and Theodore of Mopsuestia spoke more clearly in their respective *Baptismal Homilies* about baptism and its meaning to those preparing for it. Yet these catechetical addresses also emphasize the awe-inspiring character of what would take place in the font.[43] In places as far apart as Alexandria and Milan, the monk Didymus and the bishop Ambrose offered the same view that the Lord's Prayer—given to catechumens, or at least *competentes* and their equivalents, in some places—was a treasure that should be kept from the eyes and minds of those still uninitiated.[44] This view makes more sense when we consider the place of the Lord's Prayer at the center of a distinctive Christian practice of daily worship, discussed elsewhere in this book.

So these teachers differed on specifics, but all made use of a principle of mystagogy—Christian education, in effect—as well as one of catechesis or preparation. Their varied approaches are all based on a strong sense of the objective character of the sacraments received with faith, understood more as trust in God than acceptance (or even awareness) of creedal or experiential elements adequate to that trust and its ritualization. Their common concern, to draw clear lines between what was offered to the baptized and what was for instruction, reflects a new concern to define the church as a group of called and chosen believers, whose peculiar identity could no longer be imposed by civic persecution or social marginalization; the Christian, they hoped, would be the possessor of treasured knowledge and the recipient of sacramental grace.

East Syria

On the fringes of empire, straddling territory controlled by the Romans and Eastern kingdoms such as Persia, Christians of eastern Syria maintained and developed distinctive practices and understandings of baptism by means of a rich and distinctive linguistic and cultural heritage.

The most famous of the early Syrian writers is Ephraem of Nisibis, whose hymns were a liturgical vehicle for devotion, for combatting theological opponents, and for praising ascetic life. These songs often contain distinctively

43. For further discussion and texts see Maxwell E. Johnson, *The Rites of Christian Initiation: Their Evolution and Interpretation* (Collegeville, MN: Liturgical Press, 2007), 121–34.

44. Roy Hammerling, *The Lord's Prayer in the Early Church: The Pearl of Great Price* (New York: Palgrave Macmillan, 2010), 59–77.

Syrian themes and images, such as those in the seventh of his *Hymns on Virginity*, which concerns the practice and meaning of baptism:

> With visible colors
> is the royal portrait formed,
> and formed with visible oil
> the invisible picture of our invisible King.
> In those marked, baptism,
> who bears them in her womb,
> will replace the picture of the first Adam,
> corrupted, transformed into the new picture
> and birth them in the threefold pangs
> of the three precious names
> of the Father, the Son, and the Holy Spirit.

Here baptism is personified as maternal agent of regeneration; Ephraem's exposition of the invisible divine image, repainted visibly with oil within the baptized, draws upon an extraordinary range of ideas in a few words (even fewer in the original Syriac).

The prominence of the "mark" of prebaptismal anointing, which effects that restoration, continues the strong Syrian tradition of seeing anointing as a central and not merely secondary aspect of baptism. While the idea of restoration of true humanity is shared with other Christian communities, Ephraem has the tradition of this baptismal "mark" as a starting point to explain it; and while he uses the biblical imagery of baptism as new birth, the strongly feminine image of the baptismal font renders the implications of the Gospel of John's new birth into more vivid terms.

The Syrian understanding of baptism reflected here also points more directly than most Western theologies to the links with Jesus' own baptism and the messianic or royal identity it bestows. Ephraem's reference to the "King" as the one whose image is placed within the inner self of the baptized is far from the modern predilection for "king" language as a reference to losing oneself in divine glory and self-abasement; rather, Jesus' kingship was configured as the character of his mission, and the Christian participation in baptism was a share in that mission.

White Robes

The idea of the saints wearing washed white robes goes back at least to the Revelation to John (3:5; 4:4; etc.), and metaphors of conversion as reclothing, sometimes in relation to baptism itself, are also prominent in the Pauline

Letters (Gal. 3:27; Col. 3:10–12; etc.).[45] These particular clothes have wider and older associations with celebration and triumph (cf. Eccles. 9:8).

As a form of bathing, baptism of course required the removal of clothing and then subsequent reclothing. Bathing was also normally a time to change clothes,[46] and such a momentous dip would have been no exception. So the Pauline metaphor of new clothing belongs to that context, and to custom; it neither implies a ritual oddity nor merely refers to the washing itself.

Changes of clothing were not always just routine. Well-known biblical examples of tearing clothes and changing to sackcloth suggest a sort of opposite movement, from dignity to humiliation, adopted in a process of supplication or mourning (Gen. 37:29, 34; 2 Sam. 3:31). There are, however, cases where a change of clothes expresses a positive shift in status (Gen. 35:2). Public strategies of dressing the body to express need were also known in Greco-Roman society;[47] so too was the changing of clothes at an important transition such as maturity. The *toga virilis*, symbolizing via dress adult male citizenship in the Roman world, was a white robe of sorts whose significance may have been known to early hearers of the Pauline argument in Galatians, where baptism and maturity are linked.[48] Paul himself already theologizes the action of reclothing, just as of immersion itself.

We do not know just when this necessary element of the baptismal ritual became consciously or explicitly theologized through the provision of a new and/or white garment. The explicit evidence comes as late as the fourth century; before that there is ample use of clothing imagery, as in the NT documents, but in no earlier case can we be clear that the "garment" or the process of donning it is not metaphorical, with baptism itself the referent (see the Pseudo-Clementine *Homilies* 8.22; Clement, *Paed.* 1.6.32; etc.). However, the fact that this, like anointing, was the interpretation and elaboration of a prosaic part of the bathing practice underlying the baptismal rite means that any quest for a specific origin may be pointless.

Even the fourth-century evidence is not unambiguous. The account of Constantine's baptism includes the statement that immediately after the rite— administered, as we noted, on his deathbed—the emperor "donned shining royal garments, brilliant as the light" (*Life of Constantine* 4.62); these may have

45. See now Martin F. Connell, "Clothing the Body of Christ: An Inquiry about the Letters of Paul," *Worship* 85 (2011): 128–46.

46. See Garrett G. Fagan, *Bathing in Public in the Roman World* (Ann Arbor: University of Michigan Press, 2002), 10–11, 210 fig. 29.

47. F. S. Naiden, *Ancient Supplication* (New York: Oxford University Press, 2006), 58–60.

48. J. Albert Harrill, "Coming of Age and Putting on Christ: The Toga Virilis Ceremony, Its Paraenesis, and Paul's Interpretation of Baptism in Galatians," *Novum Testamentum* 44, no. 3 (2002): 252–77.

been his own version of the baptismal robes.[49] Cyril of Jerusalem also speaks of the newly baptized as "shining in body" (*Procatechesis* 15) but does not discuss the clothing rite in his mystagogical text. Chrysostom discusses the "new garment" of baptism but actually means Christ or the imperial garb of a new nature given by God in Christ (*Baptismal Homilies* 5.18; 8.25); the literal robes are more like props for his use in the exhortation than a matter for actual mystagogy. Farther west, Chromatius, who was bishop of Aquileia in Italy around this time and in fact a friend of Chrysostom, uses a similar pedagogical strategy; but Chromatius more clearly references the actual robes, moving between the literal or physical garments and the oil of anointing, encouraging his hearers to believe that both unction and robe are theirs always, if they persist in the grace given at baptism (*Sermon* 14.4).[50]

Confirmation

African theologians such as Augustine and Optatus of Milevis had a strong or high view of (postbaptismal) anointing; they called both baptism and chrismation "sacraments." Cyprian had also used the term "sacrament" for laying on of hands centuries before (*Letter* 72; cf. Augustine, *Answer to Petilian* 2.105.239). This did not mean these actions could or should all be performed separately; each was something like a "sacramental ritual act," still joined in the complex baptismal rite. However, the naming of these distinct actions as individual "sacraments" foreshadowed a later Western tendency to separate them.

The idea that part or all of the postbaptismal ceremonies constitute a separate rite of "confirmation" appears in mid-fifth-century texts from what is now southern France.[51] By that time, the growth of Christian numbers, and the emergence of a more complex structure of local congregations related to a bishop, meant that bishops themselves were no longer the expected ministers of baptism or Eucharist. A local presbyter administered the washing; elsewhere, notably in the eastern Mediterranean but perhaps in northern Gaul, too, the presbyter also administered whatever other ritual elements were regarded as proper, typically with oil (chrism) blessed by the bishop.

In southern Gaul there was uncertainty about whether presbyters should perform the single postbaptismal anointing that completed initiation, and

---

49. Ferguson, *Baptism in the Early Church*, 450.
50. Ibid., 691.
51. Gabriele Winkler, "Confirmation or Chrismation: A Study in Comparative Liturgy," *Worship* 58, no. 1 (1984): 2–17.

about how the bishop's traditional involvement and continuing oversight should be expressed. Councils held at Riez (439), Orange (441), and Arles (ca. 450) all refer to a *confirmatio* that the bishop was expected to perform at some time after the baptism itself; it is unclear whether this included a delayed form of postbaptismal anointing or was simply the laying on of hands already well known in African and Roman practice as a distinct action.

A homily attributed to Faustus, who was bishop of Riez not long after the council held there, offers a classic statement of "confirmation" as a distinct rite centered on the laying on of hands, expounding the story of Pentecost:

> What the imposition of the hand gives to individual neophytes in confirmation, the descent of the Holy Spirit then gave to a whole group of believers. . . . Therefore the Holy Spirit, who descends upon the waters of baptism in a saving flow, gives in the font a fullness for innocence; in confirmation, the Spirit abounds with an increase for grace, because in this world we must go forward and prevail among invisible enemies and dangers our whole life. (*Homily on Pentecost* 1–2)[52]

This theology has fully exploited the "seams" left in the Western tradition by the identification of the various ritual elements of baptism as distinct "sacraments"; the way forward to separate "confirmation" is not hard to discern.

Foot Washing

John's Last Supper

The distinctive story of Jesus' Last Supper in John's Gospel is well known. Where the Synoptic Gospels place the story traditionally regarded as the institution of the Eucharist, the Fourth Gospel instead narrates Jesus' washing of his disciples' feet (13:1–15).

> And during supper Jesus, knowing that the Father had given all things into his hands, and that he had come from God and was going to God, got up from the meal, took off his outer robe, and tied a towel around himself. Then he poured water into a basin and began to wash the disciples' feet and to wipe them with the towel that was tied around him. . . . He said to them . . . "If I, your Lord and Teacher, have washed your feet, you also ought to wash one another's feet. For I have set you an example, that you also should do as I have done to you." (vv. 2b–5, 12b, 14–15 NRSV, modified)

52. CCSL 101.337–41.

John's Gospel is notoriously difficult to assess as a source of early Christian practice, whether for actions it reflects or those it prescribes. Some commentators see its references to water as virtually all baptismal, but others have claimed this Gospel is "anti-sacramental."[53] If these extremes both contain a measure of anachronism, there is little to suggest what point between them best reflects the Gospel's original setting and intention.

In this case, the foot washing that Jesus performs and prescribes could be one of at least three things: an allusion to baptism, a symbolic reference to mutual service and charity, or a literal command to wash feet. The middle possibility is clearest, and not exclusive; there is certainly a message here about the type of service and leadership exercised by Jesus himself and urged on his followers.

If the precise significance of the story for the author(s) of the Fourth Gospel remains inaccessible, the way the text was subsequently received and used is at least as important for our purposes; it is from other texts—not this one—that we can gauge what was actually done in response to it. In the first century or so after its writing, the Fourth Gospel was widely read in circles beyond what would become normative or orthodox Christianity, not least by the followers of Valentinus, a philosophically minded teacher esteemed by some contemporaries but regarded by Irenaeus and later critics as beyond the pale. The rich symbolism of the Gospel—including dualisms of flesh and spirit, light and darkness, and so forth—lent itself to esoteric reading and rewriting, reflected in some of the "gnostic" documents of the Nag Hammadi library.

Tertullian and the fourth-century Codex Sinaiticus are among very ancient witnesses who knew a version of John 13:10 wherein Jesus said to Peter simply, "One who has bathed does not need to wash, but is entirely clean. And you are clean, though not all of you." Other witnesses had an extra phrase qualifying the statement; the bathed person is said to be clean "except the feet." This is generally included in modern translations, but noted as uncertain. For us, determining an original text of John is probably as difficult—or better, beside the point—as an original intention of the author; there are multiple readings and understandings as soon as this text comes to light. Certainly one of these may have been that foot washing was literally to be practiced in the community, despite or in addition to what was accomplished in baptism; the additional phrase might have supported that notion.[54]

53. Famously, Rudolf Bultmann, *The Gospel of John: A Commentary*, trans. G. R. Beasley-Murray (Philadelphia: Westminster, 1971).

54. Martin F. Connell, "*Nisi Pedes*, Except for the Feet: Footwashing in the Communities of John's Gospel," *Worship* 70 (1996): 517–31.

Washing the Martyrs' Feet

Foot washing was, like anointing, not a ritual peculiarity in the ancient Mediterranean world but was performed by all kinds of people as a practical and hospitable act, and for Christians to do so for one another might actually have been unremarkable in itself.

And there are early references to Christians washing feet, but not in the primarily symbolic way that tends to be read out of the Gospel text. One poignant example comes from Tertullian, who indicates that imprisoned Christians might have this service performed as part of the care offered by their visitors. The point is made in the course of an argument against a Christian woman marrying an unbeliever, and lists problematic practices to which a believer might be called:

> For who would allow his wife, for the sake of visiting the brethren, to go around from street to street to others' dwellings, and indeed the poorer ones? Who will willingly put up with her being taken from his side for nocturnal meetings, if need arise? Who, finally, will calmly accept her absence all night at the observance of Pascha? Who will, without suspicion, let her go to attend that Lord's Banquet that they defame? Who will endure her creeping into prison to kiss a martyr's chains, or for that matter to meet with the brethren to exchange the kiss, to offer water for the saints' feet, to share a little of her food, from her cup, to yearn for or remember them? (*To His Wife* 2.4.2–3)

This example places the care of the martyrs (still living witnesses at this stage) within a broader context of relief for the poor; there is a discernible devotional flavor to the treatment of the persecuted prisoners, but it is laid over the basic meeting of their bodily needs.[55] Prisoners in the Roman world were kept in squalid and inhumane conditions, where dirt and hunger had to be addressed in more than sacramental ways.

This was, however, unmistakably a ritual act; modern assumptions about the relationship between the ritual and the real do not survive the scrutiny such performances suggest. Tertullian's fulsome and confronting list of distinctive acts also indicates that there was considerable scope for ministry by women, although he saw it as properly performed in domestic spheres more than communal ones; but of course he, as well as others, knew of exceptions.

---

55. On the care of the living martyrs, see further Andrew B. McGowan, "Discipline and Diet: Feeding the Martyrs in Roman Carthage," *Harvard Theological Review* 96 (2003): 455–76. The discussion of the accoutrements of foot washing in Tertullian's *On the Soldier's Crown* 8 does not imply a communal or liturgical setting; he is merely arguing that Christ's use means these are available to Christians, even if they have pagan associations too.

In the later *Apostolic Constitutions* (ca. 400), deacons, who have a particular responsibility for social service, are instructed to wash the feet of the sick and infirm, presumably because these are unable to do so for themselves (3.19). As monastic rules emerged, they might also specify foot washing as an act of hospitality to visitors, affirming and interpreting the custom in the newly constructed social relations of the community (see John Cassian, *Institutes* 4.19). Many or all of these foot washers would have understood themselves to be imitating and obeying Jesus in these acts of service; and it is entirely possible that they were doing just what John 13:10 indicated.

Foot Washing and Baptism

The story of Jesus washing his disciples' feet was also widely interpreted as having baptismal significance. The Persian teacher Aphrahat (ca. 270–345) interprets John 13 as the institution of baptism (*Demonstrations* 12.10); however, this is Aphrahat's exegetical strategy for the text, not a reference to any liturgy he knew. Nearby Syrian texts and images similarly suggest that the story of the washing was interpreted baptismally, but they give no reason to think it was imitated in performance. The clearest evidence for a communal and ritual form of foot washing related to baptism comes not from the East but the West; churches in Spain, Gaul, northern Italy, and Africa all knew of a form of washing feet connected with the ritual of baptism.

A curious reference in one of Cyprian's letters may be the first hint of this practice. Another African bishop, Fidus, apparently wanted to delay infant baptisms until the eighth day, in imitation of the Jewish practice of circumcision. Among reasons offered in support, Fidus held that "the foot of an infant in the very first days after his birth is not clean, so that any one of us would be disgusted at the thought of kissing it" (*Letter* 64.4.1). The reasons for this particular repugnance are hard for moderns to grasp, but the fact of it is clear enough. Although the notion of purity that Fidus invokes was couched in terms of Jewish custom, it probably reflects his Roman colonial milieu; newborns may have been seen as marginal beings until a certain amount of time had elapsed, and only then their existence and survival were recognized ritually and otherwise.[56]

In any case, this exchange of letters implies that the feet of the baptized may have been attended to in particular ways; kissing rather than washing is mentioned, but the washing should probably be understood too. So the feet

---

56. G. W. Clarke, "Cyprian's Epistle 64 and the Kissing of Feet in Baptism," *Harvard Theological Review* 66, no. 1 (January 1, 1973): 147–52.

of infants—and others—were apparently washed and kissed as part of the baptismal ritual in Roman Africa. By implication, infant baptism was also well known at this place and time.

Half a century later in Spain, things become a little clearer on baptismal foot washing. A collection of canon law attributed to the Council of Elvira (just after 300) forbids payment for baptisms, and one of these *Canons of Elvira* (Canon 48) adds that clergy should not wash the feet of the baptized. This curious injunction tells us at least that both these things had been happening, and the link made between them implies that foot washing was perceived as a servile act, connected with the payment. Since this canon is among those possibly added to the minutes of the council considerably later, it is good evidence for baptismal foot washing in Spain, but not for any date much before 300.[57]

Sin, Serpent, and Sacrament: Diversity in Italy and Africa

In the church of Milan in the late fourth century, foot washing was certainly an additional ritual connected to baptism. Ambrose commented on this, acknowledging it was not a universal practice—unknown at Rome, notably:

> We are aware that the Roman church does not have this custom, although we always follow that church as an example and model. Nevertheless, they do not have this custom of washing the feet. Look, perhaps they have decided against it because of popular opinion. There are, however, those who try to excuse this because [foot washing] need not be done as a sacrament, not at baptism or in the regeneration, but rather in the way that the feet of a guest have to be washed. But one of these things is a matter of humility, the other a matter of sanctification. So, hear how it is a sacrament and a sanctification: "Unless I wash your feet, you have no part with me." I say this, not because I am criticizing others, but to commend my own use. (*On the Sacraments* 3.5)

So Ambrose is aware of the other sort of Christian foot washing, "a matter of humility," and offers support for it too; but it is not, he says, the same thing. And he puts his own episcopal foot down where the difference from Roman practice caused him some embarrassment; the Milanese did this not just to maintain custom but because, he says, this is a "sacrament" (*mysterium*), and because Jesus said so. The Romans, not the Milanese, were the ones who ought to be embarrassed.

57. Hess, *Early Development of Canon Law*, 41–42.

Other reasons for washing feet are in his mind too. In *On the Sacraments* Ambrose uses a colorful mythological narrative to elucidate the practice; the feet are washed because the ancient serpent had tripped Adam and, in doing so, spread venom on his feet; additional cleansing and protection were thus needed for this part of the body. There could be a connection here with the objections of Fidus in Africa more than a century earlier, but this is unclear.

In his work *On the Mysteries*, however, Ambrose gives what initially seems a different explanation: "Peter was clean, but had to wash his feet, for he had the sin of the first human by succession, from when the serpent tripped him and led him into error. Therefore the feet are washed, to take away inherited sin. Our own sins are forgiven through baptism" (*Myst.* 32). Although the story of the serpent tripping Adam features again, Ambrose here sees the foot washing as remedy specifically for inherited sin, which the influence of his protégé Augustine would later make the center of baptism. This older transmitted fault may have been behind the dramatic image of the serpent's venom in *On the Sacraments* too. For Ambrose, baptism itself was basically about the sins the candidates themselves had accumulated as conscious adult actors, not the remedy for an inherited fault. Augustine probably underwent this additional "sacrament," since he was baptized in Milan according to local custom in 387, but he was to attribute Ambrose's understanding of the foot-washing ceremony—its effectiveness against inherent sin—to the central baptismal rite itself.

When he went on to hold a similar responsibility for instructing catechumens and others on the sacraments, Augustine also referred to fundamental differences of opinion about whether foot washing should take place at all. He too refers to different patterns of its administration and implicitly advocates a delay between the rite and the baptismal bath proper:

> As for the washing of feet: since the Lord commended this as a symbol of the humility that he came to teach, just as he himself later demonstrated, the question has arisen of what time seems best for enacting it, and this [Easter] time is when it would make the most profound impression. Many, however, have not accepted this as a custom, lest it should seem to belong to the sacrament of baptism; quite a few have not hesitated to dismiss it as a mere custom. Others, however, so that they might commend it at a more sacred time, and at the same time distinguish it from the sacrament of baptism, have chosen to perform it either the third day of the eight [days of Easter week], because the third number stands out in many sacramental acts, or on the eighth day itself. (*Letter* 55.18.33)

Augustine is probably hinting at the Roman church in saying that some "dismiss" the custom, knowing their opinion of the Milanese practice. His own attitude seems to be strongly in favor, granted circumspection about both the meaning and the timing of the rite. Presumably the church at Hippo was using one of these times later in Easter week to wash the feet of its neophytes, presenting the ritual as a model of Christ's humility, but not as a supplementary baptism, nor even as an additional part of the baptismal rite proper, like hand laying or anointing.

Foot Washing: The Washers and the Washed

It would be intriguing to think that a ritual or sacramental practice of initiatory foot washing had continued from the example of Jesus through to Ambrose and Augustine. Yet while there is some possibility the Johannine community actually did something like this, the evidence is too weak to support the idea of it as more than a passing, if poignant, curiosity.

Foot washing was not Jesus' invention, nor presented as such by the Gospel of John. People in the ancient Mediterranean did wash feet and have their feet washed. What is distinctive and striking in these Christian cases is really the identities of the washers and the washed, not the ritual itself. These examples of practical service suggest a genuine attempt to embody the example of humility provided by the Gospel, not so much as a communal ritual or as a primarily symbolic act but in response to the needs of those at risk. In the case of the martyrs, this opened a wider and more ambiguous set of power relations, since they were both vulnerable and authoritative. In the case of postbaptismal washing, the clergy who seem to have performed the action were physically abasing themselves to those whom they led—causing at least some bishops to feel discomfort.

So the earliest cases of foot washing after the Gospel narrative are thus not really "liturgical" in the sense of being symbolic communal acts; yet they are not merely prosaic, either. The washing of the feet of those facing suffering and death, either by violence or the ravages of time itself, was a powerful act whereby the Christian participant, giving or receiving it, entered into a powerful mimesis of Christ. Those acts of service seem to have a slightly different history from foot washing related to baptism. The latter may be a focused development from the former or a conscious but constructed imitation of the Johannine supper narrative. In neither case, however, should we imagine a continued ritual of Christian communal foot washing stemming directly from the Gospel of John.

Conclusion

Both continuity and change are evident across the first few centuries of Christian baptismal practice. There is certainly a contrast between the spontaneous semipublic bathings of the NT narratives and the ceremonial splashing of infants and well-prepared adults in the fourth century; but some of the shifts—regarding water and preparation, at least—seem very early, and the stories such as we find in Acts may have been past ideals rather than present models, even when written down. The shift toward infant baptism across this period is also striking; but this was a trend regarding the typical, rather than an innovation in terms of the possible. Many adults were still being baptized in the fourth century; infant baptism may not have been completely normative before the sixth.[58]

Meanings also grew and changed, or at least shifted focus. John's original call for repentance has its perennial force radicalized, if anything, in Augustine's nexus between baptism and sin. The solidarity of the believer with Christ in his mission, the sense of entering and leaving the Jordan with him to fulfill divine adoption and vocation, is stronger in the ancient church—especially but not exclusively in Syria—than in the modern West, where Paul's focus on Jesus' saving death has held sway. These images are not, however, mutually exclusive, nor would any of our ancient writers and baptizers have seen them as such; baptism was divine mystery in whose waters one could dive without plumbing its depths.

The accompanying elaboration of baptismal ritual, and the growing prominence of oil, hands, clothes, and other accoutrements, is not merely a story of ceremonial development or overlay but an enacted quest for meaning. Accepting the command to baptize, Christians had in effect to tell themselves and others why they did so, beyond mere obedience. Each aspect of the ancient bath became itself something for reflection, a text for exegesis, in both word and practice.

---

58. Ferguson, *Baptism in the Early Church*, 627–33.

6

⁓

PRAYER

Hours, Ways, and Texts

They devoted themselves to the apostles' teaching and fellowship, to the breaking of bread and the prayers. (Acts 2:42)

A minority religious group provokes curiosity among their neighbors, not least because of their habits concerning ritual and prayer. Their women are conspicuously veiled; they gather for meetings whose mysterious conduct and message lead to anxiety. They stop even in their daily routine to pray, facing a specific direction, and using a set formula given by their founder as a mark of their faith.

Presumably this description brings Islam more quickly to mind than Christianity, which in modern form often sees prayer as largely an activity of the inner person, a matter of thought, feeling, and affect. Although there are some continuing Christian traditions of set prayer (often disparaged as a poor substitute for the spontaneous), the idea of prayer as a distinctive kind of ritual performance at fixed times through the day may be surprising; so too, the use of the body—its orientation and posture assumed as a means to private and public prayer—has largely been forgotten outside a few traditional contexts, such as in monastic communities. Yet the description given above is

183

indeed of ancient Christian prayer, for the average believer as much as for the specialist. Prayer for the first Christians involved far more than forming and expressing individual ideas or words; it was profoundly communal as well as highly personal, and a matter of body as well as mind.

Jewish Origins and Early Christian Prayer

"Worship" and Prayer

Understanding the undoubtedly Jewish origins of Christian liturgy is made harder by the assumption that "worship" was a distinct activity in both traditions and that primitive Christian "worship" practices were derived from Jewish ones. Yet "worship" in the modern sense did not quite exist, either for ancient Jews or Christians. Ancient Christian identity was expressed and supported by a variety of quite different ritual practices, individual and communal. "Worship" was not one sort of weekly corporate activity but the devotion to God that filled the whole of life. This included particular bodily expressions of that devotion, performed privately or communally from day to day, as well as the deepest dispositions of heart and mind expressed in some moments of conscious adoration or thanksgiving; worship took shape in such particular events but was not limited to them.

Because Eucharist, baptism, and daily prayer originated in quite different ways and for different purposes (not as variations on a single theme of "worship"), there are quite different answers to how Jewish origins are important to understanding each. In the case of prayer, Jewish practice was indeed the immediate and organic starting point for much that early Christians did, and it is fundamentally important to understanding it thereafter. Yet not all ancient Jewish texts and models of prayer known to us provide evidence relevant to the prayer of Jesus' first followers or that of the earliest church. Since Judaism, like Christianity, has changed over time, rabbinic materials from later centuries such as the Mishnah, and even more so the Talmuds, show how certain strands of Jewish prayer developed alongside distinctive Christian practice (and sometimes in conversation with it) but do not directly reveal its sources.

Jewish Prayer and Christian Prayer

The Acts of the Apostles depicts the first Christian believers sharing in specific patterns of prayer, among a characteristic set of communal practices: "the apostles' teaching and fellowship . . . the breaking of bread and the prayers" (2:42). The depiction in Acts (2:42; cf. 1:14) of the first Christians sharing together in "*the* prayers" already suggests something more than prayer in general.

However, the same sources also have the first Christians continuing in wider observances in common with (other) Jews. They are depicted as going to the temple to pray after becoming believers in the crucified and risen Lord (Luke 24:53; Acts 2:46). In one instance, the apostles Peter and John are depicted "going up to the temple at the hour of prayer, the ninth hour" (Acts 3:1 AT), implying not just that the temple was a convenient or appropriate place but that they joined in collective prayers held at that time in connection with daily sacrificial offerings.[1] Christians also seem to have continued to participate in synagogue assemblies (Acts 9:20; 13:14–45), but these were not necessarily the normal place for daily prayers; if attendance at the temple for daily prayer was impractical for many pious Jews, home was the likely alternative venue.[2]

Since first-century Judaism itself was diverse, and its forms of prayer reflected this variety, different elements of communal prayer need not have been in great tension for these first believers in Christ. The mere fact of distinctive prayers for an(other) identifiable movement—including in this case a focus on the person and work of Jesus—was not necessarily so remarkable.

Some features of the Jewish prayer shared by these first Christians in home or temple are well attested. A pattern of prayer in the morning and the evening, prescribed already in Deuteronomy (6:7), centered on the formula known by its opening in Hebrew as the Shema ("Hear"): "Hear, O Israel: The LORD is our God, the LORD alone. You shall love the LORD your God with all your heart, and with all your soul, and with all your might" (Deut. 6:4–5). Jewish authors of the first century confirm the importance of prayer at morning and evening (see Philo, *Spec. Laws* 4.141; *Contempl. Life* 27; 1QS X, 10; cf. Josephus, *Ant.* 4.8.13 §212). Later, the Mishnah explicitly links this twofold pattern with the recitation of the Shema (*m. Ber.* 1.4), and this may already have been the case in the first century too.

Morning and evening were not the only recognized times set for prayer; the midafternoon "ninth hour," at which Peter and John went to the temple (cf. Acts 10:30), was the time the "evening" sacrifice was really offered (Josephus, *Ant.* 14.4.3 §65).[3] Even after the destruction of the temple, both Jews and Christians

---

1. Daniel K. Falk, "Jewish Prayer Literature and the Jerusalem Church," in *The Book of Acts in Its Palestinian Setting* (Grand Rapids: Eerdmans, 1995), 267–301.

2. Ibid., 274.

3. Josephus is not referring to a supposed change of time, but elsewhere refers to this really as at the "closing" of the day; see *Ant.* 3.10.1 §237; cf. *m. Pesaḥ.* 5.1.

would continue to see the real or supposed times of those cultic offerings as appropriate for prayer. The sentiment linking sacrifice and prayer is familiar from Psalm 141: "Let my prayer be counted as incense before you, and the lifting up of my hands as an evening sacrifice" (v. 2). The most common patterns in first-century Judaism may therefore have been private or domestic morning and evening prayers, and public prayers related to the twice-daily offerings for Jerusalemites.[4] This mixture of patterns may help explain the appearance of a threefold structure—of morning, daytime, and evening prayer—attested in the book of Daniel (6:10) and the apocryphal *2 Enoch* (51:5).[5]

The brief Shema was the center of such prayer rather than its whole. Some Jews apparently recited the Ten Commandments with it (*b. Ber.* 21a). The elaborate prayer known as the Tefillah ("the Prayer"), an expanded Shema with attached petitions or blessings (*berakot*), was also emerging during the first century, but was not a universal or fixed formula in Jesus' time. Such blessing prayers of *berakah* type are very prominent in rabbinic texts and much older than them, emerging already in biblical texts (Gen. 24:27, etc.). They tended to have the form "Blessed be the LORD," followed by naming some basis for the blessing, such as recollection of God's gracious actions.[6] The early evidence from the rabbis indicates how this form developed in their distinct strand of Judaism in the first and second centuries, but that cannot be assumed to reflect the typical experience of all praying Jews at the time of Jesus or Paul.[7]

Another form of prayer was based on thanksgiving, praise, or acknowledgment, expressed as direct address to God, as in: "I thank you" and similarly (see Ps. 138). These *hodayot* (from *hodah*, "to give thanks" or perhaps "acknowledge" or even "confess," hence "thanksgiving," *hodayah*) were also found in biblical and early Jewish contexts. A whole collection of *hodayot* was found among the Dead Sea Scrolls (1QH[a] and other manuscripts), which probably reflect the concerns and practices of the sectarian Essene community. The prominence of thanksgiving in early Christian prayer (on which more below) confirms that similar themes and forms were important to the origins of specifically Christian practice.

Such prayer was normally performed standing (see Luke 18:11; cf. *m. Ber.* 3.5), with hands outstretched (1 Tim. 2:8). New Testament texts depicting the

---

4. Falk, "Jewish Prayer Literature," 297.

5. *2 Enoch* is a work of uncertain date; its pattern could also reflect Christian influence.

6. Bradshaw, *Daily Prayer*, 1–11; Bradshaw, *Search for the Origins*, 39–44.

7. Ruth Langer, "Early Rabbinic Liturgy in Its Palestinian Milieu: Did Non-Rabbis Know the *Amidah*?," in *When Judaism and Christianity Began: Essays in Memory of Anthony J. Saldarini*, ed. Alan J. Avery-Peck, Daniel J. Harrington, and Jacob Neusner (Leiden: Brill, 2004), 2:423–39.

prayers of those in desperate need suggest that kneeling was also well known but was specific to such situations rather than the everyday practice (Acts 9:40).[8]

Jesus and Prayer

Jesus' own prayer was quickly identified as a model by his followers. While ancient commentators, like more recent ones, reflected on various aspects of the practice and theory of prayer attributed to Jesus in the Gospels, the "Lord's Prayer" (Matt. 6:9–15; Luke 11:2–4) was generally seen as the most important part of this teaching.

There are parallels between the petitions of the Lord's Prayer and the eighteen blessings (*Shemoneh Esreh*) added to the Shema to make up the Tefillah, as well as the prayer known as Kaddish prominent in later Judaism; both emphasize the praise of God and the acknowledgment of God's holiness. The Lord's Prayer is not derived from these, however, but reflects a shared milieu, at least with the Tefillah; the Kaddish is attested only much later.

The first readers of the Gospels did not think of the Lord's Prayer primarily as a model or primer *about* prayer, although it may have been that too; for them, the first point was actually to *say* it. This was already explicit in the teaching from the Sermon on the Mount in Matthew, where the set prayer is contrasted with the "heaping up of words" (6:7). Jesus' example and teaching also reflect concern for the communal dimension of prayer and for the role of the temple (Mark 11:17 and parallels; Luke 2:17; 18:10), as well as a more solitary aspect (Matt. 6:5–6; cf. Mark 1:35; Luke 5:16). Both of these strands, public and private, were pursued in subsequent Christian practice.

Both the differences and the similarities between the Matthean and Lukan versions of the Lord's Prayer are noteworthy; the pithier version in Luke might well reflect an original form, the longer one in Matthew may come closer to the original language (granted it would be a Greek rendering of an Aramaic original).[9] Yet we may not need to think of a single "original"; beyond those two obvious canonical types, actual Gospel manuscripts provide as many as six different versions.[10] The form of the Lord's Prayer in the early Christian compilation of regulations for church life known as the *Didache* is quite like

8. L. Edward Phillips, "Prayer in the First Four Centuries A.D.," in *A History of Prayer: The First to the Fifteenth Century*, ed. Roy Hammerling (Leiden: Brill, 2008), 48–49.

9. John P. Meier, *A Marginal Jew: Rethinking the Historical Jesus*, vol. 2, *Mentor, Message, and Miracles*, ABRL (New York: Doubleday, 1994), 291–301.

10. D. C. Parker, *The Living Text of the Gospels* (Cambridge: Cambridge University Press, 1997), 49–74.

the version of Matthew's Gospel, but probably reflects the prayer as said in the compiler's own community. These differences of detail, on the one hand, and the similarity of core, on the other, are both important indicators of the significance and use of the prayer in the earliest decades. Diversity provides evidence that the Lord's Prayer was widely used and that communal use provoked adaptations to liturgical texts, then as now; commonality confirms the very wide use and importance attributed to the prayer and the author.

Times of Prayer

The Acts of the Apostles describes the first Christians praying, alone or together, at specific times (10:9; 12:5; 16:25). We cannot be sure whether Acts reflects a pattern for many Christians, or if these times have more to do with the account of the early Jerusalem community, and reflect the significance of the temple for that particular group. Another very early but partial account is that of Pliny the Younger, whose inquisition into Christian practice indicates that there was a morning assembly of some kind including prayer and praise,[11] in addition to the eucharistic meal; no other times of prayer are mentioned (*Letters* 10.96).

Many of the earliest Christians, like (other) Jews, certainly saw prayer as something to be performed a certain number of times during the day, and that number was often three. Again and again in the ancient sources, one version or another of the same pattern occurs: morning prayer, midday prayer, and afternoon or evening prayer. The precise origin of this pattern is unknown—it is attested before the emergence of a distinctive Christian community—and as we will see, there were variations.[12]

Different theological connections would later be made with one "hour" of prayer or another, but these are later interpretations of the expected times rather than their real origins. The use of prayer as a means of structuring the day could be seen as a sort of prayer "without ceasing" (1 Thess. 5:17; see Clement of Alexandria, *Strom.* 7.7) or as expectation of the kingdom of God.[13] While an earnestness about disciplined and regular prayer is apparent in many cases, the times themselves make more sense as a desire to interpret the day itself, not least its natural patterns of light and dark, as a sign of God's power

11. Specifically an "oath," which some scholars have associated with baptism; see Alistair Stewart, "The Christological Form of the Earliest Syntaxis: The Evidence of Pliny," *Studia Liturgica* 41, no. 1 (2011): 1–8.

12. J. H. Walker, "Terce, Sext and None: An Apostolic Custom?," in *Studia Patristica 5* (Leuven: Peeters, 1962), 206–12.

13. Bradshaw, *Daily Prayer*, 37–39.

and presence.[14] Here (as often) the practice itself is older than any articulation of sophisticated theological rationales.

Prayer and Fasting in the Didache

Around the end of the first century, the *Didache* provides a clearer picture of how and when one early Christian community or tradition (or some of its leaders) actually wanted its members to pray. The basic prescription is simple: say the Lord's Prayer three times a day (8.3). The times are not specified here; clearer than the "when" of prayer is the "what"—namely, the use of the Lord's Prayer. The *Didache* does not indicate whether or not these Christians actually gathered for those times; their characteristic communal assembly seems to have been for the Eucharist.

The *Didache* generally urges ritual practices comparable to Jewish ones; the lack of reference to specific times of prayer could imply these were not particularly distinctive or controversial, and that there were Jewish precedents for a threefold pattern; still, there may be an effort here to distinguish the Christian group from (for example) a twofold Pharisaic tradition marked by morning and evening prayer only, or from the dual temple-sacrifice pattern, by "outpraying" the rival group. Posture for prayer is not mentioned in the *Didache*, but the near-contemporary Clement of Rome speaks in terms of "outstretched hands" (*1 Clem.* 2.29) as does 1 Timothy (2:8), both echoing the Psalms (134:2; 141:2) and presumably showing another element of continuity with Jewish practice.

An association between prayer and fasting is common in ancient Christianity. The *Didache* proposes that its readers fast on Wednesdays and Fridays (8.1), in contrast to the Monday and Thursday fasts of unknown (but possibly Pharisaic) "hypocrites" (cf. *m. Ta'an.* 2.9). Monday and Thursday fasts seem, from the rabbinic evidence, to be understood as a means to increase or assure the efficacy of prayer. Yet the fact of fasting as an adjunct to Christian prayer appears with more persistence than consistency of reasons. Some who observed fasts on special days were apparently seeking not just effective prayer but revelations; such attempts at mystical technology were also criticized by others who saw fasting primarily as a means to saving money for charity, foregoing food to feed others (see *Herm. Sim.* 5.1). So fasting itself seems not to have a single or simple meaning, but to mark the individual or community praying as somehow set apart in a liminal state that might have different purposes or meanings but distinctive spiritual power.

---

14. Gregory W. Woolfenden, *Daily Liturgical Prayer: Origins and Theology* (Burlington, VT: Ashgate, 2004), 9–24.

Forms of Prayer

Ancient Christian prayer included both set pieces and more personal or situational compositions. Just as Jewish use of the Shema as a core in the later definitive prayer or Tefillah did not exhaust the prayers that could be offered both privately or communally, the Lord's Prayer was a core text (not merely a model) associated with and grounding other prayers. This at least is a pattern that emerges more explicitly in second- and third-century sources, and is likely to have been older.

There were other prayers, composed extempore in some cases but with recognizable forms, offered at set times and otherwise.[15] The NT writings almost certainly contain prayers and hymns that have made their way into the text; we cannot be sure of every case, but such poetic and prayerful compositions give some idea of what situational Christian prayer and praise were like.[16] The content of such prayer seems to focus on petition or intercession, on the one hand, and on praise and thanksgiving, on the other. The language of thanks or confession generally prevails over that of blessing, which we have seen coexisting in contemporary Jewish sources.[17]

Reference to Jesus and the idea that prayer was offered "through Jesus" is also characteristic of early Christian texts (Rom. 1:8; Heb. 13:21; 1 Pet. 2:5; Jude 25) and presumably therefore of the actual practice of prayer. Paul's writings also refer to prayer addressed jointly to God as Father and to Jesus (1 Thess. 3:11–13), and to Jesus particularly (Rom. 10:9–13; 2 Cor. 12:8);[18] Pliny's report on Christian practice as prayer to "Christ as God" (*Letters* 10.96) also suggests christocentric prayer or praise, recalling Jewish forms such as the *hodayah* but with a new focus.[19]

Prayer in the Second and Third Centuries

Praying in Carthage: Tertullian

Late in the second century, Tertullian provides a simple formula of Christian prayer in his commentary *On [the Lord's] Prayer*: "It is right, after rehearsing the prescribed and regular prayer [i.e., the Lord's Prayer itself] like a foundation,

---

15. Bradshaw, *Daily Prayer*, 27.

16. Bradshaw, *Search for the Origins*, 57–59; see also the discussion in chap. 4 above.

17. Bradshaw, *Daily Prayer*, 30–33.

18. Larry W. Hurtado, *Lord Jesus Christ: Devotion to Jesus in Earliest Christianity* (Grand Rapids: Eerdmans, 2005), 138–42.

19. See further Hurtado, *Lord Jesus Christ*.

to build on it a structure of other petitions for occasional needs" (10). He also indicates formal patterns for use of the Psalter with prayer, apparently the Hallel Psalms in particular, with communal responses or antiphons: "The more conscientious in prayer are accustomed to add to their prayers *Alleluia* and psalms of that type, to which those who are present may respond with the endings" (*On Prayer* 27). This exemplifies two important and persistent elements of Christian prayer: the use of the Lord's Prayer as core text, already noted, and the Psalms (or some of them) as a resource.

There were quantitative as well as qualitative considerations in Tertullian's implied readers' minds. How often do I pray, and when in particular? He at first suggests a relatively unconstrained view of the "when": "No rule at all has been laid down, except of course to pray at every time and place" (*On Prayer* 24). By lack of a "rule," however, it turns out he means not absence of norms but lack of a strict scriptural warrant for what were in fact well-established times. For Tertullian goes on to indicate that the third, sixth, and ninth hours of the day (roughly speaking 9:00 a.m., noon, and 3:00 p.m.) are useful, even though derived (in his own mind at least—a Jewish observer might have sought to correct him) from secular observances, since these "hours" may have been announced by city heralds to mark the business day in Carthage and other Roman cities; they were at least a matter of public note (cf. *On Fasting* 10). In fact, Tertullian then tries to establish that the same hours had good apostolic credentials too, related to stories in Acts (2:15; 10:9; 3:1). The result is that "we may worship not less than at least thrice a day, being the debtors of three, the Father, the Son, and the Holy Spirit, in addition of course to our proper prayers, which without any reminder are owed at the coming in of daylight and night" (*On Prayer* 25).

Tertullian thus suggests a sort of "3 + 2" pattern, where three sanctioned and shared hours of prayer—a trinitarian pattern even—complement a more personal duty of prayer on rising and retiring. Both of these have antecedents in Judaism, and it is plausible that the twofold element is actually a different version of the first and last hours of the threefold one.[20] By this time, however, they are understood as quite different in character, and Christian writers are clearly seeking to present the threefold pattern in more distinctive terms, even in relation to the threefold nature of God.[21]

20. Alistair Stewart-Sykes, "Prayer Five Times in the Day and at Midnight: Two Apostolic Customs!," *Studia Liturgica: An International Review Quarterly for Liturgical Research and Renewal* 33 (January 1, 2003): 1.

21. Phillips, "Prayer in the First Four Centuries A.D.," 44–45.

In his later work *On Fasting*, Tertullian again offers both biblical and secular reasons for a threefold pattern:

> Since in the same commentary of Luke the third hour is shown as an hour of prayer, at which time those who were initiated by the Holy Spirit were taken to be drunks; and the sixth, at which Peter went up onto the roof; and the ninth, at which they went into the temple; why then should we not understand that, without concern, we must pray always, and everywhere, and at every time of day; why, however, should these three hours, being more prominent in human affairs, and that divide the day, that order business matters, that resound publicly, not be especially solemn ones for sacred prayers? (10.3)

This time, however, he goes on to add that the ninth hour has a basis even more profound than the apostolic models he had cited years before; it was the hour of Jesus' own death (10.5; cf. Mark 15:33 and parallels). Tertullian even claims—more movingly than plausibly, perhaps—that this was why Peter himself had prayed at that time.

The fact that Tertullian was by this time part of the movement known as the New Prophecy, and hence taught and lived in some tension with what would elsewhere come to be regarded as "catholic" Christianity, does not mean his views were idiosyncratic[22]—far from it; such reflections on Jesus' passion and the hours of prayer would be elaborated over the following centuries.[23]

Tertullian sees form and content of prayer as closely related—he seems to refer to both in beginning *On Prayer*, with the idea that the new covenant offers a new "form" of prayer—not only the Lord's Prayer itself but also its own meaning, implicit teaching, and patterns of use (chap. 1). Indeed, he sees the Lord's Prayer as a summary of the whole gospel, emphasizing the will and reign of God (chaps. 4–5) as the foundation of Christian prayer and of the gospel itself. Thus he can summarize: "In 'Father' the honor of God, in 'name' testimony to the faith, in 'will' the offering of obedience, in 'kingdom' the remembrance of hope, in 'bread' the quest for life, confession of debts in deprecation, care regarding temptations in the search for protection" (chap. 9).

The Praying Body

Carthaginian Christians prayed with the whole body. Standing and kneeling were both used and had strong connotations of praise and penitence,

22. See further Andrew B. McGowan, "Tertullian and the 'Heretical' Origins of the 'Orthodox' Trinity," *Journal of Early Christian Studies* 14 (2006): 437–57.

23. For a summary of pre-fourth-century issues, see also Bradshaw, *Reconstructing Early Christian Worship*, 102–6.

respectively. Tertullian—never one to leave an opinion unclear, let alone unsaid—insists that kneeling is not appropriate either on Sundays in general or through the fifty-day period between Easter and Pentecost; this stance on standing was not a mere inherited custom but a marker of faith, a "solemnity of exaltation," the Christians' joyous insistence on their own bodies' stake in the resurrection (*On the Soldier's Crown* 3; *On Prayer* 23).

Kneeling and even prostration have his fierce support as well, however—in the right places and times. Even during periods of communal "exaltation" there was room for private "deprecation"; this included physical prostration, which he recommends at the private prayer opening the day, and kneeling during the communal prayers at times of fasting, including the "station" days (*On Prayer* 23).[24]

The erect stance with extended arms and eyes raised—referred to as *orans*, "praying"—was, however, the typical posture for prayer, found in plentiful examples in art a little after this period.[25] Although shared with other communities and traditions, it came to be interpreted in specifically Christian terms; a near contemporary of Tertullian, Minucius Felix, defends the cross itself as a Christian symbol because of its similarity to the posture of prayer: "It is a sign of the cross when someone with extended hands reveres God with a pure mind" (*Octavius* 29). Tertullian himself makes the same connection in a more sobering, even brutal, way, bearing in mind that crosses were still used when the Roman Empire punished its enemies; he says "let crosses hang us, fires light us, swords cut our throats, beasts attack; the actual stance of the praying Christian is ready for every kind of punishment" (*Apol.* 30.7).[26]

This cruciform praying body was then further marked with the cross as an additional act of physical prayer, in the gesture that has become known as the sign of the cross. Tertullian says, "At every step and stage, at every entry and exit, putting on clothes, putting on shoes, washing, dining, at evening, in bed, sitting down, wherever daily life takes us, we etch the sign of the cross into our foreheads" (*On the Soldier's Crown* 3). While the *orans* stance was an inherited and shared posture that had subsequently been interpreted by Christians in terms of the cross, this sign invisibly "engraved" into the forehead by constant use was something new, an unequivocal statement that marked the Christian's allegiance on the body as on a canvas or chattel. It may also

24. On "stations" see chap. 7.

25. Jensen, *Understanding Early Christian Art*, 35–37.

26. The threat seems to have been general rather than particular; Timothy Barnes finds no actual evidence for use of crucifixion against early Christians. See "Were Early Christians Crucified?," in *Early Christian Hagiography and Roman History* (Tübingen: Mohr Siebeck, 2010), 331–42.

have been a recapitulation of the baptismal ritual, during which such a sign was by this time being made, repeated not to doubt but to evoke and reinforce the power of the original initiatory act.

Orientation was also important to prayer; Tertullian refers to a rumor that Christians are actually sun worshipers because they pray toward the east, and implies that this relates to the sunrise (*Ad nationes* 1.13). The only possibly earlier text reflecting this practice clearly is one Tertullian knew (in some form at least) and criticized, the apocryphal *Acts of Paul*; there the apostolic hero is depicted, just before his martyrdom, praying: "Then Paul stood with his face to the east and lifted up his hands to heaven and prayed a long time, and in his prayer he shared in the Hebrew tongue with the fathers, and then stretched out his neck without speaking again" (*Acts of Paul: Martyrdom of Paul* 5).[27]

Far to the east, Clement of Alexandria provides a more explicit rationale for the same orientation, combining generally held ideas about the east as source of new light and life with his own theological emphasis on knowledge: "And since the sunrise is an image of the day of birth, and from then the light increases that first 'shone in darkness,' there has also dawned on those wallowing in ignorance a day of the knowledge of truth; in accordance with the logic of the sun's rising, prayers are made toward the breaking dawn" (*Strom.* 7.7.43). Clement is interpreting the practice rather than advocating it, so it was apparently well known and uncontroversial to him. The precise origins of turning to the east are unknown; there are, of course, many biblical images and traditions that contributed to the understandings reflected in it.[28] It may be that in fact Christians who faced the east were continuing a Jewish practice of praying toward Jerusalem, which for the Mediterranean diaspora was generally to the east (Dan. 6:10; *m. Ber.* 4.5; *t. Ber.* 3.15–16), but were reinterpreting that action in terms of a horizon less geographical than eschatological.

Praying in Alexandria: Clement and Origen

Clement knew the same three hours of prayer (third, sixth, ninth) as Tertullian, but also urged enlightened Christians to constant prayer (*Strom.* 7.7). Clement speaks of "the distribution of the hours into a threefold division, honored with as many prayers," implying that three prayers were offered at each

27. See Wilhelm Schneemelcher and R. McL. Wilson, eds., *New Testament Apocrypha*, vol. 2, *Writings Relating to the Apostles; Apocalypses and Related Subjects* (Louisville: Westminster John Knox, 1992), 216–18.

28. Uwe Michael Lang, *Turning Towards the Lord: Orientation in Liturgical Prayer* (San Francisco: Ignatius Press, 2009), 47–53.

of the prescribed times (*Strom.* 7.7.40), but says nothing of what the prayers were; the most likely explanation may be three recitations of the Lord's Prayer. Clement also advocates prayer at mealtimes, as had Tertullian (Tertullian, *On Prayer* 25; Clement, *Strom.* 7.7), indicating that this familiar Christian custom has very ancient roots—there were of course Jewish precedents too.

Clement's slightly later compatriot Origen also sees prayer as a constant activity, not just a protracted one; for him this does not mean simply praying often or at length, but suggests a disposition that extends through life, including not just devotional acts and words of prayer but ethical and just behavior:

> A person prays "without ceasing"—since the performance of actions enjoined by virtue or by the commandments is also a constituent part of prayer—who combines prayer with right actions, and becoming actions with prayer. For we can only accept the saying "pray without ceasing" as possible if we may speak of the whole life of a saint as one great continuous prayer. (Origen, *On Prayer* 12.2)

This ambitious notion also reflects the understandings of "worship" that we have noted elsewhere, as a means of referring not specifically to communal gatherings or ritual acts but to the whole of service to God. However, this notion of a "great continuous prayer" is also a stepping-off point for Origen to consider the familiar question of particular times, and some familiar apostolic examples are prominent in his answers:

> What is usually termed "prayer" is indeed a part of this prayer, and ought to be performed at least three times each day, as is plain from the account of Daniel who, in spite of the grave danger that threatened him, prayed three times daily. Peter, when he goes up to the housetop about the sixth hour to pray on that occasion when he also saw the vessel that descended from heaven let down by four corners, provides an instance of the middle prayer of the three, that spoken of by David: "In the morning shall you hear my prayer: in the morning will I present myself to you and keep watch." The last [prayer time] is indicated in the words: "the lifting up of my hands in evening sacrifice." However, we shall not spend the night properly without such prayer, as David says: "at midnight I arose to make acknowledgment to you for your righteous judgments," and Paul, as it is said in the Acts of the Apostles, along with Silas offers prayer and praise to God "about midnight" in Philippi so that the prisoners also heard them. (*On Prayer* 12.2)

So although Origen advocates "continuous" prayer, he also teaches specific prayers at morning, noon, and evening; and although he gives scriptural examples of prayer performed later at night, he offers them primarily to argue for the "last," or evening, prayer, which then allows the Christian to "spend the night properly." Of course this still allows for further prayer (since, after all, one can or should pray at all times), but it is not strong evidence for another set time of prayer in the middle of the night.[29]

Origen and Tertullian may have been reading from the same prayer book, so to speak. One difference might be that Origen places the third and last hour at the evening, rather than midafternoon, but this variance may be superficial. Not only was the "evening sacrifice" to which he refers actually offered at midafternoon (*m. Pesaḥ.* 5.1), in a world without much artificial lighting that time could really be understood as the close of the day.[30] Further, where Tertullian calls his third prayer time (the ninth hour of the day, midafternoon) the "last" (*suprema*), Origen also calls the third (evening) hour the "last" (*teleutaia*). Origen may therefore have known just the same pattern of the third, sixth, and ninth hours as Tertullian, or a slight variation, with the last of the three times closer to the evening.

But what to pray? Origen, like Tertullian, gives his expansive instruction on prayer in general when commenting on the Lord's Prayer; it was apparently recited in Alexandria, as in Carthage half a century earlier, as the core of Christian prayer at these set times. Yet Origen does not imagine even the formal times of prayer stopping with simple recitation of the Lord's exemplary text. Origen in fact offers a five-part pattern for each time of prayer, the most expansive known up to this time, with some clear indications of proper content: one should begin by glorifying God, move to thanksgiving, then confess sin, intercede, and finally ascribe praise (*On Prayer* 33). This is clearly intended as practical advice, and is accompanied by biblical texts possibly also for recitation, focused on the Psalms, as in some earlier examples.

Origen's discussion of the Lord's Prayer includes his reflection on the mysterious expression usually translated "daily" (*On Prayer* 27); the Greek text seeks from God our *epiousios* bread, which could mean something like "for time to come" or "superessential." The word, although apparently a straightforward Greek construction from common roots, is unknown before the NT

---

29. Thus also Eric Jay; see Origen, *Treatise on Prayer: Translation and Notes with an Account of the Practice and Doctrine of Prayer from New Testament Times to Origen*, ed. Eric George Jay (London: SPCK, 1954), 115–16.

30. The first-century Jewish writer Josephus, whose work Origen knew, provides evidence both for time of sacrifice and for the understanding that the ninth hour was potentially seen as the "closing" of the day in any case; see *Ant.* 14.4.3 §65; Bradshaw, Johnson, and Phillips, *Apostolic Tradition*, 214. See also, however, *Ant.* 3.10.1 §237, which indicates that this was not a question of the sacrifice being "moved."

text. Origen considers its apparent etymology and prefers one possibility—its relation to what is essential—to suggest that Christians are praying not for material bread at all but for the bread of life of John 6: Jesus himself.

Origen also resembles Tertullian in thinking of standing as the appropriate posture for prayer, but regarding kneeling as proper for confession. Strongly influenced as he was by contemporary Platonism and its priority on intellectual and immaterial things, physical posture is for Origen an expression of the inner life; the one praying should dispose the inner self first, "extending the soul before extending the hands" and "before standing, raising the mind from the earth" (*On Prayer* 31.2).

Cyprian

Meanwhile, back in Carthage, Origen's contemporary Cyprian provides further evidence for a "3 + 2" pattern of daily prayer—and yet again does so in the course of writing a commentary on the Lord's Prayer, further evidence that this remained the heart of much Christian daily prayer.

Unsurprisingly, Cyprian knows and affirms the pattern of the third, sixth, and ninth hours, and provides a near-identical set of explanations to Tertullian's related to the career of Peter, along with the additional connection between the ninth hour and the death of Jesus, familiar references to Daniel, and a link to the Trinity (*On the Lord's Prayer* 34).

But Cyprian also feels the need to reflect on the twofold pattern of prayer at dawn and dusk, as well as the three commonly observed hours during the day:

> But for us, dear brothers, besides the hours of prayer observed of old, both the intervals and the sacraments have now increased in number. For we must also pray in the morning, that the Lord's resurrection may be celebrated with morning prayer. And this the Holy Spirit once pointed out in the Psalms, saying, "My King, and my God, because to you I will cry; O Lord, in the morning you shall hear my voice; in the morning will I stand before you, and will look up to you." And again, the Lord speaks through the prophet: "Early in the morning shall they watch for me, saying, Let us go, and return to the Lord our God." Also at the setting of the sun and at the end of day, of necessity we must pray. For since Christ is the true sun and the true day, as the sun and day of this world depart, when we pray we ask that light may come to us again, we pray for the advent of Christ, which shall give us the grace of everlasting light. (*On the Lord's Prayer* 35)

Just as for Tertullian in the same city decades earlier, the pattern of three hours of prayer involved a sort of public or communal recognition. Cyprian, however, still feels the need to exhort his community to an additional set of private prayers—calling each of these observances a "sacrament," using the term more generally than later texts and authors would—aligned not with the publicly announced hours of the day but with the basic rhythms of their own waking and retiring, and of the coming of light and dark.

These further prayers at the outer edges of the day seem to be undertaken by individuals wherever they find themselves. Outwardly, at least, they are personal rather than communal, so that some can even refer to this period as an era of "private devotion."[31] Yet the middle three hours of prayer belong to a community bound together by these practices, and which does not see them as merely private efforts; thus Cyprian, for instance, says, "The Teacher of peace and the Master of unity would not have prayer to be made singly and individually, as for one who prays to pray for himself alone. . . . Our prayer is public and common; and when we pray, we pray not for one, but for the whole people, because we the whole people are one" (*On the Lord's Prayer* 8). Yet even these "public and common" three hours were not always or even typically spent in meetings of Christians but were offered by individuals—forming part of a body of the saints—wherever they happened to be.

So these writers of the late second through the mid-third centuries provide a quite consistent picture of Christian prayer, granted some variation and development. The Lord's Prayer was its center, but not its limit, and teaching about this prayer often gave rise to reflection on various issues, including and especially the proper times to say it and to pray in general. Variable wording of the Lord's Prayer, even just in Africa, confirms the "private" aspect of this common prayer—it was unlikely to have been used as a sort of choral recitation at the Christian gatherings, as in later times.[32]

And while a threefold pattern of shared prayer was widely known,[33] there was also a more private strand linked to waking and sleeping. We have also seen evidence for prayer at meals and during the night. All of these were elements of a shared Christian vocation to constant prayer, but the three daily prayer times had a special and communal character, even when not said by believers gathered in the same place.[34]

---

31. Juan Mateos, "The Origins of the Divine Office," *Worship* 41 (1967): 477.

32. Alistair Stewart-Sykes, ed., *On the Lord's Prayer* (Crestwood, NY: St. Vladimir's Seminary Press, 2004), 38–39.

33. See Walker, "Terce, Sext and None."

34. On the possible origins of a fivefold pattern, see further Stewart-Sykes, "Prayer Five Times in the Day."

Daily Prayer in the *Apostolic Tradition*

Editing Prayer

The *Apostolic Tradition* provides rich material that reflects third- or early fourth-century practice, but with some accompanying puzzles. For daily prayer, as for other Christian communal practices, it seems to gather and edit material from different sources, whether from different communities or simply reflecting the development of practice in one place across time. As a result we can see different layers or patterns in many of its materials, not least regarding communal prayer.

A first set of instructions for daily prayer begins:

> The faithful, as soon as they wake up and have risen, before beginning work, shall pray to God, and then hurry to their work. And if there is any catechesis in the word, he shall give this priority and go there and hear the word of God for the comfort of his soul. He shall hurry to go to the assembly, where the Spirit flourishes. (*Ap. Trad.* 35)

The form and significance of that teaching assembly following personal prayer is discussed elsewhere. The same instruction for morning prayer is repeated almost verbatim in chapter 41, but a longer version of the exhortation to study now appears, along with an extended explanation of the familiar third, sixth, and ninth hours:[35]

> If you are in your house, pray at the third hour and praise God. If you are in another place and that time comes, pray in your heart to God. For in this hour Christ was seen nailed to the wood. And thus in the Old (Testament) the law instructed that the showbread be offered at every hour as a type of the body and blood of Christ; and the sacrifice of the speechless lamb was a symbol of the perfect lamb; for Christ is the Shepherd, and he is also the Bread that came down from heaven.
>
> Pray also at the sixth hour. Because when Christ was attached to the wood of the cross, the day was divided and there was a great darkness. Thus they should pray a powerful prayer at this hour, imitating the cry of him who prayed and made all creation dark for the unbelieving Jews.

35. Bradshaw, Johnson, and Phillips, *Apostolic Tradition*, 48. The shift from plural to singular even within the shorter version may be a sign of a still-earlier editorial process. The shorter version (35) is preserved in the fragmentary Latin, the longer only in Sahidic (Coptic) and other translations, so it is hard to be sure whether the resolution achieved by referring to faithful men and women separately in 41 comes from the same editorial hand that added the explanation of the hours or from the Coptic translator.

> Let them make also at the ninth hour a great prayer with great praise, so
> you may know the way the soul of the righteous praises the Lord, the true God,
> who remembered his holy ones and sent his Word to them to enlighten them.
> For in that hour Christ was pierced in his side, and blood and water came out,
> and the rest of the day, he gave light until evening. Hence in beginning his sleep
> he made the dawn of another day; he completed a type of his resurrection.
> (*Ap. Trad.* 41.5–9)

We have seen that a common thread in older discussions of the hours of prayer
was the example of various biblical heroes. These models have now given way to
explanations centered on the death of Jesus himself. The theological reflection
offered by the editor who expanded the brief instruction now includes both
a pattern of reflection from the story of the passion and biblical typologies
focused on the worship of the Jerusalem temple, including the time the show-
bread was offered (see Exod. 25:30) and the curious idea of a "speechless" (or
even "irrational") lamb (cf. Isa. 53:7). There may be a connection here with the
Jewish pattern of communal prayer at times of sacrifice;[36] the appearance of
these motifs also shows that Jewish influence, and efforts made by Christians
to negotiate their relationship with that tradition, are not limited to the origins
of Christian liturgical practice but continue across the first few centuries.

Just as Origen and Tertullian had referred to the prayer of the ninth hour as
"final," and/or as of the "evening," the later version of this *Apostolic Tradition*
material links the midafternoon observance to the night and to sleep. Prayer
on actually going to bed is then also urged in far more simple terms, like the
instruction for prayer on rising, and may have been part of the older source.

The earlier version or source of the *Apostolic Tradition* (chap. 35) may have
already reflected the same synthesis that Tertullian and Cyprian make more
explicitly, of a set of personal prayers on rising and sleeping set alongside a
more public pattern of prayer at the third, sixth, and ninth hours—even if the
first two may originally have been another version of the first and third "hours"
that others were used to observing during the working day.[37] The persistence
of this linkage between the two patterns shows them as complementary but
qualitatively different forms of prayer. The forceful exhortation to the times of
quasi-public prayer in the *Apostolic Tradition* 41, added or at least expanded
by the editor, suggests that their observance was harder to maintain.

36. L. Edward Phillips, "Daily Prayer in the Apostolic Tradition of Hippolytus," *Journal
of Theological Studies* 40 (1989): 393–94. Despite some commentators' observations, there is
no particularly "sacrificial" theme extending through the interpretations here.
37. Ibid., 399.

Prayer at Night

A curious set of instructions for prayer at midnight has the complexity that is characteristic of the later editor that we have just considered:

> Rising around midnight, wash your hands with water and pray. If your spouse is present, pray together. But if your spouse is not yet a believer, go into another room to pray, and then return to bed. Do not be hesitant to pray, for one who has been joined in marriage is not impure. Those who have bathed have no need to wash again, for they are pure [cf. John 13:10]. By signing yourself with the moisture of your breath and catching your spittle in your hand, your body is sanctified, even to the feet. For the gift of the Spirit and the outpouring of washing, when it proceeds from the heart of the believer as though from a font, sanctifies the one who has believed. Thus it is necessary to pray at this hour.
>
> For those elders who handed [it] to us taught us that in this hour every creature is silent for a moment so they may praise the Lord. Stars and trees and waters stand still for an instant, and all the host of angels serving him, together with the souls of the righteous, praise God. This is why all those who believe should hasten to pray at that hour. Also testifying to this, the Lord says thus, "Behold, a cry was made around midnight, saying, 'Behold the bridegroom is coming! Arise to meet him!'" And he adds, saying, "Watch, therefore, for you do not know at what hour he is coming." (*Ap. Trad.* 41.11–16)

Just as for the daytime prayers, a mixture of theological grounds is provided; the theme of watchfulness for the bridegroom is familiar, but the tradition from the "elders" about a still point in the heavenly realm is less so.[38]

More emphatic even than the instruction to prayer itself are the pastoral admonition not to be put off by any supposed impurity from sexual activity and the instruction for another kind of embodied prayer—use of the "spirit" (breath) or spittle (water) imbued at baptism (cf. *Ap. Trad.* 20.8)—as a remedy against evil.[39] The immediate context of anxiety about sex eases the apparent contradiction between the earlier command to "wash your hands with water and pray" and the loose citation of John 13:10, which of course implies there is no need to wash.

38. Perhaps Wis. 18:14 is in mind: "while gentle silence enveloped all things, and night in its swift course was now half gone." Less likely is a proposed connection with the apocryphal *Testament of Adam*; see ibid., 397–98. There may also be a connection with the emphasis on silence in the fragmentary hymn from Oxyrhynchus, P.Oxy. XV 1786; see the discussion in chap. 4.

39. See the discussion of this confused passage in Bradshaw, Johnson, and Phillips, *Apostolic Tradition*, 204–5. The contradiction between the instruction to wash and the statement that washing is unnecessary could suggest editorial layers, but may also be a clumsy citation of John 13:11.

Hand washing as an adjunct to prayer was known elsewhere but seems to have been a patchy or even controversial practice. Decades earlier in Africa, Tertullian had dismissed it as unnecessary or superstitious, reporting skeptically that liturgical hand washers explained their scrupulosity as an imitation of Pilate's ablutions at the trial of Jesus (*On Prayer* 13).[40]

Despite the interest shown here in the passion as a basis for specifics of prayer practice, Pilate gets no mention; hand washing is assumed and passed over without comment in favor of dealing with the more pressing question of purity after sex. The Gospel text is quoted not to muddy the question of physical cleanliness but to address a concern that sexual intercourse might render prayer ineffective or improper in a subtler and more profound way than mere physical soiling; this source or editor in the *Apostolic Tradition* not only dismisses such squeamishness but also suggests ritual performances to reinforce the power of baptismal washing, which is presented as the true source of purity for the Christian. Believers are thus urged to "seal" themselves, according to some ancient versions, or perform a "consignation," both of which probably mean making the sign of the cross, to evoke their baptismal identity before praying. These physical actions were presented as helpful; by implication sexual intercourse was not a source of impurity and should not be a source of anxiety. The need for this teaching, however, reflects the fact that not all were of that opinion.

The complexity of the explanation for midnight prayer recalls the elaborated version for the three hours of daily prayer; while there could have been an ancient pattern of late-night prayer in the older source,[41] earlier material from writers such as Origen had encouraged prayer at (incidental) wakeful times in the night rather than presenting this duty in the same way as the set hours. For that matter, the three "public" hours were actually shared (even if observed alone) because these times were announced, known, and observed "communally" in a sense; but these night prayers seem more genuinely private, linked not to objective or external signs like the passage of light and dark, or public announcements of the time, but to changeable and personal experiences.

The reasons given for prayer at certain times of day and night in the church of the first three centuries are many and varied; we may need, as often, to separate reasons from origins. When a variety of explanations for a liturgical practice is given, the actual cause or origin of that practice may well be none

40. Phillips, "Prayer in the First Four Centuries A.D.," 51.
41. Paul F. Bradshaw, "Prayer Morning, Noon, Evening, and Midnight—An Apostolic Custom?," *Studia Liturgica* 13 (1979): 57–62.

of those.[42] The pattern of threefold daily prayer is arguably older than the Christian church itself, as is the twofold pattern of personal prayer at morning and night; so while neither actually needs a specifically Christian explanation, both attracted a variety of subsequent reflections. That variety reflects the richness of potential sources—Scripture, nature, and patterns of human life itself—for thinking about existence before God and about communal prayer as acknowledgment of that reality.

Prayer in the Fourth Century

The Ascetics

The emergence of an organized ascetic movement—monasticism—was to have enormous importance for the history of Christian worship and spirituality alike. Long before the fourth century, an ascetic impulse was already afoot in Christianity; while marriage and family life were usually affirmed as positive, celibacy and poverty were extolled as higher ideals, and those who embraced them as a lifestyle were honored. Those who accepted such callings held a special authority as models for prayer. The first of these monastics seem to have been women.

Communities of committed ascetic women—virgins or widows—appear even in very early texts. Widows in particular could be seen as having a vocation for prayer (1 Tim. 5:3–16). These became the first religious "order" within the Christian community, in the sense of a subpopulation with a particular role and status, and they remained so for centuries; the *Apostolic Tradition* even has to clarify that widows are not to be ordained, implying that their dignity is comparable to that of clergy (chap. 10).

Given what we have already seen about the "hours" of prayer in the third century, these ascetic women were among the most likely to fulfill the hope expressed by writers like Tertullian and Origen for continuous, or at least consistent, prayer (see also *Ap. Trad.* 23), generating a kind of sustained spiritual power in exchange for the community's economic support. This duty might often have been undertaken in a domestic setting; so the Syrian *Didascalia Apostolorum*, not far in time from the *Apostolic Tradition*, depicts the widow who "sits at home and meditates upon the Lord day and night, and, without ceasing, at all times offers intercession and prays with purity before the Lord" (3.7[15]).

42. Bradshaw, "Ten Principles," 11–12.

Prayer in the Desert

During the fourth century, ascetic tendencies in Christianity flourished, driven in part by the significant social changes during and after the reign of Constantine the Great (272–337). By the late third or very early fourth century, men as well as women seem to have been organized as communal ascetics;[43] while the roots of monasticism precede Constantine, wider toleration of Christians, and indeed some considerable material and political support for the church, meant that it had the scope to expand and to proclaim its message more freely. Without such, there could hardly have been new and large residential communities of monks or a collection of hermits large enough to make "the desert a city" (see Athanasius, *Life of Anthony* 14). Yet the growth of monasticism also reflected disquiet with what was gradually becoming a superficially "Christian" society, where the distinctiveness of authentic faith actually seemed harder to find, even in churches.

Many men and women thus sought solitude and prayer as a means to assurance of salvation; despite this retreat from the wider world, the patterns of prayer conducted away from the wider population were to become vastly influential in the rest of the Christian population.

This movement comes into focus with the activity of the Egyptians Anthony (ca. 251–356) and Pachomius (ca. 292–348), who have traditionally been seen as pioneers of solitary and communal monasticism, respectively; in fact, these men catalyzed existing patterns of ascetic life rather than invented them. The solitary monks sought to fulfill the scriptural imperative to constant prayer as literally as possible, and so their ideal pattern of prayer was not necessarily marked by observance of specific times, and was accordingly hard to document. There were, however, quasi-communities of solitaries (odd as that may initially seem) around Scetis, Nitria, and Kellis in lower Egypt who spent much time alone in their cells but also came together for certain assemblies. From reports of these, including the famous *Sayings of the Desert Fathers*, we have some idea about their patterns of praying.

These desert "fathers"—and "mothers"—seem to have offered two sets of daily prayers, early morning and late afternoon, which consisted largely of psalms. Where earlier use of the Psalter in Christian worship had centered on the use of specific psalms in communal praise, probably both at the eucharistic meal and in other prayers, the monks used the whole Psalter for a more intense sort of

43. E. A. Judge, "The Earliest Use of *Monachos* for 'Monk' (P. Coll. Youtie 77) and the Origins of Monasticism," *Jahrbuch für Antike und Christentum* 20 (1977): 72–89.

personal prayer, interpreting them as their own story; if a monk is to "take them as directed to himself, he will recognize that their thoughts were not only fulfilled once by or in the prophet's life, but that they are enacted and fulfilled daily in himself" (John Cassian, *Conferences* 10.11). This amounted to a "psalmodic movement," a new burst of interest in the use and meaning of the Psalms, that made them arguably the most popular and widely used part of all Scripture.[44]

Stories of the ascetics suggest the recitation of long series of psalms, in canonical order, for meditation. One pattern was praying the Psalms at each hour of the day and night, a logical if demanding extension of earlier forms that expressed the call to constant prayer at particular times. Reality seems to have led to these "hours" of psalmody being clumped into two groups, twelve at morning and the same at evening, marked by as many psalms.[45] Since the monks were otherwise praying at their own pace and were at different points in the Psalter at the time of this gathering, or synaxis, the twelve were probably particular psalms set for these events rather than just part of the wider pattern of continuous recitation.[46]

Like earlier forms, monastic prayer was not simply a mental exercise but involved the use of the whole body, including the voice. The quasi-communal psalmody of the desert was apparently a form of song as well as of prayer; an early monastic tourist, Palladius, likened the sound of the Nitrian monks singing to the sound of paradise (*Lausiac History* 7). John Cassian, another ascetic sightseer who sought to use the Egyptian monks' practice as a model for communities in Gaul, describes these prayers in terms that reveal their embodied character:

> When the psalm is ended they do not rush to bend the knee, as some do in this region, . . . but before they bend their knees they pray briefly, and standing spend a longer time in prayer. So after this, they prostrate themselves on the ground for a moment, as though worshiping such divine mercy, then rise together promptly again and, upright with outstretched hands, pray standing as before while remaining intent upon their petitions. . . . But when the one who is going to collect the prayer has risen from the ground they all get up similarly, so that no one would presume to bend the knee before he bows, nor to remain when he has risen from the ground, in case he is thought to have celebrated his own prayer instead of following the leader to the conclusion. (*Institutes* 2.7)

44. See in particular James W. McKinnon, "Desert Monasticism and the Later Fourth-Century Psalmodic Movement," *Music & Letters* 75, no. 4 (1994): 505–21.

45. Robert F. Taft, *The Liturgy of the Hours in East and West: The Origins of the Divine Office and Its Meaning for Today* (Collegeville, MN: Liturgical Press, 1986), 72.

46. Stig Simeon R. Frøyshov, "The Cathedral-Monastic Distinction Revisited Part I: Was Egyptian Desert Liturgy a Pure Monastic Office?," *Studia Liturgica* 37, no. 2 (2007): 198.

Although Cassian's account has been idealized and simplified for his own purposes, the general impression is clear enough, and impressive. The monks are praying, with their whole bodies, not so much as a community but as a collective self. Unlike in later forms of urban prayer, where roles were clearly defined and the diverse members of the community contributed their voices and presence distinctively, the monks of the desert immerse their individuality in a sea of prayer.

The Community of Pachomius

More communal forms of monasticism had their own liturgical observances, as well as a more clearly social orientation for prayer than their desert con-temporaries. These communities were at first prominent farther up the Nile near the ancient city of Thebes, where Pachomius established what could be called the first "monastery" in the classic sense of the word. His followers, who included women as well as men in separate establishments, lived in households within a larger ascetic community where they worked at various trades and punctuated the day with distinctive prayer.[47]

The community gathered at a morning signal for their synaxis, an assembly where work (weaving rushes into baskets, ropes, or mats) and prayer were combined. Pachomius said he had instituted this discipline to keep the ascet-ics from individualistic or self-indulgent prayer or practice ([*First Greek*] *Life of Pachomius* 38); so this was not merely a continuation or borrowing from other forms but a new way of holding individual prayer in company—"less," as one scholar has put it, "a liturgical ceremony or service than a meditation in common."[48]

The assembly focused on hearing Scripture read, interspersed with the Lord's Prayer, signing the forehead with the cross, and silence.[49] Unlike the hermits of lower Egypt, Pachomian ascetics emphasized not the Psalms per se but the memorization of Scripture in general, the literate ones such as Pachomius himself teaching others the verses (*Gr.*[1] 58; cf. 34), although the Pachomian *Precepts* (one of the early rules associated with the movement) indicates that the ascetics were encouraged to learn how to read (*Precepts* 139–40). Scripture

47. See Taft, *Liturgy of the Hours*, 62–65; and for more detail see Armand Veilleux, *La liturgie dans le cénobitisme Pachômien au quatrième siècle*, Studia Anselmiana Philosophica Theologica 57 (Rome: Herder, 1968).

48. Taft, *Liturgy of the Hours*, 66.

49. Philip Rousseau, *Pachomius: The Making of a Community in Fourth-Century Egypt* (Berkeley: University of California Press, 1985), 80–86.

was also recited at different times through the day, while coming or going from other activities (*Precepts* 28).

After that morning synaxis and a main meal, the monks worked in groups at their crafts. On some days, after a lighter evening meal, the abbot gave instruction followed by a prayer (*Gr.*[1] 77); otherwise the monks retreated to their houses for an instruction from the household leader, with discussion and the "Six Prayers," another distinctively Pachomian service consisting of portions of Scripture for meditation (*Precepts* 121).[50] Night vigils could follow, but these were a matter for individuals. Only on Sundays was actual singing of the Psalms specified (*Precepts* 15–16).

The Pachomian monks represent a midpoint between the efforts of their solitary contemporaries and the experience of other, less ascetically ambitious Christians. They spent a great deal of the day praying, so that an aspiration to "continuous prayer" is clear; but this life was also one of work and of social interaction. They were not fleeing human society as such, but recreating it. Unsurprisingly, their communal prayer was another form of the ancient pattern of prayer morning and evening, shared with Judaism and typical of the life of many Christians in the cities and villages.

The Cappadocians

The group known as the Cappadocian theologians exemplifies a different form of communal ascetic prayer life. While the Cappadocians Basil of Caesarea (ca. 329–79) and his brother Gregory of Nyssa (ca. 335–ca. 395) are the more famous siblings, along with their friend Gregory of Nazianzus (ca. 329–89), in life the brothers deferred to their sister Macrina (ca. 330–79), who presided over a kind of monastic manor house:

> She persuaded [her mother] to live on an equal footing with the servant women, so as to share with them in the same food, the same bedding, and in all aspects of life, without any regard to social standing. . . . There was no work they pursued, nothing additional, only attention to divine things and the unceasing round of prayer and endless hymnody, extending along with time itself, night and day, so that for them this was work, and work was rest. (Gregory of Nyssa, *Life of Macrina* 11)

Macrina and her companions stand in continuity with earlier communities of ascetic women such as the widows who lived in the midst of the urban church.

---

50. Armand Veilleux, ed., *Pachomian Koinonia*, Cistercian Studies Series 46 (Kalamazoo, MI: Cistercian Publications, 1980), 2:191.

Gregory's idealized biography of Macrina gives the Psalms special prominence in her own version of "prayer without ceasing":

> Nor was she unaware of any part of the writings of the Psalms, but at set times she recited every part of them. When she rose from bed, or engaged in household duties, or rested; when she took food, or left the table; when she went to bed, or rose in the night for prayer, everywhere psalmody was a good companion that never left her. (*Life of Macrina* 3)

Macrina's ancient convent may also have been influenced by the prayer patterns of the desert ascetics; Basil had visited them and sought to promote monastic life in Cappadocia. The new prominence of the Psalms (in Gregory's ideal, and presumably in some genuine sense in his sister's community) in daily prayer is one clue that these patterns are related.

Basil's own writings, as well as Gregory's biographical picture of their sister, paint a picture of a transformed community life in its original and normal setting, where family and other ties remained but were renewed. Rather than the Pachomian model of new communities or households created by monastics called away from their own lives, this was an existing household community renewed along monastic lines, and its prayer was both monastic and familial.

The City of God

The Church in the City

The change in the relationship between church and empire that had allowed (or provoked) monastic responses also made significant differences to the practice of the Christians whose lives continued more conventionally. Gatherings that had previously taken place in houses or in prosaic adapted spaces or halls could now be held in the basilica, which was a center for public business in the empire and which quickly became a model for church architecture.

Eusebius of Caesarea, a bishop and historian whose enthusiasm for the new regime and its benefits was almost unbounded, pictures the new liturgical situation:

> For the fact that throughout the whole world in the churches of God at the early rising of the sun and in the evening hours hymnody, singing of praises, and truly divine joys are offered to God, is no trivial sign of God's power. For the joys of God are the hymns sent up through the earth in his church at the morning and evening hours. Therefore it has been said somewhere "Let my praise be sweetened

for him," and again "May the lifting of my hands be an evening sacrifice," and "Let my prayer become like incense before you." (*Comm. Ps.* 64)[51]

The *Apostolic Constitutions* reflects changes in assumptions about what Christians could and should do for their daily prayers in this changed reality within the Roman Empire. They confirm not only that the new pattern of public communal prayer Eusebius implies did take hold widely but also that it had certain common elements beyond the mere fact of times of day. In this new set of circumstances, the bishop is to urge the people

> to come constantly to church morning and evening every day, and by no means to forsake it on any account, but to assemble together continually. . . . Assemble yourselves together every day, morning and evening, singing psalms and praying in the Lord's house: in the morning saying the sixty-second Psalm, and in the evening the hundred and fortieth, but principally on the Sabbath day. (*Ap. Const.* 2.59)

Today most readers and singers have Bibles using the Hebrew numbering, and thus know the psalms mentioned above as 63 and 141. Intriguingly, Psalm 141 (140) is also one of those cited by Eusebius, which suggests it was indeed widely used. Half a century later, John Chrysostom also knows the same two psalms as the core of morning and evening prayer (*Commentary on the Psalms* 140.3); he interprets them, and the times of prayer, in terms of the ancient theme of the morning and evening sacrifices of the temple.

This different use of the Psalms, focused on specific texts deemed apt for the particular time of prayer, illustrates an emerging urban pattern, different from the inexorable repetition of the whole Psalter among the desert ascetics, or even from the daunting groups of twelve psalms prayed there in common. While the monks had used their synaxes to punctuate a life wholly dedicated to prayer, and recitation of the whole Psalter (or significant other portions of Scripture) exemplified this vocation to prayer, the populations of urban churches prayed in ways that reflected the basic pattern of the day itself, taking up the natural symbolism of light and darkness. And while the monks generally used the whole collection of psalms in long sequences, only a small handful of psalms were used in these city church events, chosen for their "fit" with the time, and repeated day after day; so while the Psalter itself structured prayer in the desert, the urban liturgy interpreted and selected from the Psalter

51. PG 23:639; see further Taft, *Liturgy of the Hours*, 33–34.

to fit the day. Although in some ways perhaps new, this more selective and occasional approach to use of the Psalms is reminiscent of earlier evidence for Christian use at times of prayer.

Another striking difference between the two models involves the way community itself is figured and formed in the practices of prayer. We already saw that the monks prayed as a sort of collective person; the specific roles taken by lectors or other leaders were minimal, and clergy status played little or no part. No "props" were used, silence was valued, and the use of space itself was indifferent. In the city churches, however, something more clearly "liturgical" was emerging; roles were varied, clergy were prominent, and objects and spaces became important to the celebration.

There was, however, constant interaction between desert and city; the practices of the ascetics were influential. Athanasius' *Letter to Marcellinus* provides evidence for the centrality and popularity of the Psalter in this period. It prescribes to its recipient on his sickbed a set of psalmodic remedies that cover virtually every need and a set of occasional psalms for everything from different life experiences to days of the week:

> Do you want to give thanks on the Lord's day? You have the 24th; if on a Monday, recite what is in the 95th; and if you wish to praise on a Friday, your hymn is in the 93rd, for it was when the cross took place that the house of God was built, even though enemies sought to prevent it; and so it is proper to sing to God the words spoken in the 93rd. . . . Do you want to sing on a Wednesday? You have the 94th; for the Lord, when handed over, began to execute the judgment of death, and his glorious triumph. (*Letter to Marcellinus* [PG 27:36])

This treatise thus illustrates a meeting point between the thick recitation of the whole Psalter as a body by the ascetics and the occasional use of the Psalms by the urban Christians.[52]

Prayer in Jerusalem

The prayer of the Christianized city is portrayed with particular color and movement in the accounts of the liturgies in the great Church of the Resurrection (later known in the West as the Church of the Holy Sepulcher) built by Constantine in Jerusalem. For these we have the remarkable witness of the pilgrim Egeria, a Western ascetic who like so many others of this period was

52. See further James D. Ernest, *The Bible in Athanasius of Alexandria* (Leiden: Brill, 2004), 332–36.

drawn to the East and to places made holy both by the stories known from Scripture and from the contemporary spiritual athleticism of the nearby monks.

Egeria's account, probably from a little after 380, makes daily prayer in Jerusalem seem almost carnivalesque compared to prayer in the desert:

> Every day before cockcrow all the doors of the *Anastasis* are opened, and all the monks and virgins (as they call them here), and not they alone but laypeople as well, men and women, who desire to keep a vigil early, go there. And from that hour until it is light, hymns and psalms are sung responsively and antiphons similarly; and prayer is made after each of the hymns. For presbyters in twos or threes, and similarly deacons, and monks take it in turn every day to say prayers after each of the hymns or antiphons. But when day breaks they begin to say the morning hymns. Then the bishop arrives with the clergy and immediately enters into the cave, and from within the rails he first says a prayer for all; he commemorates those names he wishes; he then blesses the catechumens. Then he says a prayer and blesses the faithful. And after this as the bishop is going out from within the rails, everyone approaches his hand, and he blesses them one by one as he goes out, and thus the dismissal takes place by daylight. (Egeria, *Journal* 24.1–2)

Perhaps because of the presence of so many ascetic pilgrims and residents in and near Jerusalem, a similar (but less emphasized) set of prayers was also offered at the sixth and ninth hours, although this pattern was not widely followed.[53] The evening prayers, however, were more elaborate:

> Now at the tenth hour, which they call here *Lychnikon*, or as we say "Lamplight" [*Lucernare*], all the people similarly assemble at the *Anastasis*, and all the candles and tapers are lit, and there is a great light. The light is not brought in from outside, but taken forth from the cave, where a lamp is always burning day and night—that is, from within the rails. The lamplight psalms and antiphons are also said, lasting for a considerable time. Then the bishop is summoned, and he comes and takes a raised seat, and likewise the priests sit in their places, and hymns and antiphons are said. And when these have been recited according to custom, the bishop rises and stands before the rails—that is, before the cave—and one of the deacons makes the commemoration of individuals as is customary. And as the deacon pronounces each name individually, many little boys standing by answer with loud voices "*Kyrie eleison*," or as we say, "Lord, have mercy." And when the deacon has finished all that he has to say, first the bishop says a prayer and prays for all, then all pray, both the faithful and

---

53. Taft, *Liturgy of the Hours*, 51.

catechumens together. Again the deacon sends forth his voice and, wherever they
are standing, each catechumen bows, and so the bishop standing says a blessing
over the catechumens. Again prayer is made, and again the deacon sends forth
his voice and bids all the faithful, where they stand, to bow; again the bishop
blesses the faithful and thus the dismissal takes place at the *Anastasis*. (Egeria,
Journal 24.4–6)

This is a complex and vibrant set of rituals, with roles not only for bishop,
clergy, and laypeople but also for children as well as adults, and for ascetics as
well as those living and working in more conventional ways in the city. Space
itself has become important here too; the use of the "rails," or *cancelli*, reflect
the growing sense of ordered sacred space within the church, driven in this
case partly by the presence of the cave with the tomb of Jesus but also, as in
other churches, by the celebration of the Eucharist.[54]

Last but not least, objects have also become part of prayer: the light itself—
here the particular light kept burning in the Holy Sepulcher but elsewhere a
lamp of some type—becomes a central part of the ritual, its lighting recalling
earlier Jewish (and pagan) ceremonies of evening illumination.[55] The novelty
here for the Christians is not the lighting of lamps itself but what was effectively a transfer of the procedure from the communal suppers, whose relevance
to the whole community had been challenged over the previous century, to
another form of assembly.

A surprising omission, however—if perhaps less so, after our considering
of reading above—is Scripture itself. Although the Psalms are used, apparently
as a form of hymnody, the reading of Scripture does not seem an integral part
of these events. This does not imply a lack of interest in or respect for what
was by now a fairly well-defined canon, but shows that the event was focused
not on proclamation or education but on prayer and praise. Gatherings where
Scripture was a focus are discussed elsewhere. Egeria's account does mention
the pithy prayer *Kyrie eleison*, which would later become—still in its original
Greek—a feature of Western eucharistic liturgy, but whose earliest use seems
to have been as a response to communal prayers (cf. *Ap. Const.* 8.6.4).

The fact that assembling for prayer according to the dual pattern of morning
and evening emerged clearly, and across a wide area, as a corporate ideal for

54. See Branham, "Sacred Space."
55. There has been debate about which influence was the more important; this may reflect
assumptions that Jewish and Greco-Roman traditions were vastly different, which need not have
been the case; see Taft, *Liturgy of the Hours*, 36–37n15; cf. Gabriele Winkler, "New Study of
Early Development of the Divine Office," *Worship* 56, no. 1 (1982): 30.

urban lay Christians may be surprising given the emphasis placed on threefold daily prayer in earlier writers; but we saw that twice-daily prayer was also clearly attested in most of the same sources. While some have been tempted to read back this twice-daily pattern into greater and earlier prominence relative to the three other "hours," imagining that they were always the more basic or important pattern,[56] this urban twofold office was a striking new development in more than one respect.

While Christians had often prayed at the beginning and end of the day, the opportunity for a daily gathering for these prayers in buildings that were safe, often grand, and physically prominent in their communities was new. Eucharistic meals and catechetical or stational assemblies had previously been held only at certain times through the week, not daily, and in more private and modest settings. While the possibility of prayer at other times still existed, the new emphasis on morning and evening communal prayers became a fundamental rhythm for many Christians.

Conclusion

In and after the fourth century, a complex set of histories can be traced across Eastern and Western traditions of communal prayer; as in other aspects of worship, in having laid out the foundational elements of practice, we have come to what others may regard as the real beginning rather than an end.[57] Yet the point at which we have arrived defines the fundamental assumptions for most Christian daily prayer hereafter.

The most common typology in the study of Christian prayer from this period speaks of "cathedral" and "monastic" forms of prayer. We have seen enough to show how these are helpful ways of thinking about how different communal prayer could be, but also why they are ideal types that assist the modern interpreter, rather than fixed or clear ancient realities. Even in Egeria's Jerusalem and Macrina's Cappadocia, monastic patterns were already influencing the clergy and people of the cities, and this trend was to continue for centuries, particularly in the West through the later Benedictine tradition.

56. Some suggest the morning and evening offices are more fundamental; this depends on reading these fourth-century developments back into the earlier evidence. See Mateos, "Origins of the Divine Office," 478–79; the discussion by Woolfenden, *Daily Liturgical Prayer*, includes a synthesis of Christian thought about the pattern of the day and night.

57. See, for instance, Taft, *Liturgy of the Hours*, 219–373; Woolfenden, *Daily Liturgical Prayer*, 49–295.

Liturgists have noted (and sometimes decried) how patterns of daily prayer involving extensive use of the Psalms in meditative course—a direct inheritance from the desert—prevailed in the cities of the West over the color and movement, and simpler repetitive content, of the "cathedral" or urban model that could arguably have better served the inhabitants of later cities too.[58]

Liturgists have often wanted to find a "core" in and across this early complexity of communal prayer; again and again, scholarly discussions reveal a desire either to find a fundamental *ordo*, a single motive for complex patterns, or something that represents a "pure" or original form of Christian daily prayer. These quests are understandable but hard to combine with taking the whole diverse reality of early Christian prayer seriously. To find any such supposed touchstone is actually to choose one element and to relativize others; such decisions tend to reflect our theological commitments, which may themselves be more or less defensible, but do not emerge via immaculate conception from the messier history of the church itself.

This is not to say that the history of early Christian prayer is a wasteland for those seeking inspiration or instruction for their own choices and opportunities for prayer and worship. It would better be characterized as a rich and varied landscape that offers different vistas or standpoints than as a single or simple picture that merely needs to be retrieved from complexity by excision of extraneous elements.

In some instances we find individuals sharing in an invisible but deeply felt unity of daily prayer that is reflective and meditative in character; in others, vibrant communal gatherings are the heart of such observances. In some cases Christians use Scripture, and in particular the Psalms, as a means to impose meaning on the patterns of light and day, waking and sleeping; in others, the rhythm of life suggests a means for selecting and interpreting the Psalter. Within this diversity, the reality of prayer as a pattern, a structured reality, and a discipline that is related to rhythms of daily life is among the clearest features.

Besides this basic fact of Christian prayer as a way to offer divine structure to the lived reality of daily time, the centrality of the Lord's Prayer and the Psalter are the most consistent and distinctive elements of ancient Christian practice. The words of Jesus in the Lord's Prayer were certainly taken to inform the prayer of the early Christians, but they also constituted a sacred text—no more absolutely fixed, admittedly, than other sacred texts in the ancient church, although older than most of them—to which Christians persistently submitted their varied personal needs and circumstances. The Psalms, too, were valued not

---

58. Paul F. Bradshaw, *Two Ways of Praying* (Nashville: Abingdon, 1995).

merely as "biblical" but as expressing uniquely a range of human experience and emotion, and when (as often) interpreted christologically, they were read as reflecting the life of what Augustine called the *totus Christus*, the church and its head singing praise to God together.

These set and sacred texts, or at least their use as actual forms of prayer and not merely as messages or models, sit awkwardly with some modern practices and assumptions about prayer as best when "personal" and spontaneous; but the diversity of their uses resonates with attempts in contemporary worship settings to take questions of culture and locality seriously.

7

TIME

Feasts and Fasts

> For what is time? Who can easily and briefly explain it? Who
> even in thought can comprehend it, even to the pronouncing
> of a word concerning it? (Augustine, *Conf.* 11.14.17)

Few Christians have reflected on time as profoundly as Augustine, but all have faced persistent and difficult questions about how to inhabit it. Augustine wrote his reflection amid the daily, weekly, and yearly life of a church that he saw as a pilgrim on a journey through history. Since the flow of time characterizes life and history itself, the approach that the early Christians took to their days, weeks, and years was fundamental to the expression and creation of their identity.

The day itself, the most basic unit of time, particularly for those who must work to survive on a daily basis (cf. Matt. 20:1–15), has already been considered in relation to daily prayer. Prayer was a means to inhabit time itself and to claim its meaning for the One whose gift every day was. While daily prayer has become a purely personal matter in most modern settings, contemporary Christians are still familiar with other constructions of time that stem from ancient practice. Sunday is the most widely observed of these, but early Christians saw other days of every week as having particular significance too. The

217

year and its cycles also became a medium for the expression of hope and repentance, and the most fundamental feasts and fasts of the historic Christian
year arise in these first few centuries.

None of these elements, however—Sunday included—were always and
immediately obvious to the first generation or two of Christians. Yet none of
them emerged from nowhere or was merely imposed arbitrarily or through
some external authority. Rather, the development of Christian time is an increasingly detailed affirmation of how the structure of history, and of the
cosmos in and through which history flowed, reveals and serves God and calls
humans to God's service.

Sunday[1]

The Lord's Day

The resurrection of Jesus was generally and clearly remembered as taking
place on the "first day of the week" (Mark 16:2 and parallels; John 20:1); a
century or so later, this founding event was believed to underlie a tradition
of meeting and celebrating on Sundays. Yet the emergence of Sunday as a
characteristic observance is not straightforward, or at least not as clear as we
might otherwise expect.

Before Sunday there was the Sabbath. The very first Jewish Christians, and
many more at least for some years, would have observed the Sabbath, presumably with a festive meal on the Friday evening, when the Sabbath began according to Jewish reckoning.[2] Jesus' own attitude toward the Sabbath comes to
play a part in later arguments about its observance. The Gospel controversies
over the Sabbath (Mark 2:23–3:6 and parallels) reflect debate over its meaning,
not any implied rejection by Jesus; yet by the time these stories were written,
they may well have become fuel for the fire of more radical debates, and for
gentile Christians' justification of a different approach.

The Pauline Letters criticize anxiety about specific times related to the Jewish
calendar, including Sabbaths, but are silent about Sunday (Gal. 4:8–11; Col. 2:16).[3]

1. See further Paul F. Bradshaw and Maxwell E. Johnson, *The Origins of Feasts, Fasts,
and Seasons* (Collegeville, MN: Liturgical Press, 2011), 3–13.
2. William Horbury, "*Cena pura* and Lord's Supper," in *Herodian Judaism and New
Testament Study*, WUNT 193 (Tübingen: Mohr Siebeck, 2006), 104–40.
3. Sunday evenings are not likely to have been times for meeting; see Richard Bauckham, "The
Lord's Day," in *From Sabbath to Lord's Day: A Biblical, Historical, and Theological Investigation*, ed. D. A. Carson (Grand Rapids: Zondervan, 1982), 234–35.

Yet there are hints that Sunday could have been significant to Christ-believers (or some of them) from very early times: Paul advocates that each person set aside money for the poor on the first day of the week (1 Cor. 16:1–3), and Acts depicts the community at Troas gathering for "the breaking of the bread" on the first day of the week when Paul came and spoke to them (Acts 20:7–12).

These traces of possible interest, combined with a strong communal memory, reflected in the Gospels, of the "first day of the week" as the day of the resurrection, may have evolved to become the Sunday observance that appears clearly by the second century.[4] The *Letter of Barnabas* (ca. 100 CE) provides the oldest indisputable reference for this celebration, seeing Sunday as an "eighth day" linked to the resurrection of Jesus but also rejecting Sabbath observance:

> Furthermore [God] says to them, "Your new moons and the Sabbaths I cannot tolerate." Do you see how he speaks? "The Sabbaths are not acceptable to me, but that which I have made, in which giving rest to all things I will make the beginning of an eighth day, which is the beginning of another world." Therefore we also celebrate the eighth day with gladness, in which also Jesus rose from the dead and, being revealed, ascended into heaven. (*Barn.* 15.8)[5]

The apocryphal *Gospel of Peter*, also from the mid-second century, is the earliest text that clearly identifies Sunday as "the Lord's day," specifically because it was the day of resurrection (*Gos. Pet.* 35, 50). Other and earlier uses of "Lord's day" or merely "Lord's" are often assumed to mean Sunday also. The seer John was "in the Spirit on the Lord's day [*kyriakē hēmera*]" (Rev. 1:10). This could perhaps be an eschatological "day of the Lord" (cf. Jer. 46:10) to which John has been miraculously transported for his visions, but the fact that the same phrase does mean "Sunday" just a little later makes it likely that it does here too. However, the idea that the Revelation to John has a communal and liturgical setting, reflecting a "Sunday service" of some kind, is hard to reconcile with the idiosyncratic and ecstatic character of its visions.[6] The book does use motifs drawn from the temple liturgy and might contain smaller units that reflect prayer or praise in actual Christian assemblies; it was certainly read in them.[7]

4. Willy Rordorf, *Sunday: The History of the Day of Rest and Worship in the Earliest Centuries of the Christian Church* (London: SCM, 1968).

5. On the date and setting of *Barnabas*, see James Carleton Paget, *The Epistle of Barnabas: Outlook and Background* (Tübingen: Mohr Siebeck, 1994).

6. Bradshaw, *Search for the Origins*, 57–58.

7. David L. Barr, "The Apocalypse of John as Oral Enactment," *Interpretation* 40, no. 3 (1986): 243–56.

The *Didache* instructs its readers to gather on (or "according to") "the Lord's [something] of the Lord," an opaque phrase to say the least. There are other possible meanings for the ellipsis other than "day," such as "according to the Lord's [teaching?] of the Lord."[8] Certainly some command or example from Jesus is being invoked, and since the *Didache* is concerned with the observance of some days (see below on the set days for fasting), a reference to Sunday is possible. No comparison or contrast is made with the Sabbath, which may also have been observed by this community.

Sabbath and Sunday

The emergent Christian celebration of Sunday looked over its shoulder to the ancient Sabbath. Although its biblical origins have to do with rest rather than space for communal gatherings, by the first century some Jews were indeed gathering on the Sabbath (as well as on other days) for prayer and especially for the reading and study of Torah. Meals that commemorated the day of rest probably had a more domestic than communal focus.[9] Evidence in Judaism for a more developed Sabbath gathering that can better be described as "liturgy" is later, however. So the developing Christian and Jewish liturgical traditions and their uses of Sabbath and Sunday are better seen as taking their bearings from one another; the Jewish tradition in later form does not precede or explain Christian practice.[10]

Later in the second century, Ignatius of Antioch spoke of early Christians, who "overturning the old things came to the possession of a new hope, no longer observing the Sabbath, but living according to the Lord's [day?], in which also our life sprang up again because of him and his death" (Ign. *Magn.* 9.1). The elliptical phrase about the Lord is the same one as in the *Didache*, urging life "according to" that Lordly principle rather than just celebrating "on" it. Although it could imply "teaching" (or "life," as one manuscript suggests), Ignatius' argument with the Sabbath suggests he was making a point

8. Samuele Bacchiocchi, *From Sabbath to Sunday: A Historical Investigation of the Rise of Sunday Observance in Early Christianity* (Rome: Pontifical Gregorian University, 1977), 114n73.

9. See for instance Philo of Alexandria, *Life of Moses* 2.16; *That Every Good Man Is Free* 81–82; *On the Contemplative Life* 30–32; and the Qumran *Songs of the Sabbath Sacrifice*. See the discussion in van der Horst, "Synagogue a Place of Sabbath Worship?," responding to Heather A. McKay, *Sabbath and Synagogue: The Question of Sabbath Worship in Ancient Judaism* (Leiden: Brill, 1994).

10. Attempts have been made to argue for the early character of Sabbath worship based on the evidence for weekly Christian meetings; see van der Horst, "Synagogue a Place of Sabbath Worship?" The problem with this should be evident.

about time.[11] The reference to "our life [that] sprang up" may allude to how Romans associated the first day of the week with the sun—on which we will see more in due course.

Where the Jewish-Christian *Didache* did not dismiss or even mention the Sabbath, Ignatius reflects a clearly gentile context and an explicitly supersessionist worldview; these two days are exclusive alternatives, and their observance marks out each community. While such Christian references to Sabbath and Sunday together emphasize contrast and competition, rather than imitation or derivation, Ignatius' energetic protest does little to dispel the suspicion that a certain amount of imitation was involved; still, two patterns regarding Sabbath and Sunday, of "both-and" (*Didache*) and "either-or" (Ignatius), may themselves have persisted and competed for some time.

While some of these early texts seek to establish Sunday as an alternative to the Sabbath, this does not shed much light on the origin of Sunday observance as such. The idea that Sunday is a "Christian Sabbath" grows along with anti-Jewish polemic, but it does not explain the origin of Sunday or offer much help determining exactly *how* Sunday was kept. The emerging Christian pursuit of Sunday as an "anti-Sabbath" has curious implications, even to advocacy of ostentatious busy-ness on Saturday so as to avoid any accidental appearance of observing the Jewish day of rest. However, closer to 200, Tertullian still knows of some Christians in Carthage who believe that the Christian rule against kneeling on Sunday (as the day of resurrection) should apply also to the Sabbath (*On Prayer* 23.1–2), implying it, too, was a day of celebration. These African Christians held a "both-and" approach to Sabbath and Sunday but were neighbors of others who, by kneeling, were treating Saturday as a time of fasting and penitence—the "either-or" view of Ignatius.

The Day of the Sun

Justin Martyr is first to make an explicit link between Sunday and Christian meetings, in mid-second-century Rome:

And on the day called "of the sun," when all who live in cities or in the country gather in one place, an assembly occurs, and the memoirs of the apostles or the writings of the prophets are read, for as long as there is time; then, when the reader has finished, the president presents a verbal admonition and challenge to

11. Bacchiocchi, *From Sabbath to Sunday*, 214–18; Clemens Leonhard, *The Jewish Pesach and the Origins of the Christian Easter: Open Questions in Current Research*, Studia Judaica Bd. 35 (New York: Walter de Gruyter, 2006), 124–29.

the imitation of these good things. Then we all rise together and offer prayers, and, as we said earlier, when the prayer is ended, bread is offered, and wine and water, and the president similarly offers prayer and thanksgiving, according to his ability, and the people agree, saying Amen; and there is a distribution and participation for each from that for which thanks have been given, and it is sent to those who are absent by the deacons. (*1 Apol.* 67.3–5)

Given the association already made between Sunday and Eucharist in the *Didache* (not to mention Paul's Sunday meeting at Troas), Justin confirms that the purpose of Sunday was not just "meeting" as such—the idea of a generic "service" does not really exist at this point—but for the eucharistic meal in particular.

Sunday and its meal gatherings could be marked by other celebratory habits or bodily performances, explicitly contrasting it with times of penitence or fasting. Tertullian says, "We moreover, just as we have received it, ought to refrain not only from [kneeling] but from every attitude and practice of duty on the day of the Lord's resurrection, even putting off business in case we give opportunity to the devil" (*On Prayer* 23.2). The explicit basis for the observance of the first day in the earliest Christian sources had to do with history and the resurrection, and if there were a cosmic dimension it had to do not so much with the origins of this world but with the "new creation" of the "eighth day" (thus the *Letter of Barnabas*).

Justin gives a number of reasons for observance of this communal holy day and takes a bold step that would remain important, if controversial: "We all hold our common assembly on the day of the sun because it is the first day, on which God, having redirected darkness and matter, made the universe; and Jesus Christ our Savior on the same day rose from the dead" (*1 Apol.* 67.7). Justin's opportunistic reference to the "day of the sun"—a standard but not particularly ancient Greek or Roman label, wherein the days of the week were aligned to "planets" as then understood[12]—hints at a Christian view of time and the cosmos focused on origins and repeated cycles, not just on apocalyptic disruptions and ends. Justin's *First Apology* was itself couched as a defense of the Christians to the emperor, and throughout he takes hints from nature and culture alike that suggest a divine and Christ-oriented order underlying all of reality. In his other major work, constructed as a dialogue with a thoughtful

12. There is a helpful discussion of the introduction of the week itself and of the planetary designations for days in S. R. Llewelyn, *New Documents Illustrating Early Christianity: A Review of the Greek Inscriptions and Papyri Published in 1986–87* (Grand Rapids: Eerdmans, 2002), 113–17.

Jew, Justin also emphasizes the relationship with the Sabbath and the "eighth day" (*Dial.* 23).

Yet the coincidence of Roman and Christian understandings that was a short step from this kind of "natural theology" was seen as a liability by others; Tertullian, for instance, felt that he had to distinguish Christian observance from sun worship (*Apol.* 16.9–11; *Ad nationes* 1.13), not only because of the commonality of day but because of the Christian custom of praying toward the east. The importance of sun worship in Roman religion has been exaggerated in some accounts of how Christian views of time emerged, but it did exist; and by the fourth century, correlations between Sunday and other feasts with aspects of solar cults had become a positive thing for some Christians, a fulfillment of pagan precedents as well as Jewish ones. Eusebius of Caesarea, the emperor Constantine's biographer, thus waxes eloquent:

> The Word transferred and established the celebration of the Sabbath to the rising of the Light. He gave us a symbol of the true rest, . . . the Lord's and first day of light. . . . In this, day of light, first day and true day of the sun, when we gather after six days, we celebrate the holy and spiritual Sabbath. (*Comm. Ps.* 91)[13]

Constantine made Sunday a civic observance, according to Eusebius:

> Accordingly he legislated for all the citizens under Roman rule to observe rest on days named for the Savior, and similarly those preceding the Sabbath; in memory, I think, of what the universal Savior is recorded to have achieved on those days. And teaching all the military through zeal to honor the day of salvation, which is named for light and the sun, he granted leisure to those among them who were partakers of the divine faith, freely to accomplish their prayers without any impediment. (*Life of Constantine* 4.18)

Despite some uncertainty about its importance in the first few decades after Jesus, Sunday soon found a familiar place in the lives of Christian communities. It seems to have involved the celebration of the eucharistic meal, perhaps held on Saturday nights (counted as the first part of Sunday by Jewish reckoning) at first, thus not competing with but complementing Sabbath observance for Jewish Christians and others inclined to see the two days as complementary. The shift of the meal from an evening event to a morning one, from Saturday night to Sunday morning in modern terms, was arguably the origin of Sunday "worship" in the now-familiar sense.

13. PG 23:1169.

Fast Days[14]

Wednesdays and Fridays

Sundays were thus a focal point of the week for Christians from a very early point, but other days of the week also had special associations. Eusebius, we just saw, had lauded Constantine's magnanimity in making Friday as well as Sunday available for special observances. Some of these other weekly practices are more clearly attested in the earliest Christian literature than Sunday itself.

The *Didache* calls for fasting on Wednesdays, as well as on Fridays: "Your fasts must not be the same as those of the hypocrites. They fast on the second day after Sabbath [Monday] and the fifth [Thursday]; you should fast on the fourth [Wednesday] and on 'preparation' [Friday]" (*Did.* 8.1). Monday and Thursday were market days, used for occasional fasts in times of need by pious Pharisees (see *m. Ta'an.* 1.6; 2.9; *m. Meg.* 3.6; cf. Luke 18:12). It is usually assumed that the *Didache* is referring to weekly fasts, but this is not the only possible interpretation; it may be instructing along the lines of "when you do fast . . ."[15] The Christians of the *Didache* were by the standards of the time, and in their own eyes, just as Jewish as their "hypocritical" neighbors and rivals; different days for fasting here serve to distinguish two factions rather than two religions.

Wednesdays and Fridays in particular may have come to prominence because of other Jewish calendars whose holy days typically fell on these days as well as on the Sabbath, but there is no trace of this logic in the *Didache* itself;[16] in any case, to fast was generally a way to mark a day for prayer and penitence, not for celebration. In the third century, Wednesdays and Fridays came to be interpreted as reminiscences of the passion story, as were the hours of daily prayer; but at this point the choice was just about marking out life in a parallel universe to that of the "hypocrites."

The *Didache* is also characteristically taciturn about specific reasons for fasting at all. Later Christian practice comes to see fasting as a sort of workout for dealing with sin, but Jewish communal fasts had more to do with strength and fitness for prayer (especially prayer for rain; see *m. Ta'anit*). There is also

---

14. See further Bradshaw and Johnson, *Origins of Feasts*, 29–36.

15. See William Horbury, "Jewish-Christian Relations in Barnabas and Justin Martyr," in *Jews and Christians in Contact and Controversy* (Edinburgh: T&T Clark, 1998), 137–38; the Babylonian Talmud refers to a regular Monday and Thursday fast for the fulfillment of a vow by an individual, but again this is not an exact match for the "hypocrites"; see Leonhard, *Jewish Pesach*, 129–39, esp. 134.

16. Bradshaw and Johnson, *Origins of Feasts*, 29–30.

no indication of whether the *Didache* Christians met together for their fasts or observed them individually.

Stations

Weekday fasts became a widespread practice, and many Christians (even Greek speakers) adopted the Latin word *statio* as a name for them. The word is the military term for a sentry's station or "standing" at duty, and is first attested during the mid-second century in the *Shepherd of Hermas*, which was regarded as scriptural in some circles in the first few centuries. The narrator, Hermas, recounts visions of various kinds; one of them takes place while he is undertaking a *statio*, whose proper observance becomes the topic:

> While fasting and sitting in a certain place, giving thanks to the Lord for all he has done for me, I see the Shepherd sitting down beside me and saying, "Why have you come here early in the morning?" "Because, Lord," I answered, "I have a *statio*." "What is a *statio*?" he asked. "I am fasting, sir," I replied. "What is this fast," he said, "which you are fasting?" "As is customary, Lord," I reply, "so I fast." (*Herm. Sim.* 5.1)

The divine Shepherd is critical of Hermas' practice, or at least of his desultory explanation along the lines of "it's just what we do." Hermas' station was apparently not kept by all in the Christian community; for that matter it is not clear on what day this one takes place, although use of *statio* suggests something more than a purely discretionary exercise.

Given that this *statio* was a solitary duty, the Shepherd's criticism actually focuses on Hermas' lack of engagement with others' need. The heavenly herdsman urges: "In the day on which you fast, you will taste nothing but bread and water; and having calculated the price of the foods of that day that you would have eaten, you will give it to a widow, or an orphan, or to some person in need" (*Herm. Sim.* 5.3). The literal company of other spiritual sentries is not the Shepherd's point, even though he is concerned that Hermas remember those in need. Like daily prayer through this period, the *statio* was at first communally mandated but individually performed, the faster having a sense of connection to others but praying literally alone or, since of course most had to work during the day as well, in the course of their daily routine.

The Shepherd's advice to Hermas also indicates that fasting did not always mean abstinence from food; it could just mean eating differently. The appearance here of the proverbially simple "bread and water," along with concern for the needs of those who could not even assume access to that much, suggests an emphasis on simplicity. The problematic connotations of meat and wine, strongly related as they were to traditional Greco-Roman religion, would have encouraged dietary training like Hermas' to include demonstrating some independence from them. A few decades later, Tertullian considers fasts and dietary discipline as including not only food declined but also food utterly refused and food merely delayed (*On Fasting* 11.1).

Even if Hermas' "station" was observed alone, there were some gatherings on station days, probably at the beginning of the day and at the end, or at least the end of the business day at midafternoon, marking the end of the fast. Pliny the Younger, as the Roman governor of Bithynia, reported to the emperor Trajan in 111 CE that Christians in Asia Minor "were accustomed to meet on a fixed day [*stato die*] before dawn and sing responsively a hymn to Christ as to a god, and to bind themselves by oath [*sacramento*]" (*Letters* 10.96). This is not the Eucharist (despite the suggestive "sacramental" terminology) but some other sort of collective act of prayer and praise. Although usually seen as a reference to Sunday worship, the "fixed day" meeting may actually be one of the stations (note the resonance between *status*, "fixed," and *statio*); "Sunday" gatherings may really have been held on Saturday nights, and a shared commitment to fast for the day to come makes better sense of the reported "oath." Although there is too little information here to confirm it, the reference to an oath could otherwise hint at the ritual of baptism.[17]

Hermas' heavenly guide had provided advice about fasting, but there were other issues of ascetic etiquette on station days. Fasting was abstention not merely from some or all food and/or drink but from a variety of other normal processes too. Nearly half a century after the *Shepherd*, debates over proper practice in Roman Africa reveal more about how stations were observed there. Those who fasted did not bathe, for instance, and judging from one complaint of Tertullian's they did not kiss, either:[18] "Those fasting, having prayed with the brethren, withhold the kiss of peace, which is the seal of prayer. But what better time is there for bestowing peace with the brethren than when the prayer has ascended with the additional commendation of the action?" (*On Prayer* 18). Tertullian could have been referring to the Eucharist as "praying together," but this was more likely a different sort of assembly—perhaps daily prayer

---

17. See Stewart, "Christological Form." It could also have been Saturday, since some Christians certainly continued to observe the Sabbath and other elements of Jewish practice; see Bacchiocchi, *From Sabbath to Sunday*, 98–99.

18. See the fuller discussion of kissing in chap. 2.

observed communally because of the station day. So there was tension between good manners for the fasting individual, on the one hand, and the logic of the Christian gathering itself, on the other. Those fasting were as though "on retreat," to use a later term; if not physically withdrawn from regular life, their bodies were temporarily marked as different through abstinence from practices that made up the normal patterns of embodied relationship, even within the church itself.

Many Christians at Carthage felt a station should end midafternoon, at the publicly announced ninth hour, which was also the end of the business day and, as we have seen, a set time for Christian prayer. They measured its duration by the same biblical reference points used for daily prayer, specifically the time Peter and John went to the temple to pray (Acts 3:1). Presumably those observing stations and some others gathered to pray at this expected "evening" hour also. The followers of the New Prophecy, Tertullian among them, saw the *statio* as to be observed by all and as lasting until evening, thus linking it to the more solemn scriptural example of the death and evening burial of Christ (*On Fasting* 10).

By this time the eucharistic food was often being eaten outside the context of the evening banquet, privately as well as communally, even though the evening *cena* or *agapē* was still the main community gathering at Carthage. Station days were among the occasions when the Eucharist might be offered in the morning. This led to another clash of pious expectations:

> Similarly also regarding the station days: quite a few think they ought not to participate in the prayers of the sacrifices, because the station has to be broken by the reception of the Lord's body. So does the Eucharist cancel a devout service to God? Or rather, does it deepen our obligation to God? Will your station not be more solemn if you have also stood at the altar of God? By accepting the Lord's body and reserving it, both your participation in the sacrifice and your performance of your duty are safe. (Tertullian, *On Prayer* 19)

The objects of his criticism would have felt at home observing the solitary station with Hermas; but Tertullian, like the heavenly Shepherd, suggests that communal norms trump personal piety. Fasters should attend the morning eucharistic "sacrifices," but reserve the Eucharist for later consumption, and thus receive both an immediate spiritual benefit from proximity to the "sacrifices" offered at the altar of communal prayer and a delayed gratification from the sacrament itself. Tertullian does not quite make the literal identifications of "sacrifice" and "altar" with eucharistic practice that the later Carthaginian teacher Cyprian does. The "sacrifices" include eucharistic prayers but not those alone; and there is probably no intention to call a literal table the "altar" here.

Fasting for the Church

The Syrian *Didascalia*, some of whose sources may date to the third century, agrees with Tertullian and his enthusiastic allies that weekday fasts are communal disciplines, not matters of individual choice. The evidence for early Syrian communities often has a more ascetic tinge to it, and the African followers of the New Prophets may have been reflecting Eastern influence rather than just some peculiarity based on their own special revelations. The *Didascalia* also refers to widows' collective participation in weekly fasts as an expected service, implying that intercessory prayer was part of the purpose (3.8[15]).

Predictably, given developments elsewhere, the rationale for fasting in this case has shifted to the passion story. The Wednesday is now associated with Jesus' betrayal, and the Friday with his death (5.14[21]). The compilers of the *Didascalia* also give these fasts a further purpose: Wednesday commemorates when "the people" began "to destroy their souls" and betray Jesus, yet both fasts are offered "for them," an emphatic embodied prayer for the Jewish people from a place close to what had been ancient Judea.

The *Apostolic Tradition* negotiates similar tension about the division of ascetic labor within the community at weekly fasts: "Let widows and virgins fast often and pray for the church. Let elders fast when they want to, likewise the laypeople. The bishop may not fast except when all the people fast. For it happens that someone will wish to offer, and he cannot refuse. For having broken, he must partake" (*Ap. Trad.* 23.1–3). Geographical and cultural diversity is again evident here, even though we are not sure where on the map to place the *Apostolic Tradition*. Syrian Christians and the adherents of the Asian New Prophecy think of the stational fasts as universal and communal, while Westerners (Hermas, Tertullian's opponents—and perhaps the *Apostolic Tradition*?) are less rigorous but feel they must at least address the alternate view.[19]

Wednesday and Friday fasts were to continue in Christian practice; in Catholic and Eastern Orthodox churches today, fasts focus largely on moderation and/or temporary abstinence from specific food and drink, in conscious distinction from the Sunday festival. Better known perhaps and more widely observed by

---

19. Gregory Dix may have been right to see Eastern influence in the Western stations, or at least in their being a general rule rather than individually chosen; see Dix, *Shape of the Liturgy*, 342.

Christians of many traditions are those fasts and feasts that have to do with the year, to which we now turn.

Easter

A Christian Passover

Easter is the first Christian feast; like baptism, it is older than the church itself. We need no quest for the "origins" of Easter, because at least in one sense they are self-evident; we need rather to describe the processes of reception, interpretation, and transformation that lead from Jewish *Pesah* to Christian Pascha.[20]

The Christian interpretation of Passover goes back to the events retold in the NT. Jesus' death is connected to that feast in all four Gospels, granted their varied chronologies. Paul also writes to the Corinthians calling Christ a Passover lamb and exhorting them to a new sort of paschal celebration (1 Cor. 5:7–8). There was of course an existing Jewish feast centered on a paschal meal, which referred to the exodus story and to a season of unleavened bread (see Exod. 12–13). On the afternoon of the fourteenth day of the lunar month Nisan, the feast was prepared and observed through the evening and the next day, the fifteenth. This much Jesus and his followers experienced, and the first Christians did too.

Some scholars (not to mention recent Christians who have seen fit to celebrate some form of seder) assume that the Mishnah or other later rabbinic texts give an accurate picture of the first-century feast known to Jesus and his early followers.[21] However, the Mishnah as compiled is contemporary with Tertullian, not with Jesus or Paul; the seder familiar to Jews today was still in formation in Jesus' time, and the familiar Haggadah or liturgical narrative may not yet have even existed, at least in a fixed form.[22] Such ancient Jewish texts on Passover observance thus do not reveal much of the roots or the form of the Christian celebration of Jesus' passion, because they reflect later developments in Judaism.

Greater clarity about exactly what Christians did as a distinct group emerges (as often) when it becomes controversial. Unsurprisingly, the oldest account of a specifically Christian Easter celebration is set on Passover itself. The *Epistula Apostolorum* ("Letter of the Apostles"), probably from the mid-second century,

---

20. Bradshaw and Johnson, *Origins of Feasts*, 39–86.
21. Famously, Jeremias, *Eucharistic Words of Jesus*.
22. Leonhard, *Jewish Pesach*, 73–118.

depicts a dialogue between Jesus and the disciples after his resurrection, where the risen Savior instructs the eleven on keeping a sort of Christian Passover, while making an *ex eventu* prophecy about Peter's fate:

> And you therefore celebrate the remembrance of my death, which is the Passover; then will one of you be thrown into prison for my name's sake, and he will be very grieved and sorrowful, for while you celebrate the passover he who is in custody did not celebrate it with you. . . . And when you complete my Agape and my remembrance at the crowing of the cock, he will again be taken and thrown in prison. . . . And we said to him, "O Lord, have *you* then not completed the drinking of the passover? Must we, then, do it again?" And he said to us, "Yes, until I come from the Father with my wounds." (*Ep. Apost.* 15)[23]

So this Christian Passover meal is an *agapē*, including a vigil extending till cockcrow. The apostles wonder (on behalf of the later community of course) whether this commemoration, with its festive drinking, is really necessary or possible, given Jesus' vow of renunciation (see Luke 22:15–18). Apparently this was a real question for some Christians; the *Epistula* names "gnostic" leaders Simon Magus and Cerinthus as false teachers who might have raised such arguments (*Ep. Apost.* 1), but they may not have been the only people who ignored or opposed a Christian Passover altogether.[24] No attempt is made to avoid that difficult Gospel text about the fruit of the vine, though; although Jesus says he himself will no longer drink, they must continue to celebrate this sort of Passover until he comes from his Father "with [his] wounds."

Notably, this celebration is a single and simple fast and feast in which the death and resurrection of Jesus are celebrated together, using the Passover as a vehicle. It would be centuries before the complexity of the passion would be observed in a more "historicized" mode, with various days marking the elements of Jesus' suffering, death, and resurrection.

The Quartodeciman Pascha

During the second century another pattern for a Christian Pascha emerged; while some relied on local Jewish authorities for calculating the beginning of the feast on Passover, others were observing the Sunday closest after it, apparently as a more specific commemoration of the resurrection of Jesus. These

23. Translation from Wilhelm Schneemelcher and R. McL. Wilson, eds., *New Testament Apocrypha*, vol. 1, *Gospels and Related Writings* (Louisville: Westminster John Knox, 1991), 257–58.

24. Irenaeus' discussion (on which see further below) refers to earlier Roman bishops who "did not observe"; whether this means the feast, the fast, or the fourteenth day is unclear.

two patterns parallel the development of Sunday itself, discussed above; the Sunday after the Passover became more important as Sunday in general did, and the apparent desire to have a distinctive Christian observance parallels the anti-sabbatarian sentiment of such authors as "Barnabas" and Ignatius.

Irenaeus of Lyon wrote to the Roman bishop Victor around 190 on this question of the date, or day, of Easter.[25] Victor, whose community by this point observed the Sunday, was being confronted with a sort of liturgical multiculturalism on the Tiber, as migrants and visitors from around the empire brought to Rome their different customs, and in particular an insistence that the day of the feast (and a fast leading up to it) be aligned with the Jewish one. Practically speaking, the anxiety focused more on fasting than feasting; the Christians were united in believing that they should fast before the celebration, but the different times of breaking the fast undermined the solidarity of the believers.

Victor wanted to impose uniformity locally, and tried to demand it abroad too. Irenaeus, who had himself grown up in Asia, sought to impress on Victor how complex this might really be:

> For the dispute is not only about the day, but also about the actual form of the fast. For some think that they should fast one day, others two, others again more; some, for that matter, count their day as consisting of forty hours day and night. And this variety in its observance did not originate in our time but long before, in the time of those before us. . . . Yet all of these no less were at peace, and we also are at peace with one another; and the disagreement about the fast confirms the agreement in faith. (quoted in Eusebius, *Eccl. Hist.* 5.24.12–13)

The "Quartodeciman" ("Fourteenth [day]") position of the Asian and Syrian churches thus clashed with Sunday Pascha customs that by then applied not only in Rome but also in Egypt and Jerusalem (by then a refounded Roman city).[26] In some cases the calculation of the Quartodeciman Pascha was still made by relying on local Jewish calendars; where this was not possible or deemed inappropriate, the fourteenth day of other locally observed months was celebrated as the beginning of the festival, regardless of the day of the week.[27]

Sunday observance of Easter eventually prevailed over the Quartodeciman (and Jewish) pattern, but the actual celebration remained similar to the vigil and

25. Alistair Stewart-Sykes, *The Lamb's High Feast: Melito, Peri Pascha, and the Quartodeciman Paschal Liturgy at Sardis* (Leiden: Brill, 1998), 205n288.

26. See Eusebius, *Eccl. Hist.* 5.25.1–2 concerning these churches.

27. Thomas J. Talley, *The Origins of the Liturgical Year*, 2nd ed. (Collegeville, MN: Liturgical Press, 1986), 7–9.

liturgical breakfast described in the *Epistula Apostolorum*. So the *Didascalia*, whose sources may reflect mid-third-century Syria, instructs: "You shall come together and watch and keep vigil the whole night with prayers and intercessions, reading the Prophets, and with the Gospel and with Psalms, with fear and trembling and with earnest supplication, until the third hour in the night after the Sabbath; and then break your fasts" (5.19[21]). This may typify an Easter vigil in this period; the "Prophets" read probably included Moses, and hence the Pentateuch. One of the oldest surviving Christian sermons, from the Quartodeciman bishop Melito of Sardis in about 170, makes this explicit as it weaves together ancient observance and current interpretation:

> The writing of the Hebrew exodus has been read, and the words of
>   the mystery are made clear; how the sheep was slain, and how the
>   people were saved. Therefore, note this, O beloved:
> New and old, eternal and temporal, corruptible and incorruptible,
> mortal and immortal is the mystery of the Passover thus:
> It is old insofar as it concerns the law,
> but new insofar as it concerns the gospel;
> temporal insofar as it concerns the type,
> eternal because of grace;
> corruptible because of the sacrifice of the sheep,
> incorruptible because of the life of the Lord;
> mortal because of his burial in the earth,
> immortal because of his resurrection from the dead. (*On the Pascha* 1–3)

Easter was also emerging as an ideal time for baptisms. Neither Melito nor the *Epistula Apostolorum* refers to Easter baptism, but around 200 Tertullian indicates that Passover was the preferred (but not the only) time for baptism at Carthage. Of slightly later church orders, the *Didascalia* outlines an Easter vigil without baptism, and the *Apostolic Tradition* a baptismal vigil not specifically for Easter. The normative connection of baptism with Easter is apparently a phenomenon only of the fourth century.[28]

From Holy Day to Holy Week

As is often the case, the fourth century brings both clarity and change to Christian practice around Easter. The new possibilities for Christian communal life, including the construction of the great basilica churches in Jerusalem,

---

28. Bradshaw and Johnson, *Origins of Feasts*, 75–86.

Rome, and elsewhere, meant that Easter and the days leading up to it took on new liturgical definition and complexity. In turn these rituals gave rise to a literature that has preserved a sense of the form and meaning of these, more than for earlier centuries.

Before the fourth century, the paschal celebration was a single overdetermined reality, commemorating the various elements of Jesus' passion and resurrection (especially the former), not by historical reenactment but by reflecting on them through the unified symbol of Passover. If anything, the passion was given stronger emphasis than the resurrection in early celebrations; a popular but false etymology derived the Greek word for Easter, *pascha*, not from its real origin in *Pesaḥ* (Passover) but from the verb *paschō*, to suffer.

The Quartodeciman Pascha had exemplified this single, conceptual feast, but even the Easter Sunday keepers were historicizing their celebration only mildly—shaping it, that is, in relation to the use of time in the Gospel Passion Narratives—by linking it to the (week)day of the Lord's resurrection.

Differences even over the date of the paschal Sunday suggest a further version of this historicization; while in the later second century the Alexandrian church could celebrate its Easter Sunday as soon as the fifteenth day of the lunar month (i.e., on Passover), the Roman church was insisting on at least a day's interval, whether to avoid celebrating Passover itself or to commemorate the rising of Christ on the third day.[29]

A week of pre-Easter fasting had emerged in Syria and elsewhere, not initially a memorialization of Jesus' last week in Jerusalem, but simply a time of discipline and renunciation robust enough to do justice to the feast it preceded. Saturdays were fasting days in some places already, as were Wednesdays and Fridays; so as Easter observance became more focused on Sunday, that prior week became a canvas on which historically focused liturgies could now be sketched. Pascha thus eventually became a series of rites that corresponded to different elements of the Gospel accounts of Jesus' last days and resurrection, with the Sunday as its climax rather than its whole.

Holy Week and Easter in Fourth-Century Jerusalem

The church of Jerusalem had a unique role in these developments, predictably enough. Its locale provided the set on which sacred history had been enacted, so it was not surprising that liturgies commemorating the different elements of the story of Jesus' last days were developed and enacted in situ.

29. Talley, *Origins of the Liturgical Year*, 25.

This does not mean that all the innovations around Holy Week and Easter we know from fourth-century texts emerged in Jerusalem, however, even when the evidence consists of them being described there; Jerusalem was a crucible where the ordered chaos of theological tourism—the surge in pilgrimage there from all over the Mediterranean world—provided opportunities and demands for liturgical change.[30] In turn, this melting pot influenced the rest of the Christian world, directly or indirectly, toward the observance of what became Holy Week.

The most important source for these developments is the pilgrim journal of Egeria, which can be supplemented from nearly contemporary catecheses given to baptismal candidates by Bishop Cyril of Jerusalem (ca. 313–86). Their common witness to the celebration of Easter and preparation for it is virtually unique in this early period, providing mutual corroboration of important elements. Egeria, although unknown to us apart from her travel diary, may perhaps be compared to Macrina—an ascetic woman, whose literacy and capacity to undertake a pilgrimage from a vast distance away suggest privilege as well as commitment. Her narrative is liturgical not only in the obvious sense of its content but also because it provided her sisters with a vicarious means to enter themselves into the Holy Land through narrative. The center of activity for these accounts is the Church of the *Anastasis*, or Resurrection (or, as usually known later in the West, of the Holy Sepulcher), built by Constantine over what was taken to be the tomb of Jesus.

The liturgies of Lent (on which more below) gave way to commemorations of specific events in the passion story as early as the Saturday eight days before Easter, when the visit of Jesus to Mary, Martha, and Lazarus at Bethany was remembered at a church believed to be at that site (Egeria, *Journal* 29).[31] Jerusalem and its environs of course afforded many such opportunities, but the pattern of Holy Week was less a deliberate or systematic attempt to reenact the events of the Gospel narratives than a fulsome use of sites that the physical and architectural rediscovery or reinvention of the Holy Land in that century had provided.[32]

Palm Sunday saw a regular Sunday morning liturgy before an early afternoon assembly at the Mount of Olives, followed by an important form of universal participation in liturgy, on this day and others—namely, processions:

30. Ibid., 37–57.
31. Despite the appropriateness of the stories, times, and venues, there is a serious case that aspects of these observances were imported from Constantinople (ibid., 176–89); but cf. the discussion in Bradshaw and Johnson, *Origins of Feasts*, 115–16.
32. Bradshaw and Johnson, *Origins of Feasts*, 118–19.

> The bishop immediately rises, with all the people, and they all go on foot from
> the top of the Mount of Olives. And all the people go before him with hymns
> and antiphons, responding: "Blessed is he that comes in the name of the Lord."
> And all the children in those places, down to those who are not able to walk
> on their feet because of their tender age, are carried by their parents on their
> shoulders, all of them carrying branches, some of palm and some of olive, and
> thus the bishop is escorted in the same way as the Lord was. And from the top
> of the hill to the city, and from there to the *Anastasis*, all, even matrons and
> gentlemen, lead the bishop all the way through the city on foot in this manner,
> making these responses, going very slowly in case the people weary, until they
> arrive at the *Anastasis* late at night. (Egeria, *Journal* 31.2–4)

The following week through Thursday involved the regular pattern of daily
prayer, but Scripture readings commemorated the betrayal of Jesus and his
prediction of it. On Thursday there were two celebrations of the Eucharist, one
in the great basilica, or *Martyrium*, and the second, still within the complex of
the Church of the Resurrection, at the chapel where fragments of the cross were
kept. There is no sign that either celebration was about the Last Supper (any
more than any other Eucharist, that is); the two celebrations may have arisen
to deal with the demand from pilgrims for sharing the Eucharist before the approaching fast.[33] This precedent of multiple celebrations was to allow further
differentiation of the day's liturgies, eventually producing the widely observed
Mandatum, or Maundy Thursday evening celebration, in particular, and an
earlier celebration where oils were blessed for use at the coming Easter baptisms.

An exacting vigil with stations at the Mount of Olives and Gethsemane followed on Thursday evening, and at dawn on Friday the account of the trial of Jesus
before Pilate was read at the *Anastasis* before a pause for breath. One ritual that
could only have begun in Jerusalem was the veneration of the cross itself, the wood
identified sometime in the decades before Egeria's arrival as fragments of Jesus'
own scaffold. Pilgrims were given the opportunity to honor it quite concretely:

> The bishop, sitting, holds the ends of the sacred wood firmly in his hands, while
> the deacons who stand around guard it. It is guarded thus because the custom is
> that the people come singly, both faithful and catechumens, and, bowing down
> at the table, kiss the sacred wood and pass through. And because (I don't know
> when) someone is said to have bitten off and stolen a piece of the sacred wood,
> it is thus guarded by the deacons who stand around, lest anyone coming should
> dare to do so again. (Egeria, *Journal* 37.2)

33. For other possibilities, see ibid., 118.

This veneration was imitated in other places, partly because fragments of the actual cross were soon widely dispersed (Cyril, *Catechesis* 13.4); a few ambitious pilgrims had actually escaped the deacons' notice with a sacred splinter in their mouths, but more controlled forms of distribution had made pieces available across the Mediterranean, at least to a privileged group. Macrina, the Cappadocian ascetic pioneer, had such a fragment enclosed in a ring (*Life of Macrina* 30), but others were venerated publicly like the "original" in Jerusalem. Later, this Good Friday practice was extended to the use of any wooden cross (and much later, crucifix), making the Jerusalem archetype present by imitation rather than division, in copies rather than in chips.[34]

From the sixth to the ninth hours on Good Friday, an assembly was held in which scriptural passages related to the passion, from the Psalms and Prophets as well as the Gospels, were read, concluding with John 19:30, a prayer, and dismissal. Later there was a brief observance of the entombment of Christ, with John 19:38 read.

The Saturday was relatively quiet, with regular morning and noon prayers offered. A vigil followed, during which baptisms took place. After a postbaptismal rite in the *Anastasis*, the Eucharist was celebrated in the *Martyrium*, where the people had been observing the vigil. It was then immediately celebrated again back in the *Anastasis*, the second version including the resurrection Gospel reading (which was actually used every Sunday of the year in that church). The first (and larger?) Eucharist was for the baptismal candidates and the pilgrims, the second was the regular liturgy of each Sunday in Jerusalem.[35] After the demands of the week it is tempting to read Egeria's matter-of-fact account of Easter Day as marked more by relief than by exultation.

These liturgies were to become highly influential in places far from Jerusalem. The connections were made through various understandings of how time and space worked together. The distribution of fragments of the cross or other concrete relics of the passion allowed Jerusalem to be taken in token form, a catalyst for veneration and remembrance. In other cases, the passion and its setting were imitated rather than exported via churches that echoed the shape and dimensions of the *Anastasis* and "stations" that allowed pilgrims to walk and worship with Jesus without leaving home.[36]

---

34. Patrick Regan, "Veneration of the Cross," in *Between Memory and Hope: Readings on the Liturgical Year*, ed. John F. Baldovin and Maxwell E. Johnson (Collegeville, MN: Liturgical Press, 2000), 143–53.

35. See Egeria, *Journal* 38.1–2.

36. Robert Markus, "How on Earth Could Places Become Holy? Origins of the Christian Idea of Holy Places," *Journal of Early Christian Studies* 2, no. 3 (1994): 257–71.

This is also the preeminent case of one way that feasts turned into seasons—namely, by what has been termed "historicization" of a complex but single whole into a more elaborated and extended set of practices over hours or days. As we will see, there were other means, too, by which the fundamental importance of a feast was extended both forward and backward in time to create periods of preparation and celebration.

Pentecost

The Origins of Pentecost[37]

Like Pascha itself, Pentecost was initially a Jewish observance; the harvest-oriented Feast of Weeks, or Shavuot, was one of the pilgrim observances of the Jerusalem temple. When it does appear with a particularly Christian flavor, however, "Pentecost" tends to refer to the period of fifty days (the literal meaning of the term) between Easter and the Day of Pentecost rather than to one day at the end of that time. Although the Lukan account of the outpouring of the Spirit at Pentecost may be influenced by contemporary Jewish understandings of the feast,[38] there is little or no sign of an early Christian observance of Shavuot.

When Christian interest in this period appears, it is localized; Syrian sources, which reflect the Jewish celebration of Passover directly, show no trace of interest in Pentecost before the late fourth century.[39] Tertullian, however, indicates around 200 that African Christians could think of the period after Easter in "Pentecostal" terms:

> From then on, Pentecost is a most happy period for arranging baptisms, in which our Lord's resurrection was often made known among the disciples, and the grace of the Holy Spirit given, and the hope of our Lord's coming made known: because it was at that time, when he had been received back into heaven, that angels told the apostles that he would come in the same way he had gone up to heaven—that is, in Pentecost. (*On Baptism* 19.2)[40]

---

37. See Bradshaw and Johnson, *Origins of Feasts*, 69–74; Gerard Rouwhorst, "The Origins and Evolution of Early Christian Pentecost," in *Studia Patristica* 35 (Leuven: Peeters, 2001), 309–22; Leonhard, *Jewish Pesach*, 172–83.

38. James VanderKam, "The Festival of Weeks and the Story of Pentecost in Acts 2," in *From Prophecy to Testament: The Function of the Old Testament in the New*, ed. Craig A. Evans (Peabody, MA: Hendrickson, 2004), 185–205.

39. Rouwhorst, "Origins and Evolution," 311.

40. The Latin word *exinde* (translated "From then on" above) can mean "after" some previous thing either in temporal or logical terms; Tertullian is not necessarily saying this is a second-best time relative to Easter (day), but simply a time that comes after that.

This is more like an "Easter season" than Pentecost per se. Tertullian is happy to heap stories and themes onto his community's season of celebration; the resurrection appearances themselves, but also the ascension, the gift of the Spirit, and the expectation of Christ's return, are all continually remembered through the period. Hence this was not an outgrowth "backwards" of the Jewish Feast of Weeks but the continuation "forward" of Easter.

The growth of this Pentecost, a period rather than a day, can be attributed to as many as three unequal factors. First, there was clearly a tendency to view the season after Easter as inherently significant, a time rather than just a day of feasting. Second, the Jewish Feast of Pentecost did remain a point of reference, but mostly a literary or theoretical one that contributed to themes Christians observed. Third, the NT narratives indicating the ascension of Jesus "after forty days" (Acts 1:3) and of Pentecost as the day of the Spirit eventually encouraged a form of "historicizing" the calendar such as had taken place also in Holy Week.

This is therefore something like the first liturgical "season" in the sense that persists or has been revived in many churches today. Yet the most obvious media for signaling these observances today did not exist in the church of the early centuries; there were no liturgical colors, and for that matter no vestments or hangings to change or lectionaries to follow. The most important vehicle for conveying meaning was the body itself. Feasting and fasting were correlated with these times, and even the disposition of the body in public worship and private prayer depended on them. Tertullian—whom we have already seen testifying to how, for Sabbath and Sunday, kneeling and standing conveyed not only dispositions of penitence and celebration but also solidarity with other Christians in their marking of time—extends this past single days to these festive weeks: "We regard fasting on the Lord's day to be unlawful; so too kneeling for worship. We rejoice in the same exemption also from Easter Day to Pentecost" (*On the Soldier's Crown* 3.4).

The fundamental impulse around the creation of this very ancient Christian season is the significance of Easter itself; in carrying its meaning forward in time, these Christians were using time as a medium within which the importance of resurrection faith could be expressed qualitatively and quantitatively.

From Paschal "Pentecost" to the Feast of the Ascension[41]

The idea of Pentecost as an undifferentiated period of rejoicing sagged under the weight of varied associations and under the pressure of the historicizing

41. See further Talley, *Origins of the Liturgical Year*, 66–70.

tendency of the fourth century. The account of the ascension in the Acts of the Apostles as taking place forty days after Easter was an obvious reason for that day to be celebrated separately.

There was anxiety about proper fasting among these Christians, but corresponding enthusiasm for correct feasting. Tertullian, as we have seen, regards this "Pentecost" as a period of strict(!) rejoicing; the apocryphal *Acts of Paul*, which must also be from around 200 but is more likely to be from Asia, knows the same practice.[42] The rather later *Apostolic Constitutions* maintains an intimidating enthusiasm for communal rejoicing: "The one will be guilty of sin who fasts on the Lord's day, which is the day of resurrection, or during the time of Pentecost, or generally who mourns on a feast day of the Lord. For on those we ought to rejoice, and not weep" (*Ap. Const.* 5.20). But the *Apostolic Constitutions* also reflects change; the ascension is now celebrated after forty days, which in some places was to undermine the older sense of the paschal/Pentecostal pattern. There were those who had argued as early as 300 that the season of festivity should be ended after the forty days, when "the bridegroom was taken away," provoking bishops to legislate for liturgical jollity for the full fifty days (*Canon* 43 of Elvira). This meant not so much compulsory self-indulgence as suspension of fasting practices—avoidance of particular food and drink such as meat and wine, or of cooked food—that had much appeal for Christians of this time, as was both reflected in and fueled by the growth of the monastic movement. The negotiation of ascetic and celebratory modes clearly had both anxiety and enthusiasm attached.

Pentecost in Jerusalem

By the time Egeria visited Jerusalem, "Pentecost" referred to the fiftieth day itself (as in earlier Jewish usage), although she also indicates that even vowed ascetics did not fast during the fifty days, even on Wednesdays and Fridays (*Journal* 41). There was a special assembly on the Thursday forty days after Easter, but it was at Bethlehem and not connected with the ascension,[43] which was still celebrated on the fiftieth day.

After Sunday-morning Eucharist on Pentecost at the *Anastasis*, there were separate assembles at the traditional sites of the gift of the Spirit ("Sion"), where the Eucharist was celebrated again, and of the ascension ("Imbomon," at the Mount of Olives), with an assembly including readings and prayers; then

---

42. Schneemelcher and Wilson, *New Testament Apocrypha*, 2:251, 264.
43. Talley suggests a commemoration of the Holy Innocents; see *Origins of the Liturgical Year*, 64–65.

a procession back to the *Anastasis* and a further station at Sion completed the day. This liturgical table for the day of Pentecost was groaning unsustainably under the weight, and the eventual movement of the ascension festival to the obvious earlier date is hardly surprising.

Jerusalem therefore provides an exemplar of how Easter and Pentecost developed and would be maintained in churches of liturgical tradition thenceforth. Its own influence in this process was considerable.

Lent

The earliest pre-paschal fasts were only of a day or two (with considerable local and traditional variation, as Irenaeus had reminded Bishop Victor of Rome in 190 or so). We saw that the *Didascalia* already extended the fast for Syrian Christians to six days, describing for the first time what would become Holy Week. Its recipe for preparation was stern and literal: "You shall sustain yourselves with bread and salt and water only, at the ninth hour, until the fifth day of the week. But on the Friday and on the Sabbath fast wholly, and taste nothing" (5.18[21]).

Around the same time a different and longer pattern was emerging, of three weeks of preparation specifically related to baptisms, including but not limited to Pascha (Socrates, *Eccl. Hist.* 5.2). Later liturgical books contain vestiges of scriptural readings for three weeks before baptism at Jerusalem and, in Rome, of "scrutinies" of baptismal candidates on three Sundays prior to Easter; there are even parallels in Jewish lectionaries prior to *Pesaḥim*.[44] In other places the three weeks were not so clearly paschal as baptismal—which is not surprising, since baptisms were not yet strongly or universally connected with Easter in the third century. The gravitational tug of the paschal season may have attracted this floating three-week period of baptismal preparation into its orbit, as a proto-Lenten fast for catechumens.[45]

Yet the Lent that became universal in and after the fourth century was of forty days, not three weeks. The obvious model for such a period is the forty-day fast Jesus undertakes (Mark 1:13 and parallels), but this is not related to the

44. Bradshaw and Johnson, *Origins of Feasts*, 92–95; Lawrence A. Hoffman, "The Jewish Lectionary, the Great Sabbath, and the Lenten Calendar: Liturgical Links between Christians and Jews in the First Three Centuries," in *Time and Community: In Honor of Thomas Julian Talley*, ed. J. Neil Alexander, NPM Studies in Church Music and Liturgy (Washington, DC: Pastoral Press, 1990), 3–20.

45. Bradshaw and Johnson, *Origins of Feasts*, 96–98.

passion or resurrection in the Gospels, and hence has no obvious connection with the Pascha. Christians might nevertheless have undertaken a forty-day fast in imitation of Jesus' example, whether communally or at any set time of year. Origen, writing in the mid-third century, is aware of such a possibility:

> Those people fast, therefore, who have lost a spouse; we having the spouse with us are not able to fast. We do not say this, however, to release ourselves from the bonds of Christian abstinence; for we have forty days devoted to fasts, we have the fourth and the sixth day weekly, on which we fast solemnly. (*Homilies on Leviticus*, 10.2)

Yet this reference to a forty-day fast lacks any specific anchor in time. Was Origen thinking of, but not naming, a fixed date, or referring to a practice of undertaking various forty-day fasts according to circumstance? Christianity had undergone a shift from conversion to repentance, or perhaps from repentance to penance, with its growth and persistence across generations. Occasional periods of penitence were certainly known when pastoral need and personal failure suggested them.[46] Tertullian had written a treatise *On Penitence* a few decades before Origen, describing how a single second chance could be offered after serious postbaptismal sin if penitence were sought publicly, with ritual and humility (not to say humiliation):

> To sleep in sackcloth and ashes, to cover his body in filth, to lay his spirit low in mourning, to exchange sins committed for severe treatment; to abstain from food and drink other than simple—not for the stomach's sake, that is, but the soul's; for the rest, to feed prayer by fasting, to groan, to weep and cry to the Lord your God; to bow before the presbyters, and kneel at God's altars; to call all the brethren to be an embassy for his supplication. (Tertullian, *On Penitence* 9.4)

Origen may also have been referring to a non-paschal forty-day fasting pattern with similar strictures. Such issues did not arise only through moral indiscretions; during the time of the Great Persecution under Diocletian, the tragedy of violent suffering was compounded for the church by wrenching decisions about how to deal with those who had wavered under torture or the threat of it but who wished to return to the community of believers. Bishop Peter of Alexandria wrote that these penitents should be reconciled (not rebaptized, as others who felt the penitents had lost the grace of new birth argued), and

---

46. Guy G. Stroumsa, *Barbarian Philosophy: The Religious Revolution of Early Christianity*, WUNT 112 (Tübingen: Mohr Siebeck, 1999), 160.

that "there should be imposed upon them, as a memorial, from the time of their approach forty days—those days during which our Lord and Savior Jesus Christ had fasted although he had been baptized, and was tempted by the devil" (*Canon* 1). This reads like an occasional and pastoral measure rather than an annual observance; and of course Origen and Peter were both from Alexandria. The *Canons of Hippolytus*, a church order from Egypt after Peter's time, mentions both "the forty"—along with the Wednesday and Friday fasts in a way reminiscent of Origen—and a forty-day pattern of baptismal preparation, apparently unrelated to Easter (*Canons of Hippolytus* 12, 20).[47]

It is not hard to see the connections with what we find later in the fourth century: a near-universal forty-day period of fasting and preparation for Easter. Yet there is something of a sudden expansion and solidification of practice between the third and fourth centuries, which suggests some external or institutional influence. The catalyst may have been the emperor Constantine's initiative to standardize the date of Easter; the imposition of a single approach to the feast was perhaps accompanied by a standardization of the fast too.[48]

Saints and Time

The First Saints

The Christian year as it has persisted in many churches and cultures is framed by stories and symbols related to Jesus, but it is also decorated with the names and narratives of many other individuals. The roots of these observances also lie in ancient Christianity, but they grew circuitously from the unique experiences of early heroes to their repeated memorialization.

The first "saints" of the church were all its members, a holy chosen people by analogy with the first Israel (Rom. 1:7; 1 Cor. 1:2); but even in the earliest texts there are hints that certain individuals or a subgroup have particular significance; thus Acts refers to certain "saints and widows" called to witness the raising of Tabitha (9:41), and Matthew's Gospel refers to certain "saints" raised from death at the time of the cosmic disruption accompanying Jesus' death (27:52).[49]

The primary means by which certain individuals became "saints" in the second and third centuries of the Christian movement's life, however, was

47. Bradshaw and Johnson, *Origins of Feasts*, 100.
48. Ibid., 107–8.
49. Thus Davies and Allison suggest these are "pious Jews from ancient times"; W. D. Davies and Dale Allison, *A Critical and Exegetical Commentary on the Gospel according to Saint Matthew*, ICC (Edinburgh: T&T Clark, 1997), 3:633.

violent death. The importance of martyrdom can hardly be exaggerated, but its literal scope could be; there was no early Christian holocaust.[50] Nonetheless, the experiences of suffering and heroism under Roman persecution marked Christian experience deeply, for good and ill.

The capacity of the martyrs to inhabit and make present the example of Christ added a heavenly superstructure to the Roman world's patronage system, which included but went beyond the lives of households and families. Just as earthly patrons were needed to obtain material advantage in everyday life, the martyrs became spiritual patrons. Even before death, Christians who underwent trial and torture were perceived to have great spiritual power, including access to visions and revelations, and authority over prosaic problems besetting the church family.[51] The care of those who offered such power, yet who themselves needed material support while still among the living, was the original "cult," or care, of the saints.[52]

Dining with the Dead

Although "martyrs" soon became a term for those who had died, even feeding the martyrs did not end with their physical extinction. Since communal eating was so important to the early Christians, it may not be surprising to find them dining with the dead as well. In many parts of the ancient Mediterranean it was already customary to celebrate for (or with) the dead annually, in meals termed *refrigeria*, "refreshments." The prominence of banqueting imagery in ancient funerary art is striking, not merely decorative but evocative of hopes for what the deceased might enjoy. But where in traditional Greco-Roman belief the departed were sometimes more like clients relying on the living for remembrance and sustenance, and probably respected more than embraced, the martyrs were patrons to cultivate;[53] to dine with them was to eat with the great, and an invitation to their circle was a foretaste of the great banquet of the reign of God.[54]

Strictly speaking, aspirations expressed to the martyrs for their powerful intercession were not "prayer" to them as though to God; it was acknowledgment that faith required a community and that death was not the end of the duties or of possibilities that community gave. This Christian care of the

50. See De Ste. Croix, "Aspects of the 'Great' Persecution."

51. All these feature in the *Martyrdom of Perpetua and Felicitas*.

52. See McGowan, "Discipline and Diet."

53. Peter Brown, *The Cult of the Saints: Its Rise and Function in Latin Christianity*, Haskell Lectures on History of Religions, n.s., no. 2 (Chicago: University of Chicago Press, 1981), 5–6.

54. Candida R. Moss, *The Other Christs: Imitating Jesus in Ancient Christian Ideologies of Martyrdom* (New York: Oxford University Press, 2010), 134–35.

departed martyrs was a sort of familial duty, and all members of the church and of earthly families also required respect. Tertullian sees no hint of paganism in his insistence that a wife's duty to her deceased husband would involve cemeterial gifts: "Indeed, she prays for his soul, and requests interim refreshment [*refrigerium*] for him, and for fellowship in the first resurrection, and she offers on the anniversaries of his falling asleep" (*On Monogamy* 10.4). The *refrigerium* and "offering" here include some sort of funerary meal celebrated with the grateful dead, whether the cemetery picnic, a more institutional eucharistic celebration, or both.[55]

Through the third and fourth centuries, Christian practice combined these elements of care for and care from the dead. The distinction between this new martyr cult and older forms of dining with the departed was not always obvious, and the combination of the two made the cemetery venues often as important as churches;[56] churches were even built in the cemeteries. The decorations of the Roman catacombs, with prominent banqueting scenes, also link heavenly aspirations with earthly customs performed in front of them; African tombs with hollows for food offerings, and even holes for the direct administration of wine to the occupants of graves, go beyond evocation to enactment.[57]

A description of how Christians at Smyrna took care of the remains of their mid-second-century hero Polycarp exemplifies remembrance of the saints: "Thus we later took up his bones, more valuable than precious stones, and costlier than gold, and put them in a suitable place. There the Lord will allow us to come together as we can in gladness and joy, and celebrate the birthday of his martyrdom, both in memory of those who have already competed, and for the training and preparation of those to come" (*Mart. Pol.* 18.2–3).[58] Here are the elements of the cult of the saints known in subsequent centuries: veneration of their relics, places associated with their remains (eventually churches dedicated to them), and feasts commemorating their deaths. The last of these are referred to in the ancient martyr acts, remarkably, as "birthdays"—not the anniversary of mortal life beginning but of its end and the beginning of new, heavenly life.[59]

55. Compare his comments in *On the Soldier's Crown* 3 and *Exhortation to Chastity* 11; further, Jensen, "Dining with the Dead," 120–23.

56. MacMullen, *Second Church*, 52.

57. Jensen, "Dining with the Dead," 118.

58. The account may come from a considerably later time than the events of Polycarp's death; see Candida R. Moss, "On the Dating of Polycarp: Rethinking the Place of the *Martyrdom of Polycarp* in the History of Christianity," *Early Christianity* 1, no. 4 (2010): 539–74.

59. The ancient church seems to have been disinterested or simply negative about literal birthdays; Origen comments that in the Bible only the bad guys seem to have birthday celebrations (*Homilies on Leviticus* 8.3.2).

Saints and the Eucharist

The tradition of the Christian funerary and commemorative picnic varied but was particularly strong in Africa, where the remains of *mensae*, or tables for celebratory meals, can be seen in cemeteries and near churches. Ancient travelers might find their sensibilities challenged by the contrasts in local habits, however. Monica, mother of Augustine of Hippo, was distinguished by her piety (and home cooking), and was thus a regular sight in the local African shrines; but when visiting Milan in the 380s she discovered that the bishop there, Ambrose, had been cracking down on the Italian martyr feasts, which he thought had a tendency to become somewhat riotous (Augustine, *Conf.* 6.2.2). The Eucharist, a quite separate form of ritual meal long before Monica's time, was to many bishops the more appropriate way to establish communion and commensality with the saints. This in itself was not new; in Cyprian's time the African church had been celebrating the Eucharist to remember the martyrs, as well as the martyrs' Lord: "We always offer sacrifices for them, as often as we celebrate in commemoration the anniversary days and sufferings of these martyrs" (*Letter* 39.3). While sharing food and drink convivially or sacramentally was fundamental to celebrating saints, it was not isolated from other acts any more than the eucharistic banquet was without words and music. Songs were composed and sung in the martyrs' honor too (Tertullian, *For the Scorpion* 7.2), and there were even dances.[60]

Texts that celebrated martyrs' deeds point to another aspect of liturgical remembrance: reading. The editor of the *Martyrdom of Perpetua and Felicitas* urged reading stories as a means of grace; the reader could and should aspire to commune with the martyrs' example through the text, "lest any weakness or desperation in faith may suppose that the divine grace was present only among the ancients" (*Mart. Perp.* 1.5). Although relatively few actually underwent the spectacular cruelties described in martyr acts, reading and hearing them became another form of participation in the experience of the saints.

Some individuals would have read these acts privately for entertainment of a sort, and for personal edification too, but liturgical settings were their real home. In Polycarp's case this is implicit; the "remembrance" that the author of his *Martyrdom* referred to would have included the recitation of the story in church on that paradoxical "birthday," and the need for such a document may even have prompted its composition, years after the event.[61]

60. See the discussion in chap. 4.
61. Moss, *Other Christs*, 56–59.

For centuries such acts, which were composed carefully (how "accurately" by modern standards is another question), were read along with canonical Scripture at the Eucharist on the martyr's feast day; at these times the martyrs were other Christs, and their stories were inspired too. Explicit evidence for this comes much later, but by the time of Augustine's ministry in Africa he had to regulate martyr stories, not promote them.[62]

The number of these martyrs necessitated birthday calendars for the church families who commemorated them; Cyprian, absent in hiding during the persecution under Decius, urged his clerical colleagues in Carthage to note the anniversaries even of those who died in prison so that their days could be observed (*Letter* 12.2). Such a calendar is part of the Roman *Chronograph* of Philocalus, an almanac that includes a list of martyrs from the year 336 and the locations where their bodies witnessed as they awaited resurrection, attended by the living at annual and other celebrations. This was still a local matter; the Roman Christians were able to visit most of their saints at the sites listed, and other centers had quite different calendars based on their own local heroes.[63] Later, the exchange of stories and calendars would create a set of more general observances, although there has never been one universal list of saints and dates agreed upon across the whole church.

The end of persecution was cause for celebration, but challenged a church that had identified itself so strongly with the martyrs' cause. Where now would holiness be found? Christians knew that remarkable sanctity was not dependent on death or even imprisonment; if some had shown courage but circumstance had not offered the martyr's crown, were they not also examples to be followed? Cyprian had urged such respect for bishop Cornelius of Rome, who "must surely be accounted among the glorious confessors and martyrs" (*Letter* 55.9) despite having the mixed blessing of survival. So in time other holy persons could also be recognized as worthy of feasts and readings too.

Theotokos

Not every apostle or NT hero had been a martyr. Mary the mother of Jesus occupied a category of sanctity all her own from a very early time. Already in the mid-second century an apocryphal Gospel prequel, the *Protevangelium of*

---

62. Johannes Quasten, "'Vetus Superstitio et Nova Religio': The Problem of Refrigerium in the Ancient Church of North Africa," *Harvard Theological Review* 33, no. 4 (1940): 255–56.

63. Cf. the evidence for the sanctoral cycle in Cappadocia; see Jill Burnett Comings, *Aspects of the Liturgical Year in Cappadocia (325–430)*, Patristic Studies 7 (New York: Peter Lang, 2005), 95–120.

James, presents her own conception as miraculous (not virginal), her early life as exemplary, and her virginity as preserved even through Jesus' birth. These attributes or experiences were to remain central in the development of devotion to Mary, but in the ancient church their meaning was essentially christological. What was true of Mary was true of Jesus, who derived his humanity from her.

This applies particularly to the devotional title attested from the mid-third century[64]—Theotokos, or God-bearer, often rendered in English as "mother of God." That startling epithet would become prominent during the controversy that culminated in the Council of Chalcedon (451), but was above all an affirmation in worship of the integration of divinity and humanity in the one Christ; Jesus whom Mary bore was truly divine. Although its polemical affirmation at the Council of Ephesus in 431 catalyzed Marian devotion in new ways, "Theotokos" was certainly in liturgical and not merely academic use a century earlier, at least in Alexandria.[65] It was apparently less well known in Antioch, and the objection to it made by Nestorius, patriarch of Constantinople, is as much a clue to differences in worship practice as to doctrine.

Even before this time, Mary was viewed as prominent among that "communion of saints" whose friendship was precious and intercession effective. A third-century papyrus presents the oldest petition for her assistance, apparently a hymn or poem that would have been sung in church:

> Under your compassion we flee, Theotokos;
> Do not overlook our prayers, but deliver us from danger;
> You alone are pure and blessed. (P.Ryl. 470)[66]

Monastics, Pillars, and Pilgrims

The search for more distinct forms of holiness in the present did not leave the well-populated cemeteries altogether, but also turned to the increasingly crowded desert. The monastic movement, led by such heroes as Antony and

64. Probably not in Hippolytus, *On the Blessings of Jacob* (PO 27.6), *pace* Kilian McDonnell, "The Marian Liturgical Tradition," in *Between Memory and Hope: Readings on the Liturgical Year*, ed. John F. Baldovin and Maxwell E. Johnson (Collegeville, MN: Liturgical Press, 2000), 387, but in Origen, *Commentary on Romans* (fragment quoted in Socrates, *Eccl. Hist.* 7.32), and others; see Maxwell E. Johnson, "*Sub Tuum Praesidium*: The *Theotokos* in Christian Life and Worship before Ephesus," *Pro Ecclesia* 17, no. 1 (Winter 2008): 52–75.

65. See the list of witnesses in Johnson, "*Sub Tuum Praesidium*," 55.

66. See discussion in ibid., 62–63; the reconstruction translated here comes from Otto Stegmüller, "SUB TUUM PRAESIDIUM: Bemerkungen zur ältesten Überlieferung," *Zeitschrift für Katholische Theologie* 74 (1952): 76–82. The only reason to date the manuscript later stems from unwillingness to accept the early use of the term; paleographical factors suggest the date given here.

Pachomius, as well as its urban counterpart and communities like that of Macrina, was in part a response to the end of persecution and the quest for a new form of characteristic holiness.

Monasticism not only attracted many direct participants but also created a new sort of occasional devotion for those who led more typical lives. Other Christians looked to the holy men and women as powerful living examples whose sufferings were chosen rather than inflicted but borne through the same divine power as had supported the martyrs. Among the most spectacular objects of such attention were "stylites," ascetics like Simeon (ca. 390–459) who lived for considerable periods on columns raised high above the ground. Simeon illustrates the paradoxical popularity of the ascetics; his ascent toward heaven was motivated by a desire to escape human society, but instead became a magnet for it. His manifestation of divine power attracted those seeking healing or advice, and after initially building higher columns to escape these students of virtue, he relented and set visiting hours each afternoon. The crowds, who might come either for the sheer entertainment or the hope of intercession, in turn generated an industry in pilgrim souvenirs.[67] Pilgrimage, both to the present homes of these living saints and to places sanctified by the earthly life of Jesus, emerges as an important practice of embodied worship in this period, expressed less in cycles of time than by the crossing of space.

There were regional differences in the pursuit of sanctity; although communal monasticism soon became strong in the West, the more breathtaking performances in the oddly populous desert wastes like those of the stylites were an Eastern phenomenon, for which Syria and Egypt became famous. The "saint" in the West was still very often dead.[68]

Centripetal and centrifugal urges both swirled around the tombs of the holy. In the first case, the grave attracted architectural and performative memorialization, and shrines became centers of gravity not only for meals but also for the development of churches.[69] In Africa at least, churches related to martyrs seem often to have had baptisteries attached, suggesting that the saints may have functioned as invisible sponsors for converts, encouraging those who

67. See further Robert Doran, *The Lives of Simeon Stylites*, Cistercian Studies Series 112 (Kalamazoo, MI: Cistercian Publications, 1992).

68. Peter Brown, *The Rise of Western Christendom: Triumph and Diversity, A.D. 200–1000*, 2nd ed. (Malden, MA: Wiley-Blackwell, 2003), 173–74.

69. Not always in the same ways or to the same extent; see the review of a key site and of scholarship on the question in Ann Marie Yasin, "Reassessing Salona's Churches: *Martyrium* Evolution in Question," *Journal of Early Christian Studies* 20 (2012): 59–112.

stepped ritually through death to rebirth.[70] It also became desirable to return to these saints for one's own burial; they were, after all, family.

Yet the martyrs' graves were inherently limited in scope; they could form focal points for devotion only for locals or for pilgrims. Pilgrimage itself, by transcending the local, begged the question of its opposite; if the Christian by moving could become a pilgrim, the saint by moving could become a relic. Both practices assumed power that was only conceivable in the relative freedom of the peace of the church; and if power and wealth were required to undertake long journeys like Egeria's, they were all the more necessary when it came to dispensing the very remains of the saints. The distribution of relics (often not actual stray body parts but *brandea*, or "contact relics"—cloth or other objects placed in proximity to the saint's remains) served not only to provide more immediate access to the saint for people at a distance but also added a dimension to the role of the ecclesial hierarchy, who were now proxies for the heavenly patrons.[71]

Christmas and Epiphany

A Borrowed Feast?

Feasts of Jesus' birth or incarnation are not part of the earliest strand of how Christians sanctified time; on that, at least, there is consensus. But exactly when, how, and why Christmas and Epiphany emerged as Christian celebrations is less clear. The Gospels themselves leave conundrums even about the year of Jesus' birth, and offer nothing of significance about when in that year it took place. Neither can we find any evidence of concern for the date of Jesus' appearance for more than a century after most of the NT writings were composed.

Given this initial lack of interest in Jesus' birth, some have viewed Christmas as chosen or imposed cynically by the newly official church of the fourth century as part of its "Constantinian captivity," a thin overlay above an existing pagan solstice festival. According to one fairly recent popular work (for instance), an early Christian writer named "Syrus" (whom we are encouraged by context to imagine as a contemporary of Pope Liberius in the fourth century) is supposed to have revealed a dirty little secret about the origins of Christmas: "It was a custom of the pagans to celebrate on the same December 25 the birthday of the sun, at which they kindled lights in token of festivity. . . .

---

70. Robin Margaret Jensen, "Baptismal Rites and Architecture," in *Late Ancient Christianity*, ed. Virginia Burrus (Minneapolis: Fortress, 2005), 117–44.

71. Brown, *Cult of the Saints*, 90–95.

Accordingly, when the church authorities perceived that the Christians had a leaning to this festival, they took counsel and resolved that the true Nativity should be solemnized on that day."[72] "Syrus," however, did not exist. "He" is actually a marginal note from an unknown twelfth-century Syrian scribe (a "Syrian writer," *scriptor Syrus*, as subsequent Latin editors described him, not someone named "Syrus"), too far removed from the fourth century to know any more about the issue than we do. That medieval marginalia actually begins with some words omitted in the recent exposé: "The reason, then, why the fathers of the church moved the January 6 celebration to December 25 was this, they say." So "Syrus" was not really a spokesperson for popular, but dubious, wisdom about the origins of Christmas at all; this anonymous scribbler risked the ire of her or his local librarian not to explain the ultimate origins of Christmas but to argue about its real date.

Yet "Syrus" was right about one thing: the date now known as Epiphany—January 6—was known and liturgically observed well before December 25 was widely celebrated. And although interest in the date of Jesus' birth and even its liturgical observance may have preceded Constantine by some time, perhaps the December 25 date did not.

The Earliest Epiphany

The earliest real evidence for a "Christmas"—or better, an "Epiphany" of sorts—comes from the Alexandrian writer Clement, who around 200 reported calculations of the chronology of Jesus' birth:

> From the birth of the Lord, then, to the death of Commodus are, in total, one hundred and ninety-four years, one month, and thirteen days. And there are those who have over-curiously determined not only the year of our Savior's birth, but also the day, which they say was in the twenty-eighth year of Augustus, and on the 25th of [the month] *Pachon*. (*Strom.* 1.21.145)

Clement is also aware of calculations by a rival Christian group about the actual date of Jesus' baptism, and a curious connection appears between his birthday and that of his death:

> And those from Basilides observe the day of his baptism as a festival, keeping vigil with readings. And they say that it was the fifteenth year of Tiberius Caesar,

---

72. Richard Cohen, *Chasing the Sun: The Epic Story of the Star That Gives Us Life* (New York: Random House, 2010), 17.

the fifteenth day of the month *Tubi*; and some that it was the eleventh of that month. Regarding his passion, some with very great accuracy say it was in the sixteenth year of Tiberius Caesar on the twenty-fifth of *Phamenoth*; others say the twenty-fifth of *Pharmuthi* and still others say the Savior suffered on the nineteenth of *Pharmuthi*. Further, some of them say that he was born on the twenty-fourth or twenty-fifth of *Pharmuthi*. (*Strom.* 1.21.146)

Although references to the twenty-fifth day of various months may look promising, these are probably not related to December 25. Egyptian months were at first lunar, like the Jewish ones, unrelated to the year (or the week), but by Clement's time they had probably become fixed within the year like our Roman months but not identical to them. Apart from this interest in the date of Jesus' birth, the two important items here are the possible coincidence of Jesus' birth and death, and even more the celebration of his baptism on the eleventh or fifteenth of *Tubi*, which are the sixth and tenth of January.[73] The former of these is, of course, what was known later as the Feast of the Epiphany.

Basilides was probably from Syria, and his followers had ideas and practices more common there, and which contrasted with those of Clement's Alexandrian community.[74] Although Basilides was a speculative teacher of the type modern scholars have labeled "gnostic," later Eastern Christian liturgical traditions do associate Jesus' baptism, as much as or more than his birth, with the feast on the sixth of January. Since (particularly in Mark's Gospel) the ministry of Jesus begins with his baptism, the story wherein he is revealed as the Son of God (Mark 1:11; Matt. 3:17; Luke 3:22; cf. John 1:34), and since Christian baptism itself was often regarded as a participation in Jesus' anointed status,[75] Epiphany and baptism are not hard to relate.[76]

A version of the "Syrus" argument about borrowed solstice festivals was once made for the origins of Epiphany in Egypt, but older scholarly attempts to find a sun feast that had veered off course as far as January 6 relied on modern miscalculations as much as ancient.[77] Just as the early Pascha was

---

73. A calculation first made in Roland H. Bainton, "Basilidian Chronology and New Testament Interpretation," *Journal of Biblical Literature* 42 (1923): 96–98; see further Susan K. Roll, *Toward the Origins of Christmas*, Liturgia Condenda 5 (Kampen: Kok Pharos, 1995), 77–79.

74. Compare Clement's indignation at the use of *agapē* as a name for a Christian meal, when this term was well known in Carthage, Asia, and elsewhere; see McGowan, "Naming the Feast."

75. See the discussion of baptism in chap. 5.

76. Bradshaw and Johnson, *Origins of Feasts*, 138–41.

77. Roll, *Origins of Christmas*, 66–68. The curious evidence of Epiphanius concerning a sort of local nativity fast of the god Aion does not seem to be related to Epiphany; see Talley, *Origins of the Liturgical Year*, 103–17.

not a reenactment of one specific event but the celebration of a complex reality of Jesus' passion, death, and resurrection, the earliest Epiphany was a thematic celebration of Jesus' appearance and his sonship, not a historical commemoration of his birth awkwardly linked to an anniversary of his baptism. In Cappadocia it was known as the Feast of Lights, a concept similar to that of "Epiphany," but one that could be connected with various stories about Jesus' appearance and identity, and baptism in particular; such a conceptual focus allowed still other narrative connections—notably the story of the wedding at Cana, which John's Gospel presents as the first of Jesus' signs (John 2:11)—and hence has a similar theological force (as well as baptismal associations for early readers because of the water jars for purification in John 2:6). So when the more specific nativity feast of December 25 was introduced in the East in the later fourth century, there was still plenty of room for reflection on the basic theme of appearance, revelation, and light.

Syrian tradition retained and developed connections between birth and baptism in later liturgical texts; in the fourth century, Ephraem of Nisibis, in his *Hymns on the Nativity*, had Mary speak about birth and baptism as intertwined in a text that would be sung in churches at this time of year:

> What will I call you, you so different from us,
> Who have become one of us? Will I call you Son,
> Will I call you Brother, will I call you Spouse,
> Will I call you Lord, you who have birthed your mother
> With a new birth, in the midst of the waters? (16.9)[78]

The Death of Jesus and the Birth of Christmas

If a feast commemorating Jesus' origins was being celebrated in some Eastern communities before the fourth century, it was not quite Christmas in the modern sense, nor was it held on December 25. This familiar date took longer to become a widely observed feast.

The earliest undisputed references to December 25 either as Jesus' birthday or as a liturgical celebration are in the Philocalian *Chronograph* of 354, which refers twice to the birth of Jesus "eight days before the Kalends of January"—December 25—and even uses that date as its calendrical starting point for records as far back as 336.[79] That calendar is actually an early list of the Roman martyrs, as noted before; it is therefore surprising to see a list

---

78. On Ephraem and Jesus' baptism, see McDonnell, *Baptism of Jesus*, 194–98.
79. Roll, *Origins of Christmas*, 83–87.

of the martyrs' "birthdays" headed by the (supposedly) literal birthday of Jesus. The appearance of the Christmas date, not only as known but treated as a reference point for the whole year even in 336, raises as many questions as it answers.

Yet interest in December 25 itself may be even older. The earlier evidence concerns chronology more than liturgy. Most manuscripts of a *Commentary on Daniel*, attributed to Hippolytus and written more than a century before the *Chronograph*, mention December 25:

> For the first appearance of our Lord, in the flesh, in which he was born in Beth-lehem, took place eight days before the Kalends of January [December 25], on a Wednesday, while Augustus was reigning in his forty-second year, and from Adam, five thousand and five hundred years. He suffered in his thirty-third year, eight days before the Kalends of April [March 25], on a Friday, in the eighteenth year of Tiberius Caesar, while Fufius and Rubellius were Consuls.[80]

Assuming this is a genuine and third-century text (which is not clear), it is still evidence not for celebration of Christmas but for something akin to the speculation about Jesus' birth and baptism that Clement had reported. Although the date is different from the Eastern one, it is striking that again the dates of his death and birth, and implicitly his conception too, are related.

An African text slightly after Hippolytus, *On the Dating of Pascha* (243), comes up with a related but not identical date of March 28 for Jesus' birth and also for Passover. This confuses the picture in some ways and clarifies it in others; it shows that Jesus' birthday was not clearly established, but that it was of interest, and in this case believed to coincide with Passover. *On the Dating of Pascha* also links the same day with creation: the world itself was made, the author believes, on March 25 (the vernal equinox) and three days later—on the fourteenth of Nisan, Passover—came the sun's creation, on which day Jesus himself was also born.[81]

Later rabbinic texts also state that key events of redemption across history happened at Passover, which they too see as the date the world was made:

> It has been taught: R. Eliezer says: In Tishri the world was created; in Tishri the patriarchs were born; in Tishri the patriarchs died; on Passover Isaac was born;

---

80. The text is disputed, and the words regarding the Kalends of January are omitted in some witnesses; but the omission is as likely to be the result of tendentious scribal activity as any alleged interpolation.

81. Roll, *Origins of Christmas*, 81–83.

on New Year Sarah, Rachel, and Hannah were visited; on New Year Joseph went forth from prison; on New Year the bondage of our ancestors ceased in Egypt; and in Nisan they will be redeemed in time to come. (*b. Roš Haš.* 10b–11a)[82]

Presumably Hippolytus is referring to the same idea, and this notion of cosmic and historic patterns was shared by Christians and Jews.

One further step backward takes us to Tertullian, around 200. In another convoluted chronological quest for the date of Jesus' death, he states:

> And this passion of Christ was completed within the times of the seventy weeks, under Tiberius Caesar, in the consulate of Rubellius Geminus and Fufius Geminus, in the month of March, at the times of Pascha, on the eighth day before the calends of April, on the first day of unleavened bread on which they slaughtered the lamb at evening, just as it was prescribed by Moses. (*Against the Jews* 8.18)

This "eighth day before the calends of April" of course means March 25. Although Tertullian does not mention Jesus' birth, he draws on the same kind of tradition as Clement, Hippolytus, and *On the Dating of Pascha* in calculating Jesus' death on or about March 25—meaning that the date of Jesus' conception was also the date of his death.[83] Even the differences between these texts underscore that there was a tradition of calculating Jesus' birth and death in the West as well as the East, well beyond the peculiar mathematical labors of one or two Christian authors with too much time on their hands.

More than this, they demonstrate a quest for wider connections, both natural and historical, for the story of Jesus. It was expected that the results of these calendrical inquiries would align the story of Jesus with the structure of a universe that had been made through the one whose incarnation was being reckoned. Modern arguments about the relative importance of historic calculation and cultural borrowing may need to take this presumed alignment more seriously.

The Son and the Sun

Although earlier speculation about Jesus' birth and death had noted the structure of the solar year, it was not driven by connections with pagan solar festivals since there was initially no attempt at constructing a Christian festival;

---

82. Talley, *Origins of the Liturgical Year*, 81–83.

83. For a fuller discussion, including of the possibility that *Against the Jews* is influenced by the Hippolytan evidence, see C. Philipp E. Nothaft, *Dating the Passion: The Life of Jesus and the Emergence of Scientific Chronology (200–1600)* (Leiden: Brill, 2012), 35–56.

and evidence for such earlier solstice festivals has itself been exaggerated. The solstice for Romans did fall on December 25, but the idea of a major sun feast on that day before the Christian incarnation feast was established is probably a fantasy.[84] There was an ancient Roman cult of Sol, although its festivals were on completely different days. Interest in the sun as a divinity did grow through the same period that Christianity itself appeared, first through the cult of Mithras and then through the appropriation of the Syrian "unconquered sun," which appears as a motif on contemporary Roman coins; but there is no evidence for an existing major festival that the Christians could simply borrow or "baptize."

The reverse may even have a grain of truth in it; Julian the Apostate, the nephew of Constantine who sought to restore the "old" ways of pagan religion, seems to be the first to claim (in 362, long after the evidence of the Philocalian calendar) that the December 25 festival was an ancient Roman observance—trying to gain leverage from an established Christmas feast, and inventing a past wherein the divine sun had the prominence he, and some modern scholars, thought it really should have.[85]

So Christmas itself—not just a date but a feast—must have existed, at least in some places, before the early fourth-century sources of the Philocalian *Chronograph*. Africa may have been one such place; the church in Africa had been damaged by the Great Persecution, a brawl in 311 over authentic bishops and martyrs turning into the mess of full-scale schism, and then, by 317, persecution by the neat-minded Constantine of one dissident group, who became known as Donatists. A century later, Augustine of Hippo implies that both his Catholic flock and the local Donatists celebrated December 25, but says the Donatists did not keep January 6, which the Catholic group had meanwhile adopted (*Sermon* 202). This suggests that December 25 had already been observed before the violence and split.[86]

Earlier Christian authors had used sun imagery and sun-related ideas about time like "the day of the sun" to think about Jesus; the eventual celebration of his birth on this day was a conjunction of historical and cosmic interests rather than one triumphing over the other. More often than not, preachers of the later fourth and fifth centuries took full advantage of the idea that Christ was true sun.

84. Steven Hijmans, "Usener's Christmas: A Contribution to the Modern Construct of Late Antique Solar Syncretism," in *Die Metamorphosen der Philologie. Hermann Usener und seine Folgen*, ed. Pascale Rabault-Feuerhahn and Michel Espagne (Wiesbaden: Harrassowitz, 2011), 139–52.
    85. Ibid., 144–45.
    86. Talley, *Origins of the Liturgical Year*, 86–87.

But where Tertullian had feared that the Christian minority of around 200 could be mistakenly identified as sun worshipers, around 450 Pope Leo the Great feared that the ostensibly Christian majority really still might be paying too much attention to the sun:

> Even some Christians think it is pious to do this, so that before entering the blessed apostle Peter's basilica, which is dedicated to the one living and true God, when they have mounted the steps that lead to the raised area, turning they bow toward the rising sun, and with bent necks worship its brilliant orb. We shrink inside and grieve that this should happen, which is partly due to the fault of ignorance and partly to the spirit of paganism; because although some of them do perhaps worship the Creator of that beautiful light rather than the Light itself, which is a creature, nevertheless we must abstain even from the appearance of this observance. For if one who has left the worship of the gods finds it among us, will he not hark back again to this vestige of former opinion, as if it were commendable, when he sees it to be common both to Christians and to the impious? (*Sermons* 27.4)

Exchanging Feasts

Although Christmas had been established sometime early in the fourth century, it took the rest of that century and even more for it to spread, particularly to the eastern Mediterranean, where January 6 had long been celebrated. In turn, the January 6 feast was widely adopted in the West, but in slightly changed terms.

Although the December 25 feast was initially a Western phenomenon, the January 6 Epiphany feast was more widespread than simply in the East. Early evidence suggests that while Roman and African Christians had not known the January 6 feast, and celebrated what we know as Christmas at quite an early date (not long after 300), other Italian cities knew "Epiphany" with its older conceptual force and took close to a century to adopt the more focused historical nativity feast.[87] When the two dates were both celebrated, Western churches tended to focus single-mindedly on the visit of the Magi on the second of them, although Western lectionaries have often included the other Eastern "Epiphany" stories—the baptism of Jesus and the wedding at Cana—for reading soon after that date.

The essentially conceptual rather than historical Epiphany feast combined birth, baptism, and more, but the addition of the other feast, Christmas, encouraged a "historicization" process comparable to that around Pascha, if

---

87. Bradshaw and Johnson, *Origins of Feasts*, 152–54.

differently in East and West. In both regions there were also theological debates whose force would not have been lost on liturgical practitioners; in the East a sole emphasis on Jesus' baptism may have sat less comfortably with a church grinding its way to the recognition of trinitarian deity through the fourth century, since it could be taken to imply an "adoption" of Jesus.

This may have been the sort of benefit the great preacher John Chrysostom referred to when still having to commend the observance of the new Christmas to his listeners in Antioch in 386:

> And indeed it is not yet the tenth year since this day has become clear and known to us. . . . Thus also it was made known from above among those living in the West and has now been brought to us, and not many years ago, and has grown so densely and thus borne fruit. (*On Christmas Day*, PG 49:351)

When the nativity feast was established there in the East, Epiphany often remained a commemoration not of the Magi but still of Jesus' baptism.

It is speculative but plausible to see the rollout of the Western nativity feast in the East as catalyzed by the triumph of the Nicene party at the Council of Constantinople in 381, where the creed usually referred to now as "Nicene" was adopted (although its use in the regular eucharistic liturgy would take another century to emerge). The story of Jesus' miraculous conception and birth underscored full and eternal divinity, revealed rather than given at baptism, and thus suited the Nicene party well.

We should not imagine, however, that those Christians on the losing side of the christological debate and often referred to inaccurately as "Arians" necessarily had difficulty with any of these feasts; they were not ancient Unitarians, and acknowledged Jesus as a preexistent heavenly being as the Nicenes did, yet not as of the same being or essence as the Father. Nevertheless, the promulgation of the feast and its wide celebration and comment were an opportunity for the Nicenes to celebrate not only the birth of Jesus but also the settlement of a doctrinal controversy that had lasted most of a century.[88]

Advent

Although Advent has traditionally been regarded as the start of the liturgical year in Western Christianity, it was the last of the major feasts and seasons to emerge. In sources of the fourth century—the Philocalian *Chronograph* among them—Christmas itself was the beginning of the Christian year.

---

88. Comings, *Aspects of the Liturgical Year*, 87–90.

We noted that the origin of Lent lay in the coupling of Easter with an older tradition of prebaptismal fasting, rather than merely in the gradual extension backward of the pre-Easter fast days attested in third-century sources. Something similar may be behind the Western Advent, which eventually took the familiar four-week form under Gregory the Great (in office 590–604) but had considerable previous history.

As we have seen, Christmas in the classic Western sense may not have existed at all before around 300, and was not observed even in many parts of the West until closer to 400. Earlier evidence for fasting and preparation around this time seems to have been for pre-Epiphany fasts. So, for instance, a Spanish council in 380 prescribed that:

> On the twenty-one days from sixteen days before the Kalends of January [December 17] to the day of Epiphany, which is eight days before the Ides of January [January 6], let no one through these days absent themselves from church nor hide in their houses, nor stay in their country homes, nor head for the mountains nor walk with bare feet, but flock to church. (*Canons of Saragossa* 4)

This curious decree at Saragossa was part of a response by local bishops to more spectacular forms of asceticism that valued heroic individual performance over obedient communal observance; their second canon had been directed at similar fast-and-loose Lenten self-denial.[89] And the period of fasting is here defined relative not to December 25 but to January 6, although observance of the former date may already have begun as well.[90] For our purposes, the point is the time, as well as the character, of the desired practice; this period is somewhat like Lent, and for three weeks, just like some other early prebaptismal and pre-paschal periods.[91]

While the Spanish bishops were seeking to moderate asceticism, they clearly expected some sort of seasonal fast; so this really is Advent, of a sort. Their opponents apparently wanted to do more but at the same time, undertaking urban or rural retreats, which underscores that the parties agreed the time was ripe for ascetic performance. Advent in Spain appears thus not merely as a mark on the liturgical calendar but as a monument to the struggle that

89. See Virginia Burrus, "Ascesis, Authority, and Text: The Acts of the Council of Saragossa," *Semeia* 58 (1992): 95–108, esp. 98–99.

90. J. Neil Alexander, *Waiting for the Coming: The Liturgical Meaning of Advent, Christmas, Epiphany* (Washington, DC: Pastoral Press, 1993), 11–12.

91. Martin Connell, "The Origins and Evolution of Advent in the West," in *Between Memory and Hope: Readings on the Liturgical Year*, ed. John F. Baldovin and Maxwell E. Johnson (Collegeville, MN: Liturgical Press, 2000), 349–71.

the church had in negotiating how its individual and communal aspects were expressed, in time and otherwise. Periods of forty days' preparation before Christmas also appear in other Western centers in the fourth century, probably reflecting a connection with baptism.[92]

Pope Gregory, however, later led the influential Roman church to reduce a six-week Advent to the familiar four, and in doing so accentuated eschatological more than anticipatory themes (in keeping with the fact that this was the *end* of a liturgical year at this point, the new one beginning with Christmas), and loosening ties to baptismal preparation. While Western observance thus eventually came to focus on the "four last things" (death, judgment, heaven, and hell), in the East the period before Christmas was and is marked not so much by finality but by potential; Byzantine and Syrian traditions even continued to emphasize stories of Jesus' origins prior to Christmas itself.[93]

Conclusion

The undoubted contrast between the colorful calendars of feasts, fasts, and saints that churches of the fourth and fifth centuries celebrated, on the one hand, and the relative silence of the NT documents on times and seasons, on the other, gives pause for thought. Some of the explicit NT reflections on time are apparently critical of the observance of times and festivals, or at least those that establish and reflect Jewish identity.

That last point has sometimes been extended to suggest the earliest Christians were not concerned with time at all, except as the medium through which final judgment would arrive. According to that view, the tendency eventually to structure time through feasts and fasts is a sort of fall from primitive expectation to a kind of spiritual "settling," at best a circumspect reorientation and at worst a loss of authentic anticipation.

The reality seems different. Although the formation of characteristic practices around Sundays, Easter, Christmas, and fasting days and seasons involves distinct stories with specific questions and problems, there is a commonality here that consists not in a turn from eschatological single-mindedness to a complexity of complacency but in the gradual formation of a culture. As much as any other medium or practice, the use of time reveals that the Christians were as much a new cultural formation as a "religious" one—indeed "religion"

92. Ibid., 366–67.
93. Bradshaw and Johnson, *Origins of Feasts*, 158–59.

in our modern sense does not work well to interpret the choices the ancients made regarding their identity, allegiance, and practice. For them to inhabit time was inescapable and required structures, markers, and indicators of meaning; if the Lord of time was their Lord, then time itself must reflect that sovereignty.

The ancient evidence also suggests that debates about the relative importance of original Christian calculations and constructions versus "borrowings" from Jewish and particularly from "pagan" tradition have not been as illuminating as often assumed, either in explaining the Christianization of time or interpreting it. Across different controversies and processes, we see a common concern to relate history and nature rather than to subject one in the service of the other. Regarding the nativity in particular, hints of interest in the sun and its movement from an early period cannot be reduced to "pagan" influence, but suggest a desire to make sense of a divinely ordered universe with the tools available—scriptural, historical, and other. If there is a shift from focus on the *eschaton*, or end of time, to increasing attention to various other *kairoi*, or points in time, this is merely to affirm that Christian existence and practice had a history and not merely a beginning or end, and that Christians thought and acted in that history.

This is what we should expect, of course, since both the "folk" theology of most Christian believers and the more sophisticated discourses we rely on for most of this evidence share at least the belief that the world itself—the world of cities and of cemeteries, and of stars and planets—serves and reveals the God who made them. With characteristic pithiness, Augustine expresses this point in one of his Christmas sermons, wherein he presents Jesus as the meaning of time and times alike: "As born of his Father, he orders all days; as born of his mother, he sanctifies this one" (*Sermon* 194.1).

Epilogue

The Making of Christian Worship

This survey of early Christian worship ends without addressing some significant aspects of later liturgy. Weddings did not become typical events for church celebration for many centuries, reminding us that the "sacramental" (since marriage was from early times a sacrament in the Eastern and Western churches, prior to the Reformation at least) and the "liturgical" are not identical categories. We have only mentioned funerals in passing, although cemeteries have had some prominence; in the early centuries, the already-buried attracted as much attention as those on their way to the grave. There are no organs, no spires, no special clothes; many of the details that modern Christians may appreciate as "traditional" elements of their liturgical lives are actually later—medieval or even modern—additions.

We began by considering the difficulty of defining and understanding "worship," ancient or modern. For the authors and communities treated in this book, "worship" was not about services, but service; not about gestures that signaled belief or allegiance, but about allegiance itself. The most central and persistent acts of ancient Christian worship are thus not merely "liturgical"; their character or meaning is not grasped, let alone exhausted, by the mere fact that they are rituals or ceremonies that serve communal goals or communicate shared values. The distinctive communal actions of the Christians are, however, "worship," because they are undertaken as acts of obedience and service, and as the characteristic habitus of the followers of Jesus.

The different types of ancient Christian action and discourse come together to form a whole of communal identity and service—an embodied theory and practice of worship—via complex means; but it is hardly accidental that the two most distinctive Christian ritual actions—baptism and Eucharist—are associated with commands of Jesus. These are, while adaptations of existing ritual practices, initially more discontinuous from other ancient notions of cultus than obvious or recognizable. These acts did not so much, or not only, inhabit a generic or established ancient sense of "worship" in the liturgical sense; rather, they created one. The tension between this practice and those of others, including the Christians' initial or apparent lack of a sacrificial practice and rejection of others', was at least one basis for the tensions reflected in the works of the apologists and for the sanctions placed upon Christians into the fourth century.

Other forms of action that characterized the Christians' communal life were more readily understood relative to the religious practice of contemporaries: acts of prayer and praise that galvanized the media of human life, space, body, and time itself, and the discursive performances of reading and teaching that were their passive or receptive correlates, all had parallels in the lives of Jewish or Roman communities. They had distinctive qualities too, and were shaped by the allegiance of the emerging church to the crucified and risen one, whose stamp they believed could be discerned in the creation itself and whose Spirit inspired their utterance to him as well as from him.

Christian liturgy thus emerges neither as a single or generic whole of which these are indifferent or interchangeable parts, nor as the physical expression of what are essentially spiritual goals or commitments. Instead, it is the sum of very specific and concrete performances, undertaken because they are believed by the members of the church to be constitutive of their faith, their allegiance, and their identity. These actions, offered as service to God, constitute Christian worship.

BIBLIOGRAPHY

Alexander, J. Neil. *Waiting for the Coming: The Liturgical Meaning of Advent, Christmas, Epiphany*. Washington, DC. Pastoral Press, 1993.

Armstrong, Jonathan. "Victorinus of Pettau as the Author of the Canon Muratori." *Vigiliae Christianae* 62, no. 1 (2008): 1–34.

Attridge, Harold W. *The Acts of Thomas*. Edited by Julian Victor Hills. Early Christian Apocrypha 3. Salem, OR: Polebridge Press, 2010.

———. *The Epistle to the Hebrews: A Commentary on the Epistle to the Hebrews*. Edited by Helmut Koester. Hermeneia. Philadelphia: Fortress, 1988.

———. *Essays on John and Hebrews*. WUNT 264. Tübingen: Mohr Siebeck, 2010. Reprint, Grand Rapids: Baker Academic, 2012.

———. "Paraenesis in a Homily (λόγος παρακλήσεως): The Possible Location of, and Socialization in, the 'Epistle to the Hebrews.'" *Semeia* 50 (1990): 211–26. Reprinted in Attridge, *Essays on John and Hebrews*, 294–307.

Augustine. *Expositions of the Psalms*. Edited by John E. Rotelle. Translated by Maria Poulding. The Works of Saint Augustine: A Translation for the 21st Century. Brooklyn, NY: New City Press, 2000.

Aune, David E. *Prophecy in Early Christianity and the Ancient Mediterranean World*. Grand Rapids: Eerdmans, 1983.

Bacchiocchi, Samuele. *From Sabbath to Sunday: A Historical Investigation of the Rise of Sunday Observance in Early Christianity*. Rome: Pontifical Gregorian University, 1977.

Bainton, Roland H. "Basilidian Chronology and New Testament Interpretation." *Journal of Biblical Literature* 42 (1923): 81–134.

Barnes, Timothy D. "The Date of Ignatius." *Expository Times* 120, no. 3 (2008): 119–30.

———. "Were Early Christians Crucified?" In *Early Christian Hagiography and Roman History*, 331–42. Tübingen: Mohr Siebeck, 2010.

Barr, David L. "The Apocalypse of John as Oral Enactment." *Interpretation* 40, no. 3 (1986): 243–56.

Barton, John. *Holy Writings, Sacred Text: The Canon in Early Christianity*. Louisville: Westminster John Knox, 1997.

Bauckham, Richard. "The Lord's Day." In *From Sabbath to Lord's Day: A Biblical, Historical, and Theological Investigation*, edited by D. A. Carson, 221–50. Grand Rapids: Zondervan, 1982.

Bell, Catherine M. *Ritual Theory, Ritual Practice*. New York: Oxford University Press, 1992.

Berger, Teresa. *Gender Differences and the Making of Liturgical History*. Farnham, UK: Ashgate, 2011.

Betz, Johannes. "The Eucharist in the Didache." In *The Didache in Modern Research*, edited by Jonathan A. Draper, 244–75. Leiden: Brill, 1996.

Black, C. Clifton. "The Rhetorical Form of the Hellenistic Jewish and Early Christian Sermon: A Response to Lawrence Wills." *Harvard Theological Review* 81, no. 1 (January 1, 1988): 1–18.

Bovon, François. "*Fragment Oxyrhynchus 840*, Fragment of a Lost Gospel, Witness of an Early Christian Controversy over Purity." *Journal of Biblical Literature* 119, no. 4 (2000): 705–28.

Bowes, Kimberly. *Private Worship, Public Values, and Religious Change in Late Antiquity*. New York: Cambridge University Press, 2008.

Bradshaw, Paul F. *Daily Prayer in the Early Church: A Study of the Origin and Early Development of the Divine Office*. London: SPCK/Alcuin Club, 1981.

———. "Did the Early Eucharist Ever Have a Sevenfold Shape?" *Heythrop Journal* 43 (2002): 73–76.

———. *Ordination Rites of the Ancient Churches of East and West*. New York: Pueblo, 1990.

———. "Prayer Morning, Noon, Evening, and Midnight—An Apostolic Custom?" *Studia Liturgica* 13 (1979): 57–62.

———. *Reconstructing Early Christian Worship*. London: SPCK, 2009.

———. *The Search for the Origins of Christian Worship: Sources and Methods for the Study of Early Liturgy*. London: SPCK, 2002.

———. "Ten Principles for Interpreting Early Christian Liturgical Evidence." In *The Making of Jewish and Christian Worship*, edited by Paul F. Bradshaw and Lawrence A. Hoffman, 3–21. Two Liturgical Traditions 1. Notre Dame, IN: University of Notre Dame Press, 1991.

———. *Two Ways of Praying*. Nashville: Abingdon, 1995.

———. "Women and Baptism in the *Didascalia Apostolorum*." *Journal of Early Christian Studies* 20 (2012): 641–45.

Bradshaw, Paul F., and Maxwell E. Johnson. *The Origins of Feasts, Fasts, and Seasons*. Collegeville, MN: Liturgical Press, 2011.

Bradshaw, Paul F., Maxwell E. Johnson, and L. Edward Phillips. *The Apostolic Tradition: A Commentary*. Edited by Harold W. Attridge. Hermeneia. Minneapolis: Fortress, 2002.

Brakke, David. "Canon Formation and Social Conflict in Fourth-Century Egypt: Athanasius of Alexandria's Thirty-Ninth Festal Letter." *Harvard Theological Review* 87, no. 4 (1994): 395–419.

———. *The Gnostics: Myth, Ritual, and Diversity in Early Christianity*. Cambridge, MA: Harvard University Press, 2010.

———. "A New Fragment of Athanasius's Thirty-Ninth Festal Letter: Heresy, Apocrypha, and the Canon." *Harvard Theological Review* 103, no. 1 (2010): 47–66.

Branham, Joan R. "Penetrating the Sacred: Breaches and Barriers in the Jerusalem Temple." In *Thresholds of the Sacred: Architectural, Art Historical, Liturgical, and Theological Perspectives on Religious Screens, East and West*, 6–24. Washington, DC: Dumbarton Oaks, 2006.

———. "Sacred Space under Erasure in Ancient Synagogues and Early Churches." *Art Bulletin* 74 (1992): 375–94.

Bride of Light: Hymns on Mary from the Syriac Churches. Mōrān 'Ethō Series 6. Kerala, India: St. Ephrem Ecumenical Research Institute, 1994.

Brown, Peter. *The Body and Society: Men, Women, and Sexual Renunciation in Early Christianity*. New York: Columbia University Press, 1988.

———. *The Cult of the Saints: Its Rise and Function in Latin Christianity*. Haskell Lectures on History of Religions, n.s., 2. Chicago: University of Chicago Press, 1981.

———. *The Rise of Western Christendom: Triumph and Diversity, A.D. 200–1000*. 2nd ed. Malden, MA: Wiley-Blackwell, 2003.

Bultmann, Rudolf. *The Gospel of John: A Commentary*. Translated by G. R. Beasley-Murray. Philadelphia: Westminster, 1971.

Burkert, Walter. *Ancient Mystery Cults*. Cambridge, MA: Harvard University Press, 1987.

Burrus, Virginia. "Ascesis, Authority, and Text: The Acts of the Council of Saragossa." *Semeia* 58 (1992): 95–108.

Castagno, Adele Monaci. "Origen the Scholar and Pastor." In *Preacher and Audience: Studies in Early Christian and Byzantine Homiletics*, edited by Mary Cunningham and Pauline Allen, 65–87. A New History of the Sermon 1. Boston: Brill, 1998.

Clark, Gillian. "Victricius of Rouen: Praising the Saints." *Journal of Early Christian Studies* 7, no. 3 (1999): 365–99.

Clarke, G. W. "Cyprian's Epistle 64 and the Kissing of Feet in Baptism." *Harvard Theological Review* 66, no. 1 (January 1, 1973): 147–52.

Cohen, Richard. *Chasing the Sun: The Epic Story of the Star That Gives Us Life*. New York: Random House, 2010.

Cohen, Shaye J. D. "Is 'Proselyte Baptism' Mentioned in the Mishnah? The Interpretation of M. Pesahim 8.8." In *The Significance of Yavneh and Other Essays in Jewish Hellenism*, 316–28. Tübingen: Mohr Siebeck, 2010.

Collins, Adela Yarbro. "The Origin of Christian Baptism." In *Living Water, Sealing Spirit: Readings on Christian Initiation*, edited by Maxwell E. Johnson, 35–57. Collegeville, MN: Liturgical Press, 1995.

Comings, Jill Burnett. *Aspects of the Liturgical Year in Cappadocia (325–430)*. Patristic Studies 7. New York: Peter Lang, 2005.

Connell, Martin F. "Clothing the Body of Christ: An Inquiry about the Letters of Paul." *Worship* 85 (2011): 128–46.

———. "*Nisi Pedes*, Except for the Feet: Footwashing in the Communities of John's Gospel." *Worship* 70 (1996): 517–31.

———. "The Origins and Evolution of Advent in the West." In *Between Memory and Hope: Readings on the Liturgical Year*, edited by John F. Baldovin and Maxwell E. Johnson, 349–71. Collegeville, MN: Liturgical Press, 2000.

Cosgrove, Charles H. *An Ancient Christian Hymn with Musical Notation: Papyrus Oxyrhynchus 1786: Text and Commentary*. Studien und Texte zu Antike und Christentum [Studies and Texts in Antiquity and Christianity]. Tübingen: Mohr Siebeck, 2011.

———. "Clement of Alexandria and Early Christian Music." *Journal of Early Christian Studies* 14, no. 3 (2006): 255–82.

Cox, Patricia. "Origen and the Witch of Endor: Toward an Iconoclastic Typology." *Anglican Theological Review* 66, no. 2 (1984): 137–47.

Cunningham, Mary, and Pauline Allen. Introduction to *Preacher and Audience: Studies in Early Christian and Byzantine Homiletics*, edited by Mary Cunningham and Pauline Allen, 1–20. A New History of the Sermon 1. Boston: Brill, 1998.

Dalby, Andrew. *Siren Feasts: A History of Food and Gastronomy in Greece*. London: Routledge, 1997.

Davies, W. D., and Dale Allison. *A Critical and Exegetical Commentary on the Gospel according to Saint Matthew*. 3 vols. ICC. Edinburgh: T&T Clark, 1997.

Day, Juliette. *The Baptismal Liturgy of Jerusalem: Fourth- and Fifth-Century Evidence from Palestine, Syria and Egypt*. Liturgy, Worship and Society. Burlington, VT: Ashgate, 2007.

De Ste. Croix, G. E. M. "Aspects of the 'Great' Persecution." *Harvard Theological Review* 47, no. 2 (1954): 75–113.

Detienne, Marcel, and Jean Pierre Vernant. *The Cuisine of Sacrifice among the Greeks*. Chicago: University of Chicago Press, 1989.

Dewey, Joanna. "From Oral Stories to Written Text." In *Women's Sacred Scriptures*, edited by Pui-Lan Kwok and Elisabeth Schüssler Fiorenza, 20–28. Concilium. London: SCM, 1998.

Dix, Gregory. *The Shape of the Liturgy*. New ed. London: Continuum, 2005.

Dodd, C. H. *The Apostolic Preaching and Its Developments; Three Lectures, with an Appendix on Eschatology and History*. 2nd ed. New York: Harper, 1954.

Doig, Allan. *Liturgy and Architecture: From the Early Church to the Middle Ages*. Liturgy, Worship and Society. Burlington, VT: Ashgate, 2008.

Donfried, Karl P. *The Setting of Second Clement in Early Christianity*. Supplements to Novum Testamentum 38. Leiden: Brill, 1974.

Doran, Robert. *The Lives of Simeon Stylites*. Cistercian Studies Series 112. Kalamazoo, MI: Cistercian Publications, 1992.

Draper, Jonathan A. "Pure Sacrifice in Didache 14 as Jewish Christian Exegesis." *Neotestamentica* 42 (2008): 223–52.

———. "Ritual Process and Ritual Symbol in Didache 7–10." *Vigiliae Christianae* 54, no. 2 (May 2000): 121.

Dunbabin, Katherine M. D. *The Roman Banquet: Images of Conviviality*. New York: Cambridge University Press, 2003.

Dunn-Wilson, David. *A Mirror for the Church: Preaching in the First Five Centuries*. Grand Rapids: Eerdmans, 2005.

Edwards, O. C. *A History of Preaching*. Nashville: Abingdon, 2004.

Eisen, Ute E. *Women Officeholders in Early Christianity: Epigraphical and Literary Studies*. Collegeville, MN: Liturgical Press, 2000.

Elliott, J. K. "Manuscripts, the Codex and the Canon." *Journal for the Study of the New Testament* 19, no. 63 (1997): 105–23.

Epp, Eldon Jay. "The Oxyrhynchus New Testament Papyri: 'Not without Honor except in Their Hometown'?" *Journal of Biblical Literature* 123 (2004): 5–55.

Ernest, James D. *The Bible in Athanasius of Alexandria*. Leiden: Brill, 2004.

Fagan, Garrett G. *Bathing in Public in the Roman World*. Ann Arbor: University of Michigan Press, 2002.

Falk, Daniel K. "Jewish Prayer Literature and the Jerusalem Church." In *The Book of Acts in Its Palestinian Setting*, 267–301. Grand Rapids: Eerdmans, 1995.

Ferguson, Everett. *Baptism in the Early Church: History, Theology, and Liturgy in the First Five Centuries*. Grand Rapids: Eerdmans, 2008.

Foley, Edward. *Foundations of Christian Music*. Piscataway, NJ: Gorgias Press, 2009.

Frøyshov, Stig Simeon R. "The Cathedral-Monastic Distinction Revisited Part I: Was Egyptian Desert Liturgy a Pure Monastic Office?" *Studia Liturgica* 37, no. 2 (2007): 198–216.

Gamble, Harry Y. *Books and Readers in the Early Church: A History of Early Christian Texts*. New Haven: Yale University Press, 1995.

García Martínez, Florentino, and W. G. E. Watson. *The Dead Sea Scrolls Translated: The Qumran Texts in English*. Leiden: Brill, 1996.

Garnsey, Peter. *Food and Society in Classical Antiquity*. Cambridge: Cambridge University Press, 1999.

Grafton, Anthony, and Megan Hale Williams. *Christianity and the Transformation of the Book: Origen, Eusebius, and the Library of Caesarea*. Cambridge, MA: Harvard University Press, 2008.

Haines-Eitzen, Kim. *Guardians of Letters: Literacy, Power, and the Transmitters of Early Christian Literature*. New York: Oxford University Press, 2000.

Hammerling, Roy. *The Lord's Prayer in the Early Church: The Pearl of Great Price*. New York: Palgrave Macmillan, 2010.

Harrill, J. Albert. "Coming of Age and Putting on Christ: The Toga Virilis Ceremony, Its Paraenesis, and Paul's Interpretation of Baptism in Galatians." *Novum Testamentum* 44, no. 3 (2002): 252–77.

———. "Servile Functionaries or Priestly Leaders? Roman Domestic Religion, Narrative Intertextuality, and Pliny's Reference to Slave Christian Ministrae (Ep. 10,96,8)." *Zeitschrift für die neutestamentliche Wissenschaft und die Kunde der älteren Kirche* 97, nos. 1–2 (2006): 111–30.

Harvey, Susan Ashbrook. *Song and Memory: Biblical Women in Syriac Tradition*. The Père Marquette Lecture in Theology 20. Milwaukee: Marquette University Press, 2010.

Hess, Hamilton. *The Early Development of Canon Law and the Council of Serdica*. Oxford Early Christian Studies. New York: Oxford University Press, 2002.

Hijmans, Steven. "Usener's Christmas: A Contribution to the Modern Construct of Late Antique Solar Syncretism." In *Die Metamorphosen der Philologie. Hermann Usener und seine Folgen*, edited by Pascale Rabault-Feuerhahn and Michel Espagne, 139–52. Wiesbaden: Harrassowitz, 2011.

Hippolytus. *On the Apostolic Tradition*. Edited by Alistair Stewart-Sykes. Crestwood, NY: St. Vladimir's Seminary Press, 2001.

Hoffman, Lawrence A. "The Early History of the Public Reading of the Torah." In *Jews, Christians, and Polytheists in the Ancient Synagogue: Cultural Interaction during the Greco-Roman Period*, edited by Steven Fine, 44–56. Baltimore Studies in the History of Judaism. New York: Routledge, 1999.

———. "The Jewish Lectionary, the Great Sabbath, and the Lenten Calendar: Liturgical Links between Christians and Jews in the First Three Centuries." In *Time and Community: In Honor of Thomas Julian Talley*, edited by J. Neil Alexander, 3–20. NPM Studies in Church Music and Liturgy. Washington, DC: Pastoral Press, 1990.

Holmes, Michael W., ed. *The Apostolic Fathers: Greek Texts and English Translations*. 3rd ed. Grand Rapids: Baker Academic, 2007.

Hopkins, Keith. "Christian Number and Its Implications." *Journal of Early Christian Studies* 6, no. 2 (1998): 185–226.

Horbury, William. "*Cena pura* and Lord's Supper." In *Herodian Judaism and New Testament Study*, 104–40. WUNT 193. Tübingen: Mohr Siebeck, 2006.

———. "Jewish-Christian Relations in Barnabas and Justin Martyr." In *Jews and Christians in Contact and Controversy*, 127–61. Edinburgh: T&T Clark, 1998.

Horsley, G. H. R. "Epitaph for a Jewish Psalm-Singer." In *New Documents Illustrating Early Christianity*, 1:115–17. North Ryde, NSW: Ancient History Documentary Research Centre, 1976.

Hurtado, Larry W. *At the Origins of Christian Worship: The Context and Character of Earliest Christian Devotion*. Grand Rapids: Eerdmans, 2000.

———. *Lord Jesus Christ: Devotion to Jesus in Earliest Christianity*. Grand Rapids: Eerdmans, 2005.

———. "Manuscripts and the Sociology of Early Christian Reading." In *The Early Text of the New Testament*, edited by C. E. Hill and M. J. Kruger, 49–62. Oxford: Oxford University Press, 2012.

Jeffrey, Peter. "Monastic Reading and the Emerging Roman Chant Repertory." In *Western Plainchant in the First Millennium: Studies in the Medieval Liturgy and Its Music*, edited by Sean Gallagher, James Haar, John Nádas, and Timothy Striplin, 45–103. Burlington, VT: Ashgate, 2003.

Jensen, Robin Margaret. "Baptismal Rites and Architecture." In *Late Ancient Christianity*, edited by Virginia Burrus, 117–44. Minneapolis: Fortress, 2005.

———. "Dining with the Dead: From the Mensa to the Altar in Christian Late Antiquity." In *Commemorating the Dead: Texts and Artifacts in Context; Studies of Roman, Jewish, and Christian Burials*, edited by Laurie Brink and Deborah Green, 107–43. Berlin: Walter de Gruyter, 2008.

———. *Understanding Early Christian Art*. New York: Routledge, 2000.

Jensen, Robin Margaret, and J. Patout Burns. "The Eucharistic Liturgy in Hippo's Basilica Major at the Time of Augustine." In *Augustine through the Ages: An Encyclopedia*, edited by Allan Fitzgerald and John C. Cavadini, 335–38. Grand Rapids: Eerdmans, 1999.

Jeremias, Joachim. *The Eucharistic Words of Jesus*. London: SCM, 1966.

Johnson, Luke Timothy. *The First and Second Letters to Timothy: A New Translation with Introduction and Commentary*. Anchor Bible 35A. New York: Doubleday, 2001.

Johnson, Maxwell E. "Martyrs and the Mass: The Interpolation of the Narrative of Institution into the Anaphora." *Worship* 87 (2013): 2–22.

————. *The Rites of Christian Initiation: Their Evolution and Interpretation.* Collegeville, MN: Liturgical Press, 2007.

————. "*Sub Tuum Praesidium*: The *Theotokos* in Christian Life and Worship before Ephesus." *Pro Ecclesia* 17, no. 1 (Winter 2008): 52–75.

Johnson, William A. "Toward a Sociology of Reading in Classical Antiquity." *American Journal of Philology* 121 (2000): 593–627.

Jones, F. Stanley. "The Pseudo-Clementines: A History of Research." *Second Century* 2 (1982): 1–33, 63–96.

Judge, E. A. "The Earliest Use of *Monachos* for 'Monk' (P. Coll. Youtie 77) and the Origins of Monasticism." *Jahrbuch für Antike und Christentum* 20 (1977): 72–89.

————. "The Early Christians as a Scholastic Community." *Journal of Religious History* 1, no. 1 (1960): 4–15.

————. "The Early Christians as a Scholastic Community: Part II." *Journal of Religious History* 1, no. 3 (1961): 125–37.

Karris, Robert J. *Luke: Artist and Theologian; Luke's Passion Account as Literature.* Theological Inquiries. New York: Paulist Press, 1985.

Kasser, Rodolphe, Marvin Meyer, and Gregor Wurst, eds. *The Gospel of Judas.* 2nd ed. Washington, DC: National Geographic, 2008.

Kivy, Peter. *The Performance of Reading: An Essay in the Philosophy of Literature.* New Directions in Aesthetics 3. Malden, MA: Blackwell, 2006.

Klinghardt, Matthias. "Gemeindeleib und Mahlritual: *Sōma* in den paulinischen Mahltexten." *Zeitschrift für Neues Testament* 27 (2011): 51–56.

————. "A Typology of the Communal Meal." In *Meals in the Early Christian World: Social Formation, Experimentation, and Conflict at the Table*, edited by Dennis E. Smith and Hal Taussig, 9–22. New York: Palgrave Macmillan, 2012.

Kloppenborg Verbin, John S. "Dating Theodotos (CIJ II 1404)." *Journal of Jewish Studies* 51 (2000): 243–80.

Koester, Helmut. "The Text of the Synoptic Gospels in the Second Century." In *Gospel Traditions in the Second Century: Origins, Recensions, Text, and Transmission*, edited by William L. Petersen, 19–37. Christianity and Judaism in Antiquity. Notre Dame, IN: University of Notre Dame Press, 1989.

Kraabel, A. T. "The Disappearance of the 'God-Fearers.'" *Numen* 28 (1981): 113–26.

Kraeling, Carl H. *The Christian Building.* Vol. 2 of *The Excavations at Dura-Europos* VIII, edited by C. Bradford Welles. New Haven: Dura-Europos Publications, 1967.

Krautheimer, Richard. *Early Christian and Byzantine Architecture.* 4th ed. New Haven: Yale University Press, 1986.

Lang, Uwe Michael. *Turning Towards the Lord: Orientation in Liturgical Prayer.* San Francisco: Ignatius Press, 2009.

Langer, Ruth. "Early Rabbinic Liturgy in Its Palestinian Milieu: Did Non-Rabbis Know the *Amidah*?" In *When Judaism and Christianity Began: Essays in Memory of Anthony J. Saldarini*, edited by Alan J. Avery-Peck, Daniel J. Harrington, and Jacob Neusner, 2:423–39. Leiden: Brill, 2004.

Larson-Miller, Lizette. "The Liturgical Inheritance of the Late Empire in the Middle Ages." In *A Companion to the Eucharist in the Middle Ages*, edited by Ian Levy, Gary Macy, and Kristen Van Ausdall, 13–58. Leiden: Brill, 2011.

Latham, Jacob A. "From Literal to Spiritual Soldiers of Christ: Disputed Episcopal Elections and the Advent of Christian Processions in Late Antique Rome." *Church History* 81 (2012): 298–327.

Lattke, Michael. *The Odes of Solomon: A Commentary*. Edited by Harold W. Attridge. Hermeneia. Minneapolis: Fortress, 2009.

Leonhard, Clemens. *The Jewish Pesach and the Origins of the Christian Easter: Open Questions in Current Research*. Studia Judaica Bd. 35. New York: Walter de Gruyter, 2006.

Levine, Lee I. *Ancient Synagogue: The First Thousand Years*. 2nd ed. New Haven: Yale University Press, 2005.

Leyerle, S. Blake. "Clement of Alexandria on the Importance of Table Etiquette." *Journal of Early Christian Studies* 3 (1995): 123–41.

Llewelyn, S. R. *New Documents Illustrating Early Christianity: A Review of the Greek Inscriptions and Papyri Published in 1986–87*. Grand Rapids: Eerdmans, 2002.

Luijendijk, AnneMarie. "Sacred Scriptures as Trash: Biblical Papyri from Oxyrhynchus." *Vigiliae Christianae* 64 (2010): 217–54.

MacMullen, Ramsay. *Christianity and Paganism in the Fourth to Eighth Centuries*. New Haven: Yale University Press, 1997.

———. *The Second Church: Popular Christianity A.D. 200–400*. Atlanta: Society of Biblical Literature, 2009.

Madigan, Kevin, and Carolyn Osiek, eds. *Ordained Women in the Early Church: A Documentary History*. Baltimore: Johns Hopkins University Press, 2005.

Magness, Jodi. *The Archaeology of Qumran and the Dead Sea Scrolls*. Grand Rapids: Eerdmans, 2003.

Marcus, Joel. "Passover and Last Supper Revisited." *New Testament Studies* 59 (2013): 303–24.

Markus, Robert. "How on Earth Could Places Become Holy? Origins of the Christian Idea of Holy Places." *Journal of Early Christian Studies* 2, no. 3 (1994): 257–71.

Mateos, Juan. "The Origins of the Divine Office." *Worship* 41 (1967): 477–85.

Mayer, Wendy, and Pauline Allen. *John Chrysostom*. Early Church Fathers. New York: Routledge, 2000.

Mazza, Enrico. *The Origins of the Eucharistic Prayer.* Collegeville, MN: Liturgical Press, 1995.

McDonnell, Kilian. *The Baptism of Jesus in the Jordan: The Trinitarian and Cosmic Order of Salvation.* Collegeville, MN: Liturgical Press, 1996.

———. "The Marian Liturgical Tradition." In *Between Memory and Hope: Readings on the Liturgical Year,* edited by John F. Baldovin and Maxwell E. Johnson, 385–400. Collegeville, MN: Liturgical Press, 2000.

McGowan, Andrew B. *Ascetic Eucharists: Food and Drink in Early Christian Ritual Meals.* Oxford Early Christian Studies. Oxford: Clarendon, 1999.

———. "Discipline and Diet: Feeding the Martyrs in Roman Carthage." *Harvard Theological Review* 96 (2003): 455–76.

———. "Eating People: Accusations of Cannibalism against Christians in the Second Century." *Journal of Early Christian Studies* 2 (1994): 413–42.

———. "Eucharist and Sacrifice: Cultic Tradition and Transformation in Early Christian Ritual Meals." In *Mahl und religiöse Identität im frühen Christentum,* edited by Matthias Klinghardt and Hal Taussig, 191–206. Texte und Arbeiten zum neutestamentlichen Zeitalter 56. Tübingen: Francke, 2012.

———. "'First Regarding the Cup . . .': Papias and the Diversity of Early Eucharistic Practice." *Journal of Theological Studies* 46 (1995): 551–55.

———. "The Inordinate Cup: Issues of Order in Early Eucharistic Drinking." In *Studia Patristica* 35, 283–91. Leuven: Peeters, 2001.

———. "'Is There a Liturgical Text in This Gospel?': The Institution Narratives and Their Early Interpretive Communities." *Journal of Biblical Literature* 118 (1999): 73–87.

———. "Naming the Feast: The Agape and the Diversity of Early Christian Meals." In *Studia Patristica* 30, 314–18. Leuven: Peeters, 1997.

———. "Tertullian and the 'Heretical' Origins of the 'Orthodox' Trinity." *Journal of Early Christian Studies* 14 (2006): 437–57.

McKay, Heather A. *Sabbath and Synagogue: The Question of Sabbath Worship in Ancient Judaism.* Leiden: Brill, 1994.

McKinnon, James W. "Desert Monasticism and the Later Fourth-Century Psalmodic Movement." *Music & Letters* 75, no. 4 (1994): 505–21.

———. "The Meaning of the Patristic Polemic against Musical Instruments." *Current Musicology* 1 (1965): 69–82.

———. "On the Question of Psalmody in the Ancient Synagogue." *Early Music History* 6 (1986): 159–91.

McKnight, Edgar V. "Form Criticism and New Testament Interpretation." In *Method and Meaning: Essays in New Testament Interpretation in Honor of Harold W. Attridge,* edited by Andrew B. McGowan and Kent Harold Richards, 21–40. Atlanta: Society of Biblical Literature, 2011.

Meier, John P. *A Marginal Jew: Rethinking the Historical Jesus.* Vol. 2, *Mentor, Message, and Miracles.* ABRL. New York: Doubleday, 1994.

Mitchell, Leonel L. *Baptismal Anointing.* Alcuin Club 48. London: SPCK, 1966.

Moss, Candida R. "On the Dating of Polycarp: Rethinking the Place of the *Martyrdom of Polycarp* in the History of Christianity." *Early Christianity* 1, no. 4 (2010): 539–74.

———. *The Other Christs: Imitating Jesus in Ancient Christian Ideologies of Martyrdom.* New York: Oxford University Press, 2010.

Murphy, Catherine M. *John the Baptist: Prophet of Purity for a New Age.* Collegeville, MN: Liturgical Press, 2003.

Murray, Penelope. "Dance." In *The Oxford Encyclopedia of Ancient Greece and Rome*, edited by Michael Gagarin and Elaine Fantham, 355–58. Oxford: Oxford University Press, 2009.

Myers, Susan. "Initiation by Anointing in Early Syriac-Speaking Christianity." *Studia Liturgica* 31 (2001): 150–70.

Naiden, F. S. *Ancient Supplication.* New York: Oxford University Press, 2006.

Neusner, Jacob. *The Classics of Judaism: A Textbook and Reader.* Louisville: Westminster John Knox, 1995.

Niederwimmer, Kurt. *The Didache: A Commentary.* Edited by Harold W. Attridge. Translated by Linda M. Maloney. Hermeneia. Minneapolis: Fortress, 1998.

Nothaft, C. Philipp E. *Dating the Passion: The Life of Jesus and the Emergence of Scientific Chronology (200–1600).* Leiden: Brill, 2012.

Old, Hughes Oliphant. *The Reading and Preaching of the Scriptures in the Worship of the Christian Church: The Biblical Period.* 7 vols. Grand Rapids: Eerdmans, 1998.

Olivar, Alexander. "Reflections on Problems Raised by Early Christian Preaching." In *Preacher and Audience: Studies in Early Christian and Byzantine Homiletics*, edited by Mary Cunningham and Pauline Allen, 21–32. A New History of the Sermon 1. Boston: Brill, 1998.

Origen. *Treatise on Prayer: Translation and Notes with an Account of the Practice and Doctrine of Prayer from New Testament Times to Origen.* Edited by Eric George Jay. London: SPCK, 1954.

Osborn, Ronald E. *The Folly of God: The Rise of Christian Preaching.* Vol. 1 of *A History of Christian Preaching.* St. Louis: Chalice, 1999.

Osburn, Carroll D. "The Greek Lectionaries of the New Testament." In *The Text of the New Testament in Contemporary Research: Essays on the Status Quaestionis*, edited by Bart D. Ehrman and Michael William Holmes, 61–74. Grand Rapids: Eerdmans, 1995.

Page, Christopher. *The Christian West and Its Singers: The First Thousand Years.* New Haven: Yale University Press, 2010.

Paget, James Carleton. *The Epistle of Barnabas: Outlook and Background*. Tübingen: Mohr Siebeck, 1994.

Parker, D. C. *The Living Text of the Gospels*. Cambridge: Cambridge University Press, 1997.

Parker, Robert. *On Greek Religion*. Ithaca, NY: Cornell University Press, 2011.

Paverd, Frans van de. *St. John Chrysostom, The Homilies on the Statues: An Introduction*. Orientalia Christiana Analecta 239. Roma: Pont. Institutum Studiorum Orientalium, 1991.

Penn, Michael Philip. *Kissing Christians: Ritual and Community in the Late Ancient Church*. Divinations. Philadelphia: University of Pennsylvania Press, 2005.

Peppard, Michael. "Musical Instruments and Jewish-Christian Relations in Late Antiquity." *Studia Liturgica* 33 (January 1, 2003): 20–32.

———. "New Testament Imagery in the Earliest Christian Baptistery." In *Dura-Europos: Crossroads of Antiquity*, edited by Lisa R. Brody and Gail L. Hoffman, 103–21. Chestnut Hill, MA: McMullen Museum of Art, Boston College; distributed by the University of Chicago Press, 2011.

Phillips, L. Edward. "Daily Prayer in the Apostolic Tradition of Hippolytus." *Journal of Theological Studies* 40 (1989): 389–400.

———. "Prayer in the First Four Centuries A.D." In *A History of Prayer: The First to the Fifteenth Century*, edited by Roy Hammerling, 31–58. Leiden: Brill, 2008.

———. *The Ritual Kiss in Early Christian Worship*. Alcuin/GROW Liturgical Study 36. Cambridge: Grove Books, 1996.

Pickup, Martin. "Matthew's and Mark's Pharisees." In *In Quest of the Historical Pharisees*, edited by Jacob Neusner and Bruce David Chilton, 67–112. Waco: Baylor University Press, 2007.

Porton, Gary. "Midrash and the Rabbinic Sermon." In *When Judaism and Christianity Began: Essays in Memory of Anthony J. Saldarini*, edited by Alan J. Avery-Peck, Daniel J. Harrington, and Jacob Neusner, 2:461–82. Leiden: Brill, 2004.

Quasten, Johannes. *Music and Worship in Pagan and Christian Antiquity*. Translated by Boniface Ramsey, OP. NPM Studies in Church Music and Liturgy. Washington, DC: National Association of Pastoral Musicians, 1983.

———. "'Vetus Superstitio et Nova Religio': The Problem of Refrigerium in the Ancient Church of North Africa." *Harvard Theological Review* 33, no. 4 (1940): 253–66.

Regan, Patrick. "Veneration of the Cross." In *Between Memory and Hope: Readings on the Liturgical Year*, edited by John F. Baldovin and Maxwell E. Johnson, 143–53. Collegeville, MN: Liturgical Press, 2000.

Roll, Susan K. *Toward the Origins of Christmas*. Liturgia Condenda 5. Kampen: Kok Pharos, 1995.

Rordorf, Willy. *Sunday: The History of the Day of Rest and Worship in the Earliest Centuries of the Christian Church*. London: SCM, 1968.

Rousseau, Philip. *Pachomius: The Making of a Community in Fourth-Century Egypt*. Berkeley: University of California Press, 1985.

Rouwhorst, Gerard. "The Origins and Evolution of Early Christian Pentecost." In *Studia Patristica* 35, 309–22. Leuven: Peeters, 2001.

———. "The Reading of Scripture in Early Christian Liturgy." In *What Athens Has to Do with Jerusalem: Essays on Classical, Jewish, and Early Christian Art and Archaeology in Honor of Gideon Foerster*, edited by Leonard Victor Rutgers, 305–31. Interdisciplinary Studies in Ancient Culture and Religion 1. Leuven: Peeters, 2002.

Rutherford, Richard, and Tony Barr. *The Death of a Christian: The Order of Christian Funerals*. Collegeville, MN: Liturgical Press, 1980.

Schneemelcher, Wilhelm, and R. McL. Wilson, eds. *New Testament Apocrypha*. Vol. 1, *Gospels and Related Writings*. Louisville: Westminster John Knox, 1991.

———. *New Testament Apocrypha*. Vol. 2, *Writings Relating to the Apostles; Apocalypses and Related Subjects*. Louisville: Westminster John Knox, 1992.

Skarsaune, Oskar, and Reidar Hvalvik. *Jewish Believers in Jesus*. Peabody, MA: Hendrickson, 2007.

Smith, Dennis E. *From Symposium to Eucharist: The Banquet in the Early Christian World*. Minneapolis: Fortress, 2003.

Smith, John Arthur. *Music in Ancient Judaism and Early Christianity*. Farnham, UK: Ashgate, 2011.

Spinks, Bryan D. *Early and Medieval Rituals and Theologies of Baptism: From the New Testament to the Council of Trent*. Liturgy, Worship and Society. Burlington, VT: Ashgate, 2006.

———. *The Sanctus in the Eucharistic Prayer*. Cambridge: Cambridge University Press, 2002.

Stanley, Christopher D. "'Pearls before Swine': Did Paul's Audiences Understand His Biblical Quotations?" *Novum Testamentum* 41, no. 2 (1999): 124–44.

Stanton, Graham N. *Jesus and Gospel*. New York: Cambridge University Press, 2004.

Stark, Rodney. *The Rise of Christianity: A Sociologist Reconsiders History*. Princeton: Princeton University Press, 1996.

Stegmüller, Otto. "SUB TUUM PRAESIDIUM: Bemerkungen zur ältesten Überlieferung." *Zeitschrift für katholische Theologie* 74 (1952): 76–82.

Stemberger, Günter. "The Derashah in Rabbinic Times." In *Preaching in Judaism and Christianity: Encounters and Developments from Biblical Times to Modernity*, edited by Alexander Deeg, Walter Homolka, and Heinz-Günther Schüttler, 7–21. Studia Judaica: Forschungen zur Wissenschaft des Judentums 41. New York: Walter de Gruyter, 2008.

Stendahl, Krister. *The School of St. Matthew, and Its Use of the Old Testament.* Philadelphia: Fortress, 1968.

Stewart, Alistair. "The Christological Form of the Earliest Syntaxis: The Evidence of Pliny." *Studia Liturgica* 41, no. 1 (2011): 1–8.

Stewart-Sykes, Alistair. "Bread and Fish, Water and Wine: The Marcionite Menu and the Maintenance of Purity." In *Marcion und Seine Kirchengeschichtliche Wirkung/ Marcion and His Impact on Church History*, edited by Gerhard May, Katharina Greschat, and Martin Meiser, 207–20. Berlin: Walter de Gruyter, 2002.

———. *From Prophecy to Preaching: A Search for the Origins of the Christian Homily.* Leiden: Brill, 2001.

———. *The Lamb's High Feast: Melito,* Peri Pascha, *and the Quartodeciman Paschal Liturgy at Sardis.* Leiden: Brill, 1998.

———. *On Pascha: With the Fragments of Melito and Other Material Related to the Quartodecimans.* Crestwood, NY: St. Vladimir's Seminary Press, 2001.

———, ed. *On the Lord's Prayer.* Crestwood, NY: St. Vladimir's Seminary Press, 2004.

———. "Prayer Five Times in the Day and at Midnight: Two Apostolic Customs!" *Studia Liturgica* 33 (January 1, 2003): 1–19.

Stockhausen, Annette von. "Christian Perceptions of Jewish Preaching in Early Christianity?" In *Preaching in Judaism and Christianity: Encounters and Developments from Biblical Times to Modernity*, edited by Alexander Deeg, Walter Homolka, and Heinz-Günther Schüttler, 49–70. Studia Judaica: Forschungen zur Wissenschaft des Judentums 41. New York: Walter de Gruyter, 2008.

Stowers, Stanley K. "The Diatribe." In *Greco-Roman Literature and the New Testament: Selected Forms and Genres*, edited by David E. Aune, 71–83. Sources for Biblical Study 21. Atlanta: Scholars Press, 1988.

———. "Social Status, Public Speaking and Private Teaching: The Circumstances of Paul's Preaching Activity." *Novum Testamentum* 26 (1984): 59–82.

Stroumsa, Guy G. *Barbarian Philosophy: The Religious Revolution of Early Christianity.* WUNT 112. Tübingen: Mohr Siebeck, 1999.

Taft, Robert F. *The Liturgy of the Hours in East and West: The Origins of the Divine Office and Its Meaning for Today.* Collegeville, MN: Liturgical Press, 1986.

Talley, Thomas J. "From Berakah to Eucharistia: A Reopening Question." *Worship* 50 (1976): 115–37.

———. *The Origins of the Liturgical Year.* 2nd ed. Collegeville, MN: Liturgical Press, 1986.

Taussig, Hal. *In the Beginning Was the Meal: Social Experimentation and Early Christian Identity.* Minneapolis: Fortress, 2009.

Trevett, Christine. *Montanism: Gender, Authority, and the New Prophecy.* Cambridge: Cambridge University Press, 2002.

Tripolitis, Antonia. "Φῶς Ἱλαρόν: Ancient Hymn and Modern Enigma." *Vigiliae Christianae* 24, no. 3 (September 1, 1970): 189–96.

Van der Horst, Pieter W. "Was the Synagogue a Place of Sabbath Worship before 70 CE?" In *Jews, Christians, and Polytheists in the Ancient Synagogue: Cultural Interaction during the Greco-Roman Period*, edited by Steven Fine, 56–82. Baltimore Studies in the History of Judaism. New York: Routledge, 1999.

VanderKam, James C. *The Dead Sea Scrolls Today*. 2nd ed. Grand Rapids: Eerdmans, 2010.

———. "The Festival of Weeks and the Story of Pentecost in Acts 2." In *From Prophecy to Testament: The Function of the Old Testament in the New*, edited by Craig A. Evans, 185–205. Peabody, MA: Hendrickson, 2004.

Veilleux, Armand. *La liturgie dans le cénobitisme Pachômien au quatrième siècle*. Studia Anselmiana Philosophica Theologica 57. Rome: Herder, 1968.

———, ed. *Pachomian Koinonia*. Vol. 2. Cistercian Studies Series 46. Kalamazoo, MI: Cistercian Publications, 1980.

Walker, J. H. "Terce, Sext and None: An Apostolic Custom?" In *Studia Patristica 5*, 206–12. Leuven: Peeters, 1962.

Werline, Rodney. "The Transformation of Pauline Arguments in Justin Martyr's Dialogue with Trypho." *Harvard Theological Review* 92, no. 1 (1999): 79–93.

White, L. Michael. *Building God's House in the Roman World: Architectural Adaptation among Pagans, Jews, and Christians*. Baltimore: Johns Hopkins University Press, 1990.

———. "Synagogue and Society in Imperial Ostia: Archaeological and Epigraphic Evidence." *Harvard Theological Review* 90, no. 1 (1997): 23–58.

Wilkinson, John, ed. *Egeria's Travels*. 3rd ed. Warminster, UK: Aris & Phillips, 1999.

Williams, Michael Allen. *Rethinking "Gnosticism": An Argument for Dismantling a Dubious Category*. Princeton: Princeton University Press, 1999.

Willis, Geoffrey G. *St. Augustine's Lectionary*. London: SPCK, 1962.

Wills, Lawrence. "The Form of the Sermon in Hellenistic Judaism and Early Christianity." *Harvard Theological Review* 77, nos. 3–4 (1984): 277–99.

Winkler, Gabriele. "Confirmation or Chrismation: A Study in Comparative Liturgy." *Worship* 58, no. 1 (1984): 2–17.

———. "New Study of Early Development of the Divine Office." *Worship* 56, no. 1 (1982): 27–35.

———. "The Original Meaning of the Prebaptismal Anointing and Its Implications." *Worship* 52 (1978): 24–45.

Woolfenden, Gregory W. *Daily Liturgical Prayer: Origins and Theology*. Burlington, VT: Ashgate, 2004.

Wright, David F. "Augustine and the Transformation of Baptism." In *The Origins of Christendom in the West*, edited by Alan Kreider, 287–310. Edinburgh: T&T Clark, 2001.

Yarnold, E. J. "The Baptism of Constantine." In *Studia Patristica* 26, 95–101. Leuven: Peeters, 1993.

Yasin, Ann Marie. "Reassessing Salona's Churches: *Martyrium* Evolution in Question." *Journal of Early Christian Studies* 20 (2012): 59–112.

Yegül, Fikret K. *Baths and Bathing in Classical Antiquity*. New York: Architectural History Foundation; Cambridge, MA: MIT Press, 1992.

Yuval, I. J. "Easter and Passover as Early Jewish-Christian Dialogue." In *Passover and Easter: Origin and History to Modern Times*, edited by Paul F. Bradshaw and Lawrence A. Hoffman, 98–124. Two Liturgical Traditions 5. Notre Dame, IN: University of Notre Dame Press, 1999.

Index of Subjects

Index of Modern Authors

Index of Scripture and Other Ancient Writings